What Are the Arts and Sciences?

edited by Dan Rockmore

What ARE THE

Arts AND Sciences?

[a guide for the curious]

Dartmouth College Press | Hanover, New Hampshire

Dartmouth College Press

An imprint of University Press of New England

www.upne.com

© 2017 Trustees of Dartmouth College

All rights reserved

Manufactured in the United States of America

Designed by Mindy Basinger Hill

Typeset in Adobe Caslon Pro

Chapter-opening illustrations by Annelise Capossela

For permission to reproduce any of the material in this book,

contact Permissions, University Press of New England,

One Court Street, Suite 250, Lebanon NH 03766;

or visit www.upne.com

Hardcover ISBN: 978-1-5126-0101-5

Paperback ISBN: 978-1-5126-0102-2

Ebook ISBN: 978-1-5126-0103-9

Library of Congress Cataloging-in-Publication

Data available on request.

5   4   3   2   1

Contents

Preface
vii

What Is
African American Studies?
DERRICK E. WHITE
I

What Is Anthropology?
SIENNA R. CRAIG
13

What Is Art History?
ADA COHEN
27

What Is Astronomy?
RYAN HICKOX
46

What Is Biology?
AMY GLADFELTER
62

What Is Chemistry?
F. JON KULL
74

What Is Classics?
ROGER B. ULRICH
83

What Is Computer Science?
THOMAS H. CORMEN
96

What Is Ecology?
MARK A. MCPEEK
108

What Is Economics?
CHRISTOPHER SNYDER
120

What Is Engineering?
VICKI V. MAY
136

What Is English?
THOMAS H. LUXON
150

What Is French?
ANDREA TARNOWSKI
160

What Is Geography?
RICHARD WRIGHT
170

What Is Geology?
WILLIAM B. DADE
183

What Is History?
ROBERT BONNER
192

What Is Linguistics?
JAMES N. STANFORD
204

What Is Mathematics?
DAN ROCKMORE
220

What Is Music?
LARRY POLANSKY
232

What Is Philosophy?
ADINA L. ROSKIES
244

What Is Physics?
MILES BLENCOWE
254

What Is Political Science?
RUSSELL MUIRHEAD
274

What Is Psychology?
THALIA WHEATLEY
286

What Is Religion?
SUSAN ACKERMAN
297

What Is Sociology?
JANICE MCCABE
306

What Is Theater?
DANIEL KOTLOWITZ
316

What Is
Women's and Gender Studies?
IVY SCHWEITZER
328

Acknowledgments
339

Notes
341

For More Information
349

Contributors
357

Preface

This book is meant to be a brief tour through our evolved world of ideas. It is very much inspired by W. H. Gombrich's *A Little History of the World*, a wonderful book that I read to my son Alex when he was eight. Gombrich's book is a friendly, condensed world history meant for young inquisitive minds, but it's written in that avuncular Victorian-in-the-armchair manner and so is pretty erudite in many ways, perhaps too erudite for most contemporary American eight-year-olds. I didn't know that, though—and was aware of the many gaps in my own world history knowledge—so we read the book together, chapter by chapter, and enjoyed it and both learned a lot. I am grateful for the opportunity it afforded to sit in the big rocker in his room, to read aloud and chat about big ideas and events like the Big Bang, the Roman Empire, colonialism, World War II, and lots of stuff in between and beyond.

It made me think about how most of us—if not all of us—irrespective of age, don't really know what the big subjects of inquiry are about, but we want to know! We get some sense through the usual educational trajectory, but even those who choose to go to college and even "the academy" enter higher education not knowing what kinds of things a professor of *x* thinks about, and leave only getting a sense of a few. Every year I sit with prospective students, or the children of friends wondering about university, and am asked the question, "What do mathematicians do?" My colleagues all across the campus have analogous conversations about their own disciplines. These kinds of conversations are hardly limited to those looking for colleges or careers. They happen between adults and even between colleagues. In the best of cases they are driven by a sincere interest in the world of ideas.

With these thoughts in mind, I arrived at the idea of collaboratively writing a book, analogous to Gombrich's, but explicitly organized according to ideas rather than time. So this collection of essays is the result of that initial rocking chair–inspired idea, which could be viewed—as per the title—as collection of answers to a broader question, "What are the arts and sciences?" It is by design organized by subjects, written by various of my colleagues, who are in turn, by the nature of the organization of our college and almost any other, sorted into disciplines of which each of us are professors of various ranks and stripes. This organization of the academy (why we have the departments we do) has its own interesting evolutionary story, too long to go into here. On the level of metaphor, I like to think it resembles the universe: ever expanding, replete with beautiful, dynamic, and diverse clusters of coherence, linked across time and space, whose overarching structure is born of simple forces—in this case, the urges to understand, create, and even predict.

This book is in some sense also a brief introduction to the subjects of today's liberal arts by members of a faculty at a liberal arts college. The liberal arts ethos is built on a curiosity about the world at large and a belief in the importance and necessity of inspiring and fostering that broad-based curiosity. The kinds of flexible minds and critical thinking engendered by such an education have perhaps never been more in need than they are today. While the labeling of subjects might suggest that there are strict disciplinary boundaries, in fact all of the subjects represented here are now frequently pursued in an interdisciplinary fashion, and the present-day organization of the academy and almost every university reflects those porous boundaries too.

Throughout my time at Dartmouth I have always been grateful to have so many colleagues happy to patiently explain their work to me or to answer my naive questions about their discipline. I am lucky to have so many colleagues eager to share the love of their subject with their students and beyond, for without them this idea would have died on the vine. I apologize in advance to those whose disciplines are missed herein. Constraints of space, not of interest or import, make it impossible to explore all the worlds comprised by the universe of any university. Similarly, at the next scale, each essay here is but a doorway opening into a world of fascinating ideas within a given subject, rather than an exhaustive study, shaped (sometimes more, sometimes less) by the interests and expertise of the author.

But of course, this collection is not meant to be an end, but rather a beginning. Suggestions for additional reading and viewing materials appear at the end of the book. The subjects that appear here are only a sampling of those that we study here at Dartmouth and at other institutions of higher learning. The essays are written—again, as per the title—for the curious person of any age, and with that intention, citations have been placed as notes at the back of the book. We hope that you enjoy the collection and that this brief tour starts or continues a lifetime of exploration of ideas.

Dan Rockmore
HANOVER, NEW HAMPSHIRE
NOVEMBER, 2016

What Are the Arts and Sciences?

African American Studies?

Derrick E. White

What if I told you that most of the great American histories were half-truths and some were outright lies? Many of the great American heroes fell far short of heroism. In the "land of the free and home of the brave" slavery and cowardice reigned. The American Revolution was not for all.

A central reason for the falsity of many great American histories has been the minimization or exclusion of African Americans (and other ethnic minorities) from this history. Many Americans can recall the deeds of the Founding Fathers in the country's rebellion from British colonial rule. But few Americans remember that the first person killed in the 1770 Boston Massacre, which sparked the American Revolution, was Crispus Attucks, a man of African and Native American descent. The United States' political, economic, and cultural expansion was not solely the province of white Americans, but was intertwined with the institutions of slavery, segregation, and racism. When one considers the legal impact of the civil rights movement, true American democracy is barely five decades old. America looked and looks different with African Americans at the center of the story.

The great abolitionist, statesman, and former slave Frederick Douglass declared in 1857, "If there is no struggle there is no progress. Those who profess to favor freedom and yet deprecate agitation are men who want crops without plowing up the ground; they want rain without thunder and lightening . . . This struggle may be a moral one, or it may be a physical one, and it may be both . . . but it must be struggle. Power concedes nothing without demand. It never did and it never will." Unlike many academic disciplines that trace their origins to the early reaches of the Western tradition, African American Studies was born from the struggle for African American civil and human rights in the late 1960s.

After America's founding, its government, courts, and majority-white population treated African Americans (and other ethnic minorities) as either noncitizens or second-class citizens. Supreme Court Justice Roger Taney encapsulated the majority of white American thought when he declared in 1857 that African Americans had "been regarded as beings of an inferior order, and altogether unfit to associate with the white race" and they "had no rights which the white man was bound to respect." The institutions of slavery and later Jim Crow segregation denied African Americans citizenship rights. Emboldened by the antifascism of World War II, however, black reformers were determined to make the United States live up to its "all men are created equal" credo. The civil rights movement of the 1950s and 1960s made African Americans equal, legally. Through a combination of the legal victories, protests, and political agitation African Americans slowly ended their unequal legal status.

However, many activists realized that each legal and political success revealed additional layers of American racial thinking and ideology. Frustrated by the slow pace of change, the stubbornness of the American public, and the revelation of the pervasiveness of American racism, both interpersonally and institutionally, some reformers advocated for Black Power, which was a declaration of black humanity in the face of white supremacy and a demand for African Americans to take immediate control of their lives and destiny. When civil rights and Black Power crusaders turned their attention to changing America's racist culture, they knew that education, especially higher education, was a central issue.

The modern American university is the product of the convergence of several socioeconomic forces that were in play after the end of World War II. First, the us government's GI Bill (officially the Servicemen's Readjustment Act of 1944) provided monies that allowed more than 2 million men to attend college or gain additional training. Take, for example, the student population at the Ohio State University (OSU) before and after the war. OSU was already one of the largest universities in the country, with more than 15,000 students attending in the 1930s. In 1943 the loss of men to military service reduced OSU's student body to 8,000, the lowest number since 1926. Three years later enrollment soared to more than 26,000. Colleges nationwide had similar stories of rapid growth. Second, the civil rights movement opened doors for more African American to attend predominately white colleges. Southern white colleges, which had barred African Americans before the 1950s, started to enroll small numbers of African American students. Other universities in the North and the West, which had a variety of racial policies ranging from exclusion to integration, expanded their black student population. Finally, in the 1960s students of all races questioned college policies on dress, curfew, and politics. A generation of student activists, inspired by the civil rights movement, used the tactics of the movement to create new university practices.

The first African American Studies program emerged in this changing university context. Former civil rights activist Jimmy Garrett led the San Francisco State University Black Student Union, which joined with the Latin American Students Organization, the Filipino-American Student Organization, and El Renacimiento (an organization for Mexican students) to form the Third World Liberation Front in March 1968. The student leaders organized a series of protests, including a general strike from classes that in 1969 led to the first Black Studies Department and the first Ethnic Studies Department. By the early 1970s Black Studies departments and programs were appearing on campuses nationwide. The field has many names in the modern university—Black Studies, African and African American Studies, African and African Diaspora Studies, Africana Studies—but despite the variety of department and program titles, the goal is the same: the understanding of the black experience. African American Studies is an interdisciplinary field, meaning it uses a variety disciplinary analytical methods from the social sciences, arts, and humanities.

The field of study puts race and racism at the center of its analysis. Broadly speaking, this occurs in three interrelated ways. First, African American Studies attempts to understand how the belief in black inferiority emerged and infected American social, political, and cultural institutions. African American Studies analyzes how exclusionary policies became law and custom, how these legal and extralegal practices colored interracial interactions, and how racism shaped cultural norms. African American Studies suggests that no American institution has been unaffected by racism, racist policy, or racial discrimination. Most social, political, economic, and cultural institutions have been influenced by all three. Thus, African American Studies scholars see racism as ideological, interpersonal, and institutional.

Second, African American Studies examines the sociopolitical terrain of black struggle. As Frederick Douglass suggests, African Americans refused to accept America's racist prescriptions. As individuals and as communities, African Americans resisted interpersonal violence, challenged legal proscriptions, and produced alternative democratic visions of America. The field looks at individual acts of struggle, ranging from Frederick Douglass and Harriet Tubman in the nineteenth century, to W. E. B. Du Bois and Zora Neale Hurston in the twentieth, to Barack Obama and Bree Newsome in the twenty-first. In addition, African American Studies looks closely at the black institutions created to launch deep challenges to America's racist democracy. The sociopolitical nature of black struggle reflected various interdependent political ideologies and philosophies, including black liberalism, black nationalism, black Marxism, black conservatism, and black feminism. Scholars pay attention to diversity in ideology and strategy, noting that African American communities were often contradictory and divided on the best ways to oppose American racism.

Finally, African American Studies explores the cultural creations that have maintained black communities in an often inhumane world. Black literature, music, humor, religion, and art are not separate from the sociopolitical struggle, but also reflect black humanity. At times African American cultural production is explicitly political, critiquing white artistic assumptions of beauty and culture. At other times, African American artists translate love, hate, passion, and other feelings common to humanity. In the end, African American Studies analyzes the lived experience of blackness. Let's examine these three points a little deeper.

The Origins and Path of Racism in America

Race is not real, but racism shapes life opportunities. Scientists have concluded that the minor genetic differences that account for the varieties of skin tone do not mean that the races are different subspecies of *Homo sapiens*. This scientific conclusion, however, is a recent one. For more than five hundred years leaders of Western nations and cultures espoused an evolving philosophy in which racial distinctions signaled a racial hierarchy. The creation of a racial order forms a core belief behind racism.

Modern racism's roots stem from the religious hierarchies of the Middle Ages (approximately 476 to 1499). Medieval European Christian leaders divided the world between Christians and non-Christians, which primarily consisted of Jews, Muslims, Greeks, and Romans. Religious status, rather than skin color, organized the Christian Europe. Yet the Middle Ages wrote the first draft for modern racism. Christianity's extreme discrimination toward European Jews went further than the faith's opposition to heretics. The bigotry took the form of expulsion, demonization, and murder. The Black Death pandemic in the fourteenth century fueled the worst aspects of this protoracism. Still, the medieval Christian hierarchy wasn't racist in the modern sense, for it ostracized numerous groups—lepers, African Muslims (Moors), and Slavic peoples. This religious hierarchy was not only the province of Christianity. Medieval Islam discriminated against nonfollowers as well. Christian authorities mapped the division between believers and nonbelievers onto concepts of good and evil.

The late Middle Ages provided the closest relation to modern racism. Spain discriminated against Jewish converts to Christianity, called *Conversos*, based on the belief that their blood was impure. Until the late fifteenth century, Christians, Muslims, and Jews had coexisted in Spain, but the relative tolerance devolved into riots. Anti-Semitic violence, laws, and the threat of expulsion led to waves of Jewish conversion to Christianity in the fifteenth century. Unable or unwilling to assimilate hundred of thousands Conversos and *Moriscos* (the name for Muslims forced to convert to Christianity), Spanish authorities introduced the concept of purity of blood (*limpieza de sangre*) to create new racialized hierarchies. The racial order was policed by the Spanish Inquisition, which persecuted Conversos and Moriscos and ultimately succeeded in effectively removing all Jews from Spain (either through expulsion, forced conversion, or execution). For over one hundred years, the category of "pure blood" increasingly linked Christians lacking nobility with those of noble birth into a new class. Common Christians, trapped in a feudal economic system, now had a means for upward mobility based on their pure-blood status. New jobs, such as conquistador, were available only to pure-blooded Christians.

Simultaneously, Spain and Portugal led explorations to sub-Saharan African (1442) and the New World (1492). These Iberian explorers encountered human populations whose presence, in the case of sub-Saharan Africans, had been rumored, or in the case of the New World Native Americans, mislabeled as Indians. Iberian explorers, the nobility of Portugal and Spain, and the Catholic Church developed theories to incorporate these—from the European perspective—newly "discovered" peoples. Using the existing categories, sub-Saharan Africans and Native Americans were classified using a combination of bloodlines and religion as racialized nonbelievers. Christian religious leaders defined the newfound territories as *terra nullius*, "no-man's-land." By slotting African Americans and Native Americas into the racial and religious hierarchy of the late Middle Ages, these people of color, from the European perspective, were, as non-Christians, inferior and exploitable in terms of the period's emerging political economy.

As European nations outside the Iberian peninsula—Great Britain, France, the Netherlands—sent expeditions to the Western Hemisphere, Indians and then Africans were the sources of exploited labor. While these sixteenth-century Caribbean colonies initially employed white indentured servants, over time racial slavery replaced indenture. Native Americans (including the indigenous peoples of the Caribbean and South America) supplied the original sources of slave labor, but the introduction of new diseases by Europeans and Africans and colonial violence quickly reduced the native population. Enslaved Africans replaced the Native American labor force. Between 1526 and 1867 approximately 10.5 million Africans were transported to the New World. An additional 2 million died in transport. Europeans capitalized on a system of slavery already in existence in Africa as a part of the intracontinental conflicts. The sudden appearance of new European slave buyers in the fifteenth and sixteenth centuries exacerbated local rivalries, leading to wars between African ethnic groups, sometimes to provide the human cargo for the Europeans.

As the transatlantic slave trade increased from 277,500 people in the sixteenth century to a high of 6.6 million people in the eighteenth century and 3.8 million people in the nineteenth, blackness and slave status became associated in European and American thought. The rampant disregard for human life that was New World slavery required intellectual justifications that needed constant revision. In the fifteenth century the religious claim of heresy defended Native American and African slavery. When word got back to Spain about the horrifying acts of the conquistadors, heresy gave way to the Aristotelian concept of "natural slaves." The Renaissance's valuation of "man" as opposed to Christian man introduced new nonreligious explanations for the continuation of African slavery. Economic competition between nations, specious rationales that incorporated both arbitrary aesthetics and pseudo-scientific reasoning, and religious and philosophical arguments were all used to support the same conclusion: people of African descent are inferior.

Thomas Jefferson encapsulated the range of discourses justifying black inferiority in his *Notes on the State of Virginia* (1785). In the chapter on laws Jefferson muses about slavery. In considering the possibility of emancipation after the American Revolution, he argues that immediate freedom for slaves is not an ideal solution. He states that gradual emancipation, the freeing of slaves after they turn a certain age, and colonization (the removal of African Americans from the United States), are the best courses of action. After outlining the political reasons for the removal of African Americans, Jefferson turns to the "the real distinctions which nature has made." Demonstrating his command of racial discourses, Jefferson proceeds to catalogue the justifications for black inferiority.

> Science: "Whether the black of negro resides in the reticular membrane between the skin and scarf-skin, or in the scarf-skin itself; whether it proceeds from the color of the blood, the color of the bile . . . the difference is fixed in nature."

Aesthetics: "The circumstances of superior beauty is thought worthy of attention in the propagation of our horses, dogs, and other domestic animals; why not in man? Besides those of color, figure, and hair, there are other physical distinctions proving a difference of race."

Environment: "This greater degree of transpiration renders them more tolerant of heat, and less so of cold, than the whites."

Seriousness: "They seem to require less sleep. A black after hard labor through the day, will be induced by the slightest amusements to sit up till midnight,"

Reason. "Comparing them by the faculties of memory, reason, and imagination, it appears to me, that in memory they are equal to whites; in reason much inferior . . . and in imagination they are dull, tasteless and anomalous."

Conclusion: "I advise it therefore as a suspicion only, that the blacks, whether originally a distinct race, or made distance by time and circumstances, are inferior to the whites in the endowments of body and mind."

Jefferson laid bare the various components of modern racism. The roots were European and the future was quintessentially American.

The Founding Father's cold, analytic description of the various justifications for black inferiority served as a model for future American race relations. Even after abolitionists like Douglass pushed for immediate emancipation and the Civil War finally ended the barbaric practice of slavery, American leaders could replicate Jefferson's racial calculations. In the 1896 *Plessy v. Ferguson* Supreme Court decision, Justice Henry Brown spoke for the majority of the court and the nation when he wrote, "If one race be inferior to the other socially, the Constitution of the United States cannot put them on the same plane." *Plessy* legalized late nineteenth-century segregation laws and revealed that racism was as American as apple pie.

In addition to racism's notions of black inferiority, Jim Crow segregation, which began within a decade of the final shots of the Civil War, permitted whites to affirm their dominance through a series of humiliating reminders of African Americans' second-class citizenship. In the absence of slavery, Jim Crow segregation introduced a complex pattern of racial etiquette that governed daily affairs. Blacks could not shake hands with whites or look them in the eye, because that signaled equality. Blacks were expected to go to the back door of any white home or business. Whites did not use titles of respect, such as "Mr." or "Mrs."; instead they referred to black adults as "boy," "girl," or "nigger." As with the concept of pure blood in medieval Europe, racism allowed poor whites to align socially with wealthy whites in their assumptions of racial superiority. If African

Americans failed to adhere to the rules of racial etiquette, whites used violence to ensure compliance. White racial violence took the form of lynchings, beatings, incarceration, and other vile forms of control. Sadistic lynchings exemplified the kind of violence African Americans were subjected to, leading antilynching advocate Ida B. Wells-Barnett to conclude, "A Negro's life is a very cheap thing."

Agency and Activism

White Americans' racism was the belief in black inferiority and the associated violence to keep African Americans in their "place" as second-class citizens. American racism was ideological, institutional, and interpersonal. African Americans, however, did not simply accept this racist reality; they resisted individually and collectively.

As Frederick Douglass suggested, African Americans struggled against American racism. They never accepted Western racism and its associated violence. They challenged racism's logic, organized against its perpetuation, and fought for their survival in a hostile world. African Americans contested their second-class status. The second component of African American Studies highlights the resistance strategies of individuals, organizations, and communities. In addition to outlining the nature of American racism, it focuses on how African Americans challenged systemic inequality. This is described in Black Studies as *agency*. African Americans have not simply been the passive victims of racism; they have actively worked to change American democracy.

Ever since the United States' independence, African Americans, as individuals and on behalf of the larger community, challenged its racist logics. For instance, Benjamin Banneker, a free African American from Maryland and a mathematician, had helped to survey Washington, DC. Banneker also authored six almanacs, using the volumes' calculations to refute Thomas Jefferson's assumptions of black inferiority. In 1791 he wrote to Jefferson asking him to recall the time "in which the arms and tyranny of the British crown were exerted . . . in order to reduce you to servitude." Banneker continued, "This, Sir, was a time when you clearly saw into the injustice of a state of slavery, and in which you had just apprehensions of the horror of its conditions." The mathematician and astronomer chastised Jefferson and the other founders for "detaining by fraud and violent so numerous a part of my brethren, under groaning captivity and cruel oppression, that you should at the same time be found guilty of that most criminal act, which you professedly detested in others, with respect to yourselves." He told the founders "to wean yourselves from those narrow prejudices." Banneker's deliberate refutation of Jefferson, through the presentation of the almanac and by exposing the Founding Fathers' hypocrisy represented an individual's attempt to alter the life chances of African Americans.

While Banneker chose a restrained tone, four decades later David Walker lacked patience for those using the cold, analytical descriptions like Jefferson. Walker was born in Wilmington, North Carolina, in 1796 or 1797 to a free black woman and an enslaved father. As a young adult, Walker moved to Boston. He documented the effects of racism in the North and in the South and 1829 he published his *Appeal*. In the forty years between Banneker and Walker, the number of African Americans enslaved had grown from nearly 700,000 to more than 2 million. Walker asserted black humanity. The expansion of slavery, Walker sarcastically noted, was punishment "for enriching them and their country." His righteous discontent was aimed squarely at Jefferson and those who "swallowed" his racist logic in support of slavery. Walker extolled blacks, free and enslaved, to overthrow the institution, by violence if necessary.

Walker's urgency spurred abolitionists to move away from supporting gradual emancipation, and some scholars believe that Walker influenced Nat Turner's revolt in Southhampton, Virginia. Turner, a slave preacher, organized a slave rebellion in 1831 that killed more than fifty people in an attempt gain freedom. Turner's crusade, captured in the 2016 film *Birth of a Nation*, was ultimately unsuccessful, but it reflected African Americans' desire for freedom and the willingness to risk their lives for the liberty promised. Later, Douglass's call for the acceptance of physical struggle echoes Walker's demands. Individual pleas, however, were not enough to transform African Americans' status in slavery or in freedom. Collective action was needed.

Blacks created a network of organizations. During slavery, African Americans collectively fought to end the institution. Men like Frederick Douglass and David Walker and women like Frances Ellen Harper and Sojourner Truth joined these organizations, which debated a variety of strategies to end slavery. They supported escaping slaves by maintaining key locations on the Underground Railroad. Black and white abolitionists engaged in spirited debate, broke unjust laws, and, in the case of John Brown, waged war against slaveholders. Organizations were often rooted in black churches and schools. After the Civil War, churches and schools took on added significance, continuing to push for equal rights. By the twentieth century, African Americans create a host of associations designed to challenge racism, such as the NAACP (National Association for the Advancement of Colored People). Given the rampant segregation, some developed organizations that helped (and in some cases continue to help) African Americans survive American racism. Religious denominations such as the African Methodist Episcopal Church and the Black Baptist Church founded churches that tended to African Americans' spiritual, political, and economic needs. Organizations like National Association of Colored Women's Clubs, the Urban League, the National Negro Business League, Historically Black Colleges and Universities, and black fraternities and sororities all functioned to help African Americans socially, economically, and culturally. While many of these organizations attracted members of the black middle class, labor unions, like the Brotherhood of Sleeping Car Porters, and fraternal societies, such as the Colored Knights of Pythias, relied on black working-class membership. The array of organizations served a multitude of black community needs.

The civil rights movement of the 1950s and 1960s was a large-scale, public representation of the kind of political and grassroots work that had been happening in black communities for decades. For example, Martin Luther King Jr. was a member of several of political and community organizations. He was an alumnus of Morehouse College, a historically black college; a member of Alpha Phi Alpha fraternity, the first black college fraternity; and a preacher in the Baptist church, the largest denomination among African American churchgoers. These interlocking affiliations were key in generating support for the Montgomery Bus Boycott, the creation of the Southern Christian Leadership Conference, and other civil rights organizations and campaigns. These relationships and others served as the sinew that connected the national civil rights movement.

Culture

While organizational membership linked communities together, black culture sustained it. In 1944, Swedish economist Gunnar Myrdal (and a team of researchers) published a massive fifteen-hundred-page study on American racial relations titled *An American Dilemma: The Negro Problem and Modern Democracy*. The tome detailed the nature of American racism and argued that the central dilemma facing the United States was the huge discrepancy between its liberal, democratic creed and its treatment of African Americans. In his review of this book, African American novelist Ralph Ellison wrote, "But can a people (its faith in an idealized American Creed not-withstanding) live and develop for over three hundred years simply by *reacting?* Are American Negroes simply the creation of white men, or have they at least helped to create themselves out of what they found around them? Men have made a way of life in caves and upon cliffs; why cannot Negroes have made a life upon the horns of the white man's dilemma?" Behind Ellison's devastating critique of Myrdal's social science was the book's failure to take black culture seriously.

African American Studies, unlike Myrdal's race relations model, considers black cultural expressions as essential to the community's lived experience. Black culture has several functions. At one level, African Americans have used artistic culture—literature, music, art—to counter the assumption that a lack of "culture" was evidence of black inferiority. On another, black artists have captured the range of human experiences. As Ellison states, blacks have created a life. African Americans have composed spirituals that expressed sorrow and praise. They have developed a sense of humor that enables them to laugh at life and death. They have told stories that stirred the soul. They have painted, sculpted, and designed their humanity on "the horns of the white man's dilemma." African American Studies does not evaluate black cultural production based on its relation to white American or European cultural production. The field of study seeks to understand art as it relates to individuals and black communities.

Langston Hughes's 1925 poem "I, Too," for example, beautifully captures the complexity of black artistic endeavors.

> I, too, sing America.
>
> I am the darker brother.
> They send me to eat in the kitchen
> When company comes,
> But I laugh,
> And eat well,
> And grow strong.
>
> Tomorrow,
> I'll be at the table
> When company comes.
> Nobody'll dare
> Say to me,
> "Eat in the kitchen,"
> Then.

Besides,
They'll see how beautiful I am
And be ashamed—

I, too, am America.

In three stanzas Hughes is able to speak to the realities of segregation, celebrate blacks' ability to laugh at the absurdity of racism, and envision a future of equality.

Conclusion

African American Studies matters because it reveals how racism has influenced society, how African Americans have organized against its pernicious effects, and how black communities have maintained their humanity against all odds. The field continues to grow. Black feminism has pushed African American Studies to embrace intersectionality, modes of analysis that consider race, class, gender, and sexuality simultaneously. As a result, African American Studies has challenged racism and classism, misogyny, and homophobia, in theory and in practice. The Black Lives Matter movement, which emerged after the murder of Trayvon Martin in 2011, has been at the forefront of applying intersectional analysis. Another area of growing scholarship in African American Studies has been critical race theory and the analysis of mass incarceration. African American Studies has led the push for scholarly research regarding racialized policing and racism in the criminal justice system. In terms of cultural analysis, African American Studies has begun to critically examine hip-hop culture, including the technology of sampling, the intricate wordplay, and the tradition of misogyny. African American Studies is a necessary component of a twenty-first-century liberal arts education.

WHAT IS

Anthropology?

Sienna R. Craig

When I tell people that I am an anthropologist, sometimes they smile politely and say, "That's nice!," not knowing what to make of that five-syllable word. Some people ask, "Doesn't that have something to do with dinosaurs?" Other people respond, "How cool! Like *Indiana Jones and the Raiders of the Lost Ark*?" On a few occasions, people have asked me what tribe I study and if I've ever lived in an igloo or a tepee.

What is anthropology? None of these answers is exactly right, but they all contain little bits of truth about what anthropology is, or can be. In order to answer this question, we actually need to begin with another question: *What makes us human?* Is it our brain size? Our use of language? Is it our ability to build complex civilizations across Earth's many environments, as we have done for millennia? Is it how we think up rituals to mark the passage from one stage of life to another? Is it how we decide what it means to be a girl or a boy, a doctor or a shaman, a student or a teacher?

Anthropology is all of this. "Anthropo-" comes from the ancient Greek word *anthropos,* meaning "humanity" or "humankind." And as you probably know, any word with an "-ology" at the end of it means "the study of." Anthropologists study the human condition: past, present, and—as much as possible—future. We are curious about where humans came from and how we learned to create complex social worlds. We are interested in language and culture: what makes people different from each other as well as the things that we share. We want to know how human communities have changed over time, how we create meaning in our lives, and how we adapt to new social, political, or environmental circumstances.

What Makes Us Human

Some anthropologists study human evolution, nonhuman primates, and our Paleolithic past. They use scientific methods like genetics and the study of body movements and measurements as well as the fossil record to document and explain how we came to be and how we are still changing. These folks are called *biological anthropologists.* For example, you might think it is "normal" for people to keep getting taller through the generations. (Is your mother taller than your grandmother? Do you think you will be taller than her?) But that isn't always the case. One of my colleagues is really interested in how people who live in tropical rain forests have *evolved* to be shorter in stature and to be expert tree climbers. This is, in part, how they have learned to survive and even thrive in places where you might have a really tough time just walking along a trail. Such adaptations reflect not only our biology but also our shared and learned behaviors, our culture.

I asked my friend Jerry, a biological anthropologist, to explain a bit about what he does and why he thinks it is important. This is what he said:

> Biological anthropologists like to think about really big questions—questions like "Who are we?," "Where did we come from?," and "Why are we the way we are?" These are tough questions to answer and so we rely on many different methods for studying humans today and humans in the past. Some of the more interesting questions for me are: Why do humans walk on two legs instead of four? Why do we have such gigantic brains? And what did our ancestors look and act like?
>
> Biological anthropologists use evolution to frame our questions. Evolution proposes that every living thing on Earth is ultimately related and shares a distant ancestor, and that life and its expressions have changed over time. This doesn't mean that we came from fish or monkeys. Instead, it means that we share ancient common ancestors—sort of like great-great-great-great-great-grandmothers—with these other living things. We can use similarities and differences in DNA, the universal building blocks for all life on Earth, to determine which species are most closely related to one another.
>
> So, who is our closest relative? That would be the chimpanzee. Again, this doesn't mean we evolved from chimpanzees, but instead that we share a common ancestor with a chimp. This animal—the common ancestor of humans and chimpanzees—lived about 7 million years ago. We can hypothesize the existence of this common ancestor by studying the differences in the DNA of humans and chimpanzees.

But if *that* is true, if humans actually *did* share an ancestor with chimpanzees, then we should be able to find fossils of things that are neither human nor chimpanzee, but that are ancestral to both, buried in ancient sediments millions of years old. And in fact these fossils, called *hominins*, now number in the thousands, and they are terrifically interesting. There were many different kinds of hominins through time, eating different things, living in different environments, and moving in different ways. I have been involved in studying hominins in South Africa, among other places. Recently the team of scientists that I work with discovered a brand new species of hominin, which we have named *Homo naledi*. In one of the languages of South Africa, *naledi* means "star." We discovered this new species—an extinct species that also belongs, like modern humans, to the genus *Homo*—in a network of caves that is called "rising star." That is how this new species got its name. (And if you want to learn more about this, you can check out "This Face Changes the Human Story. But How?," a 2015 *National Geographic* article by Jamie Shreeve.)

You might be wondering about the difference between a *genus* and a *species*. A genus is a more inclusive category than a species. It can be a difficult and intriguing task to draw the line between genus and species (which generally means beings who can reproduce and have fertile offspring). This work is sometimes like being a detective, solving a mystery whose subject is the origin of human life. In studying hominins, we use the fossils themselves, DNA markers, and other methods to figure out when these beings lived and what the environment was like at that time. While DNA can tell us how living things are related to one another, fossils can tell us what our ancestors looked like, how they changed over time, and how we got to be the way we are today. Unfortunately, we cannot go back in time to study the behavior of our ancient ancestors. So biological anthropologists also study the behavior of our closest living relatives—monkeys and apes—to understand how primates survive. By studying monkeys and apes, we can better understand how large-brained, social animals figure out how to get food, how to get along with one another, and how to avoid becoming leopard food! These studies of living primates help us better understand how human ancestors survived and eventually evolved into modern, living people.

Finally, it is important to realize that biological anthropology is not some dusty old study of bones and rocks. Biological anthropology also can give us insight into human variation today. Biological anthropologists wonder why some of us digest milk, but others cannot; why humans around the world have different skin tones; and why childbirth can be so difficult for women.

As Jerry explained to me, while biological anthropology can provide some answers to these questions, it cannot answer all of them, or even answer any of them completely. Humans are very complicated animals, and understanding our biology and our evolutionary history is just one piece of a much larger anthropological puzzle.

Why Study the Past?

Other anthropologists study the material remains of past human societies, from those without written histories to those with complex written records and monuments. Think about cuneiform tablets from Egypt, Mayan temples, Mesopotamian irrigation canals, ancient rock art, and southwestern pueblos. These folks are *archaeologists*. (Yes, like Dora the Explorer's mother!)

Since I'm not an archaeologist, I asked my friend Jesse, who is, to tell me a bit about what archaeologists do and why it is fun. This is what he said:

> Archaeologists are interested in figuring out what people's lives were like in the past and how cultures—unique expressions of human behavior—have changed over time. They study everything from the food ancient people ate and the tools they used to how they traveled, traded, and fought with each other.
>
> A lot of people think that archaeologists study dinosaurs, but scientists who study dinosaurs are called paleontologists, and they examine fossils left behind by extinct animals. Archaeologists, on the other hand, study ancient people, and they do it by examining the things people left behind, usually in or on the ground. Anything that people made or used in the past is called an *artifact*, and it's lucky for archaeologists that pretty much everyone who ever lived left some artifacts behind. Some artifacts can be huge, like the remains of an ancient palace that is now in ruins, and some artifacts are really beautiful, like a gold statue. But most artifacts—in fact, almost all of the artifacts archaeologists study—look pretty ordinary. We find a lot of broken dishes, pieces of stone or metal used to make tools for hunting, farming, or religious rituals, bones from the animals that ancient people ate, the remains of old houses, and other things that are basically really old trash. However, by studying artifacts carefully, whether they are the kind of thing you see in museum or just a small piece of a broken pot, we can learn a lot about ancient people.
>
> A big part of an archaeologist's job is to explore the world looking for ancient artifacts to study, and there are many different ways they do this. Some archaeologists try to find the remains of abandoned cities, towns, or other places people

used to live—these are called "archaeological sites." Archaeologists look for sites by carefully studying the ground for clues, like places where there are many artifacts, crumbled pieces of old buildings, or changes in the soil and plants on the Earth's surface. Sometimes they use pictures taken from planes or satellites to help them find sites.

We can find sites all over the world: in forests, deserts, below modern cities, or even underwater! Once in a while archaeologists find a site that is particularly interesting—maybe it is unusually old, or especially big, or located somewhere that was important in the past   and then they might decide to dig into or "excavate" the site. Archaeological excavations have to be done very carefully and slowly, recording exactly where everything is found. Today we use computer programs to help us map sites. All the artifacts are collected, labeled, and studied to figure out how old they are, what they were used for, and where and how they were made. We even collect microscopic samples that can show what kinds of plants people ate, how the environment was different in the past, or how healthy ancient people were.

Sometimes archaeologists find beautiful artifacts that might end up in a museum. Maybe you have even seen ancient Egyptian mummies or pieces of an old temple or really really old necklaces and earrings when you've been to a museum. But the most important goal of archaeology is to recover and interpret *information* about ancient cultures, and that is something we can do even without particularly rare artifacts. Putting all these finds together, archaeology can tell us many things about human history that we wouldn't be able to know otherwise, and that is what makes it an exciting and important thing to do!

My father was trained as an archaeologist. When I was growing up in Southern California, he worked with Native Americans who call themselves the Chumash. He was interested in learning about the history of the Chumash civilization. How and where did they fish along a stretch of Pacific Ocean near the Channel Islands? What else did they eat? How big were their villages? He wanted to understand how they created and took care of sites that were sacred—places where they buried their dead and honored their ancestors, places not unlike a church or synagogue or cemetery you may have visited with your family. Just like Jesse described, part of how my father learned about such questions was by carefully digging and sorting through dirt. Lots of dirt. And piles of really old garbage that archaeologists call "middens." But he also learned about the past by talking to descendants of the ancient Chumash, people who carry on the knowledge of their forebears, even though they live in quite different circumstances today, and even though their and their ancestors' lives were dramatically changed after North and South America was colonized by people from Europe, and shaped by the Atlantic slave trade.

It is sometimes really important for archaeologists to talk with living people who might be able to shed light on how things were in the past or where sites and artifacts might be located and what they mean. Archaeologists can also learn about the past by reading what has been left behind—often written on ʋʟʋɯ tɑhlɑtʃ or papyrus—by our human ancestors. And this leads us to the importance of language.

Why Is Language So Important?

Our ability to use abstract verbal symbols to communicate with each other and to make those symbols meaningful is one of the things that makes us uniquely human. These are some of the things *linguistic anthropologists* study. How do we come to understand that "tree" or "nose" or "snow" mean specific things? Why do the traditional songs from one group of people carry specific knowledge about places as well as history? What do we mean when we say that something is "lost in translation"? How does the language we use—to call someone a "good girl," for example, or to say that someone is a "bad egg"—shape the ways people treat each other?

I asked my friend Sabrina, who is a linguistic anthropologist, to tell me a little bit about why she thinks the relationship between language and culture is such an important thing to study. This is what she shared:

> Language is one of the most important things that makes us human. It is deeply connected to who we are, as individuals and as members of our social worlds. The ways that we speak can often indicate where we are from, our generation, our gender, our education, our ethnicity, and more. In other words, language helps us figure out where and to whom we belong. Linguistic anthropologists study the sounds people make, the words people invent, and rules we make up for how those words go together (yep, that would be *grammar*), along with the "body language" we use. What makes all of these things patterned, predictable, and socially important? How do we learn how to behave by speaking or listening to language? What happens if we don't follow those rules? Unlike most grammar teachers, linguistic anthropologists are not interested in what is right and wrong according to a textbook or dictionary. Instead, we are curious about how real people actually

speak as they go about their daily lives, and what their language means to them, how it shapes who they are.

Language is everywhere, so there are endless topics linguistic anthropologists can study. For example, some of us have conducted fieldwork in schools to see how children use slang to mark themselves as members of a particular clique or group of friends. Can you think of an example from your own life? Other linguistic anthropologists study indigenous communities that are losing their *heritage language*—the language of their parents and grandparents—in favor of a more dominant one like English or Spanish. In these contexts, linguistic anthropologists may observe how adults talk with children, or how children speak with each other, to understand why fewer and fewer people are speaking the heritage language.

Linguistic anthropologists are also curious about how languages and language use are changing today, due to globalization and the use of social media. We want to know answers to questions like this: How do words and phrases such as *hashtag* or *OMG* come into common use, and what does using these terms say about the people who use them? How do people mix languages they know to express where they come from and who they are now?

Many linguistic anthropologists are concerned with language and inequality, or how some languages or dialects are more valued by society than others. These linguistic anthropologists are not only interested in describing and understanding language use; they may also be dedicated to helping change the situation.

Languages, especially those of indigenous people, are the vehicles on which cultural traditions, scientific knowledge, and environmental understandings get passed from generation to generation. We often think about what it means for a plant or animal to be endangered or extinct, but what does it mean for a *language* to be so threatened? Did you know that there are ninety separate identifiable indigenous languages alone—just in the state of California? Or that there are more than eight hundred languages spoken in New York City? You might also be shocked to realize that there are sixty-five hundred languages in the world, but that as many as half of them will no longer be in use by the end of the twenty-first century.

In New Zealand, the heritage language of the Maori people went through a period of serious decline after Europeans first settled on the islands that Maori call Aotearoa (which means "Land of the Long White Cloud"). They brought with them new plants, new diseases, and new belief systems like Christianity. But they also brought English. And with that, as well as the political and social power that these new immigrants came to hold over many Maori communities, the Maori language began to decline. This was not something Maori people were happy about, but it happened. Maori kids were not allowed to speak their own language in school, and they were told it was bad. This was not true—their language is beautiful and important and makes the world a richer place—but that is how things were for a while. In more recent years, Maori communities have reversed this trend and even used the tools of linguistic anthropology to help convince the government of New Zealand to support the revitalization of their language, in part through *kohanga reo*, or "language nests" that start at preschool or kindergarten and allow new generations of Maori people to learn and cherish their language—and, with it, their unique culture.

As Sabrina and other linguistic anthropologists have explained to me, their work helps us understand how language use creates distinctions between and connections among people. At the same time, linguistic anthropology has the potential to shed light on social problems and inequalities all around us. Understanding these social problems clearly and in ways that come from knowing a language can also help people for whom these social problems matter most to effectively address them. Imagine, for example, if you were trying to create a school system that welcomed children from all over the world, but you did not pay any attention to the ways that language shapes how kids learn, how they play, how girls and boys talk to each other, or how they are taught to speak to a teacher. As was the case in New Zealand, this remains a *really* crucial issue around the world today because war, economic troubles, and climate change are pushing more and more kids and their parents away from home, into new societies as migrants and refugees.

What Is Culture and Why Is It So Important?

Sociocultural anthropologists like me study contemporary societies and consider how our human communities differ in terms of our culture. But what is *culture*? I've been talking about it throughout this chapter but I haven't really defined it.

Culture is not (just) what grows in petri dishes. Culture is not (just) the things you see in a museum or a play. Culture is like the air we breathe as humans. It is the stuff that gives our lives meaning, but I also the stuff that tells us what is "normal" and what makes sense, what is beautiful and what is dangerous. It guides how we know what to do when we are sick and who we want to take care of us. Culture teaches us about how we grow food, or what we think counts as "food," how we invent and manufacture iPhones, how we divide ourselves up into different "races" (even though we are really only *one human race*), and how each of these things shapes our daily lives, values, systems of government, and methods of exchange (which means money but also other ways we get and receive things we need or want), and much more.

In summary, culture means all of the things that we take for granted but that we live by: the rules, the ideas, the ethics and moral frameworks that guide our lives. But culture is not stagnant, and it is not always something that people agree on. Ideas about what should or should not define our cultural identities can cause big arguments and can change dramatically in short periods of time. Culture encompasses our efforts to be creative, to share, and to pass things on. A famous anthropologist named Clifford Geertz said, "Man is suspended in a web of significance that he himself has spun. I take culture to be that web." I really like that definition of culture.

Sometimes sociocultural anthropologists study how families work (we call this "kinship") and other kinds of social relations. We think about how gender (which is different than biological sex, those X and Y chromosomes that make our bodies different) shapes societies. We think about how people come up with different systems of government and how those systems work, or how they fail to work and then change. We think about what it means to move from place to place, either as a strategy for hunting and gathering or as a response to war and famine. Sometimes we study the relationship between nature and culture.

For example, Laura, one of my cultural anthropologist friends, has spent years with alligator hunters in the mangroves of Florida's Everglades, thinking about what this beautiful place means to the people who live there, who rely on it for survival, who want to study its biodiversity, and who want to preserve it as a national park. I study medicine and healing, especially in the Himalaya and Tibet. I work with Tibetan doctors, spending time with them to learn about the plants, minerals, and animals they use to make medicines, and also how they diagnose diseases by taking their patient's pulse, asking questions, and looking at illness. I talk with them about *how* they know what they know and how this knowledge is changing from the times of their grandfathers to the worlds their grandchildren will inherit.

Understanding, making sense of, and valuing human difference is crucial to all of anthropology, but particularly to sociocultural anthropology. We encourage people to use the tool of *cultural relativism* to think about this difference. This term basically means being curious and, as much as possible, nonjudgmental about why people who are different than you do things in the way that they do. It might not seem normal or right to you, for example, to eat bugs or to bury your dead relatives by having Buddhist monks cut up their bodies and then letting vultures eat the remains. But people do these things, and they make sense in their cultural and environmental contexts. They have integrity. No matter how weird such practices might seem to you, chances are there are good reasons that other people do things differently. Part of an anthropologist's job is to help people understand that to be different than others is *not* to be wrong. We should appreciate cultural difference rather than judge people by it. The opposite of cultural relativism is *ethnocentrism*, which basically means thinking that the way you do things is the best way for everyone to do things, regardless of what environment they live in, what their history is, or what values they find most important. Being ethnocentric makes your world smaller, not bigger. Things get boring pretty quickly if you think there is just one way forward in life.

Anthropology as an academic discipline began in Europe and North America in the nineteenth century. It grew out of a few core ideas about wanting to understand humanity in all its complexity. It also emerged from other disciplines, like biology, linguistics, and the study of our European classical roots and political philosophies. But, like all academic disciplines, it grew up in a specific time and place.

Around this time, Charles Darwin was traveling the world by sailing ship, developing his theory of evolution through empirical (meaning "directly observed") studies of our vast and diverse world. When Darwin was doing his research, human communities were starting to live in ways that they never had before: in large, industrialized cities. This was a *huge* change for us as human beings, and it was impacting everything, from what money was useful for to how we fed ourselves, to how we organized our societies and did the work required to keep families and communities together.

Both explorers like Darwin and the changes brought on by the Industrial Revolution were connected to the ways that Europeans (and eventually North Americans who came from Europe) had begun colonizing may other parts of the world. To "colonize" means, essentially, to take over for oneself what belongs to another. In the case of European and American *colonialism*, this meant taking over vast areas of the world where native people lived. (We might also use "indigenous," "aboriginal," or "first nations" people to describe the communities that European settler colonists encountered.) Colonialism extended like a huge net over land and water and included the extraction of natural resources like gold and silver, crops like cotton, spices, timber, and even people (as slaves). These resources were all put to use to make colonizer societies more wealthy and powerful.

This is a difficult truth of human history—one that still affects us, and connects to the history of anthropology. Some early anthropologists did research or held beliefs, for example, that today we recognize as scientific racism. They made the argument that different races were more or less intelligent than others, and that we could map humanity onto a line that ran from "savage" to "civilized" based on the shapes of skulls. These are some of the difficult legacies of our discipline—beliefs that have been rejected. In fact, we now recognize that this concept called "race" is very socially and politically significant but that, biologically speaking, we are all part of only one "race"—the human race. Did you know that there is more genetic diversity *within* a group we might define as a "race" based on something like skin color than *between* groups? This is a powerful concept to realize.

Back in the early days of anthropology, encounters with human difference also planted the seed of the best that anthropology has to offer. It led to people like the famous anthropologist Franz Boas, a German Jewish émigré to the United States, who argued convincingly against scientific racism, using empirical evidence from around the world. These early efforts led people like a famous student of Boas, Margaret Mead, to help Americans understand that the ways we experience puberty and adolescence is different than how someone in Samoa or Papua New Guinea might go through this same life transition. It has led to the work of people like Paul Farmer, the physician-anthropologist who founded Partners in Health, to address, with a sense of cultural humility and a strong understanding of history and politics, the reasons some people die from diseases that other people stopped dying from long ago—and how to respond to these problems, arguing that access to health care should be a basic human right. All really important stuff.

How Do We Do Anthropology?

This little introduction to each of the different subfields of anthropology leads us to another question: *How do anthropologists learn?* We use many different methods to explore the human experience and the lives of our nonhuman ancestors. Sometimes we do laboratory experiments. Sometimes we listen to people tell stories. But one of the things that unites different forms of anthropology is our commitment to *fieldwork*: going out there into the world and talking with people, interacting with the environment, observing how things work.

For one of my friends, fieldwork means getting on a boat and traveling up the Amazon River to spend time with an indigenous community of hunters and gatherers. For another person I know, it means climbing into the mountain grasslands of Ethiopia to observe *gelada*, an Old World primate, watching how they play and mate and fight with each other. At one point for me, it meant interviewing Tibetan women about what having a "safe" pregnancy and birth meant to them. Recently, it meant going to Flushing, an area in Queens, New York, where many people from Nepal and Tibet now live, and observing a Buddhist ritual sponsored by a Chinese businessman. Here I did *participant-observation*, which basically means hanging out with people, learning about their lives by doing things with them, but also systematically paying attention to what is happening and asking questions about why people do what they do.

Archaeologists might use trowels and toothbrushes, gridlines drawn in the dirt, and screens to sift soil and recover shards of pottery or arrowheads. But they also use drones to fly overhead and take pictures of ancient settlements, and Global Positioning Systems (GPS—yes, like what might be in your family's car) and infrared technology to figure out where sites are and what lies beneath the surface. Biological anthropologists might strap a device onto someone's chest to measure how much oxygen they use or energy they spend while running or climbing or harvesting rice. Linguistic anthropologists might spend hours recording and transcribing old songs, or making lists of words with young kids or elders.

Depending on where the fieldwork takes place, it may involve learning a new language. This is especially true for linguistic and sociocultural anthropologists, but can be equally important for archaeologists and biological anthropologists. We often rely on audio and video recordings, as well as our field notes, so that we can go back later and review exactly what people said and how they said it. Then we may create what is called a transcript—a written word-for-word representation—of what was said. For linguistic anthropologists, this might go along with any important features of sound or gesture that seemed important.

All of these are useful methods to gather anthropological knowledge. More and more these days, anthropologists are doing these sorts of things not just *on* people in communities where we conduct research, but *with* people who have a stake in what we learn about them. We believe that it is ethically important that the people we work with, or their living relatives in the case of archaeological work, be a part of how their histories, communities, and cultures are described. While some of the knowledge we gain through fieldwork (as well as other methods) end up in scientific articles, many of us also write books. Sometimes these books are histories of ancient sites—like the Mesoamerican city of Téotihuacan, located right beside what is now one of the biggest metropolises on the planet, Mexico City. Other times these books might be about what it means that we share 98 percent of our DNA with chimpanzees, as one biological anthropologist has written.

Sociocultural anthropologists usually do *ethnography*, and then write up the results of this work as a book or even a film. *What is ethnography,* you ask? Well, just to throw in one more lesson in etymology (that is, the study of word origins, not the science of insects), "ethno-" comes from the Greek word *ethnos,* meaning a group of people or a culture, and "-graphy" is another Greek form that means an art or science concerned with writing, representing, recording, and describing something. Think about *biography, geography,* or *choreography,* as other examples of related words. Ethnography is the systematic study of people and culture. Ethnographies are a kind of writing that can feel "science-y" because we try to represent things as clearly and with as much neutrality as possible. But ethnographies should also be good and complex stories. We hope to be "holistic" in our representations of times, places, problems, relationships, and changes in human communities. We try to capture not only what people *say* they do when we interview them, but also what they *actually do* during their daily lives, and why this is important to them. As you might imagine, sometimes these things can be different. If I asked you, for example, how often you clean your room, you might say, "Oh, I clean it every Saturday." But if I were to live in your house, I might learn that you don't clean your room every week, even though you are supposed to. I might also learn that your mom helps you clean your room sometimes but that you help her empty the dishwasher or fold the laundry, and that she gives you an allowance for that work . . . and that you like to spend that money on soft-serve ice cream, especially in the summer . . . and that what you love the most is your pet iguana and the way your baby sister smiles at you when you tickle her feet . . . and on and on.

What Have We Learned?

So, what have we learned about anthropology? I hope you will remember that anthropology is about exploring the world with an open mind and being ever curious about the diversity and history of humankind. Anthropology is one of the most wide-ranging subjects you can study in the liberal arts. Even if you don't plan on becoming a professional anthropologist, the lessons of this discipline will never leave you. People who study anthropology go on to be designers and technology engineers, doctors and nurses, architects and artists, novelists and lawyers—as well as traveling many other paths. Whatever field you choose to pursue as you become an adult, anthropology leaves you prepared to observe, participate in, and analyze the world in a unique and powerful way.

WHAT IS

Art History?

Ada Cohen

For many people, thinking about art starts and ends with a trip to a museum. There for a few hours or maybe even a day, while going through the galleries, the museumgoer is pulled into many different worlds as she encounters various objects and ideas: a serene impressionist riverscape; the victory implied by a jewel-encrusted Ottoman sword; the energetic build-up of drips, lines, and dots on an abstract expressionist canvas; the regal ceremony enacted on an ancient Assyrian relief; or the absorbing narrative of a Japanese painted scroll. One of the pleasures of being a professional art historian is the opportunity to explore worlds other than one's own through the in-depth study of artworks—and not only for a couple of hours. Art helps us learn things about others as well as ourselves, and museums facilitate our study by serving as custodians of works of all sorts and making them available to the public. Much of world art, however, resides outside the confines of the museum, and art historians pursuing their subject may find themselves in such different places as a Buddhist cave temple in northwestern China, a cathedral in Paris, a mosque in North Africa, or the cemetery for foreigners in Rome.

Art historians engage with both art (material objects but also intangible images such as videos) and history (different times and places). Unlike "art appreciation," art history is perhaps history above all because it asks questions like what happened and when it happened, for whom, by whom, and why. But it asks these questions in light of a very particular activity in human life—art, a visual medium—and in this sense it is a separate field of its own, distinct from history. One thing is clear: art historians do not make art; they study it, both in itself and in its relations to the times, places, and people who produce, look at, and even use it. Art is a form of culture, but also a lens into a culture. When you study art history, all these many facets emerge, expanding your field of vision.

It used to be thought that art is very tightly connected with certain forms of skill and that its traditional media are the "high" (i.e., the most prestigious or most important) arts of painting, sculpture, and architecture. But art historians may now study things like pottery, photographs, and quilts. Many more things count as art today, but someone must first think that this is the case, that a work is worthy of being called art. Who gets to make that decision? Usually someone with power and influence, especially institutions like museums, which bring art to the attention of the public and shape tastes and attitudes, but also professional art critics and sometimes academic art historians. These kinds of issues were perhaps most famously exposed when a number of forces contributed to making a urinal one of the icons of twentieth-century sculpture. First, the French artist Marcel Duchamp reoriented a bought object (a urinal), gave it the signature "R. Mutt" and the date 1917, and submitted it under the title *Fountain* to an art exhibition. Second, certain art critics and art historians recognized this as a significant move and agreed to engage with the object and write about it. Third, museums expended funds to purchase and exhibit replicas of the object, inviting visitors to linger, think, and react.

Duchamp's work was provocative and history-making, but it was not beautiful. It used to be thought that art is beautiful and that beautiful things are art. Although many people, especially those who have not studied art history, continue to think that art and beauty go together, for art historians the connection is no longer automatic, and influential artists like Duchamp participated in this development. Don't get me wrong: art historians still study very beautiful and very skillfully made works, like the *Mona Lisa* in the Louvre Museum in Paris or the frescoes in the Sistine Chapel in the Vatican, but they may also study very simple or unbeautiful works that someone somewhere and for some reason has considered art. I will say more about these matters later. But for the time being keep in mind that some older definitions of art allowed only the beautiful and the skillful, while newer and more inclusive definitions give the designation art to any human-made object or intangible image (like a video) that is designed to communicate ideas in a visual manner. The careful examination of questions such as what kinds of work are received as art and why and how that changes over time, space, and culture (and, indeed, how that in turn changes culture and society) is a part of art history.

Such questions, considerations, and debates make their way into dating the "beginnings of art." Most art historians believe that the Paleolithic cave paintings of Western Europe, like those in Chauvet (ca. 30,000 BCE, or Before the Common Era) or Lascaux (ca. 15,000 BCE) in France, are among the earliest examples of art. Others, however, argue that these are not "real" art, because we do not know anything about what the people who painted them thought. We have no written records to tell us what the paintings, often of animals, meant and how they were used. The same scholars who bring up this point would exclude from the history of art those cultures that seem not to have had a special word for art, which, they believe, means that the people had no concept of art. Some put the beginning of art in the Renaissance; some put it as late as the eighteenth century in the West, when the idea of "fine art" or "art for art's sake" (art without immediate practical function) emerged.

Together with many others, I disagree. I think that all human cultures with a certain level of complexity display signs of creativity and all make art, though the art may take many different forms, serve many different purposes, and hide behind various terminologies. Clearly, not all works of art were made for museums; not all were made "for art's sake." You find art in churches and other religious buildings; you find art in tombs, where it accompanies the dead. It is the job of the art historian to study these different forms and purposes of art. That is a lot of material to study! The history of art is inexhaustible, and, by pursuing this field of study, maybe you will contribute something new to it one day.

You might now ask how old art history is. This question too has many answers. An early version of art history goes back at least as early as Greek and Roman antiquity. Some writers, most famously the author and naturalist Pliny the Elder, who lived in the first century CE, discussed important artists of the past and their works in some sort of chronological order. The artist Giorgio Vasari in the sixteenth century, in the Italian Renaissance, wrote about the lives and works of famous Italian artists, organizing them from earlier to later, and in his view from less to more accomplished. He considered his contemporary Michelangelo the pinnacle of excellence and praised him above all artists. Yet another "beginning" for the history of the discipline lies in the eighteenth century, a period known as the Enlightenment, and is associated with the German art historian Johann Joachim Winckelmann. Winckelmann is often considered the first professional art historian. He spent lots of time in Rome and wrote about, among other ancient cultures, the art of Greek antiquity, which he admired above all and set up as a model for the artists of his own time.

Early art historians wrote with tremendous self-confidence in their own judgment and included fewer works in their "canon" (the group of monuments they considered worthy of study) than we do today. Today we are much more willing to incorporate a lot of different types of works in our canon of art. As the field becomes more and more expansive, the question "What is art?" becomes all the more interesting. In fact, it would be impossible to embark on an exploration of what art history is without first considering the question "What is art?" It is a difficult one to answer (considerably more difficult than the question "What is history?"), and it has become increasingly more complicated since the beginning of the twentieth century, when the category "art" became much more fluid and encompassing than it had been previously.

Assuming for now that we agree on what art is, then what, you may ask, do art historians do with art? To begin, they must assemble the straightforward facts of its creation. When was it made? What is it made of? Who made it, for whom, and for what reason? Who paid for it and who had access to it? Finding answers to these factual questions becomes more and more difficult the older the art is. In some cases, as with undated or unsigned art, working on these questions is like working on a puzzle. Actually, some art historians operate as if the work itself, rather than just some aspect of it, is a puzzle and see themselves as detectives in pursuit of a single "solution." Others object to the notion that works of art are problems in need of decipherment, preferring more straightforward readings. In the present context I use the metaphor of the puzzle only in a limited sense having to do with a work's precise location in time and place. Even if you do not solve this puzzle completely, there are things you come to understand and things you can say about a work of art through careful looking.

Indeed, much of what art historians do is grounded in deliberate looking. They must look at the work itself and describe what they see as part of a process known as visual analysis. Try doing that and you will find that it is less simple than it sounds. We use our eyes all the time in our everyday life, and there is a certain "self-evidence" in what we see—that is, we take what we see for granted. When working as an art historian you must forget that self-evidence, try to pay purposeful attention, and notice details.

Looking is only half the process. You must also put what you see into words. Not only do you need to find the right words to communicate what you perceive; you also need an orderly way for presenting this information, discussing, for instance, the main points first and the details later without jumping around from here to there and back and forth again. One of the challenges of describing is that, without being aware of it, we usually interpret while looking. Difficult though this is, a good description must consciously try to keep facts separate from interpretation and somehow signal when moving from one type of consideration to the other. Description takes time and requires patience.

I will now briefly explore a few aspects of the process of "doing" art history. Although some of my examples are likely to be unfamiliar to you, the angle I use—the family—will be quite familiar. Let us start with figure 1, an ancient Egyptian limestone sculpture, thirteen inches high, from the tomb of an official who lived around 2500 BCE and was buried near the Great Pyramid at Giza. Today this sculpture is in the possession of the Egyptian Museum in Cairo. We see a man and a woman seated frontally, side by side, on a rectangular bench. The woman embraces the man supportively, and both have faint smiles and alert expressions on their faces. His torso is nude, while she wears a long tight-fitting dress. His skin tone is brown, while hers is white. Notice that the man is a dwarf, with very short arms and legs, but the composition of the sculpture (i.e., the way its elements are organized) and the fact that he sits cross-legged minimize the effect of his deformity. Parallel to the woman's legs, and in the area where the man's would have been if they were fully sized, stand two small nude children, male and female. Like their adult counterparts, the male child is brown-skinned and the female white. Both stand frontally and rigidly and bring their index finger to their mouth. The boy has a long sidelock of hair.

The funerary context of the work (the tomb) and the hieroglyphic inscriptions that are carved on the cubic block of stone and elsewhere in the tomb inform us that the adult male is Seneb, the dead individual, and the other figures are his wife and children. Even if we did not know that this is a family group, attention to the compositional arrangement and the gesture of embrace would have allowed us to make this leap and helped us understand the subject matter of this sculpture. Art historians refer to the identification of a work's subject matter as "iconography," a pursuit especially associated with the twentieth-century German art historian Erwin Panofsky, one of the pioneers in the field, who permanently moved to the United States in 1934, fleeing the Nazis.

Iconographic analysis is sometimes a simple and other times a difficult task, depending on how well we understand the historical context of a work. In one of his best-known essays on iconography, Panofsky pointed out that an Australian bushman or an ancient Greek would not understand a man's lifting of his hat as the greeting it was meant to be in early twentieth-century Europe. I suspect

FIGURE 1 *Dwarf Seneb and His Family*, painted limestone, H. 13⅜ inches, Old Kingdom Egyptian, fourth dynasty, ca. 2500 BCE, from the Tomb of Seneb, Giza, Egypt. Cairo, Egyptian Museum, JE 51280. Photo Gianni Dagli Orti / The Art Archive at Art Resource, NY

you might not understand this either, which is why noticing this gesture in a painting would lead you to undertake research. Similarly, an ancient Egyptian would immediately know that the index finger on the mouth of the two smaller figures in the Seneb group identifies them as children, but we, twenty-first-century viewers, need to do some work to uncover this symbolism.

So art historians do not describe works of art simply for the sake of describing. They do so as a step toward understanding and in order to communicate essential information to others, help them notice and become aware of important details that ultimately confer meaning to a work. Visual analysis addresses not only what the work depicts but also how (in what manner) it (re)presents its subject. Art historians call this aspect "style." I mentioned that the poses of the figures in the Seneb group are "rigid," which is a descriptive point but one that may also offer us clues toward interpretation. In an Egyptian context, that is, rigid postures seem to have served as signals of eternity and eternal life. Furthermore, the embrace of Seneb by his wife, the expressions, and the compact composition suggest confidence in the ties of the family unit and the hope that they will remain together forever. Note too that we are made aware of the block of stone out of which the figures were carved. This is typical of Egyptian sculpture and serves to ground the figures, giving them an additional aura of stability and permanence. Interestingly, the more we know about the context, the sooner this type of interpretation enters into our descriptions.

If description is a necessary part of studying art, interpretation is where the fun lies. With careful looking and equally careful description, a work of art can be a doorway into an entire culture. Works of visual art offer innumerable opportunities for interdisciplinary research that help interpret and situate them in a variety of frameworks. Seneb, for example, who is represented several times in his tomb, could be studied in light of his personal biography. Or he could give occasion to an art historian to explore the issue of dwarfism in ancient Egypt from a biological perspective, from a psychological perspective, or a social perspective. In regard to the latter, I note that among Seneb's many titles inscribed in his tomb one is "overseer of dwarfs," which is a rather particular appointment and raises interesting questions about the position of dwarfs in the culture and the respect that seems to have been given to some of them. An art historian could use this statue of Seneb as a starting point for an exploration of the topic of physical handicaps in ancient Egypt by comparing it carefully with other Egyptian works.

Comparing the female figures in the group with others shows that light skin was given more or less consistently to ancient Egyptian women because of their sex. This does not mean that they were all necessarily light-skinned but, rather, that this was the feminine ideal in that culture, as it was in other ancient Mediterranean cultures. We can see then that art history, with its careful looking, detailed description, and layers of interpretation, opens a window into culture and society. Although art historians typically begin with a work of art, their object of study, from it they branch out in a variety of directions.

As I indicated just now, some directions are revealed through comparison, a key method in art history. Usually comparisons are undertaken in light of works from the same culture or period for the purposes of classifying them, putting them into groups, and thus formulating broad principles. Less commonly, but in my mind more interestingly, comparison may involve works from different contexts, which, however, display some commonalities, for example by subject matter. In such cases comparisons help us not only because of the common features but also because of the differences, which highlight for us the choices an artist made in one case but possibly avoided in another. A comparative work, that is, expands our thinking, alerts us, and gives us ideas. This is especially important because when confronted with a completed work of art we tend to assume that this is the only way in which it could have been made.

Let us undertake some comparative work by looking at another family from a time much later than that of Seneb's and in a different medium: a painting on canvas from the middle of the eighteenth century by the German painter Johann Zoffany, who mostly worked in England (figure 2). The title of the painting, which today is in the J. Paul Getty Museum in Los Angeles, describes the subject matter: *John, Fourteenth Lord Willoughby de Broke, and His Family in the Breakfast Room at Compton Verney* (an English residence). The room is sumptuously decorated and the family richly dressed, so we immediately realize that we are looking at a wealthy group. Because of the attention to the environment in which the people are situated, we figure out their elite status more quickly than we do when looking at Seneb's family.

Zoffany's painted family is posed informally. The father leans casually on the back of the chair in which his wife sits. His glance and his gesturing finger direct us to the focus of his attention, the little boy on the left foreground, who reaches to grab a piece of toast or cookie from a dish on the table. His father's admonishing gesture tells us he is doing something he is not supposed to do. His brother on the right is pulling a wheeled toy horse, making eye contact with us, the viewers. The youngest child, a girl, is held upright by the mother and is the one looking at us most directly. But wait: did I say that the two children in

FIGURE 2 Johann Zoffany, *John, Fourteenth Lord Willoughby de Broke, and His Family in the Breakfast Room at Compton Verney*, oil on canvas, 40⅛ x 50⅛ inches, ca. 1766. Los Angeles, J. Paul Getty Museum, 96.PA.312. Photo J. Paul Getty Museum

the foreground are boys? How can that be when they, like the girl, are wearing long white dresses? In fact, at that time boys and girls in European countries were dressed in the same way until the age of five or so and sometimes even later.

In addition to the clothing of the members of this aristocratic family, an art historian might study their hairstyles; might notice the Turkish rug, the particular style of the porcelain tea set, or the embellishments on the fireplace. These painted objects might in turn lead us to explore the patterns of trade that could have brought them into the household. The bright colors and shiny materials might encourage us to ask how much the objects represented in the painting actually cost back then and to explore the attendant implications.

The informality of this painting, a type known as a "conversation piece," was important to its meaning. Zoffany wanted to give the impression that we are dropping into a private moment in the life of this aristocratic family, without their being aware of us. Two children, however, as we saw, are very much aware that the viewer is there. Indeed, the play of gazes within an image, as well as with the viewer, is a matter with great communicative potential and a matter of concern to art historians. Contrast the casual air of this work with the stiff, frontal poses in the Egyptian sculpture. Of course, there too we noted the affectionate embrace of the couple, but it is a more formal embrace, as if the woman is presenting the man to us.

Although a piece of sculpture, the Egyptian work seems to deny the third dimension, creating instead a shallow sense of space. Although a flat painting, an aggregate of tiny brushstrokes, Zoffany's work aims to give us the illusion of depth by subtly using the principles of linear perspective and creating the impression that we are looking through a window into the space of the room. Note too that this painting makes us suspect that the people in it actually resembled their portraits, whereas we cannot be sure of that in the case of the sculpture.

Do any of the differences I mentioned (and there are many others, as well as several similarities) mean that one work is better, more accomplished, than the other? Not at all. Each gives us a glimpse into the society that produced the work, the values of the people, aspects of their lives (and afterlives). Can we take either work to be an accurate representation of these lives, those relationships among family members, those worlds of the past? That is a tricky and very interesting question. Even when expressing informality, works of art tend to be carefully composed. In that sense they are highly selective and show us only what they want us to see. Art historians do not take what they see at face value. With study and practice it becomes easier to know what to believe and what to suspect. Yes, chances are that boys in eighteenth-century England wore dresses like this and played with toy horses like that. Chances are that dwarfs could attain positions of power in ancient Egypt. But were women really so much lighter in skin tone than their husbands? Were the Egyptian children that much smaller than their parents or so well behaved?

These kinds of considerations activate two very general theoretical approaches to the study of pictorial art. The first lingers on art's referential qualities—that is, its relationships and correspondences with reality. From this perspective art is seen as a reflection of (or at least in dialogue with) something out there in the real world. The other approach, by contrast, looks at art as a system of signs or conventions (such as the white skin arbitrarily assigned to females and the brown skin assigned to males in Egyptian art). In practice most art historians resort to both of these approaches at different times, depending on the specifics of their projects and the philosophical frameworks they employ.

We have so far looked at a sculpture from a funerary context and a painting from a secular context. The funerary work is also religious, because it is religion that typically shapes people's views of death and the possibility of life afterward. Seneb's statue is a manifestation of the Egyptian belief in an afterlife that was an extension of life on earth. In fact the statue could serve as a substitute for Seneb's real body in the afterlife—to be inhabited by his "spirit"—so you can see the religious implications. But I want briefly to turn to a more straightforwardly religious work, one that could become the focus of daily worship among the living. This turn will show that some of the objects art historians study once were, and often still are, the center of very intense rituals and emotions.

In order to maintain focus on family relationships, I have chosen a painting on a wood panel from the Monastery of St. Catherine in the Sinai, dated tentatively in the sixth century (figure 3). People familiar with the Christian tradition immediately recognize the enthroned woman as the Virgin Mary and the child sitting on her lap as the baby Jesus. Others outside this tradition might only see a woman holding a child, or a mother and a child, until they research the iconography and learn about its religious significance. Mary sits frontally, presenting her baby. Her eyes, however, are slightly averted to the side, maybe because the painter wanted to create a sense of distance between her and us. The baby Jesus sits upright but comfortably in his mother's embrace. Both wear round golden haloes around their heads, suggesting their divinity and importance, as do the two saints who flank Mary and the baby. Each saint holds a cross, symbol of the future crucifixion of Jesus, which is at the center of the Christian faith. Two angels are shown in the back looking upward, drawing our attention to a disembodied hand that comes down from above, the hand of God.

If you look closely, you will notice that there are different styles, different ways of rendering the figures represented in this painting. Notice how soft and rounded the face of Mary is. The painter has subtly "modeled" the face in light and shadow, making it look as if it were three-dimensional. This is also true about the angels. But then look at Mary's body and, especially, the bodies of the two saints. Look how flat, elongated, and weightless these appear. This aspect increases their otherworldly effect and elevates them above the ordinary. Generally artists use naturalism to create an illusion of physical reality and more "stylized" (more abstracted) approaches to create a sense of difference or distance from the viewer. In this particular case, we are not sure why a more naturalistic style is used side by side with a more stylized approach, but we suspect that there must be a reason with religious significance.

Over time painters came to vary the manner in which they depicted the

FIGURE 3 *Virgin and Child with Two Saints*, Byzantine icon, encaustic on
wood, 27 x 18⅞ inches, sixth century CE. St. Catherine Monastery, Mount Sinai,
Sinai Desert, Egypt. Photo Erich Lessing / Art Resource, NY

bond between mother and child. Sometimes Mary presents the child to us in a formal way; other times she nurses him; yet others she lovingly draws him close to her cheek and almost kisses him. Whereas the baby usually surprises us with his maturity and adult-like composure, which announces his divine status, some artists imagine him as more playful and childlike at that phase of his life. Different choices convey different views of baby Jesus and, with that, different religious attitudes and beliefs.

In iconography, the Mt. Sinai painting shows an otherworldly Christian "family." In function it is an "icon." It was made not only to be looked at but also to be used as aid for meditation and worshipped by the faithful: Christians of the Byzantine empire, which ruled the eastern Mediterranean world in the medieval period until the middle of the fifteenth century. By serving as a sort of substitute for the divine, icons were very powerful in Byzantine culture, so much so that some people became worried. In the eighth century and for a period of over a century, a movement known as iconoclasm ("breaking of icons") and embraced by many influential people (notably the Byzantine emperor) destroyed most icons (this one escaped) and prohibited the making of new ones. Iconoclasm was eventually defeated, and icon-making resumed.

I mention iconoclasm here because it shows how central works of art may be within a culture and how much power they may hold. Otherwise, why bother to destroy them? Icons are still made today and are venerated by Orthodox Christians (and Catholics) around the world. In addition to churches and some households, today you may find icons in many of the world's museums. Even though they were not originally intended as works of art, over time some essentially became works of art for a variety of reasons, including their beauty and affective qualities.

You might ask whether the French artist Jules Dalou's now-lost life-sized sculpture *Maternal Joy*, originally of 1872, also showed the Virgin Mary and the baby Jesus. You might have seen one of the porcelain versions of this work, twenty inches tall, in one of your museum visits (figure 4). The fashionable woman (notice her beautiful shoes) cradles a baby in her arms and nurses it attentively. As fashionable versions of Mary do exist in many periods (and, as already noted, versions that show her nursing Jesus also exist), it would be reasonable to identify this woman as Mary. I have no quick explanation as to why this is not the case here, other than to say that experience with the history of art helps you decide when a woman holding a baby is the Virgin Mary and when she is not. But you get the idea: things that look similar do not necessarily mean the same thing.

Dalou wanted to show an average modern woman of the nineteenth century but also wanted the modern woman to represent the abstract idea of motherhood. Consider also that things that look very different may have similar meanings. For example, a prehistoric statuette from a tomb at Mycenae in Greece, about five inches tall, is much more abstract than Dalou's work but shares some meanings with it (figure 5). The statuette shows a female figure in colorful dress carrying one baby in her arm and another on her back, protecting both with a parasol. This too points to the joys and challenges of caring for the young but does so without interest in naturalism. By contrast, an artist contemporary to us, the Australian Ron Mueck, concentrates on the challenging experience of birth in a shockingly

FIGURE 6 Arshile Gorky, *How My Mother's Embroidered Apron Unfolds in My Life*, 1944, oil on canvas, 40 x 45¹⁄₁₆ inches. Seattle Art Museum, 74.40, Gift of the Virginia and Bagley Wright Collection. Photo Susan Cole

realistic manner. His sculpture *Mother and Child* (2001–2003) shows a naked woman, strikingly lifelike but significantly under life-sized, with her newborn baby resting face down on her belly in their first encounter with each other.

In further contrast to Mueck's hyperrealism, some artists, beginning in the early twentieth century, have come to feel that abstract ideas, experiences, and emotions like joy, pain, or sadness are best communicated abstractly. So they avoid the human figure and the natural world altogether, even though they are perfectly capable of producing naturalistic work. The American artist Arshile Gorky could clearly work in both styles. An immigrant from Armenia, he painted a famous frontally posed figural portrait of himself next to his mother. Both are clearly recognizable. Two versions are actually known, one in the Whitney Museum of American Art in New York and the other in the National Gallery of Art in Washington, DC. Both were begun in 1926 and were closely patterned after a photograph of 1912, taken in Armenia when Gorky was still a child. At a later time, when he wanted to evoke his feelings and private memories of his

FIGURE 7 Jules Dalou
(French, 1838–1902), *Study for
Maternal Joy (La Maternité)*,
terra-cotta, 9¾ x 4½ x 3¾ inches,
1872. Collection of Middlebury
College Museum of Art, Vermont,
1987.005. Purchase with funds
provided by the G. Crossan
Seybolt '77 Art Acquisition Fund.
Photo Ada Cohen

mother, who, as a refugee, had died in 1919 of starvation, Gorky opted for an abstract mode of painting. In *How My Mother's Embroidered Apron Unfolds in My Life* (1944) at the Seattle Art Museum (figure 6), he presents a lively mixture of colors, lines, and shapes and challenges us to find traces of his mother and her dress among them. Both his figural paintings and his nonfigurative help us imagine the lasting influence she had on him.

I said earlier that art historians do not make art. They do, however, have to know how art is made. For example, an art historian interested in Gorky would want to understand how he built his brushstrokes, in what combination of accident and deliberation. Another interested in the sculpture of Dalou would study a small terra-cotta model at the Middlebury College Museum of Art (figure 7). Here you can see how the artist worked out his idea, adding one little ball of clay to another, giving shape to his figures. Dalou rendered the final product in various materials and sizes, from small to life-sized, through different artistic processes.

Although in Dalou's case the baby is likely a girl and the models possibly the sculptor's wife and daughter, he wanted them to stand for something more general than themselves. By contrast Flip Schulke's black-and-white photograph

of Myrlie Evers and her son (figure 8), dated 1963, is meant to be very specific. It was taken in the aftermath of the murder of a civil rights activist, Medgar Evers, who was shot in the driveway of his home in Mississippi. The assassin, a white supremacist, was not found guilty of his crime until 1994, and the photograph of members of Medgar Evers's grieving family has come to serve, among many other things, as a reminder of this particular injustice. Of course nothing prevents us from reading it more broadly, as a symbol of the loving bond and shared destiny of his wife and children.

You might ask whether this work of documentary photography belongs in an art museum or an art history textbook. Certainly it was not taken for the purpose of art, but its deliberate composition, its sophisticated exploration of an identifiable artistic theme, and its black-and-white medium, which today is seldom used except by art photographers, have elevated its status. Who knows, maybe some of the countless selfies people take today will survive into the very distant future. Maybe future art historians will think that "Look at me" is sufficiently complex a thought or sufficiently characteristic of twenty-first-century visual codes to be considered art, a case of serial self-portraiture.

FIGURE 9 Achilles Painter, Servant bringing baby to mother, Athenian white-ground *lekythos*,
height 14½ inches, second quarter / mid-fifth century BCE. Berlin, Antikensammlung,
Staatliche Museen, F 2443. Photo Johannes Laurentius / Art Resource, NY

A. DETAIL, SERVANT

B. DETAIL, MOTHER

In this short discussion I presented a few specific works of art that share a general subject matter. But I also used terms like the "medieval period" or "Byzantine art." In addition to studying individual works (or individual artists), art historians group them into periods and cultures, focusing on the various characteristics shared by works made in one time and place. So the fifth-century BCE vase of figure 9, which shows a seated mother (9b) ready to receive her gesturing child from the hands of a female servant (9a), is many things: an example of Classical Greek art; of art produced specifically in ancient Athens; of the work of a painter known conventionally as the "Achilles Painter"; a member of a class of vases known (because of their shared background color) as white-ground *lekythoi*, typically made to be placed in a tomb; a scene with multiple social and gender implications. Like every other work I mentioned, this vase opens up many lines of inquiry, which art historians love to pursue as part of the wider effort of interpreting the world and understanding its many cultures and ideologies, past and present.

Art historical theories and approaches have changed significantly over time. Some decades ago the art history curriculum presented students with *The Story of Art*, to use the title of a hugely influential textbook first published in 1950 by the well-known art historian Ernst Gombrich. Today, more and more, we speak about *stories of art* or *histories of art*. But despite the diversity in subject matter, questions asked, and interpretive frameworks employed, art historians still participate in a single, if ever-evolving, discipline, experienced by students through the similarly evolving college curriculum.

WHAT IS

Astronomy?

Ryan Hickox

Astronomy, at its heart, is exploration on the grandest scale. Humans are natural explorers, and intrepid adventurers have now journeyed to the deepest ocean trenches and the highest and most remote mountains. We have even sent a handful of people to the moon, and our robotic surrogate explorers have now reached the edge of the solar system. These achievements are fascinating to people of all ages—in elementary school I learned by heart every book in the library about the *Apollo* missions to the moon and the *Voyager* probes to the outer planets. As I got older and studied math and physics I began to focus my exploration inward, and my college senior thesis used data from a particle collider to study the world on the smallest subatomic scales. However, in my heart I always remembered that our home planet comprises only a tiny portion of the much, much larger universe. In my final semester of college I was fortunate to take a wonderful course on astronomy, which set me on a path to exploring beyond our backyard into the vast expanses of reality.

By carefully observing the sky, astronomers discover new stars, planets, galaxies, and gas clouds. I'm particularly interested in huge black holes that reside at the centers of galaxies, and much of my work involves searching for the signatures of these massive and exotic objects. However, we astronomers don't simply look to see what's out there—we also seek to *understand* what we find, using the knowledge of physics we have determined here on Earth. In this way *astronomy* is broadly synonymous with *astrophysics*, and indeed astronomers have a boundless curiosity about the greater universe around us as well as deep appreciation for the principles of physics that explain the fundamentals of the natural world. We have little hope of actually traveling to faraway stars and performing experiments on them, so how do we explore the universe while staying

FIGURE 1 The universe is teeming with a wide variety of wonderful objects.
This is a Hubble Space Telescope image of Stephan's Quintet, a group of five galaxies in
the direction of the constellation Virgo. The *galaxies* contain huge clouds of gas known
as *nebulae* (shown as blobs, particularly visible in the galaxy to the upper left). The small,
bright objects (such as the one halfway up the image on the left edge) are *stars* in our
own Milky Way galaxy that we see in the foreground. Courtesy of NASA

at home? The answer is simply by *looking*, using telescopes as enormous eyes to
detect and study the light from faint, distant objects.

What are the objects we see in the cosmos? An image showing several interesting objects is shown in figure 1. The most familiar objects are *stars*, huge
balls of gas like our sun powered by nuclear fusion in their cores. Orbiting the
stars are *planets*, rocky bodies like the Earth or gaseous giants like Jupiter. We

can now identify and study billions of stars and many thousands of planets, but these represent just the tip of the iceberg of what we can observe with telescopes. We see the huge nurseries in which stars and planets form, diffuse clouds of gas known as *nebulae*, and we see the remnants of dying stars as they puff off their outer layers forming beautiful patterns of gas, or explode and drive shock waves into the surrounding space. These stellar explosions produce exotic objects known as *neutron stars* and *black holes*, in which material the mass of the sun is compressed into a size of less than ten kilometers. Rotating neutron stars can create radio-wave "lighthouses" known as *pulsars*, while black holes have such strong gravity that they dramatically warp the space around them and even light cannot escape.

When we look deeper out into space we see *galaxies*, enormous "cities" of billions of stars like the Milky Way galaxy in which we reside. Some galaxies are beautiful pinwheel spirals like the Milky Way, while others (the elliptical galaxies) are smooth and round like rugby balls. Galaxies are collected together into a vast *cosmic web* of which the densest regions are massive *clusters* of thousands of galaxies. Inside almost every galaxy resides a huge black hole, weighing from a million to a billion (or more) times the mass of the sun. Sometimes these black holes "eat" surrounding gas, which is heated to hundreds of thousands of degrees as it falls down to the black hole and glows extremely brightly, producing *quasars*, the most powerful (and if you ask me, the most interesting!) objects in the universe.

Making Maps of the Universe

In studying all these remarkable objects, one of the biggest challenges is the enormous distances. If we shrank the sun down to the size of a grapefruit, the star that is its nearest neighbor, Proxima Centauri, would be four thousand miles away! Indeed, when thinking about astronomy people often remark that they "can't wrap their head around" the scales involved. Astronomers have this problem too; we can't intuitively conceive of the distance to a far-off galaxy, in terms of meters or kilometers with which we are familiar. So how do we build our understanding of the universe? We use *relative* scales, considering each successive distance in terms of how many times larger it is than the next smaller one. So we can think of the distance to the nearest star not as 30 trillion kilometers, but as about 200,000 times the distance from the Earth to the sun. These relative scales are much easier for our minds to comprehend.

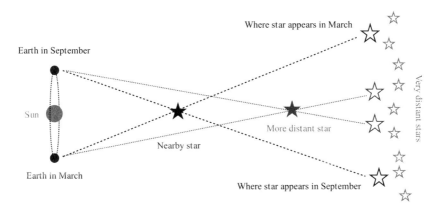

Where star appears in March

Earth in September

Sun

Nearby star

More distant star

Very distant stars

Earth in March

Where star appears in September

FIGURE 2 The schematic illustrates the basic concept of the parallax method
for measuring distances to stars. As the Earth orbits around the sun over the course of the
year (shown at left), we will view nearby stars at different angles. This causes the positions
on the sky of nearby stars to change relative to very distant stars in the background.
A nearby star will have a larger change in its apparent position, compared to a
more distant star. By measuring how much stars move on the sky over the year,
we can directly determine their distance.

But how do we actually measure these enormous distances in the first place?
It is easy to tell in which direction in the sky an object lies, but much more
challenging to tell how far away it is. An object can be right next to another on
the sky but be millions of times more distant! So we need a 3-D view of the sky,
and to do this we can take inspiration from our own naked-eye vision. Since
our eyes are slightly separated from each other, each eye views a scene from a
slightly different angle, so the images produced by each eye are offset by a small
amount. For objects that are closer to us, this offset is larger—you can verify
this by holding a finger up in front of your face and moving it closer and farther
away, while opening and closing each eye. These changing offsets with distance
allow our brain to process this "binocular vision" and to see the world in 3-D.

Thankfully, we also have this binocular vision on Earth, because we happen
to reside on a planet that is orbiting around the sun! So for two points separated
by six months in the year, when the Earth is on opposite sides of the sun, we
see the sky from two quite different angles. If we observe a star over the course
of the year, we will see the star appear to move around on the sky, relative to
background stars that are much farther away, as shown in figure 2. This effect
is called *stellar parallax*, and the angles are amazingly small: the angle for the

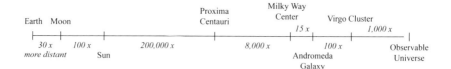

FIGURE 3 A schematic illustrating the relative distance scales to a number of well-known astronomical objects. The distance to the moon is expressed in terms of the radius of the Earth; otherwise each distance is expressed in terms of the next nearest distance. Note that these relative analog are still highly compressed (the relative distance to Proxima Centauri compared to the distance to the sun is *much* larger than the relative distances to the sun and moon). All images from NASA, except the Observable Universe schematic, made by A. Colvins (Creative Commons license BY-SA 3.0)

nearest stars is around one arcsecond (or 1/3,600 of a degree), which is about how large a penny appears at a distance of 4 kilometers! However, using a highly sensitive telescope, these angles are measurable. A parallax angle of one arcsecond corresponds to a distance of one *parsec* (which is the standard distance measure used by astronomers, corresponding to about 3.26 light-years) and the smaller the angle, the larger the distance. Starting with direct distances from parallax, we build up a range of ways of determining the *relative* distances to objects, and can measure distances all the way to the edge of the observable universe.

Let's take a tour of the universe, pointing out the relative distances to some of best-known landmarks (figure 3). The distance to the moon is about 30 times the diameter of the Earth, and the sun is 500 times farther away than that. Proxima Centauri, the nearest star after the sun, is another 200,000 times more distant, corresponding to three *light-years* (one light-year is the distance light travels in a year—and remember, it travels 186,000 miles in just one second!) from the Earth. The supermassive black hole at the center of our Milky Way galaxy is another 8,000 times further still. Beyond these scales, the relative scales get a bit more manageable: the nearest large galaxy, Andromeda, is about 2 million light-years away, or only about 15 times farther away than the size of the Milky Way, and the nearest large cluster of galaxies is another 100 times larger than that. If then we go out only 1,000 times farther in distance, we reach the size of the entire observable universe! This scale is enormous (it would take light many billions of years to traverse that distance), but by thinking of things in terms of these relative distances, we can begin to intuitively understand the scale of the entire cosmos that we can observe.

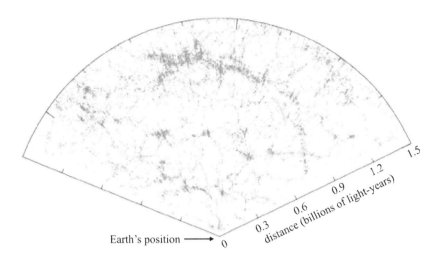

Earth's position ⟶ 0

0.3   0.6   0.9   1.2   1.5

distance (billions of light-years)

FIGURE 4 A three-dimensional map of galaxies in the universe made by the Sloan Digital Sky Survey. The position of the Earth is at the bottom, and the most distant galaxies shown in this map are about 1.5 billion light-years from the Earth. The map clearly shows the large-scale "cosmic web" and large clusters of galaxies at the densest parts of the web. Sloan Digital Sky Survey collaboration

Once we have accurately measured distances to astronomical objects, we can begin to make 3-D maps—"surveys"—of the universe. Huge new surveys have produced some of the most exciting astrophysical discoveries of the past decades. Around the turn of the twenty-first century, advances in telescope and computing technology and the advent of large international collaborations allowed us to dramatically expand the scope of sky surveys. Today, the Gaia space telescope uses parallax to chart the 3-D locations of billions of stars in our Milky Way galaxy, and the Kepler mission has discovered the locations of thousands of planets around other stars. Zooming out to larger scales, the Sloan Digital Sky Survey has used a purpose-built telescope in New Mexico to make a map of many millions of galaxies, illustrating the cosmic web that represents the largest structures in the universe (figure 4). Recently, extremely long exposures over a small patch of sky with the Hubble Space Telescope have produced a map of galaxies to nearly the edge of the observable universe.

What do we do with these maps? For one, they tell us how cosmic structures formed—if you look at a map of the roads on Earth, you get a sense of the connections between places and can build a picture for how cities grew and developed over time. Likewise, by seeing how different types of stars are distributed in our Milky Way, or how galaxies are distributed in the cosmic web, we can deduce the processes by which these objects formed. Second, sky surveys give us a complete census of stars and galaxies. They show us, for example, that the most common stars in our Milky Way are significantly smaller than the sun and that the Milky Way is a very typical sort of galaxy. Often the most interesting discoveries come from the rare, exotic objects that turn up in our maps and challenge our understanding of how stars and galaxies work.

As we look to the future, ever-larger international collaborations of astronomers are working on larger and more powerful survey telescopes. The Large Synoptic Survey Telescope, currently being constructed on a mountain in Chile, will use a huge digital camera to map the entire sky every few days, producing a remarkable 15 terabytes of data per night that will require new big-data technologies just to process the results. A new space observatory, the Wide-Field Infrared Survey Telescope, is being planned that will enable Hubble-like observations over a much wider area of the sky, giving astronomers ultrasharp images across the full extent of the cosmic web.

Fingerprints of the Cosmos

With every new map of the sky, we gain an increasingly detailed view of what is out there in the universe around us. However, astronomers are not just mapmakers, but also *physicists*—once we find astronomical objects we want to understand how they work, by uncovering the kinds of physics that govern how these objects behave. For example, imagine we perform some observations of an object such as the Orion Nebula (shown in figure 5). The fact that this object looks like an extended blob, rather than single point on the sky, tells us that it is a diffuse cloud of gas that is filling the space between stars. We can determine the diameter of the cloud simply by how far away it is (determined via parallax, as described above) and how wide of an angle it appears to cover on the sky. Both a larger distance and wider angle would correspond to a larger physical size.

However, we want to know not only what this cloud looks like and how big it is, but what is it made out of, how hot it is, how fast it is moving, and how massive it is. Since the nebula is about a thousand light-years away, we cannot go grab some of this material and bring it back to a lab to analyze. However, by carefully studying the light it emits and by applying the principles of physics, we can determine its properties.

To give you a very brief physics primer, different kinds of light (radiation)

FIGURE 5 The Great Nebula in Orion, the nearest large region in which stars are rapidly forming, is the middle "star" in the "sword" of the constellation Orion, the Hunter. The nebula is a large cloud of gas. The detailed structures in the image and the shape of the object's spectrum allow astronomers to understand its physical nature. NASA

comes in different wavelengths. Long wavelengths are at the "red" end ("infrared" and "radio" are even longer than red), and short wavelengths are at the "violet" end ("ultraviolet" and "X-ray" are even shorter than violet). In order to figure out what we are looking at we do a careful analysis of the kind of light the object emits. This is accomplished using something like a prism at the end of the telescope to split the light from astronomical objects into the rainbow of its component wavelengths. Telescopes have come a long way since Galileo used simple optics to get a good view of the moon and some of the relatively nearby planets. Modern telescopes receive all kinds of light, including observatories such as the Chandra X-ray Observatory, Spitzer Space Telescope, and Jansky Very Large Array, that cover wavelengths (X-ray, infrared, and radio, respectively) that are well outside the limited visible range that our eyes can see. Each of these telescopes can decompose the light into its component wavelengths, known "spectroscopy," and the brightness of the light observed at each wavelength is called the object's "spectrum." This spectrum gives us clues about the atoms and molecules in the object, each of which emits or absorbs light at very specific wavelengths. In other words, the spectrum of an object has distinct lines that serve as fingerprints of its composition.

For example, in the spectrum of the Orion nebula we see thousands of lines, but the most prominent ones can be easily recognized as belonging to hydrogen, helium, carbon, nitrogen, and oxygen, so the gas cloud is primarily composed of those elements. The atomic lines of most elements are well-known from studies in a lab here on Earth, but it is worth noting that since helium is difficult to isolate on Earth, it was actually first discovered due to the presence of unknown lines in the spectrum of the sun! Hence it is named after Helios, the Greek god of the sun.

In addition to using spectral lines to determine composition, atomic and molecular physics tells us that the *relative* brightnesses of lines vary with temperature. Thus the details of the line spectrum tell us that the gas we see in Orion is hot, with a temperature of about 10,000 degrees Celsius. We also notice that the lines emitted by some parts of the nebula are at slightly shorter or longer wavelengths than we observe for the same type of atoms sitting at rest in a lab on Earth. This change in the wavelength reflects the motion of the gas toward or away from us, due to the *Doppler Effect*. In just the same way that an ambulance siren is higher-pitched when moving toward you and lower-pitched when moving away, so the "pitch" (and thus wavelength) of the spectral lines gets shifted when the gas clouds are in motion. By carefully measuring this shift, we can see that the gas in Orion is moving at 36,000 kilometers per hour!

Finally, we can use this motion to determine the mass of the cloud. Isaac Newton developed his theory of universal gravitation to explain the motion of the moon and planets, and it tells us that the velocity of an object in orbit around a larger object is determined by the distance between the objects and the total mass. Thus by measuring the velocity of a gas cloud in the Orion Nebula due to the Doppler shift, and the distance from that cloud of gas to the center, we can determine the total mass of the nebula to be 4×10^{30} kilograms, or two thousand times the mass of the sun. By using similar reasoning, we can determine the properties of all sorts of astronomical objects, from nearby planets and stars to the most distant galaxies.

Telescopes as Time Machines

As we have seen, using new telescopes we can map out and characterize objects throughout the universe, so now we are ready to ask perhaps the most fundamental question. *How did the universe come to be?* Our understanding of physics allows us to trace the history of an object back in time, to understand the process by which it formed. For example, by knowing the basic principles of hydrodynamics (the physics of fluids and gases), nuclear physics, and gravity, we can build a model for the formation of stars that reproduces the properties of stars that we see today. This type of theoretical modeling is essential for understanding the formation of stars, planets, gas clouds, and galaxies.

However, astronomy provides an even more powerful way to learn where things come from: with our telescopes we can actually *look directly back into the past*. As we mentioned earlier, the huge distances to astronomical objects means that it takes light many years to travel to us. That is, we receive the light now, but that light started elsewhere and had to travel to us. If the time it arrived was a year after it started, then it came from an object that is one light-year away. So we see the Orion Nebula not as it is now, but as it *was* a thousand years ago.

One thousand years is a blink of the eye in cosmic time, but once we get out to distant galaxies, the light-travel times become billions of years. This is a timescale that is a significant portion of the age of a galaxy. So if we're peering into distant space—for example, using deep Hubble Space Telescope observations (figure 6)—then what we are seeing are the "baby pictures" of galaxies as they form and evolve at different stages in cosmic time. (For example, if a galaxy was a billion light-years away and it was billion years old, then we would actually be seeing its birth pictures!) So observing galaxies at different distances in the universe is like taking pictures of human children of different ages and comparing them to see how children grow over time. On any given day we cannot watch the development of any one individual child, but by examining many children of different ages, we can draw great insights into how a typical child grows over its lifetime. By exploring back in time in the deep universe and studying galaxies at various stages in their development, we can perform a similar trick with galaxies like the Milky Way.

What we see using our cosmic time machine is quite extraordinary. The early universe was a very different place than today—the young, adolescent galaxies we see in the distant sky are denser, messier, and they contain more of the interstellar gas from which stars form. In the Milky Way there are currently about two stars forming out of gas clouds per year, but in the early universe a similar galaxy forms stars ten or even one hundred times more quickly! As we observe galaxies closer and closer to us (which are also closer to us in time), we see the galaxies slowly decline in the rate at which they form stars as the universe expands and cools. Sometimes we also see galaxies colliding with each other to produce even more massive systems. Through careful analysis of the universe at different distances, we are nearing a complete picture for how galaxies like our Milky Way came to exist.

A Night in the Life of an Astronomer

Hopefully this chapter so far has given you a sense of what we can learn from astronomy, and why it is so interesting. But what is it like to actually *be* an astronomer?

Let's imagine that you are an astronomer interested in measuring the properties of a galaxy system prosaically named UGC 11185 (as it is the 11,185th object in the Uppsala General Catalog of Galaxies). This system (shown in figure 7) is interesting because it consists of two merging spiral galaxies, both of which contain growing supermassive black holes that produce copious radiation. This radiation lights up gas in the galaxies that glow like a fluorescent lamp (particularly visible as the clouds in the lower half of the image). My research group at Dartmouth College was fortunate to recently observe this object and publish the results in a prestigious journal. Here we'll walk through the steps of carrying out and interpreting these observations.

First off, observing is not accomplished just anywhere. There are only a limited number of telescopes large enough to carefully observe galaxies such as UGC 11185. One of these is the 2.4-meter diameter Hiltner Telescope at MDM Observatory on Kitt Peak in Arizona (figure 8). Now, you can't just drive out to the observatory and knock on the door and say, "Hey, I'd like to use your telescope to look at a cool star!" You have to write a proposal that explains to the people running the telescope why you think this is important (in this case, you want to study the nature of these colliding galaxies), and if they agree they schedule you some precious nights of time on the telescope to carry out these and other observations.

FIGURE 6 The Hubble Ultra Deep Field, the part of the sky
that was observed most deeply by the Hubble Space Telescope. This
image covers a small patch of sky (if you held a dime at arm's length,
it would be about the size of Roosevelt's eye!) but contains many
thousands of galaxies. Almost every object in this image is a distant
galaxy, and some of the small ones are located near the edge
of the observable universe. NASA

FIGURE 7 A Hubble Space Telescope image of the interacting galaxy
pair UGC 11185. The blobs on the galaxy at left represent gas excited by
radiation from the growing supermassive black hole at its center. NASA

FIGURE 8 The 2.4-meter Hiltner Telescope at MDM Observatory
on Kitt Peak, Arizona. Photo by R. Hickox

Our target galaxies in UGC 11185 are in the constellation Lyra, which is visible high overhead from much of the Northern Hemisphere. Due to the orbit of the Earth around the sun, different constellations appear overhead at different times of the night throughout the year, and Lyra is best viewed in the summer. Therefore we schedule our observations for sometime in July, and at the appointed week, we fly to Tucson and drive the hour and a half through the desert up to the observatory on top of Kitt Peak, always hoping for clear weather. In the afternoon before the observing begins, we carry out technical checks and calibrations on the telescope to make sure it is set up for the night. Finally, as the sun disappears below the horizon and the sky gets dark, it's time to begin the observations.

In the control room, we enter the sky coordinates of our pair of galaxies (273 degrees East and 42 degrees North) into the system's computer and the telescope turns to point at that position on the sky. Once we've centered on this position, the telescope will continue to slowly turn to account for the motion of the sky over the course of the night due to the rotation of the Earth and keep the galaxies within view. Now we begin our exposures—you use the computer to open the shutter on the giant digital camera attached to the bottom of the telescope, and set it to pass the light from the galaxies through a prism to spread the light out into a spectrum. The camera then digitally records a series of spectra of the galaxies.

We carry out similar observations of other galaxies throughout the course of the night, and as dawn approaches we retire to our rooms in the on-site dormitory, complete with blackout shutters, and sleep for the day. After several nights of successful observations, our run is over, so we head back down the mountain for home.

Once back at home we can carefully analyze our spectra of UGC 11185 to determine the composition of the clouds of gas that are lit up by the growing black hole. How bright the light from these clouds appears in the spectrum depends not only on how bright the cloud actually is, but also on the diameter of the telescope, since a larger telescope lets in more light and so makes fainter objects appear brighter (just as how your pupils dilate to allow you to see better in the dark). The brightness also depends on the exposure time, since leaving the shutter open longer lets in more light. Accounting for these variables, you obtain an accurate measurement of the brightness of the fluorescent radiation produced by the gas in this spectrum. By measuring the wavelengths of the lines in the spectrum, we can also measure how fast the gas is moving, as described above.

By combining a number of different spectra of these two galaxies, we can map out the velocity and brightness of their gas cloud. This gives us important clues about the radiation from the growing black hole that illuminated the gas, as well as insight into how the collisions of galaxies may help trigger the growth of their central black holes. Having made this discovery, we present our results at conferences around the world (astronomers do a lot of traveling!) and work with colleagues to produce an article for submission to a journal of astrophysics. In the meantime, we plan even more observations, always thinking about how we can use telescopes to discover and understand new components of the universe.

What Do We Know Now?

With all these powerful astronomical techniques to understand the universe, what do we know about the universe now? We know that the specks of light we call "stars" are giant balls of gas like our sun, powered by nuclear fusion in their cores. We know that stars come in a whole range of masses, sizes, and temperatures. We know that stars form out of enormous clouds of interstellar gas, and that when the most massive stars die, they explode and leave behind extraordinarily dense and powerful objects called black holes.

We know that our Milky Way galaxy takes the form of a giant flat spiral, like a pinwheel, and that it is just one of billions of such galaxies in the larger universe. We know that the universe came into being in a "Big Bang" about 14 billion years ago and has been expanding ever since, and that galaxies like the Milky Way formed and grew over that cosmic history. We know that these galaxies reside inside a gigantic "cosmic web" that grows over the lifetime of the universe under the influence of gravity and is made primarily of a mysterious substance called dark matter that makes up most of the mass in the universe. We also know that there is an even more mysterious substance called "dark energy" that is driving galaxies apart, accelerating the expansion of the universe.

Closer to home, we now know that many, if not most, stars have planets orbiting them and that planets come in a dazzling array of masses, sizes, and temperatures, including some completely different from what we have in our own solar system. Recently, we have discovered that about a quarter of stars like the sun host planets the size of Earth, so that there may be billions of planets like the Earth just in our own Milky Way galaxy.

What Are the Big Questions Left to Answer?

Many of these discoveries have come in only the past one or two decades, and the pace of discovery in astronomy is extraordinarily rapid. So as we look to the future, what are the big questions on the horizon?

One addresses how the largest structures in the universe formed. We still do not know the nature of the dark energy that is driving the expansion of the universe, but it has a profound effect on the growth of the "cosmic web." Through enormous new surveys such as the ground-based Dark Energy Survey and the Euclid space telescope, which will map the sky with unprecedented precision, we will directly observe how cosmic structures grow and evolve over time, and gain key insights into the mysterious energy that dominates the evolution of the universe.

Another important question addresses how galaxies came to exist. While we understand the general picture of galaxy formation quite well, the details are still very challenging to understand. In particular, the processes that regulate the formation of stars are complex and interrelated. One important role appears to be played by enormous black holes that reside at the centers of galaxies and release energy as they grow through eating interstellar matter. However, the details of how this process works remain quite unclear. Deep observations with

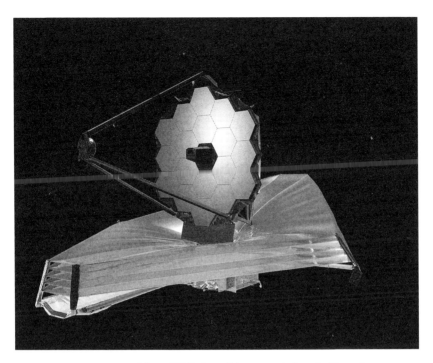

FIGURE 9 NASA's James Webb Space Telescope, to be launched in 2018. The science goals of JWST include exploring the youngest, most distant galaxies and searching for signatures of life around other planets. NASA

new observatories such as the Atacama Large Millimeter Array and the James Webb Space Telescope (figure 9), along with advances in theoretical models for the formation of galaxies, will enable an increasingly clear picture of this process.

This brings us to the last, and perhaps most profound, question, regarding the presence of life on other planets. We now know that there are countless other planetary systems that could potentially harbor life, but have not yet detected evidence that life actually exists. With large and powerful new telescopes, we will be able to directly perform spectroscopy of Earth-like planets around other stars and look for chemical signatures (for example of oxygen) in the atmospheres that could indicate processes due to life. These observations could provide the first evidence that we are not alone in the universe.

The next generation of astronomers will tackle some of the grandest and most fundamental questions that can be asked by humankind. By mapping the sky and understanding the nature of the objects they discover, these new explorers will produce an ever-deeper understanding of the vast universe we live in.

WHAT IS

Biology?

Amy Gladfelter

In nearly every nook of the planet there are molecules, cells, and tissues that when mixed together are alive. We feel it with the sensation of our own heartbeat; we witness it in the plants and animals that share our homes. Biology is part of every moment of our every day. Yet how often do we actually step back to marvel that life happens at scales from the tiniest bacterium to the majestic oak tree? The diversity and dynamics of life are complex, fascinating, and even (dare I say) beautiful. *Life* is in us and all around us—and the study of life and what makes things alive is the province of *biology*. The study of biology is about asking good questions about life and figuring out clever ways to find the answers. Each question and each answer leads to new questions, new answers, and, with that, new mysteries.

There are as many flavors of biologists and biology as there are scales and kinds of life. Areas of biology are sometimes based on the creatures the biologists study. There are microbiologists, who study bacteria; entomologists, who study insects; mycologists, who study fungi; or plant biologists, who study, well, plants. We can also carve up the world of biology according to the type of approaches biologists use to tackle problems. There are geneticists, who manipulate DNA; biochemists, who study the activity of proteins; physiologists, who look at tissue behaviors; bioinformaticists, who look for patterns in genomes; and ecologists, who look at how organisms interact with each other in the environment. Most biologists find a "scale" at which their brain likes to think. The biochemists like working at the nanometer (one-billionth of a meter) scale of proteins, while the ecologists like the kilometer scale of the savannah. However, none of these categories are tight, and basically most people who end up being biologists cross back and forth to a certain degree between different organisms, different approaches, and even different scales. They go where their questions and new data lead them!

I am a *cell biologist*, which means (as you might expect) I study cells. I'll refresh your seventh-grade vocabulary to remind you that cells are often called the "fundamental unit of life," which means that all living things are made up of them. There are big cells like our neurons or those that comprise our muscles, and there are tiny cells like the bacteria or plankton that whales snack on. Cells can be round, long, square, pointy, hard, or soft. Cells can make signals, receive signals, compute, react, grow, divide, and even make decisions. The diversity of life-forms and functions begins even at the scale of a single cell.

In this essay I'm going to focus on the study of cells and how cells may act together in communities. I hope that through this you will get a sense of how exciting and interesting it is to think about life at the cellular scale.

I'll begin with giving you a sense of what it is like inside a cell, then explain how we probe and imagine this world. I'll pitch some exciting unsolved problems biologists are actively tackling that revolve around cells. After you are finished, I think you'll agree that the practice of biology is alive with the spirit of exploration and creativity.

What Is It Like Inside the Cell?

Close your eyes and imagine a cell. What do you see? It may be that cartoon picture of a cell that you saw in seventh grade. If so, then what pops to mind is probably a lumpy, amorphous sac that appears to be filled with water and dotted with strangely shaped islands floating in suspension. This is unfortunate and well, wrong! Sorry! These static pictures do not begin to capture the whirring, dense jungle of molecules, the fluxes of energy, or the constant transport and rearrangements of compartments.

It's something like the disconnect between the maps you find on the inside of some favorite fantasy books and the stories that follow. That first impression you get belies the complexities of the world represented by the map, a world that comes to life as soon as you start reading. Maybe the kingdom becomes populated with a dysfunctional royal family, forests, wars, dragons, unicorns, and some magical object that is lost but must be found. After I finish book like this, I always go back to that map on the inside cover—especially when it's a really good book that I don't want to end. I replay my favorite parts of the story with the visual cues of the imaginary geography and recall my favorite scenes in the context of the simple map. Suddenly, the mountains feel more desolate, the seas more treacherous; the walls of the castle are higher, the forests sparkle with magic, and there are secret relationships traversing the boundaries of the lands. Once our imaginations are primed, the map becomes a dynamic, Technicolor panorama. In the best such books, you might just feel the cold mist of the sea, the smell of smoke from the plundered village, and the soft touch of the moss underfoot in the woods.

The map comes to life with the help of an imaginative storyteller—the author. A good author often has more than pure imagination to help with her story. Research and life experience can add detail and texture to create a living world made with words. In our case it's the cell biologist who vivifies the picture of the cell. But the cell biologist doesn't work by pure imagination—although imagination is important! Her work will be enabled and amplified by experiments and technologies with which we can probe and sometimes even look inside the cell. Let's now bring that cartoon map to life.

Microscopists: Cartographers of the Cell

The first question you might ask is "How do we know what's going on in there?" Well, as the great philosopher Yogi Berra once said, "You can observe a lot just by watching." We look very closely and very carefully at the cell using microscopes, a technology that continues to transform our understanding of the cell.

Microscopes are one of the oldest tools of the cell biologist. The most famous pioneer microscopist (a person whose research centers around the use of a microscope) was Anton van Leeuwenhoek, who worked in the mid-seventeenth century. His early work and drawings of what he saw in the cell changed the way we understood life, much as Galileo's use of the telescope changed our understanding of the solar system.

Van Leeuwenhoek's basic idea of using finely tuned lenses and visible light as the underpinnings of a microscope carried the day for about three centuries, and was responsible for a host of important advances in our understanding of cells. However, as new generations of cell biologists tried to see smaller and smaller objects, visible light no longer could do the trick. That is, as you may know, light is a kind of wave, and you start to run into problems as you try to see things that are smaller than the wavelength used to illuminate the field of view. Before the middle of the last century biologists were limited by the wavelengths of visible light to distinguish among things in the cell closer together than, say,

300 nanometers. By analogy, this would be like a camera that produces a picture in which two people are next to each other, when in reality there were in fact twenty people between them. In the 1950s engineers and physicists figured out a way to use electrons instead of visible light to "illuminate" the interior of the cell. These *electron microscopes* gave the first clear, highly detailed maps of the cell at the scale of nanometers. The early electron microscopists, such as George Palade and Keith Porter, were like cellular biology's Lewis and Clark: they produced extraordinarily detailed early topo maps of the cell.

But with this enhanced detail came a loss in speed: whereas light microscopes could happily observe a living cell, electron microscopes required the observed cell to be dead, so there was no way to use them to monitor any kind of dynamic process as it happened. For decades cell biologists have had to live with this "speed/detail" trade-off—either you could observe the living cell in "real time" in a fuzzy way (with little detail) or you could get a detailed static snapshot of a dead cell.

Fortunately, combinations of advances in physics and computer science and many other disciplines are bringing faster, more sensitive, and higher-resolution views to cell biologists. The ability to give a molecule a "fluorescent tag" enables us to accurately place and track single molecules moving and interacting within the context of a living cell, which can in turn be imaged using newly developed cameras that are faster and more sensitive. The fluorescent molecules can damage cells, but new optics are so strong that we need less and less of the stuff to see the tiny objects, and more images can be taken in a short time to accurately follow fast processes. Even more, new computational methods help to clean up dramatically the images. We are currently experiencing a golden era of microscopy because we can look at intracellular processes at high speed and deep detail. The things we can see now are truly extraordinary, and these new and ever-improving views of life in the cell are transforming our understanding of the cell at a rapid pace. Take a look at figure 1 for some great examples.

What Does It Feel Like Inside a Cell?

So, what is the world inside the cell? The first thing to know is that despite pictures that make it look like a weird archipelago in an ocean, in fact the cell is unbelievably crowded. A single cell is packed with *billions* of proteins. Recent estimates put the density at 2 to 4 million proteins per cubic micrometer. This would be like being on a subway car with every seat taken; people in seats would

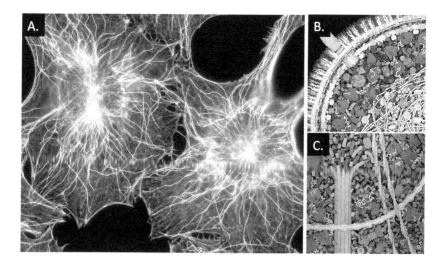

FIGURE 1 *(a)* Fluorescent light micrograph of two fibroblast cells, showing their nuclei and cytoskeleton. The cytoskeleton is made up of microtubules of the protein tubulin and filaments of the protein actin. The cytoskeleton supports the cell's structure, allows the cell to move, and assists in the transport of organelles and vesicles within the cell. Fibroblasts are cells forming connective tissue and are responsible for secreting connective tissue proteins such as collagen. Image by Torsten Wittman. *(b)* This illustration shows a cross-section of a small portion of an *Escherichia coli* cell. The cell wall, with two concentric membranes studded with transmembrane proteins, are in an arc across the top left of the field. A large flagellar motor crosses the entire wall, turning the flagellum, which extends upward from the surface. The cytoplasmic area is just below this and contains large round molecules that are ribosomes; the small L-shaped molecules are tRNA, and the white strands are mRNA. Enzymes are shown in lighter gray. The nucleoid region, which is the DNA, is shown as long white strands in the bottom right of the field. Image by © David S. Goodsell 1999. *(c)* A small portion of cytoplasm is shown, including three types of filaments that make up the cytoskeleton: a microtubule (the largest), an intermediate filament (the knobby one), and two actin filaments (the smallest ones). The large molecules with white strands associated are ribosomes, busy in their task of synthesizing proteins. The large dumbbell-shaped protein at bottom center is a proteasome, which is responsible for degrading proteins. Illustration and caption by David S. Goodsell, the Scripps Research Institute

have someone on their laps, those people would have someone on their shoulders, and the people standing would be as close as possible and also would have two people stacked on top of their shoulders. Okay, honestly, even worse than that . . . Also, like in the subway, where people would have bags, umbrellas, books, and strollers, in a cell the proteins have their own accessories, a myriad of small chemicals such as *lipids* and RNAs.

Generally, in a subway car the passengers just sit there and wait for the next stop, but in our overcrowded subway car of the cell, the passengers are in constant motion. Molecules need to move to make life happen! Imagine that you're the person crammed in the back corner of this overly overly crowded subway car and needing to make your way to the top front corner to have a meaningful conversation (exchange information) with another person and thus change that person's behavior, and to do all that in a matter of seconds. In cells, protein molecules are moving (more precisely, *diffusing*) around at the rate of about 1–5 micrometers per second. About how many molecules would a protein pass by in a second on its journey to finding an interacting protein? A safe guess would be at least 3 million! Even more, all the proteins (and all the other molecules) are also moving because much of the diffusion is being driven simply by changes in temperature. So that person you had to find keeps changing position! Plus, that person needs to find another person! And so on and so on . . . Seeing what happens is only the first step in cell biology. The next step is to understand *how* it happens.

What Kind of Mechanic of Life Are You?

How does the jumble of activity described above produce the complex and organized decision making, metabolic handling, and reproduction that is a hallmark of every cell on the planet?

We need more tools to get at what we call the "mechanism," and this is a basically a code word for "How does it really work?" A key process in the life of the cell is the interaction of proteins. When two proteins meet, does that change their ability to catalyze a reaction? Does it make them go to an entirely new location or cause their destruction?

Historically, there have been two philosophically quite distinct approaches to understand how different proteins do their jobs within a cell, one guided by biochemistry (see the "What Is Chemistry?" essay in this volume) and one guided by genetics. To get a sense of the distinction, I'll summarize a famous story (well, famous among cell biologists, at least) written by an accomplished biochemist, Doug Kellogg, and a respected geneticist, Bill Sullivan. They describe a scenario wherein a biochemist and a geneticist out for a walk come upon an auto-manufacturing plant. All the two can see are the finished cars coming off the assembly line, and they separately set out to understand how the cars are made. The biochemist gets her hands on a car and starts taking it apart, trying to see what each individual part of the car is capable of doing. The geneticist goes down to the factory and ties the hands of specific workers at different parts of the assembly process and then looks at how the cars drive, depending on which components were disabled. Ideally, at the end of these "experiments" the two would be able to reconvene outside the factory and build a model of what goes on in there.

The analogy to understanding the cell is immediate. A biochemist tries to understand a process by taking a cell apart and studying the activity of small numbers of components in isolation. A geneticist takes one or a few things away from an intact cell by making mutations in the DNA and sees what the resulting *phenotype* is (what its characteristics are) and infers the function of the missing component based on how the cells behave when that component is lost. Ideally, all cell processes are studied by both genetic and biochemical approaches. One way to think about the differences between the two ways of thinking is that biochemistry tells you what a set of molecules are capable of, and genetics tells you what they are required to do in a cell. Most people who become cell biologists seem to sort themselves toward genetics or biochemistry based on which approach feels more natural. Which way is more intuitive for you to think about a problem? Would you try to take apart the car or break the assembly line?

The genetics and biochemistry approaches might both be called "reductionist" in the sense that they look to understand the whole from a reassembling of the basic parts. The geneticist and biochemist generally look at a few proteins or genes at a time, almost in isolation. This reductionist approach has been very powerful for understanding many cell processes, but at the end of the day, amazingly, the cell has a myriad of processes that have to be controlled, coordinated, and integrated. This means that analysis of any protein in isolation may be misleading for the reality of daily life in the cell. Just like you can't really understand the workings or culture of a city with a weekend visit to one neighborhood, it is tough to truly understand how cells work by studying each process without connection to the bigger network. So in recent years a more "holistic" approach has emerged and, with it, a new breed of "systems cell biologists" who often have a strong background in computational (mathematics, computer science, statistics, etc.) methods. Systems biologists use new computational tools to analyze huge data sets that include information about all the proteins or RNAs that are changing at any given moment in a cell. Such data sets or approaches are often named with the suffix "-omics," such as genomics or proteomics, and involve experiments where every RNA or every protein that can be detected is being monitored in an experiment.

New Horizons

Let's consider now some big questions that still remain unanswered in cell biology. Many of these have been chipped away at, but we still don't really have a satisfying understanding of the "mechanism," and these will be some meaty problems for the next several years in cell biology.

HOW DOES A CELL KNOW ITS SIZE?

Life happens on many scales, from bacteria to whales. What determines how big a cell, a tissue, or an organism actually is? After an organism grows to adulthood, what determines how many cells are needed to maintain a size? The largest organism is a fungus called the "honey fungus," and a single individual of this species can be kilometers wide. The largest single cell is an aquatic alga where a single cell can be twelve inches in diameter—this is four orders of magnitude bigger than most of the cells in our bodies. A cell can't carry around a ruler in its pocket, so how does a cell or a population of cells know how big it is "supposed to be"?

It is generally thought that cells control the size at which they divide, and perhaps this is how they control their ultimate size. The idea is that a cell won't "decide" to undergo division until it reaches a certain threshold size, and once it crosses the threshold, then it will divide into two smaller cells that will grow to the threshold and divide, and so on. So, what sets this threshold, and how does the cell "know" it passes the threshold? Amazingly, some single-celled *eukaryotes* can actually change their threshold or size to be smaller or larger depending on their environmental nutrient conditions. This means there is some plasticity to the mechanism of setting cell size: it isn't necessarily hard-wired to be a single size for a given cell type.

There have been two broad ideas put forward for how a cell may "know" when it is ready to divide. One possibility is that the threshold is based not on size but on time. In this so-called timer model, cell size is not based on some physical measurement but instead reflects how much time has elapsed since the last division. You could imagine it as an alarm clock, where somehow there are biochemical timers that tick away, and after some set amount of time, the buzzer rings and triggers the cells to divide. This may be hard to imagine on a molecular level, but there is plenty of precedent for timers—our own circadian rhythms are ٭٭ ٭٭plon of biological timers that work to keep a sense of time in the backdrop of cellular reactions. It is an interesting and active area of rew٭٭٭ arch to consider all the ways a cell might be able to construct a timekeeper out of molecules. One of the fascinating complexities of this problem is that such cell-based timekeepers have to be able to keep time regardless of the temperature. Since many chemical reactions in the cell will occur at different rates depending on temperature, it can be quite tricky to wire a robust clock that can ensure division at the same size simply based on time.

Alternative and probably more widely accepted models for cell size controls are based on cells having so-called sizer mechanisms, whereby a cell "senses" its size relative to some kind of physical ruler. One intriguing model (currently being tested) is based on protein production in the cell: perhaps cells sense how fast they are making new proteins, or whether concentration of certain proteins is increasing or decreasing, or the ratio of activating and inhibiting proteins. This is a hugely fascinating question in the pure puzzle of the science of life. Understanding this size problem may be critical for one day when we use synthetic biology applications to engineer cells to provide new materials or products. Can you imagine ways that cells would be able to measure their physical size?

HOW DO SINGLE-CELLED ORGANISMS
FORM DIVERSE COMMUNITIES?

While many of us may be more inclined to study the cells of multicellular animals (like people!), there are many single-celled organisms on the planet, and increasingly their lives have attracted a lot of attention from cell biologists as well as microbiologists. We are thought to possess about as many bacteria (39 trillion) as human cells (30 trillion) in our body. Tremendous effort has been made in the last decade to map the human *microbiome*, meaning the inventory of all the microbes living in any specific area of the body, such as the skin, the GI tract, or the lungs. So far most of the work has focused on bacteria, but there are also many fungi living in these microbial networks. Many disease or unhealthy states are being linked to the composition of microbes in a person, and early success of microbiome "transplants" from healthy to diseased individuals provides further support for the idea that diverse microbes play a key role in the health of the more visible parts of the biosphere. Microbe communities are also at work throughout the natural environment, and many people are familiar with the notion that a teaspoon of soil has over a billion bacterial cells in it. But now consider that within that billion are at least tens if not hundreds of thousands of different species.

What are all these bacteria doing in our bodies and our fields and forests? How much do the different species depend on each other or compete to survive? Are they collaborating, or are they all fighting for a niche in our warm, glucose-rich crevices? Much of the recent work on the importance of the microbiome has focused on making lists of species in broad territories of a whole organ system. This is a great starting point but doesn't begin to tell you how and why all the different cells cohabitate. Learning this kind of information from currently available lists of species would be like trying to piece together a town based simply on the phonebook (these are books that everyone used to use to look up phone numbers before the Internet). Exciting future work will start looking at neighborhoods of organisms and see who is beside whom, how interdependent different species are, and whether they rent a space transiently or are permanent residents. This is where the cell biologists who are used to thinking about spatial organization in a cell can join forces with the microbiologists. These questions will take lots of clever microscopy, mathematical modeling, and chemistry to determine what microbes are where and how they communicate with each other. The conception of the microbiome as a "community" of living things has also attracted the attention of ecologists! Take a look at the "What Is Ecology?" essay in this volume for an introduction to that idea.

WHY DON'T ALL CELLS DO THE SAME THING EVEN IN THE SAME ENVIRONMENT WITH THE SAME GENES?

How often do we say in daily life, "Well, that was random"? What do we mean by that? We didn't expect it, it didn't follow a pattern, it seemed to happen by chance. Whereas we might (paradoxically!) expect that "stuff happens" as a part of life at our scale, randomness at the level of the cell is perhaps more of a surprise. For a long time the standard assumption was that everything cells do must be highly programmed, regulated, and precisely controlled so that nothing gets screwed up that might affect generations of cells to come. But actually, the randomness or *stochasticity* of life even exists down at the level of molecules inside cells. I'm not sure whether that is comforting, but it is increasingly clear that cells actually take advantage of stochasticity and that natural selection may have even selected for processes to be more random or noisy that you would expect even by chance.

What does randomness on the cell scale look like? Often it will be seen as variability in the number of molecules of a given protein in a cell, such that one cell may have ten molecules, another cell fifty, another cell five hundred, and depending on the number of these proteins, a cell may turn on different genes, have different sensitivity to a signal outside the cell, or be able to grow at a different rate. What is so surprising is that this randomness will emerge in a population of cells that have exactly the same genes and are growing side by side in the same environment. Why would cells embrace randomness? There is still a lot of work to be done here, but biologists are finding more and more places where stochasticity is at work and is important. One idea is that cells use stochasticity as a form of "bet hedging" so that if things suddenly change (stuff happens!), some members of the cell population may be "ready" for that new condition. Why do you think cells might embrace random acts of biochemistry?

Conclusion

These are just a few of many open questions right now in cell biology. With more discoveries and new technology, the lists of interesting unsolved questions keep getting longer, not shorter. New genome-editing technology such as CRISPR (Clustered Regularly Interspaced Short Palindromic Repeats) is opening up study of completely new organisms that have never been examined before at the molecular level. This will allow generations of biologists to discover totally new biology and apply this knowledge to increasingly complex problems. What is so thrilling is that this likely means that entirely new kingdoms will be created on our fantasy maps of cells. On the other hand, this now gives humanity the power to potentially edit the genomes of embryos and crops in ways that will need to be given deep reflection by not only scientists but also humanists and ethicists.

The basis for most human diseases is cellular, and the possibility of environmental health remediation involves the application and engineering of cells. Problems that we may not even know about yet will likely be solved by *synthetic biology*, where what we know about normal cells is applied to constructing specialized cells that can solve very specific practical problems. This interface of computational, physical, and biological sciences will be a really exciting place to be working as the planet changes over the next century. So cell biology—really, all fields of biology—needs all kinds of thinkers, including physicists and computer scientists. Math, physics, and chemistry are around every experimental corner: many cell biology labs are an interdisciplinary patchwork of biologists, physicists, engineers, and mathematicians all working on the same problem and trying to speak each other's languages. Technology has enabled all of these approaches to make massive strides in the past twenty years or so, and it is clear that the interface between computational science and biology will prove to be a stable and powerful association.

I hope you see that biology is far from understood and that it is a truly creative endeavor that involves linking imagination to experimental design and interpretation. For years to come (assuming that the federal government continues to support science), imagination and ethics will be the only factors limiting what biologists can do.

WHAT IS

Chemistry?

F. Jon Kull

Chemistry is the science of understanding the properties of matter and how matter forms from the basic elements that make up our universe. Chemists seek to understand how the atoms and molecules that make up matter can combine, how and when they react, and how new molecules can be synthesized. Chemistry can explain why water freezes at some temperatures, but remains liquid at others. It can explain why wood is so stable that buildings made from it can last for hundreds of years, yet a single match can reduce it to ashes. It enables us to make the drugs that keep us healthy and the polymers that shape our society. Chemistry helps us understand the basic principles of life, how proteins fold, and how DNA carries the code to make a human being. In short, chemistry helps us to understand many of the natural world's most fascinating questions.

Although chemistry is often called the *central* science, I think of chemistry as occupying an arc in a great circle of disciplines that help us understand the world we live in. To one side, chemistry is flanked by physics, beyond which is math; and I think many would agree that math edges up against philosophy. On the other side, chemistry blends into biology, beyond which is physiology, and, for humans, psychology, sociology, and, you guessed it, philosophy. So don't think of any of these fields as distinct; they are related to each other and merge into each other. You can start your journey of understanding our world at any point on the circle.

A Brief History of Chemistry

People have been fascinated with the reactions of matter for thousands of years, and the Greek philosophers were perhaps the first to try to define the nature and makeup of matter. In Aristotle's view of the world, four basic elements—earth, air, fire, and water—could be combined to form everything in the universe. This view was accepted as truth for centuries, with some slight modifications. By the 1600s, alchemists were studying materials and reactions, seeking to change matter into different forms (particularly lead into gold), and trying to create ever more perfect materials. They believed that all complex matter, for example wood or flesh, could be broken down into three basic elements: salt, mercury, and sulfur.

Among the alchemists was a young man whom many believe to be the first chemist, Robert William Boyle (1627–1691). Boyle had the clarity of thought to think beyond the common practices and beliefs of Aristotle and the alchemists and to approach the study of matter using the *scientific method*, which is based on hypothesis, experimentation, and logical analysis. Much of this is described in his 1661 book *The Sceptical Chymist*, in which he describes his skepticism, not of chemistry, but of the common premises of alchemy. The book is a fascinating read, and describes the observations and experiments Boyle conducted which convinced him that the beliefs of the alchemists were incorrect and that matter was composed of far more elements, which he called "corpuscles." For example, Boyle did not believe that gold, which was so pure and beautiful, could be made up of some combination of salt, mercury, and sulfur. In one experiment, Boyle had his gardener gather some soil and dry it in an oven. He then planted a "pompion" (i.e., pumpkin) seed, watered it using only rainwater, and let it grow over the summer. In the fall, he determined the mass of the plant and pumpkin, as well as the dry mass of the remaining soil. He was amazed to find the soil's mass had not decreased, and deduced that somehow the plant matter had been formed only from the water that was added. Of course, this presented a problem for him, as the same water and soil could produce a number of different plants, from which could be derived a variety of oils. Boyle knew there must be more going on than the alchemists could explain, and devoted his life to the study of this and other reactions, founding what is considered to be modern chemistry.

Of course, today we know that plants use not only water, but also carbon dioxide from the air, to grow, and that they do indeed extract some nutrients from the soil. However, at the time Boyle had not yet imagined that the air contained different molecules, and he does not even mention the possibility in his book. Interestingly, Boyle went on to study the behavior of gases, and to this day you will learn in chemistry class that Boyle's Law describes the inverse relationship between the volume and pressure of a gas. I expect he realized during his experiments on gases that the air had something to do with the experiment he had run years before with the plant.

Following in Boyle's footsteps, the chemists of the eighteenth and nineteenth centuries used the scientific method to greatly expand our understanding of matter and its components. They found that while matter could be converted into different forms, mass was always conserved. This led to the conclusion that the basic *elements* making up the molecules of matter were not destroyed or created during a reaction—they simply changed forms—and led to the description of the *periodic table of the elements* by Dmitri Mendeleev in 1869. The periodic table can be viewed as a codebook for the behavior of atoms. As the early chemists identified new elements, they were able to place them into the table in the proper place, arranging them such that elements in the same column have similar properties. Of course, in the early days there were gaps in the table, which predicted additional elements that had not yet been discovered. This is a great example of how the scientific process works: the best theories are predictive, and the periodic table's predictions inspired chemists to work on identifying, purifying, and characterizing the missing elements. Today the periodic table contains 118 elements, of which 94 are naturally occurring—the rest have been created by scientists in the laboratory. Of course, the nature of the table continues to predict that more elements can exist, and it is likely only a matter of time until element 119 is created.

Other early chemists studied molecules, and how they were made from the elements. For example, the chemical formula for water is H_2O, meaning it is made up of one atom of oxygen combined with two atoms of hydrogen. But early chemists did not know this, and indeed since Aristotle's time water itself had been thought to be a pure element. Experiments in the late 1700s demonstrated that water could be separated, using electricity, into elemental hydrogen and oxygen, but it took early chemists such as Proust, Dalton, Avogadro, and Cannizzaro more than half a century to develop the theory and perform many clever experiments to demonstrate that water was *always* made up of *one* molecule of oxygen bound to *two* molecules of hydrogen. While there are other ways to arrange oxygen and hydrogen atoms (HO, HO_2, etc.), only one combination, H_2O, forms water. Today we know that each molecule in nature is made up of a constant, defined proportion of elements, held together in a unique molecular structure. During a chemical reaction, the atoms in molecules are rearranged to make new molecules—importantly, the atoms themselves are neither created nor destroyed.

The Collective and the Individual

The modern study of chemistry is a combination of exploring the macroscopic and microscopic properties of matter. By macroscopic, I mean the properties of collections of molecules, such as a sample of gas in a balloon or a solution of seawater in a beaker. The gas in the balloon has a *pressure* that we can measure and a *density* that, at least if it is floating, is lower than air. But both of these properties are a result of the unique contributions of individual molecules—for pressure, the force exerted by the collisions of tens of billions of individual molecules with the side of the balloon; for density, the average mass and number of all of the different types of molecules in the balloon. Similarly, we might study a chemical reaction, such as sugar burning, and measure the amount of heat that is produced and the mass of the reactants before the reaction and the products after. Clearly, the total amount of heat produced is a result of the sum of the minuscule amount of heat released by each of the individual molecular reactions.

It is quite common that chemists study the behavior and properties of such macroscopic collections of matter in order to deduce what is going on at the level of individual molecules, what is referred to as "microscopic." Please note that molecules really exist on a *nanoscopic* scale (a nanometer is *one-billionth* of a meter, and *one thousand* times smaller than a micrometer). Nevertheless, at this level, chemists study the bonds that hold the atoms in molecules together, and the details of the mechanisms by which individual molecules interact to form new molecules. A complete understanding of matter at this level allows chemists to create new molecules or materials with different properties (think anticancer drugs, or superconducting metals).

Will It Happen, and How Fast?

Once chemists have described, discovered, or invented a new chemical reaction, there are two fundamental properties that need to be determined about it—will the reaction occur spontaneously (i.e., by itself without adding energy), and how fast will the reaction occur? Answering these two related but distinct questions makes up the very heart of chemistry and involves the concepts of *thermodynamics* and *kinetics*.

Thermodynamics is the study of the *enthalpy* and *entropy* of a chemical reaction or physical process. Enthalpy, which I'll refer to as energy for the remainder of this discussion, deals with the amount of heat energy given off or absorbed by a reaction. Entropy is the change in the disorder/randomness of the products as compared to the reactants. One can think of these two aspects of thermodynamics as being somewhat at odds with each other—in effect, a universal struggle between order and chaos. For example, all processes in nature tend to spontaneously move toward a state of lower energy, just as a ball spontaneously rolls down a hill. On the other hand, the universe is constantly moving toward increased disorder. Think about it; your room spontaneously becomes messy, and not the reverse (at least without some prodding and subsequent effort/energy). For every different chemical reaction, there exists a certain amount of energy and entropy associated with it that determines whether or not the reaction will be spontaneous. If the energy decreases, and the entropy increases, the reaction will always occur spontaneously—think about wood burning, in which the cellulose in the wood combines with oxygen, releases a significant amount of heat energy, and forms carbon dioxide and water. On the other hand, if the energy increases and the entropy decreases, the reaction will never occur by itself—you can mix water vapor and carbon dioxide together, but they will never form cellulose!

Importantly, thermodynamics tells us whether a reaction will happen, but nothing about how much time it will take. To illustrate, you can use wood, which we just said will spontaneously react to form carbon dioxide and water, to build a house that can last for centuries. How can this be? The answer is that the kinetics of the reaction determines the rate, and this reaction is occurring, but *extremely* slowly. However, as anyone who has lit a fire with a match knows, when the flame of the match, around 1,500 degrees Fahrenheit, increases the temperature of the wood, the reaction proceeds quickly and spontaneously. Furthermore, it releases a great deal of additional heat energy—indeed, enough to quickly burn a house to the ground.

Another example of the relationship between thermodynamics and kinetics addresses the age-old question of whether diamonds really are forever. The answer is, perhaps surprisingly, no! Diamond is not the lowest-energy form of pure carbon; that honor belongs to the rather less flashy form of carbon called graphite. This means that, right now as you read this, all of the diamond jewelry in the world is spontaneously turning into graphite! But there is no need to panic: although the conversion is thermodynamically favored, it is kinetically limited to be an *extremely* slow process. It does not take forever for a diamond to turn into graphite, but it probably requires more than a billion years!

Indeed, a great deal of the modern chemical research and applications of chemical theory seek to overcome the energy and rate requirements imposed by the fundamental limits of thermodynamics and kinetics. For example, above we saw that carbon dioxide and water will never *spontaneously* combine to form cellulose/wood. However, we all know that plants do this all the time. What trick do they use in order to run this reaction in reverse, the thermodynamically nonspontaneous direction? The answer, of course, is sunlight, which provides the energy necessary to, in effect, drive this reaction uphill. Similarly, if chemists want to make a reaction run in the "wrong" direction, they must discover a way to add enough energy to the process to make it happen.

In terms of reaction rates, there are some tricks chemists can use to speed things up. One you know already is that, most of the time, increasing the temperature will increase the rate of a chemical process. Think about how much easier it is to dissolve sugar or salt in hot water as compared to cold water. Or why we refrigerate our food to slow down spoilage. All chemical reactions at the microscopic level depend on collisions, and molecules at higher temperatures move faster, collide with more energy, and therefore react with each other more frequently.

A second way to increase the rate of a chemical reaction is to add a *catalyst*. A catalyst is neither a reactant nor a product of a reaction, nor is it consumed by the reaction; rather, it is something that helps the reactant and products to interact and/or interconvert more efficiently.

You have likely heard of enzymes, which are proteins that catalyze biochemical reactions. Life would not exist without enzymes, as the reactions that our bodies all depend on would simply be too slow without them. For example, eating a candy bar provides us with a quick fix of energy, largely from the sugar it contains. However, if you take some sugar and place it in a bowl, it will (according to thermodynamics) start to react with the oxygen in the air and spontaneously turn into carbon dioxide and water. Of course, since you likely have sugar in the cupboard at home, you know this does not happen at an appreciable rate. However, if you take the sugar (in the form of a marshmallow) and heat it up over a fire . . . Oh no! You got it too close and it caught on fire, almost instantly converting sugar and oxygen to carbon dioxide and water (and a bit of ash). By contrast, your body has neither the time to wait, nor the tolerance for the high temperature required, to convert sugar quickly into energy. Instead, it uses enzyme catalysts, which can speed up a chemical reaction by a million times or more, allowing you to get that sugar rush after only a few minutes!

If you will allow me a brief aside, it is the mystery of enzymes that first attracted me to chemistry and the subfield of biochemistry. As an undergraduate, I double majored in chemistry and biology because I loved the pure, basic-science aspects of chemistry and was fascinated by being able to apply mathematical and physical principles to understanding how molecules formed and reacted. And while I was very interested in the myriad processes that were described in cell biology and genetics lectures, I was somewhat baffled by memorizing and keeping straight the names, pathways, and regulatory cascades, and instead driven to understand these biological processes at the structural and chemical level. For example, I found it amazing that enzymes in our bodies can harness the chemical energy stored in a molecule of ATP—*adenosine triphosphate*, the basic energy currency found in all cells on Earth—and then use that energy to power cellular processes as diverse as replicating DNA, synthesizing proteins, carbohydrates, and lipids, or powering our molecular motor proteins (an interesting fact is that each day a person uses roughly their own weight in ATP as it is consumed to power reactions, and then remade using energy from the food we eat; for a person weighing sixty kilograms, that much ATP would cost about $3 million!). As a graduate student, I found biochemistry and structural biology to be the ideal combination of applying fundamental chemical principles to understanding complex biological questions, and I have spent all of my adult life trying to understand at the atomic level the mechanisms by which enzymes and other proteins operate.

Putting discussion of enzymes aside for now, many nonbiological chemical reactions use chemical catalysts, and these can be incredibly valuable, both in terms of reaction efficiency as well as economics. One example that we see on a daily basis is the catalytic converter used in automobiles, which helps to more efficiently and completely convert fuel into less harmful products (once again, mainly carbon dioxide and water). The catalyst in this case is usually a precious metal, often platinum, that speeds up chemical reactions, eliminating some of the nasty by-products of combustion that would otherwise be present in exhaust so they are not released into the environment.

Other chemical catalysts represent major scientific breakthroughs. For example, the *Grubb's catalyst*, typified by a complex molecule containing an atom of the metallic element ruthenium, is widely used in chemical reactions, and in 2005 Robert Grubbs, Richard Schrock, and Yves Chauvin earned the Nobel Prize in Chemistry for its discovery and application.

Chemistry Is a Diverse Discipline

Modern chemists belong to a wide range of subfields and conduct research designed to both explain the nature of molecules and use such information to improve society and the world we live in.

Physical chemists strive to understand the mysteries of individual molecules at the atomic level. They use mathematics, computers, and sophisticated scientific instruments to study how atoms bond to each other and to determine the details of the molecular mechanisms by which chemical reactions occur. They also combine the use of experiment and theory to explain the characteristics and behavior of matter, offering us an understanding of the chemical world, as well as discoveries and insights into creating new molecules and materials.

Organic chemists are the artists and engineers of the chemical world. Their research focuses on synthesizing molecules, often combining atoms in novel ways and producing molecules with incredible properties: from effective drugs against cancer, to compounds that glow in the dark, to new and effective chemical catalysts. I recently went to an organic chemist colleague of mine with a sketch of a molecule on a piece of paper and asked, "Can you help me make this?" He looked at it for perhaps a minute, grabbed a notepad, and in fifteen minutes, in a process that to me was as amazing as watching an actual artist drawing a portrait, had sketched out a multistep chemical synthesis. He ending by saying, "This molecule has never been made before, but I think this method would work." Subsequently, his insight enabled my laboratory to synthesize that very molecule, which as it turns out might be effective at preventing bacterial disease.

Inorganic chemists, including the Nobel laureates discussed above, specialize their research on molecules and reactions utilizing the many unusual properties of the transition metals from the central region of the periodic table.

Materials chemists seek to create molecules and materials that have special properties, leading to inventions such as the ink used in 3-D printers or molecular sensors that change their electrical properties when they bind to molecules found in secondhand smoke.

Biochemists, such as myself, are fascinated with the chemistry of life. We delve into questions related to how organisms such as humans keep ourselves alive by existing in a steady state where we constantly take in food and convert it to energy and the ability to do work, and at the same time are able to think, create, and dream.

Today, one of the major challenges facing chemists of all types is the topic of "green" chemistry, which seeks to minimize the impact of chemical synthesis on the world's environment. As discussed, many chemical catalysts utilize metals, which are not only very expensive, but often toxic. Furthermore, synthesis of chemicals often requires large volumes of solvents, and these solvents can also be toxic. Green chemistry seeks to develop schemes for chemical synthesis that minimize the use of toxic materials, and also to discover new methods of synthesis and catalysis. Interestingly, this has resulted in a significant shift by the largest pharmaceutical companies away from research and development of small-molecule drugs toward discovery and synthesis of *biologics*, or protein based therapeutics. Biologics are usually produced in water-based systems and therefore do not utilize organic solvents, metal catalysts, and other potentially toxic substances during their manufacture and therefore generate fewer toxic side products. Numerous biologic therapies are already available to treat a wide variety of illnesses, and their future is even more promising, for they have to potential to be customized to a particular person's illness. Being able to recognize, diagnose, and treat disease with such precision-based medicine is one of the holy grails of the biomedical field and will lead to a future where disease can be fought at the individual level, possibly even the cellular level.

Of course, there are other types of chemistry waiting for you to discover, and while chemists tend to describe themselves in terms of some of the subfields I discuss above, most chemists utilize aspects of multiple disciplines of chemistry in their research. Today many of the most interesting discoveries are made at the interfaces of these traditional disciplines. You may find your passion lies in organometallic chemistry, analytical chemistry, physical organic chemistry, chemical engineering, or bioinorganic chemistry, but no matter what flavor of chemistry you decide on, you will be studying the matter and molecules that make our world such an interesting and wonderful place!

WHAT IS

Classics?

Roger B. Ulrich

The one way for us to become great . . .
is to imitate the Greeks.

JOHANN JOACHIM WINCKELMANN, 1775

The great German scholar who wrote those words nearly 250 years ago believed that the ancient Greeks had reached a level of perfection through their art that represented the pinnacle of human achievement. Many of us would argue today that "greatness" is achieved less by copying the accomplishments of others than through innovation and fresh ideas. If innovation and fresh ideas lead to greatness, then surely Greeks—and later the Romans—have earned the distinction of being "great." We can still learn from them today (without having to "imitate" them!), building on their ideas to interpret the world around us. Those who devote their professional lives to understanding the cultures of Greece and Rome work in the field of *classics*.

From the time of the Renaissance to the present day, people interested in classical civilization have studied literary works written in the two main languages of these cultures: ancient Greek and Latin. Even though most of these writings from Greece and Rome have now been translated into many modern languages—we'll return to that development later—being able to read Greek and Latin in their original form gives us a closer understanding of ancient thought and the art of the ancient writer. By studying ancient language we can still read and hear the Greek used by Homer nearly three thousand years ago to tell the stories of the Trojan War, or the Latin spoken by Julius Caesar in his accounts of his wars against the Gauls.

Why has there been such an interest in these "dead" languages (so called because they are not spoken anymore)? And why the focus on places and events now so removed from us in time and space? Because much of the world that we experience today—especially for those of us who live in Europe or the Americas—has been shaped by the literature, art, and philosophy of ancient Greeks and Romans. In telling their stories and writing about the world around them, ancient poets, historians, playwrights, philosophers, lawyers, and architects grappled with the same issues we face today: our responsibility as citizens, the nature of religion, of good and evil, of justice, of bravery and cowardice.

To explore the ancient world the modern classicist no longer focuses only on language study. The understanding of the words and thoughts of the Greeks and Romans is still the foundation of the classical education. But today the study of classics embraces a number of other disciplines. Given the breadth and complexity of the civilizations and geographical spread of Greeks and Romans (who at one time or another dominated all of Europe, Britain, the Middle East, and North Africa), modern scholars who study the classics choose a focus. In addition to the traditional field of language and literature study there are classicists who devote their energies and inquiries to history, archaeology, drama, and philosophy. Scholars in one area can work collaboratively with colleagues in other areas to form a clearer understanding of the classical world.

Before we look at some of the various ways classicists study the civilizations of ancient Greece and Rome it is important to remember that the fact that so many people study these cultures (and many do!) does not mean we consider them perfect or somehow superior to the world we live in today. Far from it! The great achievements of the Greeks and Romans took place in societies afflicted with many of the same problems we face in modern times. Crime, war, lack of food, and disease were all a part of ancient life—and in many cases much worse than is experienced today. For a particularly egregious example, note that most Greeks and Romans viewed slavery as a normal and useful part of their daily lives—a view that we find abhorrent today.

It is also important to remember that while Greeks and Romans get the most mention, they were not the only peoples who lived along the shores of the Mediterranean Sea in antiquity. It would be unfair to these other ancient civilizations (and poor historical work!) to credit only the Greeks and the Romans with all the "Greek" and "Roman" achievements we admire today. For example, the much-studied and well-known "Greek mythology" developed in part from stories of gods and heroes that had long circulated in the lands of Mesopotamia (modern Iraq). Moreover, the stories we enjoy reading today would have been lost if the Greeks had not learned how to write from the Phoenicians. They learned by adopting the alphabet used by Phoenician traders (who lived in the land that is called Lebanon today) nearly three thousand years ago. This is just one example of the interconnectedness between diverse peoples and shared contributions that characterizes the classical world.

Nothing lasts forever, and the civilizations of Greece and Rome were no exception. The Romans in Italy fought against the Greeks in a long series of wars, and once-great Greek cities like Athens and Corinth were eventually subdued by Rome. Rome's great empire grew. Not only Greece, but countries we know of today as France, England, Spain, Egypt, and Turkey, along with many others, all fell to Rome and became part of an enormous empire. But this great empire also eventually collapsed: barbarian invasions, economic troubles, and a government that failed to look after the needs of its citizens all contributed to the fall. In the centuries that followed, much of Greek and Roman civilization was lost.

Much, but not all! A good deal of writing from these fascinating cultures and a surprising number of physical objects have survived. As I've already mentioned, the study of the classics is in practice a family of related disciplines that all share an interest in the cultures of the Greeks and the Romans. You might have already guessed that there are many different ways to study classical civilization. A person who loves poetry might devote his entire career to reading and interpreting poems written by Greeks and Romans. Another might want to examine the great battles fought by famous Greek and Roman generals. You might be interested in the religion of the Greeks and Romans: who were their gods, and what did these ancient people believe? Think of other questions you might have: What about gladiators? Or the things people ate? How were massive stones lifted into place to construct amphitheaters, temples, and aqueducts? There are probably as many questions about the ancient world as there are classicists.

Today the modern classicist begins to focus on an unanswered question or a group of related questions and spends time in libraries, museums, and archaeological sites in an attempt to find answers. This practice of inquiry—looking into and trying to answer a question—is the heart of research.

Even though there are dozens—in fact, hundreds and hundreds—of specific questions we "moderns" have about the ancient world, most classicists can place their interests under one of three basic "families" or subjects. Let's look for a minute at each of these three broad families of investigation that classicists use today: (1) literary studies (including ancient philosophy); (2) ancient history; and (3) classical archaeology.

Many classicists who have achieved expertise in reading ancient Greek and Latin in their original form devote their energies to the reading and interpretation of early texts. What exactly do I mean by "original form"? That takes us first to the interesting story of how the writings of Greeks and Romans have survived for us to read today.

Books were already precious and scarce in the Greek and Roman world, since every book had to be copied by hand. In antiquity great libraries like the ones at Alexandria in Egypt or the royal library at Pergamon (Greek in antiquity, but now a site in Turkey) held vast collections of handwritten books. Most of the great libraries fell into disuse or were destroyed in the wake of the collapse of the Roman empire. Today not a single original "book" (most would have been written on rolled scrolls) survives from the classical world, except for a few charred scrolls from the buried city of Herculaneum and fragments of papyrus from Roman-period Egypt. Nevertheless, some of the most important stories, histories, poetry, plays, and original philosophical works written in ancient Greek and Latin can still be read. Have you heard about Homer's *Iliad* and *Odyssey*, the fabulous accounts of the legendary Trojan War and the adventures of Odysseus? How did these stories survive for us to read today if Homer's original poetry and all the other great works written by Greeks and Romans have been lost or simply crumbled away into dust? We have some other early "classicists" to thank for the great texts that survived, including Muslim scholars who lived in the eastern Mediterranean and the first Christian monks who lived in the West.

In the early days of Christianity, monks spent many hours copying all kinds of books. This was long before the invention of the printing press. Old books were copied as a way of encouraging silence and concentration, and the new copies enhanced monastic libraries. Some abbots (the leaders of the monks), like Cassiodorus (sixth century CE) believed deeply that the truths to be found in the literature of the Greeks and Romans were essential for the training of the Christian monk. Each letter, every word and phrase, was carefully copied by hand onto specially prepared thin sheets of leather called *vellum*. We call these documents *manuscripts*. A similar practice was engaged in by Arab scholars working for their patrons in the Middle East, an area that had once been a center of learning in classical times.

Thankfully many of these medieval and Arabic manuscripts survive, without which the modern classicist could not do his work today. Because no single manuscript of a given work is a flawless copy of the original (copying with 100 percent accuracy is almost impossible!), or in some cases pages or sections are missing, one of the classicist's first tasks was to reconstruct texts as fully as possible from a variety of often incomplete copies. For example, there exist around three hundred medieval manuscripts of Homer's great epics the *Iliad* or *Odyssey*; each is a little different from the others.

Editors still work with old manuscripts in order to reconstruct a modern version that scholars believe is closest to the original, and classical scholars still debate the correctness of these reconstructions. High-resolution photography and scanning of old manuscripts have allowed more scholars than ever to view the original texts without having to travel extensively. Occasionally words lost from erasures can be recovered through photographing the manuscripts using different light spectrums, like infrared. Online databases of Latin and Greek allow scholars to search quickly to compare word forms, vocabulary, or grammatical constructions. This use of technology to study Greek and Latin allows work that once took weeks, months, or longer to be done in minutes. Nevertheless, it must be remembered that errors can and do occur in the building of these databases: many researchers argue that close examination of the original manuscript with the human eye is still the best way to study an ancient text.

Whereas the copying and examination of old manuscripts were at first limited to a small number of monks who lived and worked in the monasteries, a new interest in the writings (and, as we shall see, art) of Greeks and Romans exploded during the period of history we now call the Renaissance. First Italians then French, English, and Germans, studied the monks' old manuscripts. The loss of Constantinople (now Istanbul) to the Ottomans in 1453 brought to mainland Europe refugees, manuscripts written in Greek, and the knowledge of how to read Greek.

Interest in classical literature during the Renaissance also produced the first attempts by classicists to translate great works of Greek and Roman literature into the "common" (we use the term "vernacular") languages of Europe. In the sixteenth century the *Iliad* and the *Odyssey* were translated into modern Greek, Italian, French, German, and English. These attempts spawned a debate that continues today among classicists: how can an ancient text be translated into another language while being "faithful" to the original? The rhythmic "beat" (we call it the "meter"), for example, of Homer's poetry is almost impossible to render into good English. The translator of ancient Greek has to find a good balance between rendering the original Greek accurately—too accurately will make the

English sound "stilted" or artificial—and substituting English approximations ("paraphrases") that sound better to our ears but are in fact less faithful to the original. George Chapman's English translations of the *Iliad* and the *Odyssey* won great praise when they were created the sixteenth century, although the student who can read Greek will quickly see the great liberties he took in making his lines rhyme!

While rendering good translations of Greek and Latin texts into modern languages is still practiced by talented classicists today, modern classicists are also engaged in a wide variety of approaches to ancient works of literature. "Literary studies" is just a phrase for studying the beauty and art of language. Just as famous writers like Shakespeare, James Joyce, or Mark Twain used English in very different ways to express ideas, emotions, and values, so too ancient writers had their own individual styles for expressing human experiences.

A huge difference between ancient Greek and Latin and modern English is that the ancient languages are *inflected*. That means that the meaning of the sentence is conveyed by different endings on the words, not the word order. If, for example, we write, "The dog bites the man," we understand that the man is suffering from a dog bite. The word order, or *syntax*, tells us this. We would understand that sentence very differently if we wrote, "The man bites the dog." The changed word order conveys a different (and in this case rather strange!) meaning. Latin and Greek work differently. In Latin we can write: *Canis virum mordet* or *Virum canis mordet* or *Mordet canis virum*, or any such combination. Each sentence means the same thing: "The dog bites the man." We know this because of the endings (-*um*, -*is*, and -*t*) found on each of the words. This ability to convey the same meaning without worrying about word order (this is true of ancient Greek as well) gave Greek and Roman writers immense flexibility and creativity in their poetry and prose literature.

Classicists must also keep in mind that much of the ancient literature we read today, including the many plays that have survived, was composed to be performed orally, not read silently. Like most of ancient poetry, for example, Homer's *Iliad* and *Odyssey* were recited to music, and the poet sang the lines after memorizing them. The *Iliad* alone contains over fifteen thousand lines of verse. It is hard for us today to imagine the effort it must have taken to learn this amount of material by heart! At the same time, the classical scholar looks for clues in the text, such as repeated phrases or descriptions, that could have aided the performer. In other words, the oral nature of the poetry in part explains how it was composed.

One important branch of literary studies of Greek and Latin that deserves special mention is the field of ancient philosophy. Classical philosophers study the texts left by the philosophers of Greece and Rome and try to understand their reasoning. The ancient philosopher was, quite literally, someone who "loved wisdom," and as such ancient philosophy included many subjects that we think of today as distinct disciplines in the sciences, including such fields as mathematics, astronomy, and physics. Greek and Roman philosophers also thought, discussed, and wrote about large, more "abstract" questions of human existence, the nature of the human soul, and basic notions of "good" and "evil." Greek philosophers had many theories about the universe. They speculated on what the world is made of: How many elements are there, and how do they combine and separate? Are there atoms, and if so what are they like? In sum, anyone in the ancient world who looked for logical explanations of things could be considered a "philosopher."

The names of some Greek philosophers will be familiar to those who have never formally studied ancient philosophy. In school we learn of the theorem named after the early Greek philosopher Pythagoras, who lived in the sixth century BCE. Other Greek thinkers, such as Socrates, Plato, and Aristotle, have acquired a broader fame that extends well beyond the field of classics. There were many other practitioners of philosophy in the Greek and Roman world, including politicians and lawyers like Cicero and even Roman emperors like Marcus Aurelius, who also wrote a book, the *Meditations*, that is still studied today.

Many of the ways we now ask questions, use evidence, and test our theories are methods that were invented by Greek philosophers. So it is not only the questions ancient philosophers asked, but also how they went about discussing and answering those questions that we find interesting today.

Ancient History

The study of history begins with writing. That is why we call old civilizations without the knowledge of writing *pre*-historic. The modern scholar who studies ancient history works to reconstruct past events by studying ancient texts, especially those written by a group of Greek and Roman writers who recounted stories and reports about their own origins, along with past and current events. Modern studies are concerned not only with *what* ancient texts have to tell us about past events, but also *how* these events have been told. The study of how the telling of history has evolved over time is called *historiography*.

The Greek historian Thucydides, for example, wrote in the fifth century BCE about a long series of wars between two great Greek cities: Athens and Sparta. He himself fought for Athens in that war. If Thucydides wrote about this war—we call it the Peloponnesian War—offering much detail, why would a modern historian want to write about it as well? Think about an experience you might tell about yourself. You might include only the details of what happened that seemed important to you. You might not even notice things that took place that your friends who were there might have noticed about the same event. In a similar way, Thucydides wrote about a war between his home city of Athens and a powerful enemy, Sparta. His story is in part an eyewitness account, but it is not complete and only presents one point of view.

The modern classical historian reads carefully what Thucydides has to say about the Peloponnesian War, but she also tries to include other information: for example, other Greeks, like Xenophon, wrote about events of the war not covered by Thucydides. The playwright Aristophanes included allusions to the war in his dramas. Inscriptions recorded military victories. Perhaps the location of a battlefield from the war can be identified and examined. All of these clues are "evidence," and the classical historian tries to put these scraps of evidence together to form a picture in words, like parts of a gigantic jigsaw puzzle with many pieces missing. But even with the missing pieces we can have a good idea of what the picture looks like. Or in the case of an ancient event, even if we cannot reconstruct everything that happened, we can often form a pretty good idea.

While ancient wars or other "big" events from the classical world have always been of interest to classicists, the modern classical historian now also looks into questions that deal with everyday life: What were daily experiences like for average people: shipbuilders, farmers, or slaves? What about small children or women who played important roles in society but about whom little was written? Here the classical historian might have to look at more fragmentary evidence. Grave inscriptions, for example, often give much useful information about the relationships and roles of individuals within families. Other evidence may be in the form of objects found in ancient houses and workplaces. This is where the archaeologist can help.

Classical Archaeology

You have probably heard of *archaeology* and of the person who works in that practice: an *archaeologist*. "Archaeology" means the "study of old things." Instead of focusing on ancient texts, like the classicist who studies literature, history, or philosophy, the classical archaeologist's focus is on the *artifact*. An artifact is an object that has been made or shaped by human hands. Interpreting artifacts from the worlds of Greece and Rome is the core activity of the classical archaeologist.

Most artifacts are recovered through excavation, or careful digging. Over time abandoned places are buried by dust, leaves, mud, and water. Buildings fall down and bury everything beneath them. Think about how many houses, temples, schools, marketplaces, streets, and public squares of ancient Greece and Rome have been buried under many feet of dirt after having been abandoned or forgotten for twenty centuries or more. Does it surprise you to learn that many of these places are still waiting to be explored by archaeologists?

In the eighteenth and nineteenth centuries, when people first started to dig at ancient sites, there was no formal training to become an archaeologist. Wealthy men whose imaginations had been fired by reading legends and myths in the old Greek and Latin texts were determined to visit and investigate famous places of antiquity. Their efforts were clumsy, even sloppy, by today's scientific standards. Nevertheless, they introduced us to a new way of studying the past. One of the most famous of this new breed of archaeologist was a German named Heinrich Schliemann.

Schliemann was a rich businessman who loved the tales of Homer's *Iliad*. As we have already seen, the *Iliad* and *Odyssey* tell stories connected with the Trojan War. The eighth-century BCE Greeks of Homer's day thought that they had themselves descended from an age of heroes who had lived centuries before their time and fought at Troy, men like Achilles, the greatest warrior of the Greeks, and Hector, the champion of the Trojans. Schliemann believed that the old legends of the Trojan War were true. He was convinced that he could find the location of the fabled city of Troy, a place that was already little more than a legend to a poet like Homer. Schliemann was not the only man intent upon the discovery of Troy. An English expatriate and early archaeologist named Frank Calvert was also convinced that the Homeric epics were based on actual history and had already started to explore the hilltop in Turkey that would prove to be the site of Troy.

Schliemann was something of a romantic, and we can imagine how many of his friends thought his determination to find ancient Troy was a waste of time and money. But to everyone's surprise, he did find the ruins of the famous city in 1871. It was just where Greeks and Romans themselves had believed the Trojan stronghold once stood, now located on the shore of western Turkey.

Schliemann's diggers unearthed the remains of a large city protected by high walls that had been destroyed by fiercely burning fires in ancient times. He found more than just walls. His discoveries included a mass of golden jewelry that he believed had once belonged to the leader of the Trojans himself: King Priam. Now we know that the treasure found by Schliemann is in fact centuries older than when Priam was supposed to have ruled. In this case a later generation of archaeologists who returned to Troy after Schliemann, used the principles of *stratigraphy* to date the finds. Stratigraphy is the practice of studying the diverse levels at which different artifacts are found. We'll come back to this later.

Although we cannot actually prove that there was a king named Priam, or that he had a son named Hector who was finally defeated by a Greek hero named Achilles, thanks to the efforts of Calvert and Schliemann we do know that there was a place called Troy, and that it was destroyed violently, and that the destruction seems to have been remembered and passed down from father to son for many years, probably for hundreds of years, before the Greeks learned how to write and finally preserve the story. Calvert and Schliemann believed that there was at least a core of truth to these ancient stories. Their determination to discover places connected with the stories of Homer resulted in a new field of study: the Greek Bronze Age.

Today archaeologists who focus their investigations on the Greek and Roman world follow in the footsteps of men like Calvert and Schliemann. The methods used take much more time, are more expensive, and rely on computers as much as shovels. The excavation of any site is a destructive process. If mistakes are made or notes and observations are sloppy, much valuable information will be lost forever. The location of every artifact found is carefully mapped, including the notation of the layer, or *stratum*, in which it was found. Doing this helps the archaeologist work out the site's chronology. Since most archaeological sites were occupied for a long time, it is important to assign a diverse range of finds to their proper periods. All of this explains why modern archaeologists work very slowly!

One of the most important concepts for the archaeologist is keeping a record of the *context* of an artifact. That means carefully recording where the object was found in relationship to its surroundings. Unfortunately, many of the first diggers ignored context. They were looking above all for valuable or pretty objects to put in collections and museums (more on this subject later). Why is context so important? Imagine looking at a rusty chisel in a museum case. It would not be very pretty and would perhaps be of interest only to a modern woodworker or mason. But what if we knew more about the context of that artifact? Say we knew that the chisel was found in a grave next to a skeleton. Now we could guess that the grave was that of a carpenter or mason. And we might even hypothesize that the tool was buried along with the person because of a belief in an afterlife—and in the afterlife the deceased would practice the same profession he did while alive. Or maybe there were other iron tools found in the grave, too. Maybe the person was a blacksmith, and buried with samples of his trade. In this example, by paying attention to the context of a simple object, we can begin to form hypotheses about ancient occupations, identity, and even religious beliefs. What if that chisel had been found in the tomb of a woman? What might that tell us about ancient crafts and those who practiced them?

New advances in science and technology allow us to explore the ancient world in ways unimaginable even fifty years ago. For example, we can now use geophysical survey to "see" buildings that are still underground and side-scan sonar to view vivid pictures of sunken ships. Satellite images reveal "lost" roads and even entire buried cities that are in remote places or areas that are not safe (modern warfare is a big problem) for archaeologists to visit. Not so long ago, ancient pottery was scrubbed in a mild acid for cleaning. We now understand that in many cases such treatment was a mistake. Microscopic residues in some ancient pots can now be analyzed on the molecular level, giving us a window on food storage, trade, and ancient diet. A recent study of DNA fragments found inside Greek transport jars (*amphorae*) recovered from a shipwreck, for example, has shown that vessels once thought to have contained primarily wine were used for a wide range of goods, like herbs (for medicines), beans, and nuts.

We have already seen that the language databases and digital imagery accessible to scholars through their personal computers have been a great help to classicists of the present day. Computers are now essential tools at every phase of classical archaeological research, from recovery of artifacts to publication. At archaeological sites they are used for mapping and surveying, as well as keeping records on a day-to-day basis. Powerful CAD (computer-aided design) software allows for sophisticated reconstructions of buildings. Virtual reconstructions help us to visualize what ancient cities and buildings within them looked like when they were still standing. Artifacts can be scanned to produce 3-D renderings, and even physical copies for study. Excavation results and dialogue between archaeologists can now be shared rapidly through websites and online publication.

Who Owns the Past?

Recently classical archaeologists and museum curators have had to address the controversy that stems from the modern phenomenon of "collecting" ancient art.

Remember that the first explorations of archaeological sites were really just "treasure hunts" for beautiful objects. To make things more complicated, for a long time (since the beginning of the nineteenth century) archaeologists digging in countries like Greece, Turkey, and Egypt were not citizens of those countries. Their expeditions were designed to bring excavated treasures back to their home countries for display in museums. Some objects were even smuggled out of the countries in which they were found, or bought from shady dealers. Today many of the greatest examples of Greek and Roman art are found in places like Berlin, London, Paris, Copenhagen, and New York, far from their original settings. The current governments of countries like Greece and Egypt (and the others mentioned above) believe that the old practices were wrong and that the works of art should now be returned to their "homelands."

A famous example to illustrate this controversy is the collection of architectural sculpture traditionally known as the "Elgin Marbles," and now generally referred to by their place of origin as the "Parthenon sculptures." Lord Elgin, a British aristocrat, brought these marvelous statues of gods and heroes from Greece to London between 1801 and 1812. They had once decorated the most famous temple in Athens: the Parthenon. Many people, especially those who live in the modern country of Greece today, believe these sculptures should be returned to Athens. Modern Greeks see these as much more than works of art. They see them as an important element of their national heritage—akin to America's famous Liberty Bell in Philadelphia or the original document of the Declaration of Independence.

Today, this practice of removal and relocation has become a major point of controversy among classical scholars, citizens impassioned about their heritage, tourists, and governments. Some believe that ancient art should be distributed all over the world so that many people, especially those who cannot travel long distances, can enjoy it and learn from it. Protecting and displaying art in museums located all over the world can also, some argue, save art from being destroyed by countries caught up in destructive wars. Others believe just as strongly that old works of art should always be left where they were found . . . that they will always "belong" to the country in which they were discovered. These kinds of arguments have become even more charged in 2015 with the recent destruction and looting of many ancient and historically important ruins in Syria and Afghanistan and Iraq. What do you think?

What's Next?

Today you may wonder if there are any new discoveries to be made in the field of classics. You may ask, "Hasn't everything already been discovered?" Or, "What more can be possibly said about an ancient poem like Homer's *Iliad*?" After all, scores of books, many translations, and hundreds of articles have already been written on such a famous work. It turns out that every new generation has different questions to ask about our past heritage from the classical world. The civil rights struggles, the feminist movement, and Vietnam War conflict of the 1960s, for example, prompted classical scholars to reexamine classical texts and works of art for what they have to tell us about race, gender, and aggression. As our own modern society evolves, so does the way we frame questions. A relatively novel field of inquiry, known as "Reception Studies," has placed a new focus on the ways in which diverse postclassical periods and cultures have interpreted and responded to the art, literature, and history of the classical period. Each new generation brings new tools and a fresh perspective to look back on and understand the classical tradition anew. Greek and Roman poets, philosophers, historians, artists, and architects still can play an instructive and inspiring role in our twenty-first-century lives.

WHAT IS

Computer Science?

Thomas H. Cormen

Have you ever heard the saying "Information is power"? Computer science is all about information. In fact, in some places, computer science is called informatics. So computer science is all about giving people the power provided by information.

Information is a noun. What do we do with it in computer science? What verbs go along with information? The most prominent are *storing*, *accessing*, *transforming*, *transmitting*, and *interacting*. That is, computer science, at its core, is about storing, accessing, transforming, transmitting, and interacting with information. We'll see some examples of these verbs a little later, when we look at text messaging.

Storing and accessing are really two sides of the same coin. If you can store information but not access it, what good does it do you? That would be like having a piggy bank that you can only put money into but never open up.

How information is stored in a computer can affect greatly how easily or rapidly it can be accessed. Depending on the application, one scheme for storing information might be much better or much worse than another. Have you ever seen a printed phone book? It contains the names and associated phone numbers of customers in a certain area. The names are listed alphabetically by last name (in computer science, we say that they are *lexically sorted*), and the top of each page gives the names that start and end the page. Think about how that property makes it easy to find a name in the phone book, so that you can quickly determine that person's phone number. You need to look at only a few entries in the book. But what if you were to try to use a phone book to find a person's name, given only their phone number? The phone book is not organized to look up by phone numbers, so you might have to look at every single entry in the book, especially if the phone number you are searching for does not appear.

Interpreting Information

As you might know, information is stored in a computer as *binary digits*, or *bits*. A bit can have one of just two possible values: 0 or 1. Why do computers use bits instead of the digits 0 through 9 like everyone is used to? It's because information in a computer is stored as electrical charges (voltages), which are not always precise. By interpreting an electrical charge in only one of two possible ways, we can just say that the value represented by a particular charge is whichever of the two possible values it's closest to. You can think of it this way. Suppose you have a friend who lives a block away from your home, and you're going between your friend's home and yours. We can say that you are "at" your home if you're closer to your home than to your friend's home, and that you are "at" your friend's home if you're closer to it than to your own home. What if you're exactly halfway between the two homes? Fortunately, we don't have to worry about that situation in a computer, because the electrical charge is always much closer to one of the possible values than to the other.

How we interpret a sequence of bits matters a great deal. A sequence of bits could represent a number, some text, an image, audio, video, instructions for the computer to execute, or many other possibilities. Consider, for example, this sequence of 112 bits:

0000000010111110101111111011111110111111011101110000011
1011101110111111101111111011111110111111101111110001111

Does it mean anything to you? Of course not. What if you knew that it represented an image made up of black and white squares, where each 0 indicates a black square and each 1 indicates a white square? As a sequence of squares, it would look like figure 1.

FIGURE 1

That's still not helpful, is it? What if you also knew that the image had 14 rows and 8 columns and that it was stored row by row (so that the first 8 squares form the top row, the next 8 squares form the second row, and so on)? Then it would look like figure 2.

FIGURE 2

And now you know that this sequence of 112 bits represents the image of an uppercase letter *F*. Of course, real images usually are in color and much larger than 14-by-8 squares (or *pixels* on a screen). We use more complex schemes to represent them, often incorporating methods to *compress* them—that is, reducing the number of bits needed to store them. (The JPEG encoding scheme, for example, reduces image sizes to about ten times smaller than raw images.)

EXAMPLE: A TEXT MESSAGE

Something as simple as a text message gives a good example of how computers store, access, transform, and transmit information, as well as how you can interact with the information. Now, when we talk about texts, we're talking about smartphones. Is a smartphone really a computer? Absolutely! In fact, today's smartphones are many, many times more powerful than the computers that NASA used for the Apollo missions to the moon.

So, let's say that your friend Pat sends you a text that also contains a photo. Pat has to compose the text, attach the photo, and send the text. Pat's cell-service provider has to receive the information from Pat and, if you and Pat don't have the same provider, get it to *your* provider. Then your provider has to notify you that you have a new text. Once you decide that you want to see the text, it has to be sent to your phone and displayed there. Perhaps you want to view a section of the photo in more detail, so you zoom in on the photo. There's a lot going on here.

Storing and accessing information That text, including the photo, is stored in at least three places: Pat's phone, the cell-service provider's equipment, and your phone. It's stored as bits. Your phone needs to know what value each bit has— 0 or 1.

Transmitting information It's pretty obvious that Pat's phone has to transmit information to Pat's provider and your provider has to transmit that same information to your phone.

Transforming information When your phone receives the text message, it's really receiving nothing more than a long sequence of bits. Some of these bits make up the textual part of the text message, and the rest represent the photo. Your phone has to know which bits are which. That's not enough, however. Your phone also has to know how to convert groups of bits into the pixels you see on the screen.

Even something as seemingly simple as the textual part isn't so simple. It should be straightforward to represent the letter *F* with fewer than the 112 bits we saw earlier, shouldn't it? After all, my phone keyboard can produce only 26 uppercase (capital) letters, 26 lowercase (small) letters, 10 digits, and 32 punctuation characters. That adds up to just 94 different characters. To store 94 characters, only 7 bits are needed. (Why? One bit can represent two possible values, 0 or 1. Each time you add a bit, it doubles the number of possible values. With 2 bits, you can represent 4 values; with 3 bits, 8 values; and so on. With 6 bits, 64 values, which is not quite enough for the 96 characters, but 7 bits gives 128 values, which is enough.) There's one little flaw in this reasoning: a text message might include more than just the 94 characters on the keyboard. Think about characters in languages other than English, such as letters with accents. Or characters in Japanese or Chinese. Or emojis! There are several different ways to represent characters with bits, going under names such as ASCII (American Standard Code for Information Interchange) and Unicode.

And then there are images, such as the photo that Pat sent. There are several ways to represent images as bits. Many of them compress the image, in order to reduce the number of bits needed to transmit and store it.

Interacting with Information To zoom in on an image on your smartphone, you take two fingers, touch the screen with them over the image, and then spread your fingers apart while maintaining contact with the screen. Your phone has to detect the contact and motion, and it then continuously updates the image it displays as your fingers move apart. Likewise, if your fingers move closer together, your phone zooms out. Although you might take zooming in and out of an image for granted, it demonstrates that you don't always have to accept the information exactly as it's presented to you. Like many computers, your smartphone gives you the power to interactively change how you receive information.

Computation

Computers are really good at computation. Big surprise, right? But what do we mean by computation? Think of computation as a precisely described way of transforming information. Here are some examples of computational problems:

Take a list of millions of numbers, and rearrange the list into increasing order. (We call this problem *sorting*.)

Starting with a representation of all the roads in North America, find the shortest driving route from Moose Jaw, Saskatchewan, Canada, to San Luis Potosí, Mexico.

A delivery truck starts from a depot, delivers to several locations, and returns to the depot. The truck could visit the locations in any order. Figure out which order uses the least fuel. (Although this problem might seem similar to the previous one, they turn out to be *very* different.)

Given the locations of objects in a frame of an animated movie and the sources of lighting in that frame, render (draw) the image containing the objects under that lighting.

From a representation of an image, determine what objects are in the image. (This problem is the reverse of the previous one.)

Provided with an image that is claimed to be an actual photograph, decide whether it has been altered.

A robot can move in certain ways, and it must navigate around a set of obstacles. Figure out the fastest way for the robot to get itself to a target location without bumping into any of the obstacles. (The robot can be a self-driving car.)

Given the gene sequences in two strands of DNA, measure how similar they are to each other.

Take a representation of a piece of music, and make it occupy fewer bits without significantly altering the sound.

A person has spoken into a phone and produced an audio signal. Determine what words the person said. (Extra credit: Avoid getting that person into "phone jail.")

Provided with a list of known terrorists and information about which individuals have communicated with each other, decide how likely it is that a specific person will commit an act of terror.

Some sensitive information is to be transmitted. Encrypt it in such a way that the intended recipient can easily decrypt it (that is, restore the original information), but if someone else were to intercept the encrypted information, even with really fast computers, it would take years to decrypt the encrypted information.

A manufacturing company can take several raw materials and produce a number of products from them. The company knows the prices of the raw materials, how much of each raw material goes into each product, and how much profit it makes from each product. Figure out how much of each product it should produce in order to create the highest overall profit.

Find relevant pages on the web to answer a question entered into a search engine.

Can you think of some others?

Resources

Solving computational problems is not free. There are always costs. Yes, there's the cost of the computer itself, but that's a fixed cost: it's paid whether or not we have the computer solve a particular problem. What other types of costs arise when solving problems on computers? Put another way, what resources do computers use?

One important resource is *time*. Once it is spent, you can never get it back. Some computer systems have to operate in *real time*, meaning that they must finish the job within a certain amount of time, or the consequences could be dire. Consider, for example, an air-traffic control system that is supposed to determine whether two jets are on a collision course. Suppose it is possible to determine that two planes are about to collide one hundred seconds before they do, but it takes ninety seconds to alert the pilots that they are about to collide and have them change course to avoid the collision. Then that air-traffic control system had better detect an impending collision in ten seconds or less.

Even if a system does not have to meet real-time requirements, computing time matters. Suppose you ask a GPS to find the fastest route from Boston to Miami. There are a huge number of possible routes, most of which would be ridiculous to even consider. You know, for example, that the fastest route from Boston to Miami cannot possibly go through Los Angeles. The GPS must be using some clever method to find the fastest route that quickly rules out going through Los Angeles. Suppose that, instead, the GPS did consider every possible route. It would take a *really* long time to try them all. The consequences of a GPS taking, say, hours to find the fastest route are not exactly dire, but nobody would use a GPS to find routes if it took that long.

The point is that in computer science, time is a precious resource. Time matters. Many computer scientists continually try to find faster ways to solve computational problems.

Time is not the only precious resource, however. There are several others. One is energy. Computers require energy to operate, and the faster a computer runs, the more energy it uses. That's why you can put a laptop or smartphone into low-power mode, where it runs slower to prolong the battery life.

If you've ever taken your smartphone to where the reception is sketchy, then you can appreciate that communication can be another precious resource. If you've tried to download a large app, song, or video when the signal is weak, only to give up and wait until you got somewhere with a stronger signal, you can see why you might want to communicate as few bits as possible in certain circumstances.

Here's another resource that will probably surprise you: random bits. Random bits? What are they? Why would we need them? Where do they come from? Random bits are some sequence of bits where each bit has an equal chance of being a 0 or a 1, and if you've seen the entire sequence of random bits so far, you don't have better than a 50–50 chance of guessing what the next bit will be. Random bits help us protect information by helping to create *keys* that encrypt and decrypt sensitive material, anything from credit card numbers to critical details of national security. Some modern computer processors have built-in ways to generate random bits based on random electrical processes. Others generate "pseudorandom" bit streams that have all the properties of random bits but are actually generated by a computer program.

Quality of the Solution

It's not enough for a computer to use resources efficiently. It also has to solve the problem at hand. Would you rather have a GPS take one second to give you a route from Boston to Miami that may or may not be the fastest, or have it take a minute to find a route that is guaranteed to be the fastest? Because a route that is not the fastest will certainly take more than a minute longer than the fastest, most people would be willing to wait the extra fifty-nine seconds for the confidence of getting the best route.

There is often a trade-off between the resources used to compute a solution and the quality of the solution produced. When rendering images, more computing time can yield more realistic-looking results. When recognizing faces of specific individuals, more computing time can give more reliable matches.

Even more random bits can give you higher confidence in a solution. For example, many cryptography systems rely on finding extremely large prime numbers. (You probably know that a prime number is an integer, at least 2, whose only integer divisors are 1 and itself.) How large do these prime numbers need to be? *Thousands* of digits. One way to find a large prime number is to repeatedly generate a random odd number and test whether it's prime, until the test says that the number is prime. How can you test whether a number, let's call it n, is prime? You could try all possible divisors. You need to try only numbers up to $\sqrt{n}$, which has half as many digits as n. Of course, if n has thousands of digits, then $\sqrt{n}$ is also a really large number, and it would take a really long time (possibly longer than your lifetime) to try all possible divisors of n.

There's another way to determine whether n is prime, and it's much faster than trying all possible divisors. It's called the "Miller-Rabin test," and it uses lots of random numbers in the range 1 to n. If it says that n is not prime, then n is definitely not prime. But if the Miller-Rabin test says that n is prime, then there's a slim chance that n is not prime. Why would you accept a test that can make errors? Because you can control the chance of the Miller-Rabin test making an error. If you are willing to generate r random numbers in the Miller-Rabin test, then the chance that it calls a number prime when it's not is at most 1 in 2^r. For example, if you are willing to generate 40 random numbers, then the chance that the Miller-Rabin test errs is at most 1 in 2^{40}, which is about one in a trillion. Not good enough for you? Then generate 50 random numbers, and get the chance of error down to 1 in 2^{50}, or one in a quadrillion. Still too risky? Generating 60 random numbers will get you one error in a quintillion, and 70 will get one in a sextillion. You have to like *those* odds!

Algorithms

When we solve a problem on a computer, we need to be able to describe the exact steps for solving it. We call a precise method of solving a problem an *algorithm*. Here's a simple algorithm that you learned many years ago. It's how you add two numbers. Let's call the numbers to add x and y, and the result z.

1. Set the carry to 0.
2. Start at the rightmost digits of x and y.
3. Take the digit of x at the current position, the digit of y at the current position, and the carry, and add them together. You'll get a number from 0 (if the current digits of x and y are both 0 and the carry is 0) to 19 (if the current digits of x and y are both 9 and the carry is 1). If this sum is less than 10, then write it in the next digit of z and make the carry be 0. If, on the other hand, this sum is 10 or greater, then take the ones digit of this sum, write it in the next digit of z, and make the carry be 1.
4. If there are digits of x or y that have not been looked at, go back to step 3, working with the next digits to the left in x and y. Otherwise, if the current carry is 0, then you're done. If the current carry is 1, write it in the next digit of z, and then you're done.

As long as you know how to add three single-digit numbers together, with one of the numbers always being either 0 or 1, you can mechanically execute these steps, just as if you were a computer. (Of course, computers work with binary numbers, so that the sum of three bits ranges only from 0 to 3. They also have a faster way of adding two numbers, based on a clever way to determine all the carries before adding the bits in any position.)

Adding two numbers is about as simple an algorithm as you can find. Let's look at another algorithm. How about the algorithm that a GPS uses to find the fastest route? The road network consists of intersections and roads, where each road connects two nearby intersections. The GPS stores how long it takes to travel each road. (In a really good GPS, this information is updated frequently as traffic conditions change.) Let's say that you want the GPS to find the fastest route from your home to your grandmother's home. To be precise, you want the GPS to find the fastest route starting at the intersection nearest to your home (let's call it intersection S, for the starting point) and ending at the intersection nearest to your grandmother's home (let's call it intersection T, for the terminating point). For each intersection, we keep track of two things:

The fastest time found so far from intersection S to that intersection.

The intersection that you most immediately come from on the fastest route found so far from intersection S. Call it the "preceding intersection."

Initially, set the fastest time to 0 for intersection S (since it takes no time to get from intersection S to itself), and set the fastest times to ∞ (infinity) for all the other intersections, indicating that the algorithm has yet to find any way to get to them.

The algorithm, known as "Dijkstra's algorithm," dates from 1959. It simulates what happens if you can send out cars from each intersection, all going at the same speed, along each road. Start by sending out cars from intersection S along each road that leaves intersection S. Let's look at any intersection, say, intersection I. The first time a car arrives at intersection I, do three things:

1. Record the difference between the time that the car arrives at intersection I and the time that the first cars left intersection S. That's how long it takes to get to intersection I.

2. Record the intersection that the car just came from as intersection I's preceding intersection.

3. Send out a car along every road leaving intersection I.

Stop once a car arrives at intersection T.

Once a car arrives at intersection T, the algorithm can trace out the fastest route from intersection S to intersection T by tracing out the reverse of this route. Starting at intersection T, follow the chain of preceding intersections until getting back to intersection S. Reverse this chain, and you have the fastest way from intersection S to intersection T.

Implementing Solutions on Computers

It's one thing to describe an algorithm in English. We can often infer what is meant when the language is imprecise. But when we describe an algorithm to a computer, we must be excruciatingly precise. Computers execute simple instructions, such as "take the integer value stored in location A and the integer value stored in location B, add the two values, and store the result in location C." Over the years, people have developed *programming languages* as a way to express computational ideas precisely. The simple instruction above would be written in many programming languages as the statement C = A + B. Here, the equals sign is actually an operator, just as the plus sign is. The equals sign means "evaluate the expression on the right-hand side and store that value in the variable named on the left-hand side." One statement that often confuses beginning programmers is something like X = X + 1. They wonder how can X equal itself plus 1. This statement says, "Take the current value of X, add 1 to it, and store the result back into X." Just as the plus sign causes something to happen (adding two values), so does the equals sign (storing a value into a variable).

Programming languages have evolved over the decades, from simple languages designed primarily for mathematical calculations to sophisticated languages that help programmers model the physical world and answer questions. Computer programs have become more and more robust. Some are now among the most complex creations of mankind. The field of *software engineering* devises strategies for writing programs in order to manage the ever-increasing complexity, balancing the cost to produce the programs, the capabilities and correctness of the programs, and the speed at which the programs run.

LIMITS TO WHAT COMPUTERS CAN DO

As you hear each day about new things computers can do—such as driving a car—it might seem as though computers can do anything. They can do a lot, but not everything. There are some problems that we don't know how to solve on a computer in any reasonable amount of time. What might surprise you more is that there are some problems that simply cannot be solved by a computer, no matter how much time you give it! Let's look at an example of each.

The earlier list of computational problems included one about a truck delivering to several locations between starting and finishing at a depot. The question is in what order to visit the locations to use the least fuel. Imagine that you already know, for each pair of locations, how much fuel the truck uses to get from one to the other. It's not too hard to write a computer program to try each possible order of locations, summing up the fuel used in each order, and keeping track of which order uses the least. This program could take a long time—a *really* long time—to run, however. If there were just 20 locations, then even if a computer could try 1 trillion orders per second, it would take over 28 days to try out all possible orders! Maybe you're willing to wait 28 days, though who knows where you're going to find a computer that fast. Increase to 25 locations, however, and it would take a bit longer—about 491,520 years. Still willing to wait? This problem is called the "Traveling Salesman Problem," from the days when traveling salesmen would have to visit several cities, starting from and returning to home. Nobody has ever found a fast algorithm to solve it, nor has anyone ever shown that no fast algorithm can exist. We just don't know—and there are hundreds of other computational problems in the same boat.

Here's a problem that no computer can solve. It's a problem about computer programs. Specifically, can you give a computer a program P and the input to program P, and have the computer tell you whether program P, running on that input, ever runs to completion? We're not asking whether program P gives the right answer, or even whether it gives an answer at all. Just does program P, running on that input, ever finish? Believe it or not, there is a mathematical proof that no computer can ever answer this question correctly 100 percent of the time.

Computing Is in Everything

Computers are everywhere. Just look around the kitchen in your house. There's a good chance that there are simple computers in your refrigerator, microwave oven, dishwasher, range, toaster oven, and coffeemaker. Your family's car has several computers, managing the engine and dashboard controls. If you carry around a smartphone, you tote a computer with you everywhere you go.

Virtually all fields of study now use computation. Scientists use computing to model the physical and biological worlds. Social scientists use computing to understand human behavior. Even humanists use computing to gain deeper insight into literature and art—as well as to produce works of art.

You might have heard the saying "You don't know something until you can teach it to someone else." True, but you don't *really* know something until you can teach it to a computer!

WHAT IS

Ecology?

Mark A. McPeek

Before you begin reading this, take a few minutes to use all your senses and find out as much as you can about your surroundings.

How well did you take in your surroundings? Are you warm, chilled, or comfortable right now? Does the air feel dry or damp? Is the breeze moving air past you, and, if so, in what direction? Do you see or smell any food around you, and if so, is it something you'd like to eat? Are other people near you who might also like to eat that food? Can they potentially get to it before you do? Do you see any place where you could get water or something else to drink? Are any potential threats near you, like a street with traffic, a tree that's just about to fall over, a wasp that might sting you, or a large, threatening dog?

Any question about your surroundings and about how well or poorly you might do in the surroundings in which you find yourself is a question about your *ecology*. The study of ecology is the inquiry into organisms and their environment. Where are particular species found? What makes them successful in the places where they are found, and what prevents them from inhabiting other places? Which species can live together and which cannot? How do collections of species found in a particular location alter that environment? These are the major questions addressed by scientists who study ecology—*ecologists*. Questions about the species that inhabit these environment—Why these species and not others? Where did the dinosaurs go?—raise questions related to *evolution*. Ecology and evolution are fascinating subjects, and here we'll explore them both.

What Is Ecology?

Imagine that you are a cheetah on the Serengeti evaluating your surroundings. What questions would you have about your surroundings that would be important to you? Is it so hot that you need to seek shade? Is there water nearby where you can get a cool drink? What prey is around you that you might be able to subdue? What prey must you ignore because they are too well protected by their herd? Are other cheetahs present that might get to that vulnerable prey before you? Are there other larger predators that may be a threat to you personally?

In fact, just about any organism—a plant in a field, a fish in a lake, a salamander in a creek, an octopus in the sea, an earthworm in the dirt—has the same questions about its *environment*.

Some subdisciplines of ecology study the fit of an individual organism to its environment. As an illustration of this, let me first ask you what may initially seem a silly question. Why do fish live in the water? If you put a fish on the ground under a tree, it would die in only a few minutes, because many of its essential environmental requirements are missing. Foremost among those requirements is water as a medium and not air. The fish must be in a water medium because its body is built to extract essential oxygen from water and not air, namely through its gills.

This may seem a ludicrous question to ask, but it illustrates a broader issue. This question illustrates how scientists approach these questions. No fish species lives in every environment in which water is the medium. Some fish species are found only in small creeks, some only in large rivers, some only in freshwater lakes, some only in saline lakes, some in the open ocean, and some only in the polar oceans, some only where freshwater rivers enter the ocean. Most of these species are restricted to particular environments because their physiological systems operate best in only a limited range of environmental conditions defined by temperature, water salinity, or oxygen concentration.

Species are not just limited in their distribution by their physiological capabilities. For example, many salamander species live in small ponds and creeks, but are never found in larger ponds or streams where fish are present. Ecologists have examined the causes for these types of checkerboard species distributions in many environments with many different types of species.

Let's briefly explore how an ecologist might go about determining why salamanders and fish do not live together. The first thing an ecologist would do is develop a set of *hypotheses* that she could test. Then for each hypothesis she would devise an experiment to test the hypothesis and state her prediction about what should happen in the experiment if the hypothesis is true. What are a few hypotheses she might develop?

One hypothesis is that the salamanders are predators of the fish, and they are such good predators that every time salamanders and fish end up together, the salamanders drive the fish population extinct locally. This hypothesis could be tested by finding a pond with only fish in it, and then introducing salamanders to it to see if they drive the fish extinct.

Another hypothesis is the converse of the first: namely, that fish are incredible predators of salamanders and drive salamanders locally extinct every time they end up together. This hypothesis could be tested by simply doing the opposite: finding a pond with only salamanders, introducing fish, and seeing whether the fish eat all the salamanders.

Another hypothesis is that the fish and salamanders are not predators of one another at all, but rather that they both feed on the same prey, and that one of these is better at eating these shared food resources. Thus, when they end up together, one drives the other extinct because they can eat enough food to cause the other species to starve. I will leave it to you to devise a set of experiments that would test this hypothesis and specify what results would support or disprove it.

(If you want to know, the correct hypothesis is that fish are voracious predators of salamanders and will eat all the salamanders in a pond, causing the salamanders to go locally extinct.)

Ecologists also explore the causes of the *dynamics* of populations, namely how many individuals of a particular species are present at any one time and how and why those numbers change over time. Data from real populations come from myriad sources. For example, one of the most famous studies of population dynamics comes from data on the number of lynx and hare furs sold by the Hudson Bay Company from Canada starting in the 1700s. Fur trappers noticed that the number of hares they trapped for pelts went up and down over about a ten-year cycle, and the same happened for lynx. This cycling of lynx and hare abundances is clearly apparent in the number of pelts sold over three centuries, and the cycling still happens in the forests of Canada today: when the rabbits are abundant, the lynx are scarce; and when the lynx are abundant, the rabbits are scarce.

This data set has motivated a tremendous amount of mathematical modeling to see whether there are mathematical principles that can explain why the abundances of this predator (the lynx) and its prey (the hare) cycle out of phase with one another. The first mathematical biologists to explore this were the Italian Vito Volterra and the American Alfred Lotka in the early twentieth century. In fact, the mathematical model they developed independently is still the basis for modeling the dynamics of interacting species today: the Lotka-Volterra models of predators and prey and competing species.

While their models do show that cycling population abundances can emerge from purely mathematical issues, the real cause of the cycling in lynx and hare abundances is more complicated and caused by the changing physiology of the hares. When hares are abundant, lynx have more food, so the lynx increase in abundance. However, as lynx become more abundant, the hares do not decrease because the lynx kill too many. Rather, when the lynx are very abundant, the hare's abundance plummets because the hares stop reproducing. You see, when lots of lynx are around in the environment, hares are so frightened that their physiology stops producing babies. Consequently, the hare population crashes because it stops reproducing, and then the lynx start to starve.

If we compare the lynx-hare interaction to the fish-salamander interaction, you will realize that they are the same. Lynx and hare abundances are linked because they are predator and prey, respectively, but the lynx are not capable of driving the hare population to extinction. This means that the lynx and the hare *coexist* with one another. "Coexistence" is the scientific term for species being able to live with one another in the same place. Fish and salamanders do not coexist, but lynx and rabbits do coexist.

Moreover, if you walk through the forests of Canada where the lynx and hare interact, you will encounter a vast number of species of different types living together and interacting with one another. Many plants photosynthesize, converting light into simple sugars, and these sugars fuel their physiologies. These plants include everything from large trees that form the overstory of the forest to mosses, ferns, and small flowering plants in the understory. Many different types of species in addition to hares eat these plants. Mice, voles, caterpillars, squirrels, beetles, beavers, grasshoppers, porcupines, groundhogs, leafhoppers, and many other animals eat the plants. These plant eaters are called *herbivores*. Lots of *predators* in addition to lynx eat these herbivores, including foxes, wolves, spiders, coyotes, weasels, owls, dragonflies, woodpeckers, bears, centipedes, and warblers.

If you think of all these relationships about who eats whom, you are thinking about the entire *food web*. Food webs are the complex feeding relationships among all these interacting species. Modelers try to describe the dynamics of these complex dynamical systems, and empirical ecologists try to describe whether consistent patterns are apparent when food webs in different types of environments are compared.

However, the entire *ecosystem* has many other types of species in them as well. Every time plants or animals die, their dead bodies are processed and recycled by large *scavengers* like vultures and crows and by much smaller organisms such as bacteria and fungi that degrade tissues into simpler constituent molecules that can be reused by living organisms. Moreover, all herbivores and predators that eat other organisms do not completely convert consumed prey into their own biomass. They excrete wastes that they are unable to utilize, and these waste products are also recycled by bacteria and fungi, which decompose the waste. The wastewater treatment plant in your town uses these same organisms to do the same things. So an ecosystem is the food web plus all the scavengers, all the recyclers, and all the materials that they are recycling.

From what we have discussed so far, it may seem that ecologists only study the blood and guts of predators and their prey—"nature red in tooth and claw," as the poet Tennyson put it. But that is not all that happens out there in nature. Lots of organisms are very nice to one another and help each other. Ecologists study that, too.

In the summer, go outside and watch any flower, and within just a few minutes you will see bees and butterflies coming to that flower. The bees and butterflies are helping the plant with its needs, and the plant is supplying the bees and butterflies with some of their needs. This is called a *mutualism*. The plant is supplying the bees and butterflies with nectar to eat, and in return the bees and butterflies are pollinating the flowers of the plant so that the plant can make seeds. Without pollinators in their environment, plants could not make fertilized seeds, and there would be no plants next year. And without plants supplying nectar, pollinators would starve.

You can also see mutualisms if you go scuba diving on a coral reef. You have probably gotten parasites like ticks on you in the summer. Fish on the coral reefs also get parasites just like this on them. Living on the coral are shrimp that pick these parasites off of the fish. These cleaner shrimp set up shop on a spot on a piece of coral just like setting up a doctor's office, and fish come in one at a time to be cleaned of parasites. The fish benefit by having all these nasty parasites cleaned off of them, and the shrimp benefit because they eat the parasites, so they get lots of free meals. Each greatly benefits from having the other in its environment.

You are also a living mutualism yourself! In fact, you could not live without your mutualist partners. Who are those mutualist partners of yours? They are the billions of bacteria that live in your stomach and intestines. In fact, your body is made up of about 10 trillion human cells—in numbers, that's 10,000,000,000,000. But you have about 100 trillion bacterial cells in and on your body—in numbers, that's 100,000,000,000,000—or 10 times more bacterial cells than your own human cells. Also, you are their environment. The bacteria in your gut are essential to you being able to digest your food. They love living in you because you feed them every day, and you greatly benefit from having them there because they help you digest things that you couldn't otherwise.

However, you and all the other organisms do not have to just take what the environment throws at you. As you are reading this, are you sitting inside your house or your school or a library? Where did this building come from and why is it here? It's here to provide a place for you so you don't always have to sit out in the blazing sun, or the chilling rain, or the bitterly cold snow. This building was constructed by other humans so that you would have a more pleasing environment in which you could live and work. The same thing goes for your house. Humans don't just live in caves for shelter anymore. We build our own structures to protect us from some of the harsher features of the environment.

Many animals do exactly the same thing to make their environments better for them. Birds build nests to protect their eggs and chicks. Bees and wasps construct hives to live in. Beavers are probably the best animal engineers because they make new ponds where there were none before by building dams, and then they build a house for themselves on their new pond. Wouldn't you like to live in a house on a pond? Ecologists call this *niche construction*: the animals are modifying their environment in ways that make it better for themselves by constructing their own niches.

These are just some of the things that ecologists study about organisms and the environments in which they live. Ecology is all around you. In fact, ecology *is* what's all around you. There's lots of ecology to see in the woods or at the lake, but you have an ecology just sitting here reading this.

What Is Evolution?

The environments and species that ecologists study are changing all the time. The ecosystems change seasonally (mosquitos generally only bother you in late spring and summer—thankfully!), but they change over larger timescales as well. For example, where did all those dinosaurs go?

These days Chicago is a great place to see dinosaurs—not roaming the shores of Lake Michigan or wandering The Loop, but rather in the Field Museum of Natural History. Have you ever been there to stand next to Sue, the fossilized skeletal remains of the *Tyrannosaurus rex* (*T. rex* for short)? Sue was 42 feet from the end of her snout to the tip of her tail, and she weighed 7 tons when alive. That means that if you weigh 150 pounds, it would take 93 of you standing on one side of the scales to balance Sue's weight. Sue lived in what is now South Dakota about 65 million years ago.

Or have you ever walked through Terminal 1 at O'Hare International Airport and looked up to see the *Brachiosaurus* skeleton that towers over the gates? *Brachiosaurus altithorax* was a 75-foot-long plant eater that weighed over 48 tons (that's 640 of you 150-pounders) and lived in what is now Colorado about 200 million years ago.

These are only *fossils* now, the mineralized remains of organisms that lived tens to hundreds of millions of years ago. We do not have to fight off *T. rex*es today, or fence out *Brachiosaurus*es from our cornfields, because they are *extinct*. However, their fossilized remains prove that they once roamed the Earth. In fact, most of the animals and plants that lived with *T. rex* and *Brachiosaurus* are also now extinct and can be found on Earth only as fossils.

Think about that! Most of the millions of species that are alive today—including us, *Homo sapiens*, human beings—did not exist hundreds of millions of years ago, and most of the species that lived on the Earth back then are now extinct. We know where all those species went: they went extinct. But where did all the species on the Earth today come from?

All the species alive today are descendants of the species that were living with *Brachiosaurus* and *T. rex*, just like you are a descendant of your mother, and your grandmother, and your great-great-great-great-grandmother. You probably never met your great-great-great-great-grandmother, and you might not know who she was, but you do know you definitely had a great-great-great-great-grandmother. In fact, you had thirty-two great-great-great-great-grandmothers. Your dog also had a mother, a grandmother, and a great-great-great-great-grandmother. The history of all your descendants is called your *genealogy*. Since every species is composed of individuals, the same genealogical process happens in every species, which means that all the individuals in all the species today are descendants of individuals that were alive with *T. rex*.

How can it be that all the individuals of all the species alive today are descendants of individuals that were alive with *T. rex*, but very few of the species that exist today lived at the time of *T. rex*? It's because every generation, each population in each species changed just a very, very little bit, and when you add up all those very small changes over those millions of years, the animals and plants of today are not the same as those that lived on Earth 65 million years ago. At some point, the descendants become so different from their ancestors that they become new species.

How does this change happen? The original idea for how this process of change over time along the ancestry of organisms was proposed by two people in 1858. Most people know Charles Darwin. However, few people know that another Englishman, Alfred Russel Wallace, proposed basically the same set of ideas as Darwin. They each spent a good part of their lives traveling around the Earth studying the animals and plants they found in different places. Darwin spent almost five years sailing around the world on the HMS *Beagle*. Every place the ship would stop, he would get off and explore the surrounding countryside for weeks, collecting all the new and exotic species of animals and plants he found. Wallace spent four years mapping the Amazon River in present-day Brazil and collecting insects and mammals. He then spent another eight years exploring the rain forests of the Malay Archipelago (present-day Indonesia, Malaysia, Singapore, and surrounding islands). In these explorations, both were struck with the diversity of animals and plants they found, and both were dumbfounded by the differences in species they found in different parts of the world.

Both of them were struck by a simple but profound question: Why do you find different animals and plants living in different places around the world? The birds and the beetles and the trees you find in the Brazilian rain forest are completely different species from the birds and beetles and trees found in the rain forests of Borneo. American deserts have cacti, but no cacti are found in deserts in Africa; instead African deserts have plants called euphorbs, which have spines and store water like cacti, but are not cacti. The grasslands of Africa have giraffes, gazelles, wildebeests, elephants, lions, and cheetahs, but the grasslands in North America have buffalo, pronghorn antelope, coyotes, and foxes. Similar types of species are present in the same kinds of places on different continents, but they are not *the same* species.

This simple observation made Darwin and Wallace wonder why. The answer that came to both was also simple. Species living on each continent were descended from a very distant common ancestor in the past, but the very small changes that accumulated over millions of years in each place resulted in different species. Darwin described this process as *descent with modification* in his famous book *On the Origin of Species*, which was first published in 1859.

Their very great insight, though, was that the process causing the change was actually not just random. These changes happened to make the individuals in the species better at what they needed to do to survive and produce offspring. They called the process causing these changes *natural selection*, and it results in species being *adapted* to their local environment. Imagine a population of gazelles out on the African savannah. Gazelles today can run sixty miles per hour, and as Darwin's and Wallace's theory predicts, this is a good thing because cheetahs can run sixty miles per hour too, and lions can run fifty miles per hour: these two species are primary predators of gazelles. Millions of years ago the ancestors of gazelles and cheetahs and lions probably could not run that fast. However, the gazelles that could run just a little faster would be better able to outrun chee- tahs when they were attacked. Thus, gazelles that could run faster would have survived better, and ones that couldn't run as fast would have become cheetah dinners. That is natural selection in a nutshell. Some feature of the organisms make some of them better at leaving offspring to the next generation than others. We hypothesize that this is why gazelles can run so fast today.

For natural selection to work well, something else must also be true: gazelle parents that run faster must have gazelle babies that also run faster. This is called genetic *heritability*. Parents and offspring tend to have the same characteristics: tall parents tend to have tall children, and short parents tend to have short children. This is where the descent part of "descent with modification" comes in, and it is because of the *genes* that parents pass to their offspring. Genes are the genetic information that is passed from parents to offspring. In our example, every generation, the gazelle population would have gotten just a little faster, since the faster gazelles are more likely to survive and pass on genes for fast running to their gazelle babies.

This process of natural selection goes on in every species. So what would have happened to the cheetahs as they caused the gazelles to evolve to be faster over successive generations? As the gazelles evolved to be faster, the cheetahs would have gotten less food because they were not fast enough to catch most gazelles—except that natural selection also worked on the cheetahs. The cheetahs who could run faster would have been the ones who could catch more food, so they would be the ones who had the resources to have more offspring. If cheetah parents who run faster also have cheetah babies that run faster, natural selec- tion will cause the cheetahs to evolve to be faster runners. This cycle of species evolving in response to one another is called *coevolution*.

Nature offers up many puzzles just like the ones that Darwin and Wallace pondered. For example, unlike on the savannahs of Africa, the Great Plains of

North America have a very large and fast herbivore, the pronghorn antelope, which can run at sixty miles per hour, but no large predator in North America can run nearly that fast. So what was the selection pressure favoring pronghorn antelope that could run so fast? It turns out that close relatives of the cheetahs and lions lived on the Great Plains in North America until both went extinct about fifteen thousand years ago! If we had been in North America thirty thousand years ago, we would have been able to watch cheetahs and lions chasing pronghorn antelope and buffalos, just like cheetahs and lions chase gazelles and wildebeests in Africa today. In fact, North America at that time also had four species of elephants roaming around. So Kansas would have looked very much like the Serengeti does today! However, most of these big mammals went extinct for some reason in North America about fifteen thousand years ago, which is just about the time that humans walked across the Bering land bridge from Siberia to colonize North America for the first time.

In addition to the struggle for existence that all animals and plants face, another way that many organisms ensure that they have offspring in the next generation is to be more attractive to potential mates. Males of many species are bright and showy during the breeding season. Experiments in the streams of Trinidad have shown that this is why guppy males have such a dazzling variety of colors—those bright colors make these males more attractive to females. This is also why peacocks have such a fantastically exaggerated tail, and why turkey males puff themselves up to look so big. All of this is because these males are trying to attract a mate. These displays are just another way that individuals try to have more offspring, and this process is called *sexual selection.*

If you started with a population of drab guppies, why would they evolve to have brightly colored males? Natural and sexual selection are not the only processes that cause these very small changes each generation in species. Remember that genes are the genetic information that make parents and offspring resemble one another. Your genes are encoded in the DNA in your cells just like words in a book. DNA has a four-letter alphabet that stores genes in very long words in this DNA book. Every time your body makes a new cell, it has to copy this entire book of gene words so that the new cell has exactly the same DNA book as the original cell. The only problem is that your DNA book has 3.3 billion letters in it. In copying this DNA book with 3.3 billion letters a few mistakes are made. Each of these mistakes, each place where one DNA letter in the book is copied wrong, is called a *mutation.*

So let's return to the gazelles for a minute. If the DNA copy in a gazelle has a mistake in some of the words about the directions to build a fast gazelle, that gazelle's offspring who get that copy of the DNA might be able to run a little faster because of this new mutation, or instead they might run a little slower. If the mutation makes the gazelles run faster, natural selection will cause this copy of DNA to increase in the population, because this gazelle's offspring will survive better. In effect, natural selection decides the best way to spell the words in the DNA book of a species, given the options that are available for how to spell them. These mutational misspellings of DNA are important because they give natural selection the various options to choose from in its quest to leave more offspring to the next generation.

Sometimes the small changes that happen across generations occur not because it makes better individuals, but just because of the luck of the draw. Imagine a large pool in a creek on a mountain on the island of Trinidad— the natural home of guppies. Now imagine that this pool is filled with hundreds of brightly colored male guppies and lots and lots of female guppies who are looking for mates. The males show a dazzling diversity of colors among them: some are blue, some are orange, some are green and orange, some are silver and blue, etc., etc.

What if one day a hurricane came though and made it rain ten inches in an hour, causing a massive flood, and all the male guppies were swept away except for one green male and a few females? Clearly the green male did not survive the flood because he was green—that was purely random. After this population of one green male and three female guppies breed with one another, what color do you think all his sons in the next generation will be? They should all be green. So over one generation, the guppy population has changed from having a dazzling array of colorful males to a population of all green males. Moreover, this happened purely at random because of the flood. This is a process called *random genetic drift*. Even though this genetic change in the population occurred because of random processes, this change is still evolution.

The final process that can cause a population of individuals to evolve is something called *gene flow*. Have you ever gone to a small pond and seen water striders skittering across the surface of the water? Those water striders, with their ability to walk on the water, are amazing insects. If you look very closely, you will notice that some of them have wings and others do not. The ones that have wings have genes that code for making wings, and the ones without wings have genes that do not make wings. Water striders use their feet to walk on water, and their wings to fly from one pond to another. Imagine that you go to this pond one day, and you see all wingless water striders, which means that the entire population of water striders have genes that do not make wings. If you come back the next week and see a few water striders with wings (and so genes that code for wings), the simplest explanation is that these winged water striders flew to this pond from somewhere else. In this case, too, the genetic composition of the population has changed, but this was caused by individuals moving between populations. That is evolution by gene flow.

These are the processes that evolutionary biologists study about how species have changed since the beginning of life on Earth. The world and the species in it change over time. And just as species changed in the past to create the species we see today, the descendants of the species that exist today will change because of these processes going into the future. What will the Earth and those that inhabit it look like in another 65 million years?

Conclusion

As you can see, the study of ecology can take you from the world around you to the world inside you. It's a subject that you can study by tromping around in the woods with a bucket, or in front of a computer—and it's actually best studied using combinations of the two! It is a subject full of important and interesting questions about the history and dynamics of living things. Maybe you'll contribute to our understanding of it one day.

WHAT IS

Economics?

Christopher Snyder

Economics Is about More Than the Stock Market

When people I meet learn I am an economist, often one of the first questions they ask is, "What's the stock market going to do?" That's a great question. If on the day I was born my parents had invested $100 for me in Altria, the stock that has turned out to be the top performer since then, I would be a millionaire today (see figure 1). "What's the stock market going to do?" is a million-dollar question we would all like to know the answer to. The people I meet are often surprised to learn that I—and most other economists—spend very little time thinking about the stock market. This article will give you a glimpse into the diverse set of topics we do think about and, just as important, a glimpse into *how* we think about them.

All that said, I do have some wisdom to share about the stock market, but I am not going to simply blurt it out. One general area of study in economics is incentives—what drives people to make the choices they do—so I know that if I give away the answer to the million-dollar question here, you won't have an incentive to read the rest of the article. If you want my wisdom on the stock market, you will have to read through to the end of the article. Maybe you will find the other topics just as rewarding.

Fitting Economics among the Sciences

Economics is one of the social sciences, along with sociology, political science, psychology, and others, devoted to the study of human behavior. Some scientists in the "hard" sciences like physics and chemistry consider economics and the other social sciences "soft" sciences, if indeed they consider them sciences at

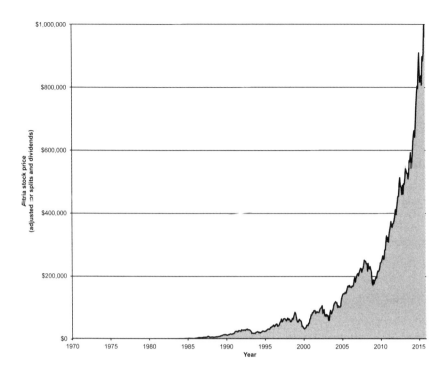

FIGURE I Huge gains from Altria stock investment. Author's calculations using historical
stock-return data from the Center for Research in Security Prices

all. I won't argue with that view. Humans are complex; they sometimes act on
whims; they certainly don't behave as systematically as particles. Organizations
of individuals such as companies, universities, or a country's whole economy
are yet more complex. Devising simple theories to explain their operation is
hard, and conducting experiments on them to test these theories is even harder.
Economists and other social scientists sometimes have to be content with looser
theories than they would like, or less-than-perfect tests. So, yes, they are "soft"
sciences. But social scientists are trying harder than ever to be rigorous both in
the theories they propose and the statistical analysis of these theories.

Economics is distinct in its focus on aspects of behavior related to people's
material well-being. Other social sciences, some covered in other chapters of
this book, might study what groups people join, how they vote, what spiritual
beliefs they hold, how they form a thought. Economics asks a different set of
questions. How do people earn a living? What do they buy with the money they
earn? These questions are not to everyone's taste. Some noneconomists might

find such questions about the "business side" of life pedestrian. For some reason economists find them fascinating. Perhaps the fascination lies in the opportunity for concrete measurement: hard data on income and spending may be easier to come by than ideas or religious beliefs. Perhaps the fascination lies in the opportunity to make material improvements in people's lives with a good answer to an economic question. Perhaps the fascination lies in the opportunity to tease out philosophical issues buried in pedestrian questions. Take the question of what people buy with the money they earn. Behind that question is the more fundamental question of what determines an object's value. Why are diamonds, mere decorations, perfectly easy to live without, so prized, while water, essential for human life, can be drunk for free from public water fountains? (Give this philosophical question some thought yourself; we will revisit it when we discuss some broad economic principles below.)

Although I have dwelled on the distinction between economics and other social sciences, the dividing lines have blurred over time. For example, crime was once the exclusive purview of sociologists and corruption of political scientists. But economists realized that fines and jail time can be thought of as different prices placed on these forms of antisocial behavior. With that, they naturally started to think about how these prices could be fine-tuned to get better deterrence while saving on enforcement costs. More directly, crime intersects with economics in a disruptive way, as any hope of enjoying the fruits of a productive economy could be summarily wiped out by a crime wave or corrupt administration. This has led some economists to suggest that the main determinant of a nation's wealth is not the richness of its natural resources or the productivity of its machines but the lawfulness of its leaders and citizens.

Art Auctions

Art provides another good example of blurred lines between disciplines. While one might think nothing could be further from the "business side" of life than art, even this has come to be a subject of economists' study. In 2015, the Picasso painting shown in figure 2 broke the record for the highest price paid at an art auction ($180 million). While economists may have few insights about the quality of the imagery or brushstrokes, they have deeper insights about the design of the auction, run by the famous New York auction house, Christie's.

For this extraordinary and important painting, the opening bid (called the "reserve price") was set at $100 million. Why was that chosen instead of some

FIGURE 2 Picasso's *Women of Algiers* sells for record $180 million at auction. Painting credit: Pablo Picasso (1881–1973), *Les femmes d'Alger* version "O" (after Eugène Delacroix's *Femmes d'Alger dans leur appartement*), © 2016 Estate of Pablo Picasso/ Artists Rights Society (ARS), New York. Photo credit: Private Collection / Bridgeman Images

lower or higher amount? Stating the obvious, the current owner should never sell a painting she values at $80 million for only $50 million, so the opening price should be set at least at $80 million (or whatever her personal valuation is). But there is a reason to set the reserve price higher than the seller's personal valuation, which is particularly important in auctions in which only limited bidder interest in the painting materializes. In such cases, an increase in the reserve price can boost the amount the highest (and presumably winning) bidder has to pay. Now this is not obvious—if there is a "winning price," then presumably it could be reached no matter where you started. But let's see if that is right.

Suppose for concreteness that only two bidders are interested in the Picasso: bidder A, who values it at $120 million, and bidder B, who values it at $90 million. Without a reserve price (in other words, starting the bidding at $0), B drops out of the auction when the bid reaches $90 million, leaving A as the winner. With a reserve price of $100 million, however, A must bid that much or lose the painting. Even if A's is the only bid the seller receives, she earns $10 million more than without a reserve price. Still better would be a reserve price close to A's valuation of $120 million; but unless the seller can somehow read the bidders' minds to determine the most each is willing to pay, the danger in setting too high a reserve price is it risks pricing even the highest-value bidder out of the market. The optimal reserve price is set so that the increased revenue when a sale is made balances the reduced chance of selling the painting.

Although bidder interest is difficult to predict in advance, in the Picasso auction it turned out to be intense. Heated competition among a pack of them drove the price to $180 million in about ten minutes. So in this particular case the reserve price may not have contributed much to the seller's revenue. Other features of the auction may have had more of an impact. Though allowed to bid in $1 million increments, at several points in the auction bidders jumped over the previous offer by $10 million. Such "jump bidding" is puzzling because it wastes the chance of winning the painting for less if other bidders drop out with incremental bidding before the price rises the full $10 million. Understanding puzzles like jump bidding is an active area of auction research. Some economists speculate that bidders learn something about the market value of the painting by looking at the number of bidders remaining active as the price goes up; a jump bid may scare other bidders off by destroying some of this market information. For now, this is just speculation, awaiting further testing using data from the Picasso and other auctions.

Of course, auctions are not restricted to art objects. Ad prices that accompany search returns on Google are set by a kind of online auction. Maybe you have engaged in an auction yourself when you bought something on eBay. The growth of online marketplaces has made the study of auctions increasingly relevant, revealing all kinds of interesting questions for economists (in collaboration with computer scientists and other scholars) to think about.

Economic Principles

Although economists study a diverse set of topics, ranging from jobs to crime to art, there are some shared some core concepts underlying their thinking. Perhaps the most central of these is the idea of *scarcity*. Scarcity means one cannot have everything; instead one has to make choices. Devoting money, property, time, or other resources to one project—say, an important project like preventing diabetes—means that some other significant project—like finding a cure for cancer—goes unserved. In determining whether a project, an action, or any other choice should be undertaken, its benefits should not be considered in isolation but weighed against its *costs*. Costs put a dollar value on what has to be given up when one choice is made over another.

One can be forgiven for thinking of economists as a "dismal" bunch, fixated on scarcity, costs, and the quantification of trade-offs when choosing between one thing and another. Economics isn't called the "dismal science" for nothing. The label dates back hundreds of years, to an appraisal of Thomas Malthus's theory of economic growth. Malthus, an eighteenth-century parson, regarded as one of the founders of economic thought, theorized that improvements in food production would not help the population rise very far above the subsistence level because any increase in food supply would just lead them to breed more, like rabbits. Commenting on this theory, Thomas Carlyle wrote, "Nowhere, in that quarter of his intellectual world, is there light; nothing but a grim shadow of hunger." A look at the currently high standard of living in Malthus's England and much of the rest of the Western world, along with the shrinking family size, suggests a problem with Malthus's theory. In any event, the label "dismal science" has stuck.

Another core economic concept is *value*. People have been thinking about value for a long time. In the Middle Ages, scholastic philosophers propounded the *just-price theory*, the idea that value is an inherent property of an object. On this view, diamonds are expensive because of their inherent quality; water is not. But this theory is not completely satisfactory. It does not explain where this inherent value comes from (if not divinely decreed), nor is it consistent with variation in prices observed across cultures and over time. Karl Marx, the father of communism, ascribed to *the labor theory of value*, holding that the value of an object is constituted by the effort workers put into its production. (Incidentally, one can see how this would have led him to advocate a worker revolution to wrest the value they create from business owners, who steal this value.) The labor theory has its own drawbacks, for example leading to the awkward conclusion that a tooth extraction taking an hour would be sixty times more valuable than one taking a minute. If you were sitting in the dentist's chair, you might disagree.

The prevailing view among economists these days is that value is neither inherent in an object nor determined by a single factor such as labor but is the result of the interaction of a number of impersonal market forces, which for a simple approximation we can reduce to those of *supply* and *demand*. Figure 3 provides a graphical representation of a market, called the "Marshallian cross" in

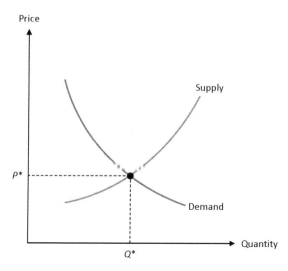

FIGURE 3 Market supply and demand.
Drawing by the author

honor of Alfred Marshall, author of the granddaddy of economics texts, *Principles of Economics*, published in 1890. On the vertical axis is "price" and on the horizontal axis is "quantity." Seller behavior is represented by the supply curve. Its upward slope (aiming toward high prices and larger quantities) indicates that at higher prices, more of the stuff is supplied as existing suppliers expand their operations and new suppliers are drawn into the market looking to make money. Buyer behavior is represented by the demand curve. Its downward slope (aiming toward low prices and larger quantities) indicates buyers are willing to purchase more at lower prices.

In our simplified market with these two "forces" affecting the price, an *equilibrium* price (value) is reached, meaning that there is no tendency for the price to move up or down, when supply intersects demand. At other points, either supply exceeds demand, in which case the price would tend to fall as sellers accepted lower prices to offload their excess inventory; or demand exceeds supply, in which case the price would tend to rise as buyers would still line up to buy at higher prices rather than do without the good. Equilibrium price determines the object's value. If mention of "forces" and "equilibrium" reminds you of what you might learn in a physics or chemistry class, you are not too far off. The work of Isaac Newton in physics and Robert Boyle in chemistry in the mid-seventeenth century influenced subsequent Enlightenment thinkers in virtually every field, including the early economists.

With this in mind, let's now go back to our water/diamond paradox. Water is in abundant supply, intersecting demand at a price near zero. At this price water is used not just to prevent one from dying of thirst but also to water lawns and wash cars. Diamonds, by contrast, are mined in only a few places in the world. The restricted supply intersects demand at an extraordinarily high price. At this price, diamonds are only put to extraordinarily high-value uses, such as sealing an engagement promise. The relative prices of water and diamonds depend not on something inherent or just one factor such as labor but on both supply and demand and everything that goes into them.

The principles discussed so far regarding costs and value, although experienced in the real world, are at heart theoretical. Early on, economics was quite theoretical, beginning as a branch of philosophy. More recently, economics research has shifted in an empirical direction, spurred perhaps by advances in information technology, allowing for the collection of rich economic data, analyzed on high-powered computers using sophisticated statistical methods.

If I had to come up with a single core principle behind modern empirical research in economics, I would say it is the push to uncover *causality* in economic phenomena—that is, to determine true causal relationships rather than to overinterpret apparent correlations as causation. Correlation is the observation of a relation between two phenomena. For example, suppose I found that graduates from Dartmouth, the college where I teach, have much higher salaries than the average college graduate. We might say that a Dartmouth degree is *correlated* with a high starting salary. But would I be justified in saying that this difference is *caused* by the purported excellence of a Dartmouth education? Or is the difference due to the higher skill of students who enroll in Dartmouth, skill that would translate into higher salaries regardless of where they went to college? The correlation between a Dartmouth education and high salaries may not be causal. Uncovering true causal relationships is difficult in economics because the opportunity to run controlled experiments is limited (although these opportunities are growing: there has been an explosion of interest in laboratory and field experiments in economics). No one has run the experiment of taking a group of students with similar profiles, randomly sending some to Dartmouth and some to other colleges, and then seeing who ends up with higher salaries. How, then, can one go about measuring how much of the salary difference is due to the college?

Economists have to think of clever ways to establish causation in nonexperimental data. To get an idea of how this is done, the rest of this essay covers two case studies. The first case study starts big, with a crisis that threatened to bring down the whole US economy: the Great Depression. The second case study explores in more depth the issue raised in the previous paragraph about whether a college like Dartmouth causes graduates to earn more, making the extra tuition worth the investment. The scope of the issues covered in the two case studies mirrors the division of economics into two broad fields: the first case study falls into *macroeconomics*, the study of the dynamics of entire economies; the second falls into *microeconomics*, the narrower focus on individual markets or decision makers.

Case Study from Macroeconomics

The Great Depression was a terrible downturn in the global economy between World War I and World War II, falling particularly hard on the United States. At the worst point of the Great Depression in 1932 and 1933, US industries were only producing half of what they did before its start. More than a quarter of the working population could not find jobs. John Steinbeck's novel *The Grapes of Wrath* famously gives a deep sense of the human suffering behind these abstract numbers. With no stable jobs in their hometowns, the novel's protagonists, the Joads, travel from place to place in search of better opportunities, but no matter where they go, they find squalid living conditions and long lines of unemployed workers queuing up for the few available low-paying jobs.

The Great Depression might seem like ancient history, but history has a way of repeating itself. In 2007, the world experienced a deep financial crisis that precipitated the worst economic slowdown since the Great Depression, which has come to be called the "Great Recession" and from which the world has yet to fully recover. Economists—particularly those concerned with large-scale changes such as the rise and fall of an entire country or world economy, called *macroeconomists*—are keen to study the Great Depression carefully to understand the measures that can be taken to prevent small downturns from turning into full-blown depressions in the future.

Among measures proposed to stimulate a national economy and thereby reverse a downturn, two have received the most attention. One general policy is to encourage banks to lend more. The thinking is that loans can stimulate an economy by financing business investment and consumer purchases of houses, cars, and other big-ticket items. The government has several ways to encourage lending. It can relax regulations on how much banks have to put aside in reserve to cover bad loans and bank runs (depositors all trying to withdraw their money at once). More directly, the government could just print more money, giving it to the banks to lend out. Either way, the policy of encouraging more lending is called *expanding the money supply*.

Another stimulus policy is to increase government spending. This is sometimes called a "Keynesian" approach after John Maynard Keynes, a British economist who had wide policy influence during and after the Great Depression and celebrity status. Here the idea is for the government to boost employment by undertaking public projects such as roads, bridges, and parks. However, there is a catch: funding for increased spending cannot come from increased taxes; otherwise the people paying the higher tax, with less money to spend, would cut back their purchases, shrinking the economy. Instead, the boost comes from *deficit spending*—spending funded by borrowing rather than taxes. Borrowing from whom?, you might ask. Foreign sources are an option. Domestic citizens whose savings sit idly in bank accounts due to the stagnating economy are another possibility (this kind of borrowing can take the form of a government bond—like a US Savings Bond). Regardless of the source, the borrowed funds will have to be paid back in the future, but the hope is that an improving economy will help make repayment relatively easy by then. While it would be better for the government to direct deficit spending toward valuable projects (the roads, bridges, and parks mentioned), Keynes was so committed to this idea that he suggested that hiring people to dig holes and fill them back in would be better than doing nothing.

Both policies were tried during the Great Depression. President Franklin Roosevelt tried to spend the country's way out through government jobs programs such as the Works Progress Administration and the Civilian Conservation Corps. The money supply also expanded. Interestingly, the expansion of the money supply was less a conscious policy decision by the US government than a by-product of political unrest in Europe. Worried about the events that ultimately led to World War II, in the late 1930s Europeans shipped their money and gold to the United States for safekeeping, adding to and vastly expanding the US money supply.

Which policy deserves more credit for getting the United States out of the Great Depression? This is a tough question to answer because in the middle of a downturn, even a milder one than the Great Depression, countries do not bother to run controlled experiments, separately changing each policy in isolation, first one then the other, to determine its effects. Instead countries are inclined to use all available avenues to escape the mess. The bigger measurement problem is that cause and effect are all muddled up.

Suppose, for example, that the government increases deficit spending to stem a downturn in the economy. Suppose the policy turns out to work—say, turning a huge 10 percent decline into a smaller 5 percent decline. If, as in this example, the decline is too severe to be completely reversed by the policy, all that an outside observer would be able to see is that the policy was implemented and a 5 percent decline resulted. What is not seen is that the downturn would have been worse without the policy. Furthermore, a bad economy can feed back to make a beneficial policy look damaging. A downturn in the economy naturally reduces the taxes the government earns from businesses and workers, increasing the deficit even if the government does not change spending on roads, bridges, or parks by one penny. This feedback effect can make it look like deficits, rather than stimulating the economy, cause downturns when in fact the reverse is true.

While governments may be loath to run economic experiments on their citizens (with a few, mostly lamentable, historical exceptions) economists have come up with some clever methodologies to tease out policy effects. In this case, Christina Romer (an expert on the Great Depression who served as the chair of the US president's Council of Economic Advisors, holding that position during the recent Great Recession) hit on the idea of looking at recessions outside the span of the Great Depression. To help separate cause and effect, she looked at the association between the decline in the economy in the year of the recession and policies undertaken *the year before*. If one change takes place before another, it is easier to argue that the first caused the second than the second caused the first (although this by no means *proves* that the first caused the second).

In every recession she examined, the depth of the recession corresponded to the decline in the money supply the year before, not the deficit. For example, the severe (8 percent) recession in 1938 followed a drastic (9 percent) decline in the money supply the previous year (a misguided Federal Reserve policy to redirect bank operations), a year in which the deficit hardly changed. On the basis of this evidence, Romer concluded that the expansion of the money supply during the Great Depression was the biggest contributor to its end, more important than Roosevelt's deficit spending on jobs programs such as the Works Progress Administration and the Civilian Conservation Corps. Further supporting her conclusion, despite the renown of Roosevelt's spending programs, the budget deficits that he ended up running were just not big enough to affect the economy much one way or the other. On the other hand, the flood of money and gold from an anxious Europe prior to World War II was big enough that, given the causal effects estimated by Romer, it could by itself have ended the Great Depression. The lessons from the Great Depression are more than an interesting historical footnote, for they suggest the appropriate policy response to the current decade's Great Recession as well as perhaps any future crises.

Case Study from Microeconomics

That completes the first empirical case study, from *macroeconomics*, the branch of economics devoted to the "big picture" (that's what the prefix "macro-" indicates) of the whole economy at once. We next turn to the case study from *microeconomics*, the branch of economics with a narrower focus ("micro-") on individual markets or decision makers. We will use some economic thinking to tackle a problem that is familiar to current (and former) students: deciding which college to attend.

There are many personal reasons for students to prefer one college over another. Some prefer a bigger college in a city; others prefer a smaller one in the setting of a college town. Some look for nationally competitive sports teams; others want excellence in performing arts. Most students would agree that if two colleges were the same on all of these dimensions, they would prefer to enroll in the more prestigious one. But what is *prestige*? If prestige is measured by the number of applications per slot, then this statement is tautological, in essence saying that more students prefer the more popular choice. Those of us who teach at highly rated colleges hope that prestige captures dimensions of quality beyond popularity. We hope that a "better" college is more effective in developing the student's mind, leading to a broader, wiser person, with the side effect of affording the student better career opportunities on graduation. Understandably, students may regard better career opportunities and higher associated pay as more than a mere side effect. If we just focus on this point, is there any way of measuring the contribution of college to career opportunities and pay? Put bluntly, is spending more to attend a better college worth the investment?

To provide a concrete example, suppose you have the choice of attending either Dartmouth College, the private Ivy League college in New Hampshire where the authors of this book teach, or UMass Dartmouth, one of the campuses of the University of Massachusetts public system. A year at Dartmouth College costs about $50,000 in tuition and fees, but a year at UMass Dartmouth costs less than half that, about $20,000 (and Massachusetts residents pay even less). Is the extra $30,000 a year for Dartmouth College—$120,000 over the four years needed for a bachelor's degree—a smart investment?

Let's put aside all of the aspects of the college experience—the vibrancy of student life, the enrichment of the student mind, and so on—and focus on the narrow question of monetary returns. By doing so I do not mean to say that the monetary return is the only reason to go to a college or even the most important reason. But it is an issue worth some thought. The company PayScale compiles salary information from a comprehensive survey of college graduates (available on the website www.payscale.com). Based on the average salaries earned by graduates in midcareer, Dartmouth College ranks 13th in the country ($119,000 average salary), while UMass Dartmouth ranks 204th ($86,000). The average salary difference of $33,000 per year adds up over the typical forty-year career to $1.3 million. This seems like a huge amount, more than ten times the $120,000 tuition difference over four years. The benefit-cost ratio is a bit overstated because the cost of the extra tuition comes up front but the benefit from the extra salary comes later, forty or more years later for salary earned close to retirement. There should be a way to give more heft to the immediate costs relative to benefits realized in the distant future. In fact, we can do that using formulas for compound interest. Sparing you the details, one can calculate that the implicit return on the Dartmouth College tuition investment is 18 percent. This is a fantastic return relative to other investments, for example, the 5 percent average return on the US stock market or the 4 percent return on Treasury bonds over the past decade.

There is a more fundamental reason, beyond formulas for compound interest, that the fantastic returns on a Dartmouth College education we just calculated may be overstated. The PayScale data tells us that the average Dartmouth College graduate earns $33,000 more than the average UMass Dartmouth graduate. Does this mean that given the choice between the two colleges, enrolling in Dartmouth College would *cause* you to earn $33,000 more on average? Not necessarily. If Dartmouth College is able to attract higher-caliber students, it may be the caliber of the student that generates high salaries, not any special contribution of Dartmouth College. Perhaps Dartmouth College students are not higher-caliber but just come from more privileged backgrounds and are able to exploit family connections to find high-paying jobs. A student facing the choice between the two colleges wants to know the causal effect of Dartmouth College on salary for a student of his or her fixed characteristics, which one cannot say using just the PayScale survey data.

Just as in the example from the Great Depression, separating true causal effects from apparent associations requires more careful work. Stacy Dale and Alan Krueger, two economists working in Princeton, New Jersey, took a clever approach to estimating the causal effect of prestigious colleges on salaries. Rather than comparing average salaries of all Dartmouth College and UMass Dartmouth grads, the authors suggest concentrating only on students who were admitted to both and compares the average salary for them. This method holds constant the nature of the student (after all, the student could have gone to either college) and better isolates the effect coming from the college. What they find is surprising: the big differences that showed up using the PayScale survey data largely disappear!

Dale and Krueger's method is not perfect. The set of students accepted at both Dartmouth College and UMass Dartmouth (or any two schools differing a lot in selectivity) may be too small to allow an accurate comparison. The decision to attend one over the other may itself be related to some unobservable student characteristic (family wealth? striving?) that drives salary differences rather than the colleges themselves. Nonetheless, the study suggests caution in basing a college investment decision on available salary data. Although it is hard for me to admit as a Dartmouth College professor, it may be an overstatement to say that Dartmouth College *causes* a $33,000 salary boost relative to UMass Dartmouth. The economic approach is a piece of the picture, but not the whole picture. Perhaps Dartmouth College has other benefits in terms of the vibrancy of student life or intellectual atmosphere that will continue to attract students so I will be able to keep my job.

Back to the Stock Market

Having patiently waded through the intervening discussion of economic principles and case studies, you are owed my promised wisdom (!) about the stock market, an answer to the million-dollar question "What's the stock market going to do?" Go back to the Altria stock chart in figure 1, showing how my parents could have made me a millionaire by now. Are you curious what Altria makes? A good guess might be something high-tech: computers, communications equipment, pharmaceuticals? No. Altria makes cigarettes. Until a recent spinoff, Altria was the parent company of Phillip Morris, manufacturer of Marlboro and other brands of cigarettes. With cigarette smoking on the decline in the United States due to high taxes and restrictions on indoor smoking, it is hard to imagine that cigarette manufacturing would be a good investment. However, cigarette smoking is on the rise in poor countries. Cigarettes are simple to manufacture, keeping production costs low. The advertising ban impedes potential competitors from entering the market, leaving the few established manufacturers to divide up the market and keep prices high. Because of these and other factors, cigarettes have been an incredibly profitable industry over the past half century.

The surprising performance of cigarettes provides a useful lesson about stock picking. It is tempting for nonprofessionals to think that careful analysis and good intuition can help them pick stocks that will provide a better return than the market average. Study after study shows this is generally not true. The current price of a stock on the market reflects the accumulated "wisdom of crowds" about its proper value, and the crowd of investors is generally much wiser than any individual. As soon as information comes out that a particular company or industry has attractive prospects, investors try to scoop up the stock at its current bargain price. With lots of people all trying to buy the stock, its price jumps up. So any positive information about a stock quickly gets reflected in the price. By time the average investor gets the information, it is already too late to profit from it. From that point on, the stock price is likely to be quite unpredictable. An investor may as well throw darts at a list of stocks and invest in the ones randomly hit rather than try to outwit the market with his or her own picks. In study after study such "dartboard portfolios" are shown to beat the personal picks of investors, whether nonprofessional or professional. Making money picking stocks is about as easy as making money picking up the hundred-dollar bills one finds lying on the sidewalk.

What strategy should the average person, someone who is not a company insider or high-speed trader, use to invest in the stock market? For every big winner like Altria there are big losers that could destroy the investors' nest egg. Rather than picking one or a few stocks, one should reduce risk by diversifying across many stocks. Mutual funds have put together market indexes that in effect allow the investor to hold a tiny share of every stock available on the market. Such indexes are a good investment, especially if they can be purchased from a mutual fund that charges investors very low markups (over the cost of acquiring the stocks in the index). Trying to time the market, buying before an expected run up and selling before a downturn, is also a generally bad idea. Instead, buying and holding a market index for a long period allows the investor to smooth out the ups and downs of the market. That's the wisdom I promised about the stock market: diversification and buying and holding. It won't turn $100 into $1 million over a short span, but it does employ economic reasoning to help the average investor earn a solid return while cutting down on risk.

So, while economics can provide useful guidance on investing in the stock market, it is about much more. The topics mentioned in this article—art auctions, corruption, overpopulation, the value of a diamond, the return on a college education, the ups and downs of national and global economies—just scratch the surface of the broad range that economists study. Economics dares the practitioner to find something fascinating in what others might find pedestrian—the business side of life—and provides a set of core principles (this article mentioned some important ones: cost, market value, careful empirical measurement separating causation from mere correlation) that can help us understand that side of life.

WHAT IS

Engineering?

Vicki V. May

What comes to mind when you think about engineering? Try it! Think about engineering for a few minutes and come up with a list of words you associate with engineering and engineers.

Maybe words like "math" and "science" come to mind? Yes, engineers often use math and science, but they also use so much more. Engineers are just as likely to use psychology, art, sociology, music, and history when they work on real-world problems. Engineering draws from many disciplines.

"Difficult" is a word that some people associate with engineering. Yes, I suppose some of the problems that engineers tackle are difficult, but working on those difficult problems can be really exciting. There are difficult tasks in every profession.

"Bridges," "phones," and "cars"—did any of these things come to mind when you thought about engineering? Yes, engineers design bridges, phones, and cars, but they also design medicines and ways to improve the taste and nutritional value of foods. They develop processes to clean up the environment and more efficient ways to convert energy. They create lasers to explore space and to improve medical equipment and communications. They work on both the microscopic scale, building devices that are smaller than the diameter of a piece of your hair, and the macroscopic scale, designing huge systems such as satellites and buildings.

Do you picture an engineer when you think about engineering? What does a typical engineer look like? What does an engineer wear? What does an engineer's office look like? Engineers tackle such a wide range of *multidisciplinary* problems that it is very difficult to come up with a single image of an engineer. Some engineers work in an office, others spend most of their time in a laboratory, and many work outside on a regular basis. Some rely heavily on mathematics and computers, while others do more writing or work with people to understand issues and needs. There is something for every type of person in engineering.

Of all the words I associate with engineering, "creative" is my favorite. Engineers are inventors and must be creative. They design and build things to meet human needs and help solve complex problems.

You can give engineering a try by designing and building something, anything: a chair or a musical instrument or an alarm for your door. Use materials you have on hand, like cardboard, tape, clay, or even twigs. Designing and building should be fun, and the possibilities are endless.

Engineers design many things: structures, materials, tools, satellites, robots, electronic devices, energy systems, chemicals, biomedical devices, and more. They also design ways to do things like reduce air pollution, create new materials, and travel through space. Rather than try to cover everything that engineers do, let's focus on a few key areas including: how engineers design the *structures* that are all around us, how the *mechanical and biomedical devices* created by engineers help us live healthier lives, and how engineers tackle issues related to *energy and the environment*.

Structures

Structures are all around us: from the chairs we sit on, to the houses and buildings we live in, to the bridges in our communities, to the cars we drive, and satellites in space. We even find structures in nature; examples include trees, caves, and beaver dams. Structures are a collection of elements that resist loads. Most solid objects (and even some not-so-solid objects) may be classified as structures.

As with most engineering design problems, an engineer must consider many different competing criteria when designing a structure, such as how the structure will be used, how it should look, what materials are available, how much it will cost, and more. How a structure will be used dictates the forces that will be applied to the structure. For example, a chair must be designed to resist the force of a person sitting on it (and maybe leaning back). A hockey stick must be designed to resist the force of a person hitting a hockey puck (or accidently hitting the wall). An airplane wing must be designed to resist the upward lift needed to oppose the downward weight of the plane and passengers and keep the plane in the air. A building must be designed to resist the forces associated with people walking around in the building as well as environmental forces such as those produced by wind, snow, and earthquakes.

Forces, forms, and materials are all related, so let's explore these relationships a bit. If you can, grab a few objects that are made of different materials—maybe a piece of chalk, a piece of string or rope, a paperclip, a ruler, and a spoon. How do the different objects behave? For each different object, try applying different forces. Apply a tension force by pulling on the object. Apply a compression force by pushing on the object. And apply a bending force by rotating each end or by applying a force perpendicular to the middle. How does each object behave under these different loads?

The kinds of questions that we are considering here are fundamental to the construction of safe and beautiful structures! Look at the great towers in Dubai or the skyscrapers of New York City or the long-spanning bridges in Japan and South America or the great cathedrals of Europe or mosques of the Near East. How are we able to design and build these structures to resist different loads?

First let's consider rope. You should find that you can pull on a rope, but can you push on a rope? When you push on a rope, it will collapse, since ropes can only carry loads in tension or when pulled. So a rope, cable, or chain is a good choice for resisting tension forces but would be a poor choice for resisting other types of forces. Where do we find tension in structures, and what forms are in tension? If you hang a rope or cable, it will naturally find the perfect form; it turns out the form a rope finds if no other loads are applied to it is called a *catenary*. The seventeenth-century mathematician Johann Bernoulli figured out the formula that describes a catenary in response to a challenge from his brother Jakob! If you hang things on the rope (e.g., clothes on a clothesline), new forms will be created. All of these forms for a rope or cable are known as *funicular forms*. The unique thing about funicular forms is that tension is the only force found in a funicular form, since a rope can only support tension. Cables and funicular forms can be found in lots of structures around you, such as suspension bridges, spiderwebs, guitar strings, clotheslines, and more.

Of course, for something like a suspension bridge we don't just build it and hope for the best! An engineer will use mathematics, physical models, and computer simulations to understand how the forms respond to different loads. Engineers are continually experimenting and learning about how structures behave. While we hope that failures are limited to the prototypes, they do occur on occasion in final structures. Failures provide opportunities for engineers to learn from their mistakes. The failure of the Tacoma Narrows Bridge is a classic example: engineers created a very efficient suspension bridge but didn't account for the area's wind gusts, which eventually set up resonance (a wave motion in the bridge generated in response to the wind) and caused the bridge to fail in a catastrophic and dramatic (but thankfully not deadly) manner (you can watch this on YouTube). While the Tacoma Narrows Bridge failure was tragic, it led to a better understanding of the response of bridges and other structures to wind gusts.

Suspension bridges and cable-stayed bridges rely heavily on metal cables. Other structures use different types of elements and materials. Stone and concrete are clearly very different from metal and would not make good cables and ropes. Consider a piece of chalk, which behaves much like stone and concrete. You can push on a piece of chalk or stone, unlike rope. How about if you try to pull on it? Or if you try to bend a piece of chalk? Can you break the piece of chalk when you push on it? pull on it? bend it? Most people are able to break a piece of chalk when they pull on it and when they bend it, but find that it is more difficult to break a piece of chalk when they push on it. Some of the chalk may flake off as you push on it, but it is likely to stay in one piece. That is because chalk (and stone and concrete) is strong in *compression* but weak in tension and bending.

Even though it doesn't perform well in tension or bending, engineers have used stone (which is not unlike chalk) to build many amazing structures, including the pyramids of Egypt, the Parthenon in Greece, the Coliseum in Rome, and the Great Wall of China. These structures share the fact that they mainly resist downward, compressive loads.

What types of forms generally work well for stone? Funicular forms would not be a good choice, since they are in pure tension, but columns do well in compression, since the weight of the column and structure above push down on the column. How about arches, vaults, and domes? Why were they so common in stone structures? The answer, again, is compression. Arches, vaults, and domes are forms that resist loads largely through compression. You might notice that an arch has the shape of a rope suspended at either end, but turned upside down, as shown in figure 1. More precisely, an inverted catenary (made out a different type of material; rope won't work) is an arch and will be in pure compression under its own weight. The arches under the roof of Antoni Gaudí's Casa Milà in Barcelona, Spain, are catenaries that were designed in part using models made of chains as shown in figures 1 and 2. If you extend an arch, you get a vault, and if you rotate an arch, you get a dome, all of which are mainly in compression. In the language of funiculars: if you invert a funicular form you create an antifunicular form and antifunicular forms are in pure compression for a given load! Engineers started using arches, vaults, and domes when designing structures because these forms do well in compression and stone was readily available.

While early engineers built arches and domes using trial and error, today engineers use mathematics and computer simulations along with physical models to design and build arches, domes, and more. Heinz Isler (1926–2009), for example, was a Swiss engineer who was famous for designing and building very thin concrete shell structures. Shell structures are a type of antifunicular form. Isler's engineering process involved first determining the form for the shell by building a series of physical models. He then tested these physical models in his laboratory by applying different loads to determine how and when they would fail. He also developed computer models to verify the failure modes determined by his physical models and further refine his designs. Finally, based on his physical and computer models, Isler developed plans from which the full-scale shells could be constructed. Isler's thin-shell concrete structures can be found throughout Europe.

You can build amazing structures out of concrete and stone, but imagine the possibilities with a material like steel, which performs well not only in tension (or pulling) and compression (or pushing), but also in bending. While there is evidence of small amounts of iron being used thousands of years ago, it wasn't until the Industrial Revolution that iron and steel began to be used more widely. Iron, a precursor to steel, was a fairly brittle material, not unlike stone. Like stone, early iron did better in compression and tended to fail without warning. The difference between iron and steel is that steel has less carbon; and because steel has less carbon, it is a more *ductile* material. Ductility is important in structures and machines: ductile materials yield or stretch, thus providing a warning that the structure may be overloaded. Taffy and Tootsie rolls are examples of very ductile "materials," as they will stretch a long way before finally being pulled apart. An English inventor and engineer, Sir Henry Bessemer (1813–1898), developed a process to create ductile steel cheaply so that it could be used more widely to build structures and machines. The Bessemer process (as it is called) involved blowing air across molten iron ore to burn off the impurities and carbon. The availability of ductile metals that could resist tension and bending meant that bridges and beams in buildings could span longer distances.

Structures today are built using a huge range of materials, from wood and manufactured lumber to concrete and steel and composites and titanium and even glass, like the all-glass Apple Cube buildings. And structures today soar to extreme heights. The Burj Khalifa in Dubai is over 828 meters tall, with over

FIGURE 1 Catenary arches
under the terrace of
Antoni Gaudí's Casa Milà,
Barcelona, Spain. Wikimedia
Commons, photo by
Wikipedia user Error.

FIGURE 2 Model of catenary arches for Casa Milà. Wikimedia Commons,
photo by Wikipedia user Etan J. Tal

FIGURE 3 Isler building. Wikimedia Commons, photo by Wikipedia user xp10

FIGURE 4 Guggenheim Museum in Bilbao. Wikimedia Commons,
photo by Mario Roberto Durán Ortiz

160 stories and all of the amenities of a city, from restaurants to offices, markets, businesses, swimming pools, and more. The amount of concrete alone used in the Burj Khalifa weighs more than 100,000 elephants! To design a building so tall requires extensive modeling and testing. The Burj Khalifa was collaboratively designed by architect Adrian Smith and engineer Bill Baker. Bill Baker writes, "Architectural design and structural engineering have a symbiotic relationship: a close and essential union in which one relies upon the other. In the ideal structure, the lines between science and aesthetic are blurred."

The symmetrical three-pronged shape of the Burj Khalifa, which was inspired by a flower, was selected by Bill Baker and Adrian Smith because it was easier to construct and had lower stresses during high winds than other designs. The engineering team built large-scale physical models of the Burj Khalifa that were tested in wind tunnels as well as numerous computer models to determine the expected behavior and stresses on the building.

Advances in computer software and manufacturing processes have made it possible to design and build ever more complex structures. Consider the Gug-

genheim Museum in Bilbao, which was designed by architect Frank Gehry. Due to the structure's mathematical complexity, engineers relied heavily on computer software to analyze the building, create drawings of it, and even manufacture parts of it. Note that the computer software that structural engineers use is typically designed and written by engineers, *computer engineers*, as well! Engineering is almost always a team effort.

Mechanical and Biomedical Devices

Early engineers didn't just design buildings and bridges. They also designed and built tools and simple machines such as ramps, pulleys, levers, and wheels. Experiment with simple machines if you have time—you can build prototypes using easy-to-find materials like cardboard, paper towel tubes, tape, and sticks. These simple machines form the basis of many of our tools and more complex machines today.

The development of ways to produce ductile materials like steel resulted in advances not only in structures but also in machines. Some of the first machines to be invented were the steam engine, power loom, cotton gin, seed drill, and plow. These machines revolutionized the way textiles or fabrics were made and how agriculture was practiced. James Watt (1736–1819), a Scottish inventor and engineer, patented a steam engine in 1791. The steam engine was used to power a large range of machines, including those in factories, and eventually trains and early automobiles. James Watt was known for having a strong theoretical understanding of math and science but also for having a good practical mechanical sense and the ability to build things. Both theoretical and practical knowledge are needed for engineers to successfully create new machines and devices.

Leonardo da Vinci was an early mechanical engineer, perhaps among the most famous in history. Leonardo da Vinci?—maybe you think of him as an artist. He was definitely a famous artist, but he was also a prolific inventor. He is credited with inventing a bicycle, a helicopter, an armored tank, and a way to concentrate solar energy. He epitomizes the Renaissance era because he had a broad range of interests that he was able to link together to his advantage. Engineering has become more and more specialized over the years, partly out of necessity, but the most successful engineers tend to be people like da Vinci and Watt: engineers with a broad range of interests within and beyond engineering.

Mechanical engineering has experienced some astounding advances in recent years. Some of the more popular machines and tools that engineers have designed and built are laser cutters and 3-D printers, tools that are becoming more widely

FIGURE 5 Leonardo da Vinci's Flying Machine. Wikimedia
Commons, file provided by Wikipedia user Sailko

available and allow users to design and build complex things. Laser stands for "light-stimulated amplification by stimulated emission of radiation." Lasers are powerful beams of light, powerful enough to cut wood, metal, and even diamonds; 3-D printers print three-dimensional objects layer by layer using "ink" in a wide range of materials, from plastics to metals to chocolate. 3-D printing is just one of a broad collection of new techniques that engineers and others are using to design and create new devices and prototypes.

Robots are specialized machines and have been around for years but are becoming more complex and capable of doing more things. Engineers who design robots must understand how the mechanical components fit together and move but must also know how to wire the robots' electrical components and how to write computer programs to control them.

Robots are fun and useful. Let's look at a few of the robots that have been and are being developed by engineers. Helen Greiner, a mechanical engineer, is the founder of iRobot, the company that brought us the Roomba, a small, autonomous robot designed to do the vacuuming, a chore most of us don't mind passing along to a robot. Helen's company went on to develop many variations on the Roomba for cleaning. But she recently moved from cleaning robots to flying robots, or drones. Engineers who design drones must use principles not only from mechanical, electrical, and computer engineering but also from aerospace engineering. Drones are being used for many different applications, from surveying to defense to firefighting to search-and-rescue missions. Drone technology is still developing, so who knows what applications will be possible in the future. Drones use a series of propellers and motors that are controlled remotely or autonomously using preprogrammed computer flight instructions. It is not too difficult to build a small drone, or flying robot; give it a try if you can.

Professor Laura Ray and her research group at Dartmouth College have developed Cool Robots, which are able to navigate rough, cold terrain such as the terrain in Antarctica. Laura's Cool Robots must be able to operate at temperatures as low as -40 degrees Celsius! Batteries do not work well at these low temperatures, so the Cool Robots rely on solar power and must be able to operate autonomously, or without human contact. The Cool Robots are being used to collect climate information and samples in cold environments. Engineers then analyze and use this data to build models to predict future climate changes.

Other engineers are designing robots that are more interactive. Professor Cynthia Breazeal's Personal Robots Group at the Massachusetts Institute of Technology is designing robots that are social and can interact with humans. Cynthia's group has developed robots that are huggable, help children learn, tell stories, and interact with children who are in the hospital. Nexi, a mobile social robot developed by Cynthia's group, was named one of the fifty best inventions of 2008 by *Time* magazine.

Many robots are being developed for medical purposes. Amy Kerdok, PhD, works for Intuitive Surgical to develop new instruments and visualization tools for robots used in surgery. The robots that Amy's group develops use sophisticated 3-D visualization tools that allow surgeons to be more precise and see better. One of the robots that Amy helped to develop, called Da Vinci, helps reduce the invasiveness of surgery by allowing the surgeon to insert robotic tools through very small openings and work inside the body using cameras as eyes. People who design and build medical devices and processes are known as *biomedical engineers.*

Professor Jennifer Lewis, an engineer at Harvard University, and others in her lab are developing machines to 3-D print using living cells as "ink"; perhaps in the future we will be able to print body parts! Professor Jane Hill, an engineer at Dartmouth, is designing devices and tools to detect diseases just by analyzing a patient's breath. Other engineers are developing super-small, nano-sized devices that are able to detect and target cancerous tumors in the body. Many engineers are designing and building prosthetic devices to replace body parts such as knees, hips, legs, and arms. And biomedical engineers working with neurologists and others have developed robotic arms that may be controlled by the brain, thus allowing paralyzed patients to once again move a robotic arm to eat chocolate or turn the pages of a book or type a message using only their thoughts.

Engineers who design and build biomedical devices rarely work in isolation, instead collaborating with multidisciplinary teams of doctors and scientists and psychologists and others. While the technical aspects of a design are important factors in its success, nontechnical factors can be equally if not more important. Take the MRI (magnetic resonance imaging) machine as an example. MRI machines are used by doctors to take images of the inside of the body to help detect diseases. Engineers who developed the MRI machine had to understand physics and mathematics as well as electrical and mechanical engineering, but also needed to work with doctors and medical professionals to understand how to create readable images. The development of the MRI machine was a major engineering achievement and has helped save many, many lives. But getting an MRI scan can be a terrifying experience, especially for children. Doug Dietz, an engineer with GE, was appalled to find that most children needed to be tranquilized before getting a MRI scan. He did not find this acceptable, so he went back to the drawing board. After observing and interviewing many children who were getting an MRI, he redesigned an MRI machine for children that made getting an MRI an adventure rather than a terrifying medical procedure! Doug was able to significantly reduce the number of children who needed to be tranquilized before an MRI scan. His design went beyond the technical details to include human factors as well—which only makes sense, given that engineers design machines and tools that are used by humans.

Environment and Energy

Many engineers today tackle challenges related to energy and the environment, areas that are interrelated, since the production and use of energy have a direct impact on the environment.

Environmental engineers are designing new ways to convert energy to electricity, provide safe drinking water, process waste, recycle materials, and reduce pollution to air and water. Environmental engineering, like most fields of engineering, is a very multidisciplinary field requiring expertise in chemistry, biology, geology, mechanics, electricity, and more.

Let's first look at energy, since we use energy every day: to heat and cool our homes, operate our lights and computers, and fuel our cars and our bodies. Engineers design and build the machines and processes required to convert, store, and use energy, from power plants to batteries to computers.

So where does energy come from? Much of the energy we use comes from the sun. The sun provides energy directly in the form of heat. But the sun also provides energy for plants, which are eaten by animals and humans. And when these animals and plants decompose, they eventually form fossil fuels like oil and coal, which are used for fuel or energy. The uneven heating of the Earth by the sun even causes wind, another form of energy. Other sources of energy include nuclear energy and geothermal energy.

Often the goal is to convert energy from the wind or sun or coal to electrical energy, which we use for our electronic devices, appliances, computers, heat, and more. Engineers have developed many ways of converting energy in other forms to electrical energy. One example is photovoltaics, which are used to convert solar energy into electricity through the use of semiconductors. Semiconductors are materials like silicon that conduct or transport electricity under certain conditions. When certain types of semiconductors are exposed to sunlight, an electric current is developed. While solar panels are becoming more widely used, they are still fairly expensive to purchase and install, so many engineers are working to make them more efficient and cost-effective. Professor Jifeng Liu, an environmental engineer at Dartmouth, is developing new coatings for photovoltaics that are designed to improve the efficiency of solar panels. Jifeng is also trying to develop lower-cost materials that may be used for photovoltaics.

Other engineers design wind turbines that convert energy from the wind to rotational motion, a form of mechanical energy. That rotational motion or mechanical energy may then be converted to electrical energy by attaching a set of conducting coils to the rotating shaft and putting the shaft inside a large magnet. Michael Faraday was the first to discover that electricity could be produced through the combination of spinning copper coils and magnets. Imagine the excitement of that discovery! Engineers have been refining and improving on ways to produce electricity since Faraday's discovery. Wind turbines use Faraday's principles, and engineers are working to make them more and more efficient by designing wind turbine blades that are more aerodynamic and batteries that can store the energy for later use. A large wind turbine with blades that are around 50 meters long can convert enough energy from the wind to provide electricity for about 150 homes.

While fossil fuels remain the main source of energy in the world, engineers are working hard to make renewable sources of energy like solar and wind more cost competitive. Even renewable energy sources have some environmental impact, and there are pros and cons to all energy sources. Solar energy produces no noise or pollution, but it takes up land and is not viable everywhere, and installation costs are still fairly high. Nuclear energy, on the other hand, produces lots of energy but produces long-lasting waste products that must be handled properly, so engineers are working on ensuring that plants operate and dispose of by-products safely. Engineers and policy makers must weigh the pros and cons of all of the different possibilities for converting energy. There is no shortage of issues for engineers to tackle related to energy and the environment!

I've focused on three areas here—*structures, mechanical and biomedical devices, and energy and the environment*—but there are many, many more areas where engineers are designing and building things and ways to do things. Engineers are designing rovers to explore Mars and other planets, telescopes and satellites to see galaxies far away, smartphones and computers for work and entertainment, animations for movies, devices that are able to send messages millions of kilometers through space, and more. Who knows what engineers will tackle in the future: human travel to Mars, new forms of entertainment, roads that heal themselves? The options are endless.

What words come to mind now when you think about engineering? I hope that many words come to mind, and that you now have an appreciation for the ways in which engineers are creative and tackle multidisciplinary challenges.

WHAT IS

English?

Thomas H. Luxon

What is English? Well, sure, you already know it's a language—maybe even the language you grew up speaking, although maybe not! In fact, English is a language spoken by millions of people all over the world. Its oldest form, Anglo-Saxon (or Old English), was spoken in England and southern Scotland beginning around the middle of the fifth century CE. By the late twentieth century, modern English—the kind that we speak now (and even that is continually changing) had replaced French as the "lingua franca," or semi-official, language of international business and law. In almost all countries where English is not the "official" language, most people will still learn English as part of their regular studies in school.

There are lots of people who think about English as a language, as one of the many languages spoken around the world. If you are an expert in *linguistics*, you might be interested in how English has changed over time and adapted to different environments. For example, the "English" that we use when we communicate on the computer or by texting is very different from the English we use where we are speaking to each other face-to-face (I hope you still do some of that!). Also, the English that we speak up here in New Hampshire might have subtle differences from the English that our friends in Illinois speak (what we call "soda," you call "pop"—and why do you do that, anyway?). Each of these variations is known as a "dialect." In addition to the words that we each use in our forms of English, it's also deeply interesting how we put those words together—that is the syntax and grammar of the language. In fact, making sense of this has enabled innovations like machines that you can talk to—like "asking" your phone to give your directions, a piece of something called "natural language processing." Yes, there is a lot you can do and hope to do by better understanding the language of English.

But when someone says "I study English," say in college, generally they don't mean any of those things; instead they'd say "I study linguistics" (read the "What Is Linguistics" chapter to learn more!) or "I study natural language processing" (which is a mixture of linguistics and computer science). "Studying English" almost always means thinking intensively about literature—poetry and prose—and English literature in particular.

First, English literature means not just works written in England, but works connected to England in some fashion. Now I don't know, that might either seem really big ("You mean everything ever written in English?") or really little ("Why just English? What about other languages?"), and you'd be right on both accounts. If you think it's too small, don't worry, we'll get to that. The kinds of questions we can ask about English literature, we can ask about any collection of writings with some shared origin. So let's talk about that first.

Like linguists, English scholars are interested in how the language works—how it encodes meaning and how readers decode it. But unlike linguists, the language users we're most interested in are those whose writings *expand* the possibilities of how the language works. Lawmakers, judges, and technical writers want language to work as precisely, simply and predictably as possible. Poets, novelists, and playwrights explore the ways language can surprise us with complicated, even contradictory, meanings. They also work hard to make the language's *sounds* interact with its *senses*. For instance, take this poem by the American poet Emily Dickinson (okay, she's not from England, but too wonderful not to include for an example!):

> There's a certain Slant of light,
> Winter Afternoons –
> That oppresses, like the Heft
> Of Cathedral Tunes –
>
> Heavenly Hurt, it gives us –
> We can find no scar,
> But internal difference,
> Where the Meanings, are –
>
> None may teach it – Any –
> 'Tis the Seal Despair –
> An imperial affliction
> Sent us of the Air –

When it comes, the Landscape listens –
Shadows – hold their breath –
When it goes, 'tis like the Distance
On the look of Death –

Besides the rhymes, which use sound to couple disparate senses like "breath" and "Death," Dickinson also plays with alliteration—"certain Slant" and "Heavenly Hurt" and "Landscape listens." In each case the sounds bring special textures to the meanings of the words. The "sibilant *c*" and "sibilant *s*" invite us to imagine sunshine making a sound as it slants through a window. "Heavenly Hurt" sounds like a soft kind of pain that leaves no scar, asking us to reconsider what kind of "Hurt" the poem considers. And the notion of a "Landscape" as a personified listener and shadows holding their breath challenge our usual beliefs about reality and logic even as the paired sounds pressure us to make some sense of words and images that defy reason. This poem invites us to think about topics reason has trouble grasping—death, heaven, and how meaning itself is produced by difference. It is more interested in radiating meanings than in nailing them down. English scholars study the ways poets like Dickinson play with sound and sense and the ways readers respond to her challenges by making sense themselves.

So, okay, it is big. But that's a good thing! It means that there is so much to learn and so much to think about. The field of English literary study is unusually broad for several reasons. First, for historical reasons: English has been used artistically, in poetry (verse) and prose, for more than fifteen hundred years, and it has taken three broadly distinct forms over that period. Old English looks to us today like an entirely alien language. The first long narrative poem (epic) in English, *Beowulf* (ca. 800–900 CE), appears unreadable to most native speakers of English today:

hwæt, we gar-dena in geardagum,
þeodcyninga þrym gefrunon,
hu ða æþelingas ellen fremedon!
Oft Scyld Scefing sceaþena þreatum,
monegum mægþum meodosetla ofteah,
egsode eorlas, syððan ærest wearð
feasceaft funden; he þæs frofre gebad,
weox under wolcnum weorðmyndum þah,
oð þæt him æghwylc ymbsittendra

ofer hronrade hyran scolde,
gomban gyldan; þæt wæs god cyning!

The last phrase can be translated "That was a good king." But as you can see, even some of the letters used in Old English are unfamiliar to us today.

One of the most famous English poets, Geoffrey Chaucer, wrote in what we now call Middle English, the second distinct form of the language, spoken from the late eleventh until the late fifteenth century, following the Norman (French) conquest of 1066. These lines from the "General Prologue" of *The Canterbury Tales* will look somewhat more familiar to modern eyes:

> Whan that Aprill with his shoures soote,
> The droghte of March hath perced to the roote,
> And bathed every veyne in swich licour
> Of which vertu engendred is the flour;
> Whan Zephirus eek with his sweete breeth
> Inspired hath in every holt and heeth
> The tendre croppes, and the yonge sonne
> Hath in the Ram his halve cours yronne,
> And smale foweles maken melodye,
> That slepen al the nyght with open ye,
> So priketh hem nature in hir corages,
> Thanne longen folk to goon on pilgrimages[.]

Words like "licour" (liquor or liquid) and "corages" (hearts) betray the French influence on an older Germanic language.

The third distinct form of English, modern English, emerged in the early sixteenth century. This is the English of William Shakespeare's poems and plays. Students today think Shakespeare's English looks and sounds old-fashioned, but it is an early form of modern English:

> When fortie Winters shall beseige thy brow,
> And digge deep trenches in thy beauties field,
> Thy youthes proud liuery so gaz'd on now,
> Wil be a totter'd weed of smal worth held:
> Then being askt, where all thy beautie lies,
> Where all the treasure of thy lusty daies;

To say within thine owne deepe sunken eyes,

Were an all-eating shame, and thriftlesse praise.

How much more praise deserv'd thy beauties use,

If thou couldst answere this faire child of mine

Shall sum my count, and make my old excuse

Prooving his beautie by succession thine.

   This were to be new made when thou art ould,

   And see thy blood warme when thou feel'st it could.

Spellings like "fortie, "askt," and "prooving" may look a bit strange when we read them, but even the slightest effort to pronounce them usually helps us recognize a modern English word. One fascinating reason that English spelling becomes far more regular in the eighteenth century is because that was the period when encyclopedias and dictionaries came into widespread use. Since they were organized alphabetically, spelling needed to become more regular. English, of course, continues to evolve to this day.

But the language didn't just evolve in place; it also spread (and that spread surely contributed to its evolution). A key historical reason for the breadth of English literary studies has to do with the expansion of the British Empire beginning in the seventeenth century. In Shakespeare's day British people spoke—and composed poetry—in English, Scots, Irish, and Gaelic, depending on where in Great Britain they were born, but today English is an official language in sixty-seven sovereign countries, from Antigua and Barbuda to Zimbabwe. The most populous of these is India, with more than 1.25 billion people. There are people in all of these countries writing verse and creative prose in English. So English literature includes Shakespeare's works, and it also includes those of Chinua Achebe, an Igbo chief from Nigeria who wrote five novels in English, the most famous of which, *Things Fall Apart* (1958), dwells on the clash between traditional Nigerian and Western cultures. The study of English literature today includes the study of scores of different cultures expressed in the English language.

Students of English literature must develop expertise in a variety of related disciplines, especially history and *theories of representation*, that is, how we represent our worlds and experiences in words. Poets, novelists, playwrights, and other creative writers in English write about religion, politics, race, history, music, science, sex, and gender, to name just a few topics. This means that someone who tries to understand how English is used to delight, instruct, and inspire readers and listeners must usually become an expert in several other academic disciplines.

Take the work of John Milton, for example. Milton's greatest poem is an epic (a long narrative poem) based on the biblical book of Genesis. *Paradise Lost* first appeared in print in 1667, a period of great religious and political controversy. Milton was a Puritan, a person who believed the English church was corrupt and needed further reformation. He also was staunchly against monarchy during a period of popular support for a recently restored king and church.

In reading Milton, there is a lot to think about! How did English Puritans like Milton read the Bible in the seventeenth century? How did they feel about adding new characters and new episodes to a story from the Bible? When we think of the story of Adam and Eve in the Garden of Eden, we're more likely to remember features of *Paradise Lost* that do not appear in Genesis, features that Milton added from various sources and his own imagination. For example, we all remember Satan was Eve's tempter, even though Genesis never mentions Satan. Milton's Adam and Eve enjoy sexual relations before they eat the forbidden fruit; nothing about that in Genesis! Milton's great English epic uses the story of the first man and the first woman as a kind of memory tree on which he hangs just about all the knowledge, wisdom, and opinions he had acquired during his remarkable life.

Milton was also an expert in political theory; he wrote scores of books and pamphlets on church politics, monarchy, and even marriage and divorce (he was in favor of divorce). All of these topics appear in his poetry. And a Miltonist (a person who specializes in Milton studies) needs to know a lot about classical literature and philosophy in Greek and Latin because Milton's poems very self-consciously refer to, imitate, and sometimes satirize the works of Homer in ancient Greek, and Virgil and Ovid in Latin, not to mention theologians and philosophers reaching back thousands of years. Milton set himself an ambitious goal: "to assert Eternal Providence, / And justifie the wayes of God to men" (*Paradise Lost* 1.25–26). Many have admired this ambition—to explain God's ways and defend him against the charge of being unfair to human beings—but others have thought such ambition unwarranted, even dangerously immoral.

What we've done just now is engaged a little bit of "literary criticism." But criticism is not only about explaining how poems and stories work (nor is it just about "criticizing" the writer!). It is also sometimes an opportunity literally to criticize, to take a reasoned ethical position about a work of art. No English author invites this more than John Milton. Perhaps this is because the biblical story of "the beginning" remains important to millions around the world, and Milton's version of the story has become, for some, more influential than the one in Genesis. The poem not only tells the story of the first man and woman, but also documents the process by which an ancient Hebrew story has been recast to support Christian ideologies, some of which are painfully anti-Jewish and anti-Islamic. Understanding seventeenth-century versions of these ideologies, still very much alive today, may help us better understand where they come from and why they persist.

Yet another reason the study of English is so broad has to do with *formal categories.* English literature takes many forms—we call them genres—and each genre sets up a different set of expectations about how it should be read and how we go about producing meaning when we read or hear it. In the broadest terms, literature may be either in verse or prose. Prose is more like spoken language and is not written in metrical lines. The metrical or rhythmic arrangement of sounds in verse has a great deal to do with how poets and their readers produce meaning in English. This stanza from Edmund Spenser's *Faerie Queene* illustrates several examples of the formal characteristics of an English romantic epic poem.

> A Gentle Knight was pricking on the plaine,
> Y cladd in mightie armes and siluer shielde,
> Wherein old dints of deepe wounds did remaine,
> The cruell markes of many a bloudy fielde;
> Yet armes till that time did he neuer wield:
> His angry steede did chide his foming bitt,
> As much disdayning to the curbe to yield:
> Full iolly knight he seemd, and faire did sitt,
> As one for knightly giusts and fierce encounters fitt.

Easy to notice is the rhyme. In the late seventeenth century most poets wrote in rhyming couplets (with important exceptions), but this earlier poem (it was written in the 1580s) rhymes in a different pattern. The first and third lines rhyme; so do the second, fourth, fifth, and seventh; and the stanza ends with a rhymed couplet. Spenser adapted this scheme from Italian poets, but in English we now call it a *Spenserean stanza.* This rhyme scheme has the effect of making the stanza appear woven together as if each line was a strand of yarn, and it often invites us to draw connections between nonadjacent lines that creatively distort the meanings of certain words. For example, "shielde," "fielde," "wield," and "yield" are all words drawn from the lexicon of battle. A knight with a shield fights on a field of battle, wields a sword, and hopes his opponent will yield him the victory.

Though we notice that the word "yield" in line 7 refers in the first instance to a horse's obedience to his rider's manipulations of the bit in his mouth, because rhyme associates it with a martial vocabulary, it acquires additional meanings, and we may well try to compare a yielding steed to a yielding enemy with interesting imaginative results.

The rhythm of this stanza is also significant. The first eight lines contain (generally) ten syllables or beats in an alternating rhythm (mostly) that we call iambic pentameter, or five feet (iambs) of two beats each with emphasis on the second beat in each foot. There are variations here that interrupt the singsongy effect, and those interruptions are artfully managed to prompt a reader to think, to interpret. For example, "deepe wounds" in line 3 interrupts the established rhythm; this happens again in line 5 with "that time." Readers will stumble a bit over these lines, especially if they are read aloud (as most poetry should be), and when they do, they will also find themselves stumbling over the sense: If the knight has never been in battle before (the sense of line 5), why does his armor have so many "old dints"? Whose armor is this, and how did this gentle knight ("gentle" in the sense of class rank, but also pretty unwarlike, even jolly?) come across this armor? Just how old is it? The interplay of sound and sense, abetted by the formal and thematic expectations of an epic romance (that is, in a roman, or novel, style), are calculated to make a reader ask these sorts of questions as she engages with the poem.

The last line has six feet (twelve syllables). This will be true in every stanza throughout the poem. We call this sort of line an alexandrine (why, I don't actually know). In this case, the first foot, "As one," draws attention to the fact that this knight, though jolly and a good horseman, is really not yet fit for jousts and fierce encounters. Will he ever be? He does, however, wear armor that has seen its fair share of bloody battles.

There's much more we could say about this stanza—its various tones, the way it imitates an older form of English than was common in the 1580s, the alliteration (front rhyme) of "pricking" and "plaine," "silver shielde," and "dints of deepe." Some scholars aim to produce close readings that exhaustively explain the effects of every formal, rhetorical, and thematic feature of the poem, but this poem (unfinished as it is) has seventy-five such cantos. For this reason, Spensereans rarely attempt exhaustive explication. Scholars more often attempt such explications with shorter forms of verse like lyric poems, hymns, sonnets, and songs.

There are many more formal considerations that affect the ways we understand poems and prose stories. Some are written for occasions; some are fiction and some not; some employ allegorical modes of thought as well as the more familiar metaphors and similes. Whole catalogs of rhetorical schemes and tropes have been compiled to help English scholars address their primary task of explaining how the language is used artistically and imaginatively to delight, instruct, and move readers' hearts and minds. The study of English literature is old and broad and deep—well worth a lifetime of reading, thinking, and writing.

When we study English literature, we also engage with history, religion, politics, even science. In book 8 of *Paradise Lost,* Milton invites us to imagine Adam talking about astronomy with the archangel Raphael (one of many episodes with no basis in Genesis). Does the sun circle the Earth or the Earth orbit the sun? Milton's angel has an interesting answer.

Most important, though, English students study the limitless ways we human beings use language, sound and sense, to produce meaning. We've only made it to the seventeenth century in our various examples, but the kinds of questions we are asking are questions that are asked of literature created at all times. Poets and scholars concern themselves with the same big questions philosophers and scientists ask—Where did we human beings come from? Why are we here? Where are we going? What makes life worth living? How do we make meaning?

In recent years, students of English literature have even helped to found new disciplines, including Gender Studies, Film Studies, Cultural Studies, and others. You will read about some of these in other essays in this book. As an academic discipline, English Studies is quite young, just over one hundred years, but the objects it studies—poems, plays, novels, films, performances—are as old as the language itself. These objects originated in oral performances; later they were written and preserved in handwritten form (manuscripts) that often were read aloud to groups of students and monks; since the late 1400s, literature has been mass-produced in print, allowing new experiences of individual reading; and now we have film and video versions of songs and stories, old and new. In the 1500s, scholars undertook the enormous task of collecting Greek, Roman, and Hebrew classics into printed books. Before print only a few could read Homer's *Iliad* or the Bible. Once printed copies appeared, tens of thousands could own and read their own copies. One result of printing was widespread literacy. Today, digital editions of classic English literature hold out the promise of another new reading experience. Dartmouth's *John Milton Reading Room,* for example, helps readers trace out Milton's many allusions and references by accessing hyperlinks to a virtual library known as the World Wide Web.

I imagine a time when digital editions will allow readers to share their reading experiences and insights with each other across time and distance, and the tools of literary scholarship will be available to anyone, anywhere in the world, at all times. Even more, with digitization come not only expanded opportunities for reading literature, but even for studying it using computational tools. Such efforts are among those included in the new field of "digital humanities." With each generation, we all renew the activity of reading as a community experience.

WHAT IS

French?

Andrea Tarnowski

Are you fascinated by the idea of speaking another language? Very early on, I was—in particular, I was eager to absorb the complexities of French. It wasn't just the mechanics of learning to communicate in French that moved me, but also the hope that this would be part and parcel of a way into French culture and history. While for me it was the French language, for some of you the "other" or "foreign" (we'll get to those terms later) language might be Russian, Swahili, Hebrew, or German. No matter what your choice, the surest and most direct path to participating in another culture is through its language.

Many of you may have experienced the truth of this statement firsthand, because you speak a language other than English at home, or have parents or grandparents who do. You know that perspectives on what is important in life, on how children should be educated, on relationships and religion, are most clearly understood when you learn them from *inside* the language the culture carries. If you don't already know a language other than English, you might aspire to because you've long wanted to understand your family's origins, or you might be excited about becoming a skilled speaker of a language your friends and relatives have never studied. In any of these scenarios, you're demonstrating a healthy desire to go beyond "tourism," where many people stop. Tourism doesn't just mean physically visiting other places for short periods of time to get a taste of what they're like; it can also be an intellectual approach. You dip into a book, or sample a philosophy. While all of us are tourists in some things—expertise in even one or two areas is a commitment!—deep knowledge of another language opens door upon door on the millions of minds that have used that language to live. Whichever language you choose, it offers a path of exploration and discovery, about others as well as yourself.

The Tower of Babel—An Origin Myth for Language

Before we get into the philosophy, practice, and results of speaking another language, we should turn to an emblematic story about languages found in the Bible's Old Testament: the tale of the Tower of Babel. This is an origin story; that is, it aims to explain why something is the way it is. In this case, the explanation addresses why the world contains a wide variety of languages, rather than a single language used by all human beings.

In the distant past, the story says, all people spoke one language, shared one speech. A group of settlers on a plain decided to build a city, marked by a tower that would reach to the heavens; their achievement would ensure their fame. They set to work, and were able to build because they could all understand one another and thus make good progress toward their common goal. But when God saw what they were doing, he wasn't pleased. He knew that if all those people set their actions to a single purpose, there was nothing they couldn't accomplish; they would succeed in their plan, and their tower would touch the skies—all because they could communicate seamlessly with one another. The heavens were God's realm; he didn't want human encroachment on his territory. So he had to devise a solution that would keep human beings from getting too close to divinity. Just destroying the tower wouldn't be enough; he had to ensure that, once razed, it could never be rebuilt. God's idea was to create a diversity of languages; this would confuse people and block mutual understanding. Rather than uniting, human beings would disperse. That is indeed what happened as soon as God divided people linguistically. Groups left the community they had built and scattered to every land on Earth. And so there is a multiplicity of languages. (Just to add some numbers to the picture, there are about 6,500 languages in existence, but only about sixty or so have more than 20 million native speakers. As for the number of languages taught in US universities, there are rarely more than thirty, and most often considerably fewer.)

While the tale of the Tower of Babel gives a reason for our linguistic diversity, the important point it conveys to us now is that language and communication are foundational to any kind of human accomplishment. There's little we can do in its absence; in fact, we could define the term "language" by saying, simply, "Language is *us*." You may be wondering whether you'd rather study Chinese, or Spanish; you may ask yourself which would be more practical, or more appealing. But step back a moment first to think about language *as such* as an all-pervasive phenomenon, no matter what variety of language you know or learn. We can't imagine ourselves without making use of it.

We Are Our Language

It's of course easy to perceive how empty life would be if you couldn't talk with your family or friends, write or send messages, or read books or signs or jokes. You'd be moving around in what would amount to a big empty space, connected to nothing and no one. The connection language provides—that connection the builders of Babel had—would be severed. But there's a more difficult and mind-bending notion at work here: without language, we might not imagine, or think, at all. If you formulate something as basic as "My name is *X*, and I have brown hair and long legs, and I love music," you have envisioned and described yourself with language. You may not say the words of the description aloud, but you do form them in your head; your mind is organized through language, and if you are doing the work of thinking, there is no way to bypass words. You think *by means of* words. Try something more rudimentary: instead of describing—whether yourself, another person, or an object—just observe. For example, you might notice a pattern of tiles in your kitchen: one white tile, one blue tile, one white, one blue, repeated all along one wall. You see the alternation of white and blue. But the fact that you think of it as an alternation, and perceive a contrast; the fact that you mentally call one color white and the other color blue; the very simple fact that you understand the tiles as being square, and that you know that they are tiles, means you have used language every step of the way. Each thing you have thought in observing the tiles, you have thought through language. Language is the threshold to being human. If you didn't have language, that line of tiles would be indistinguishable from a motorcycle, a giraffe, or a baby; any or all of those might be in your line of sight, but you wouldn't be thinking anything about them. You couldn't compare them, define them, or even recognize them. Your eyes would physically see the objects, but seeing in the sense of *insight*, of understanding and knowing, presupposes language.

Let's say you are now convinced of the omnipresence and even the omnipotence of language in human life: How do people go about acquiring it? You certainly won't remember how you did this as a child, but it's worthwhile to think of the mechanisms involved now that you're older. Especially given this daunting news: our natural language-learning ability, which is high when we're very young, starts sliding sharply by the time we hit age twelve or thirteen. If you learn a language in your late teens or early twenties, you're going to have to be deliberate and concentrated in your effort. (Side note: given that we lose the ability to acquire language as we pass from childhood into adolescence, isn't it strange that most people in the United States, if they ever study a new language, study it *after* they become teenagers? Our educational policy would seem to operate in the least efficient way possible on this score; if you're interested in language and education, maybe you will want to become an advocate for earlier and more intensive language instruction in schools.)

Two primary principles of language acquisition are association and distinction. If you put this duo into motion, you can create, and convey, meaning. In the 1800s, a Swiss linguist named Ferdinand de Saussure developed a theory called semiotics, or the study of meaning and the way language means. Like most great theories, it can be expressed concisely: nothing "means" on its own. A word only means in relation to something else. If you teach a child language by pointing to a table and saying "table," you begin to create a connection in the child's mind between the object and the word: an association. But if you then point to a picture frame and say "table," and point to a cardboard box and say "table," you'll create confusion; without a series of opposing terms to delimit or distinguish that thing called "table," the word's meaning is fuzzy at best, and perhaps nonexistent. As soon as the distinction boundaries are set up, though—*this* is a table, whereas *this* is a picture frame, and *this* is a box—the word "table" starts to be infused with meaning. There is a link between the word itself and what the word stands for—and thus, simultaneously, there is a distinction from, and exclusion of, everything that is not that object. You might think of the word "table" in this case as a sort of magnet, drawing the table-object to it—but repelling, or leaving alone, everything else.

Associate, distinguish, associate, distinguish; we do this not just at a basic level as we learn the words of everyday life in childhood, but even once we have a broad and solid foundation in our own language. As our understanding of connections grows, so does the subtlety of the distinctions we can make. Take a look at this list of words, each of which is followed by a synonym: costly, sumptuous, magnificent, exquisite, beautiful, stunning, astonishing. While the power of association allows us to marry each term to the one that precedes it, we also, even in the midst of the link-ups, register slight changes in shade of meaning; this is made obvious when we compare the words at the beginning and the end of the list, as no one would claim that "costly" and "astonishing" mean the same thing.

Studying Another Language

While you can improve your knowledge of your own language so that your mind works in both an ever-broader sweep and an always-finer grain, there is a fast and easy way to gain new perspective on what you know, and that is to study *another* language. The challenges are numerous: you may have to learn to read and write a new alphabet (Greek, Russian, Japanese), or acquire the habit of reading from right to left and/or from top to bottom (Hebrew, Arabic, Korean). You'll have to learn how diacritical marks (symbols added to letters) that don't exist in English affect pronunciation, such as the Polish *ł*, Swedish *å*, or French *ô*. Also, because you'll be beyond the age of just being able to "pick up" a new language, you'll need to acquire a clear consciousness of how language works: how the changes in verb forms called conjugations operate, and what the differences are between a verb tense (that is, past, present, future) and a verb mood (e.g., indicative to make a statement, conditional to pose a hypothesis, subjunctive to suggest doubt or uncertainty). Every time you actively acquire a new element of another language, you will have a sharper sense of the boundaries of your own—that's why English speakers might reach for the Italian term *sprezzatura* when they want to describe a kind of effortless competence or casual show of talent; it's a light, one-word formulation for something that in English requires a longer descriptive phrase.

Up to a certain point, you can consider learning another language to be something of a scientific exercise. You can memorize lists of vocabulary words and their meanings, recite categories of verbs, and deftly transpose singular nouns into the plural (English is easy in this regard, because mostly, we just add an *s* or *es* to form the plural; other languages are far more complex). What you say in the language you're learning will be either right or wrong; the answers you give on tests concerning grammar points will be either correct or incorrect. There's not a lot of middle ground. This kind of language acquisition can feel deeply satisfying; with each new set of vocabulary lists, you see your language knowledge expand. But in fact, it's beyond the "scientific" work that language gets most interesting.

Consider translation. People tend to think of it as a simple transposition of a word or phrase in one language to the equivalent in another. But it's infinitely messier than that. To use a brief example, if you're a professional translator rendering German into English, and you come across the word *Freiheit*, would you translate it into English as "freedom," or as "liberty"? Do you perceive any difference at all between the two English words? Might it be that "freedom" sits better in a day-to-day, physical realm (e.g., "freedom of movement"), whereas "liberty" sounds more intellectual, more conceptual (as in the Declaration of Independence: "life, liberty, and the pursuit of happiness")? Depending on the type of document you have before you in German, one or the other of these English terms might be a better choice. In any case, once you translate that single word, you'll go on to the next, and the next, and have to make literally hundreds of choices to translate even so much as a page. The result will necessarily be a product of your era, your priorities, your culture, your own interpretation—in short, of yourself. You cannot translate someone else's words without inserting yourself into the mix; by definition, the translator is fused into the translation. That is why, if you seek out a famous work that has been translated dozens of times over centuries—maybe Homer's ancient Greek tale *The Iliad*—you will find wildly differing versions, to the point where it may be difficult to tell if all the translators were working from the same basic text to begin with.

Fear of the "Foreign"

This is the time to bring up the term "foreign," as in "learning a foreign language"; you may have noticed its absence up until now. "Foreign" comes from the Latin word for "outside," meaning a language that is outside yourself—not a part of you, the way your native language is. "Foreign" used to be widely used, but recently it has fallen into disfavor, mostly because of the synonyms it calls up that have a negative connotation: "strange," for example, or "alien." People hesitate to "judge" a language or somehow show a lack of respect by labeling it foreign; they prefer to say they study "languages" (with no qualifier), or "world languages," or "modern languages" (the last category excludes languages that today exist only in written, rather than spoken, form, such as ancient Hebrew, ancient Greek, and Latin). In universities, languages often get grouped into academic departments on the basis of shared origins or geography; a department of Romance languages might teach Spanish, French, Italian, and Portuguese, whereas a department of Asian languages could cover Chinese, Japanese, and Korean. This kind of clustering is at once logical and free of critical overtones.

"Foreign" might be most unappealing because it suggests not only that a language is not part of us to begin with, but also that it can *never* be part of us; something foreign is held perpetually at arm's length—it can't be absorbed or embraced. And of course, if you want to learn a language, bridging distance, embracing, and absorbing are just what is required. You have to launch a counter-Babel initiative, aiming to repair in some small measure the confusion and dispersion that reign when people's modes of communication are not mutually understood.

To Culture, through Language

The language I targeted in my own initiative was French, and there were plenty of motivating factors for the choice. France is consistently the most visited country in the world, so its appeal seems lost on few (in German, the expression for living in perfect happiness translates as "living like God in France"!). For hundreds of years, French was *the* language Westerners learned to gain access to both other people and new ideas; only in the later decades of the twentieth century did it become increasingly important to speak English in matters of international politics and diplomacy (French and English were the two working languages at the United Nations when it was established in New York in 1946; today their number includes Arabic, Chinese, Russian, and Spanish). But most importantly, the cultural status and influence of French seemed unparalleled. Identities anchored in France and through the French language—eminence in literature, painting, philosophy, film, and dance, not to mention couture and gastronomy—exercised a strong attraction.

Once you've studied a language at length, incorporating aspects of its culture into your understanding; once you've gone and lived in another country, so that it is not foreign but at least partly a second home, you can take any of a number of paths to keep the crucial linguistic connection at the forefront of what you do. My interests were historical—history is another means of making the "foreign" familiar—so the evolution of French was of particular interest. You may have heard of William the Conqueror, who invaded England from France in 1066, and, in a military encounter called the Battle of Hastings, triumphed; this is known as the Norman Conquest. The result of the victory was that French became the standard language of the English court and educated circles for over three hundred years! Even today, we're aware of this legacy: about 30 percent of the English words we use have direct French origins. When we observe the types of words that look most similar in English and French, the notion that French had currency as the language of the law, of universities, and of elites is confirmed: most of our French imports concern the realm of ideas and concepts, as your immediate understanding of the French words éducation, *imagination*, and *justice* will attest. English is technically classified as a Germanic language, and German and English do share quite a few words of basic, everyday vocabulary; in addition to a bread-and-butter phrase like *Brot und Butter*, we can cite *Haus* for "house," *Hund* for "dog" (as in "hound"), and *Mann* for "man." But as soon as we leave the arena of the down-to-earth, easily discernible links decrease;

the word "justice," for example, is *Gerechtigkeit*. It is more difficult for an adult speaker of English to learn German than French.

Because I liked studying the evolution of language, my work eventually focused on the end of the Middle Ages: the decades around 1400 CE. If you deal on a daily basis with French that is six hundred years old, you're not too far from having learned yet another language; it has a different name, Middle French, and is readable only with much difficulty by modern-day speakers—as if you picked up a copy of Chaucer's *Canterbury Tales* in their original Middle English. In 1400, Paris hummed with intellectual, artistic, and commercial activity; it had a population two and a half times as large as Italy's largest city, Venice, and nearly six times that of London. Many foundational works from antiquity, on subjects such as ethics and politics, were being translated into the French vernacular for the first time (usually from Latin), and the trend in translations was accompanied by a rise in the production of sumptuous books, beautifully copied and illustrated and destined for important dedicatees. This period was still fifty years before the invention of the printing press in the West, so every element of every book was produced by hand; when you read the words of an author in that author's own script, knowing that crossed out words signal a human error or the writer's preference for a new term, there is a connection across time, through both language and the material object, with people, places, and contexts that are otherwise lost. And when the content of a book many centuries old resonates with situations you know yourself—calls to reform a society of feuding factions, or advice to those who govern on respecting the dignity of the people—it gives another dimension to reflections on both the past and present.

The principles of language study—attentive listening, fine-tuned analysis, a desire to engage in dialogue with the spoken and written word—let you approach the unfamiliar with both humility and empathy. Learning another language will take you out of yourself; you'll move toward the other person in a potential conversation, trading self-assertion for curiosity. And in the act of going beyond your original boundaries of self, you'll be more able to invest in what surrounds you. If you want to contribute to public policy on immigration, you'll be more competent and credible if you can speak with the people on the frontline. If you aspire to bring change to an existing system elsewhere—establish new healthcare methods, for example, or implant a new kind of technology—knowledge of the language of those affected will be the most stable platform for success. If you seek to understand a nationalist movement, the repercussions of colonialism, or the unique features of an economy, then the languages used among political partisans, colonial inhabitants, or businesspeople will be key to engaging productively with information. If language is the core of being human, as we've said, it follows that a particular language constitutes an individual's consciousness and experience. Setting our sights on reaching others' individuality means using a linguistic conduit.

Some Final Points, and a Paradox

When you learn language to access culture, a key way to enter a mind-set is by means of words that stay the same over generations, from person to person and group to group: traditional sayings, or proverbs. You capture culture effectively not (just) by proving your own mastery of vocabulary and grammar, but by integrating into yourself the set phrases the culture offers. Standard ways of speaking and writing change, though relatively slowly; slang and trendy expressions give the speaker a thrill about being "in the know" and up to the minute, but fade quickly and are usually relevant to only a particular slice of a population. Knowing proverbs, though, gives you a sense of membership in an enduring language community: you test what the culture values, and how it marks recurring observations on everyday life. Proverbs themselves are often untranslatable—you can't just flip the words of a saying into another language and expect that in that language the words have the same import—but they can share a basic meaning across cultures. So if, as an American, you want to express your energetic, can-do spirit by declaring, "The early bird catches the worm," to a French person you'll have to say, "Le monde appartient à ceux qui se lèvent tôt" ("The world belongs to those who rise early"). If you're sorry that you didn't start language study earlier, but still hold out hope that you'll become a fluent speaker, you might remind your French counterpart, "Mieux vaut tard que jamais" (which is in fact a direct translation of "Better late than never"). And if you recognize that you can't achieve your language goals just by wishing you were multilingual, you can console yourself with the wise old adage "You can't have your cake and eat it too." Except that in French, you'll have to accept that "on ne peut pas avoir le beurre et l'argent du beurre": "You can't have both the butter and the money from selling the butter."

The intensive study of another language is a complex process that draws on philosophy, history, geography, anthropology, and neuroscience along the way. Tourists—those who acquire just a smattering of language, like those who travel only briefly to new places—will probably find themselves yearning for more.

With a small cache of words and some rudimentary phrases, they manage a few basic exchanges that produce minimal and predictable results. You, however, can do better. The goal is admittedly a challenging one: truly to enter the culture at hand, to feel both solicited and game.

WHAT IS

Geography?

Richard Wright

"Geographer" literally means someone who writes about the Earth. It comes from the Greek *geo-* (Earth) and *graphia* (writing). That covers a lot of things, right? So just what is geography? In the Department of Geography at Dartmouth College, where I work, we've come up with this definition: "Geographers study the material and symbolic transformation of the Earth in relationship to both human and natural processes. In keeping with shifts in culture, the environment, politics, and economics, the boundaries of the geographic discipline are dynamic. For example, environmental change, international development, globalization, and new spatial technologies exemplify important arenas of study in geography."

Geography spans the social sciences (human geography) and the natural sciences (physical geography) and, I would add, even drifts into the arts and humanities. Human geographers ask questions about the political, economic, social, and cultural processes and resource practices that give definition to particular places. Physical geography focuses on the Earth systems that create the natural environment, such as weather, soils, biogeography, and Earth-sculpting processes. It is an interdisciplinary discipline, and its practitioners are expected not only to roam about in their own intellectual (and physical!) backyard but also trespass into other areas of inquiry.

Lots of disciplines traverse traditional subject boundaries. In fact, such scholarship is celebrated and encouraged in colleges and universities. So what makes geography different? While geography shares with anthropology, sociology, and economics a central concern for the study of cultures, society, and economies, and shares with geology and ecology goals of understanding natural landscapes and the nature of society relations, geography examines social and physical processes through the lenses of location, place, scale, and region.

Well, you may say, that's all well and good, but when I studied geography in fifth grade it was all about maps: we used a map to learn where things were and, worse, had to memorize state capitals. (Go ahead; take a trip down memory lane through Seterra Geography, whose website and apps let you "learn geography while having fun.") Mapping is a big part of geography. Geographers are particularly drawn to research questions about the relationships among places. Maps help us see these questions. You may therefore suspect I am going to discuss potentially boring topics like "What's the best route from A to B?" and "How many bananas are grown in Costa Rica?" Or "What is the capital of the United States?" And just where *is* Nauru?

Well, I am, but not in the ways you might think.

Getting There from Here

I recently went on vacation to the United Kingdom. My family and I flew to London and rented a car at the airport. One of the first things we had to do after we packed our luggage into our smaller-than-expected Renault was to figure out the navigation system. Almost all cars (and phones!) now come with sophisticated maps and a GPS—a Geographic Positioning System. These technologies help us find our way from one location to another—from Heathrow airport to the hotel where we were staying in Bedfordshire, for example. In more technical terms, the maps show the location of the airport (using latitude and longitude) relative to the location of the hotel about fifty miles away. And then a disembodied voice, which is part of that GPS, talks us through the drive, telling us when to turn and so on. A GPS helps us understand the relationships between places—something that is fundamental to geography.

Because GPS units depend on satellites, they are a very recent technology. How did people find their way before our cars and our phones "told" us how and where to go? They used maps printed on paper, of course. And before that they found other ways to navigate and find their way using the landscape and the positions of the sun, the moon, and the stars. Some cultures also used local knowledge and understandings to find their way in the world. Some of these ancient geographic techniques remain a mystery. For example, Westerners are still trying to understand how Polynesian mariners navigated across the Pacific using celestial bearings as well as the swell of the ocean, wind, and other natural features.

"Finding our way" is thus something fundamental to human activity. People have used maps to find their way for millennia. Earlier maps were much cruder than ones we use today, as information back then was sparser. Some of those maps used natural features to help users find their way. Some used, in part, on the interpretation of certain scriptures. A good map, of whatever vintage, should be effective and accurate. Whether the map is electronic and relies on digital data transmitted to a GPS from a satellite or drone or is a map drawn or printed on paper, a geographer helped make it. This is one of the things geographers do. And it's one of the things people who do geography do.

Because early maps were relatively simple, travelers hundreds of years ago were more likely to make mistakes moving between places. These mistakes could be in terms of direction or distance. One of the more famous examples of a distance error was when Christopher Columbus attempted to navigate to Japan in 1492. Land routes to Asia were slow and hazardous, and Columbus was seeking a safer (i.e., bandit-free) sea route so he could trade spices and silk (and become wealthy). He made two mistakes, in fact—both related to poor map usage. First, contrary to legend, it was well known that the Earth was spherical—not flat. The issue was the size of the Earth's circumference. Columbus needed a good estimate of this in planning his route. In 200 BCE, Eratosthenes calculated the circumference at the equator to within 1 percent of its correct value! Unfortunately, Columbus went with a different, smaller estimate due to the medieval Persian geographer Alfraganus. Columbus then compounded this mistake by assuming that Alfraganus was using a "Roman" mile (4,856 feet), when in fact he had used the Arabic mile (7,091 feet). He thus severely underestimated the size of the Earth, figuring the distance west from Portugal to Japan as about 3,700 kilometers, when the actual figure was 12,500 kilometers. These mapping mistakes changed Columbus's route and the history of the world.

So, five hundred years ago some geographers produced some very inaccurate maps. Today we are far better at locating places, people, and things, and thanks in large part to some geographers, our maps are much more accurate. But all maps are simplifications of reality. All cartographers make decisions about what to include and what to exclude, as well as how to depict regions and places. So while new technology makes it possible to add details about roads or elevation or some other physical features, the world will never be entirely mapped. There will be always new features of interest or new questions to consider, and those inquires will motivate people to produce new maps. Generally speaking, mapping involves linking place to some variable of interest, and what is "of interest" can change over time. For example, a generation ago we did not concern ourselves much with patterns of CO_2 levels. But now, with climate change and global warming, we do. In short, if you can measure something and tie that measurement to a location, then you can map it.

Technology has revolutionized cartography, way finding, and how we think geographically; it's also changed the nature of the journey. Thanks to technological advances like GPS or Google Maps, journeying between many places is far easier than it was five hundred years ago, or even fifty years ago. The physical distances between places have not changed, of course, but the time it takes to get between places has declined dramatically, depending on the quality and type of connection. Geographers have their own term for this process: *time-space compression* (or *time-space convergence*).

You don't have to be a geographer to think of distance in terms of time. In fact we all do it, all the time. When you leave home for school is not a matter of miles but a matter of time. When you leave one classroom and rush to the next class is not a matter of meters but rather a matter of minutes (or seconds!). When I get in my car and plug in my phone, Siri has learned to tell me that it's, for example, twenty-nine minutes to Plainfield and the traffic is light. There's little point in telling me the distance in miles. I'm far more interested in the traffic flow; is it congested around the local school, or has there been an accident en route? It's not surprising that census data on commuting reports travel time between home and work, not the distance in miles. On the other hand, if I'm going for a run, it's still about distance. Google Maps even lets you indicate whether you are walking, biking, driving, or taking public transportation when it plans a route, so travel mode also comes into play here.

And that reminds us that we move between places using different modes of transportation, along different networks of roads and rails. Even sea transport is networked, as is air travel and the Internet. By combining thinking about different modes of transport and some very clever cartography, you can remake the map of the world in an innumerable number of ways. You can start doing a little geography yourself! Your only limit is your imagination. Princeton's Non-Geographic Mapping website will give you a good idea of what I mean.

Spatial Diffusion, and the Geographies of Bananas, Horses, and Germs

So, geographers don't just measure the world; they also think about how our conception of mapping it can change the way we think about the world. For example, geographers think deeply about the implications of technology's "conquest" of distance. The world really is smaller in many ways—but of course not physically! Think about the integration of different places in the world because of changes in connectivity. This has implications for culture, society, and economics. The issues shift from technology and distance to culture and politics.

Take our taste in food, for example. A colleague of mine became very interested a few years ago in how Western consumers have changed their ideas about perishable foods and just what is "fresh" and desirable. A few decades ago, some restaurants attached mileage totals to menu items to signal the exotic origin of the food that the diners enjoyed. A fruit cocktail's ingredients registered about eight thousand miles, while those in a vegetable salad covered more than twenty-two thousand miles to arrive on the diner's plate. Today, however, due to environmental concerns, fine dining and supermarket shopping often involves different geographic sensibilities, where we celebrate local sourcing—the *short* distances from farm to table.

Supermarkets and restaurants are usually stocked with both local products and those that were sourced globally. Perhaps you like bananas. Perhaps the last one you ate was grown in the Caribbean. It is now a global fruit. It originated in Southeast Asia and is now grown all over tropical lands. And it is consumed globally. Some people refer to this process of the integration of local markets with global markets as *glocalization*. This clever portmanteau makes one think geographically—how the local and global work together (or against one another). (As an aside, it's also worth noting that today many people can eat bananas year-round—so not only has distance been vanquished, but technology has also got rid of seasons!)

Talking of globalization, let's go back to those Europeans sailing from Spain in the fifteenth and sixteenth centuries. Yes, they were interested in trading goods and securing wealth for themselves and their sponsors. But they brought other things with them. For example, horses. No one in the Americas had seen a horse before Europeans began to settle in what the Europeans called "New World." Of course, the so-called New World was only new to Europeans—it had had a long and rich history prior to their arrival. It wasn't until almost 150 years after Europeans arrived in what they called the Americas (after Amerigo Vespucci, who like Columbus was an Italian explorer) that a relatively isolated tribe of Native Americans, known in English as the Comanche, began to encounter horses. Within a few generations, the relationship between the Comanche and the newly discovered horses transformed the Comanche into one of the most powerful Native American peoples in North America. They ruled the Great Plains and amassed wealth mostly in the form of horses (perhaps 2 million!).

We know how those horses got from Europe to the Americas, but how did they get north to Comancheria (the Comanche's historic territory)? This is a great question for a geographer to ask! Answering it requires thinking about the spread of this breed of animal over time and space. We call this *spatial diffusion*.

The concept of spatial diffusion is relevant for the study of many kinds of phenomena. For another example, let me tell you a brief story about feral pigs. The first feral pigs in continental North America deserted from the expedition of Hernando de Soto, the Spanish explorer, in the 1540s. In a 2005 *New Yorker* magazine article, Ian Frazier writes, "Wild pigs that got away from Spanish colonists in Florida survived in the woods and swamps so successfully that today some of their descendants represent the only modern examples of old Spanish breeds that long ago disappeared in domestication." They are very adaptable; now they are in over half the US states, and their populations continue to expand their range.

Spatial diffusion is not just relevant for animals or plants (e.g., the invasive species mentioned in the "What Is Ecology?" essay in this volume). It is also important for the study and understanding of the spread of people and the spread of what people spread! Europeans didn't just bring horses to what they called "the New World"; they also brought germs that produced illnesses to which many Europeans had, over time, built up tolerances and immunities. The people they encountered in the Americas had had no such chance to develop such defenses. Many people indigenous to North and South America suffered terribly from the introduction of smallpox, chicken pox, and measles. Whole societies were severely weakened or even wiped out entirely.

At that time people had little idea how diseases spread. They did have theories of germs (and many were off the mark, such as the miasma theory, which held that diseases such as cholera or the Black Death were caused by "bad air"). At least in Europe and the Americas, it really wasn't until the mid-nineteenth century that doctors realized that many germs were found in water. It was then that one man, thinking like a geographer and making a map, made one of the most important discoveries and, with it, gave birth to the field of epidemiology—the rigorous study of the spread of disease through populations.

In this era people in London suffered from several terrible outbreaks of cholera—an acute and highly virulent disease of the digestive system. Hundreds of people were dying each week, but the death rates were particularly high in certain parts of town. John Snow, a London doctor, had an idea about how cholera was transmitted, and it was not through the air. He thought it had something to do with the water supply—specifically, one certain water pump in London's Soho District. He produced what has become a very famous "dot map" to show how cases of cholera were centered on that pump. The Broad Street pump is the dot in the middle of the map (figure 1). And this map, along with many others, helps show one of things that fascinates geographers—spatial patterns. To this day geographers continue to use maps just like Snow's to identify patterns (using math, statistics, and computing power!) and then decipher what processes produced those patterns. So maps help geographers and epidemiologists develop theory. They also help practitioners design strategies to counter epidemics.

Of course germs, people, plants, and animals aren't the only things that spread. Information spreads, customs, habits, and culture spread. Spatial diffusion is an important concept in understanding the workings of the world.

Snow's map illustrates another important geographic principle, known as "Tobler's First Law of Geography": *All things are related, but near things are more closely related than distant things.* You can see from Snow's map that incidence of cholera is associated with that water pump on Broad Street. The farther away from that polluted pump, the lower the incidence. Waldo Tobler is not some nineteenth-century doctor or a long-dead explorer. He's a geographer still living (as of July 2016) in Santa Barbara, California. This law might only be several decades young, but the principle he captures in that statement is old and universal. Some other geographers talk about it using different language, such as "distance decay": in other words, that incidence (in this example, cholera) declines—decays—with distance.

To show why Tobler thought this idea worthy of being called a law, think about things that do decline with distance. I'll give you several examples to show the range and breadth of this subject we call geography.

Migration systems: People move from one location to another for all sorts of reasons, and some people indeed move very long distances. But if you map out many migrations—say, movement of people in the United States—you'll find that more people move within a state than between states, or that the rate of moving between counties is higher than the rate of moving between states. In fact, many forms of spatial interaction follow this principle.

Wind speed from the center of hurricane: For a low-pressure system to be called a hurricane, it must have sustained winds of over seventy-five miles per hour.

FIGURE 1 Maps of the 1854 cholera outbreak in London. (a) Original map by
John Snow. (b) Spatial analysis showing "density" of cholera deaths using contour lines
and shading. *Robin's Blog*, "John Snow's Cholera Data in More Formats," map adapted
by Lucinda M. Hall, Dartmouth College Library, Dartmouth College

But the farther away from the main system you measure wind speed, the lower it is—distance decay. (At the very center of the storm system—the eye of the storm—winds are light [and there are no clouds!], but that's a story for another time.)

The dispersal of helicopter seeds from a sycamore tree: The wind speed and direction influence where those seeds end up, but on average, most will fall close to the tree, and a few will land at more distant locations.

Spatial Scale: Racial Segregation and Diversity, and the Capital of the United States

You may have noticed that in our discussion of Tobler's First Law, our examples spanned many levels of "scale." You may be familiar with this from looking at a map, where you may see a little inset that says something like "Scale: 1:63360," which means that one inch of the map corresponds to 63,360 inches of the real world—which is one mile! When I use the word "scale" here, I mean more about the level of analysis. Going from smallest to largest, Tobler's First Law as seen for helicopter seed dispersal would require us to consider the phenomenon on the scale of feet or inches. Hurricanes are measured in terms of miles, so they're studied on the scale of some fraction of that. Finally, migration patterns for people are apparent at even larger scales and even using different notions of scale. It's the last of these that I'd like to discuss in this section.

I'm a population geographer, and as such I research the spatial distribution (and redistributions) of various human populations. I consider this at specific times as well as how it changes over time. This work could be at the scale of countries (for example, national mortality rates) or at finer scales (rates of mortality by state or metropolitan area). Consider the racial diversity of a place. Take the United States. Fifty years ago, about 12 percent of its population identified as black and another 1 percent as Native American. There were a number of Asian Americans and Latinos, but not very many compared to today. Because most recent immigrants to the United States are Latino or Asian, whites constitute a declining share of the population, dropping from 76 percent in 1990 to about 64 percent in 2010. By contrast, the Latino population almost doubled, increasing from about 9 percent to about 16 percent over the same period. Asians/Pacific Islanders constituted about 5.5 percent of the total in 2010. Blacks expanded their population share from 11.8 percent (1990) to 12.8 percent (2010). Native Americans made up about 0.75 percent of the total in 1990 and 1.2 percent in 2010. The country is becoming more racially diverse.

The trend toward increasing racial diversity also can be seen at the state scale. All of the US states have become more racially diverse in the last few decades, but some are more diverse than others. Vermont, New Hampshire, and Maine are between 97 and 98 percent white. Hawaii, on the other hand, has an Asian/Pacific Islander majority, and New Mexico is majority Latino. States like Texas, New York, and California, traditional gateways for immigrants, are far more diverse than Hawaii or those northern-tier New England states.

Shift scale again, to the metropolitan scale (such as big urban areas): if you think about racial diversity within those metro areas, and you get a different picture. Some places in the United States, such as metropolitan Washington, DC (where we find the nation's capital!), have many neighborhoods that are far more racially diverse than they were twenty years ago, yet at the same time, they also have an *increasing* number of neighborhoods that are over 80 percent black. How can this be? How can you have increasing diversity in some parts of town and increasing segregation in other parts of town? Well, it's happening in Washington, DC (and some other cities, such as Atlanta and Houston), and it occurs because while attitudes toward racial minorities among the white majority population have generally become more tolerant over the last fifty years, some groups, especially blacks, remain the subjects of particular forms of racism. We see this in the protests we've had over policing, but we can also see it on maps—in patterns of residential segregation (and diversity) in cities.

But these geographies are not just about mapping difference and different places. Racially diverse places are important locations; they represent the polar opposite of neighborhoods where intergroup living and interaction is impossible because one group lives in isolation from others. The sociologist Thomas Pettigrew described residential racial segregation as the "structural linchpin of US race relations." The physical separation of racialized groups is not in and of itself a bad thing in the absence of racism. But although overt discrimination in housing and labor markets is outlawed, racism continues to shape life outcomes and is far from absent in US social relations (see, for example, Ta-Nehisi Coates's stirring Pulitzer Prize–winning work *Between the World and Me*). Diverse residential spaces offer the promise of places where notions of being on the "wrong side" of the tracks/river/town have no meaning. That is, racially diverse places promise more democratic outcomes in not only housing markets but also other key, related institutions: schools, the labor market, and the criminal justice system. Racially undiverse places—segregated spaces—promise the opposite: unfair and unequal access to education, jobs, and policing.

Let's go back to scale for a bit—did you see what I just did? I grouped different parts of the Earth into different regions. The first region I mentioned was the United States as a whole. Then I talked about states, then cities, and then neighborhoods within cities. Each of those areas involved me grouping geographical information into appropriately sized units for analysis. And that's a pretty good definition of what we can call a region. As my example about the racial makeup of a place shows, the scale of the region can vary greatly.

Here's a different definition: a region can be defined as an area of land that has a consistent or easily recognizable set of features. And this second definition should make you realize that a region can illustrate both physical features or cultural traits. My last example was about human attributes in the United States—the different races a society assigns to people (and the racial groupings people assign to themselves). But you may know regions as geographic areas defined by, say, their lack of water—no, not California in 2015, but rather deserts. Or mountain ranges—such as the Himalayas. Scale is complex and hierarchical. And geographers think a lot about how processes at one scale play out at other scales.

Why the Location of Nauru Matters

Some demographic trends occur through subtle mechanisms. Some are more dramatic and even horrific. As I write this essay in summer 2016, we are in the midst of the largest refugee crisis since World War II. The forced displacement of people falls squarely again in the realm of geography. What could be more geographical than people moving from one place to another? The details are alarming. A few years ago Syria had a population of about 17 million. Then a civil war erupted there, and the country has fallen apart. In summer 2016, about two-thirds of that population has been displaced, meaning that they now live someplace other than their homes. About 5 million people have been displaced internally—within the borders of the country we used to understand as Syria. Another 6 million have fled to other countries. Most moved the short distances to neighboring counties: Turkey, Jordan, and Lebanon. One to 2 million have tried to move farther afield to find refuge. The political ramifications of these diffusions are significant. Many Syrian refugees have sought protection in Europe. The European Union (EU) has reacted by closing internal borders, rescinding the Schengen agreement, which allowed for uninhibited passage among many member states.

The swell of migrants attempting to access the EU doesn't just originate with the refugees from the Syrian apocalypse; people are attempting to access the EU from all over the world. The context of their migration—their passage and reception—has the potential to change the very nature of the EU. Fears about migrants in the United Kingdom fueled some of the historic Brexit vote in Britain in summer 2016.

Exclusion from a political union is one (geographical) way to try to address the issue migrants. Another way that some EU member states and others deal with people seeking political refuge is to detain them remotely, on islands. Italians use the island of Lampedusa as just such a site. The United States has used Guantanamo Bay (on the island of Cuba) for just such a purpose and today uses, among other places, Guam. And that gets us to Nauru (which—drumroll, please—is in Micronesia) because it is here (and other places, like Christmas Island) that Australia detains many people who have sought protection from political or religious persecution in Australia. Why would states use geography to manage refugee flows in this way? The answers are insidious. Remote island locations are far away from the public eye, and access is difficult for lawyers and human rights activists seeking to assist migrants. Detention on islands reduces the chances of refugees reaching sovereign territory. States, when they can, often keep migrants, deemed out of place, at a distance.

I learned about this island detention strategy from a scholar who once was a student of mine. She saw patterns on the land that no one else had seen and, with the support of a large grant awarded by the National Science Foundation, built the Island Detention Project to draw attention to, and critique, this strategy.

Geography—The Big Picture

Seeing like a geographer involves seeing or (re)imagining patterns on the land and using them to ask questions about the Earth, regions, and places. These questions can be "big," like the uneven effects of a warming planet Earth on the weather and climate of different places at different scales, or the questions can be "small," perhaps confined to a more localized space, and concerning the geographically uneven effects of removing an old mill dam from a river in Massachusetts or the impacts on human and natural ecosystems of building a new dam in Zambia.

When answering the question "What Is Geography?," the Royal Geographical Society answered this way: "Geography is, in the broadest sense, an education for life and for living. Learning through geography—whether gained through formal learning or experientially through travel, fieldwork and expeditions—helps us all to be more socially and environmentally sensitive, informed and responsible citizens and employees." Geography is thus a wonderfully interdisciplinary discipline—an unruly discipline, even: we range all over the place. New technologies have perhaps made geography a more exciting field as we develop terrific ways to visualize our planet. But as I hope you've learned, this discipline is not just about mapping and visualization. Geographers use their understanding of place and space to address the massive challenges that we all will have to grapple with throughout our lives: climate change and rising sea levels, racial and cultural integration, endangered species and endangered languages, and global integration and inequality. As we continue to write the history of our ever-changing world, geography matters more than ever.

WHAT IS

Geology?

William B. Dade

Geology is about asking, and attempting to answer, questions concerning our planet, our home, the Earth. How did the Earth come to be? It sounds grand, but perhaps you've already asked these kinds of questions while hiking in the woods or picking up a shiny rock in a local park, or maybe even sitting in the movies and seeing a view of the Earth from outer space. We can readily see that the Earth is made up of solid parts (rocks) and liquid parts (deeply buried molten material that sometimes erupts onto the Earth's surface; surface waters in oceans, lakes, and rivers; and the overlying atmosphere). What are its different parts made of, exactly, and how are they arranged? How has the Earth's makeup and arrangement changed and, at the same time, how has life developed over millions, even billions, of years of Earth history and possibly influenced that process?

The lucky people who tackle such questions in a scientific way, with some training in mathematics, physics, chemistry, and biology, are called geologists. That is, geologists base their answers to these and other questions on observations of the natural world that can be interpreted in a rational framework and can be used to yield predictive insight. Their scientific perspective requires no explanations arising from special belief systems or worldviews, and the answers geologists seek are rigorously tested, confirmed, and ultimately accepted by a worldwide community of investigators with similar technical training and dedication to rational thought. This approach makes geology different from the nonscientific ways throughout most of human history, such as mythology and the interpretation of religious scripture, that people have used to address questions about the form of our Earth and the processes that underlie it.

Geology is a natural science, and one full of opportunities for wonder, so some geologists jokingly describe themselves as "wonder-full" (okay, and also "wonderful"!) people. We typically share an appreciation for exploring the outdoors, our greatest classroom, and like to get together with other geologists at the end of the day to debate and laugh about our ideas. All are full of amazement and share a humble curiosity about the natural world we live in.

It's about Time

We now know that the Earth is a little over 4.5 *billion* years old. It is difficult to grasp the magnitude of such a number, so think about it this way: Imagine that all Earth history, just over 4.5 billion years, could be condensed to a walk the length of a 100-yard football field. With this visualization each yard represents about 45 million years. If you begin walking steadily from the home-team goal line, you see the first signs of single-cell life somewhere around the near, home-team 22-yard line; the rise of photosynthesis and the resulting introduction of oxygen into the ancient atmosphere occurs somewhere around the 25-yard line; the earliest multicellular life appears just past midfield, and sexual reproduction kicks in around the far 27-yard line of the away team. The first known footprints (of any kind!) on land appear around the far 11-yard line, and the first land plants appear around the 9-yard line. The age of dinosaurs runs from the 7-yard line to about 1.5 yards from the far goal line. The first grasses and songbirds show up at around the 1-yard line. Our earliest humanlike ancestors emerge in Africa at less than two inches from the far goal line. And Europeans arrive in eastern North America at less than one-thousandth of an inch from the goal line.

How did we arrive at this humbling understanding? It's not like there was a stack of calendars to look at—or chalk marks on a wall marking time, as a castaway on a desert island or a prisoner in a cell might have. Or is there? That is, are there some clues in the rocks around us? Indeed there are! You just need to know how to look! Using chemistry we can detect in rocks small amounts of certain naturally occurring elements that decay at known rates compared to other, readily detectable elements. Such elements are naturally *radioactive*, meaning that they spontaneously emit energy from, and thus alter, their own atomic structure to become a different, "daughter" element. Radioactive elements, and especially their unique rates of decay, are well studied. So, by precisely measuring the relative amounts of "parent" and "daughter" elements in a rock, geologists can determine the age of that rock.

But this is just one piece of evidence. Geologists are like detectives who, using a broad toolkit of scientific, statistical, and mathematical tools, solve crimes by following clues. These "geo-detectives" have reconstructed the Earth's history from many overlapping lines of evidence. With this information in hand, geologists further piece together the story of ongoing environmental change and the development of life that has taken place over immense stretches of geologic time by studying the fossils, chemical makeup, and structure of many rocks of known ages and from around the world.

It's about Change

Geo-detectives also track the evolution of environments at the Earth's surface over the great expanse of Earth history. For example, suppose you were lucky enough to be hiking around the Sandia Mountains outside of Albuquerque, New Mexico. Sandia Peak is at almost 10,000 feet! Looking out beyond the city you see a vast, flat, almost desert-like expanse with more mountains in the horizon. But now look down at your feet. It won't take too much luck to find little seashell-like fossils! Was this high-desert landscape once under the ocean?!

A sandstone of a certain age with marine fossils indicates to the geologist that at that time in the past, the environment at that location was indeed likely to have been a beach or a sandy, shallow sea. Similarly, a limestone embedded with fossil corals and shells indicates that, at some time in the past, the environment at that location was likely to have been a coral reef; a mudstone or shale can suggest a deep-sea setting. By mapping out the sequence and location of rock types around the world, we have come to understand that the Earth's surface has *always* been undergoing slow but significant environmental change over its geologic history. Some of the rocks underlying the rolling hills of Britain and the Appalachians of the Eastern United States, and even some of those exposed in the high peaks of the Himalayas, the Alps, as well as in the Rocky Mountains (and mentioned above), are made of sands and muds originally deposited in ancient seas.

Among the more dramatic changes recognized in the Earth environment are the occurrence of *ice ages*, during which continent-spanning sheets of ice a mile or more thick covered one or more land masses. Geologists think there were at least five different ice ages during Earth history, the most recent beginning about 2.5 million years ago (corresponding to about two inches from the goal line in our stroll down the football field) and ultimately reaching its last, greatest extent about twenty thousand years ago (at 0.015 inch, or just under one-half millimeter, from the goal line). During this most recent time, over several nearly regular intervals of about two hundred thousand years, an ice sheet up to several miles thick covered most of northern North America, extending from the Arctic south to about the latitude of New York City, and most of northern Europe. In many high mountain ranges around the world, smaller glaciers nestled among the peaks were also common. Landscapes in these settings have many features resulting from the slow grind of the thick accumulation of snow and ice as it collapsed under its own weight or down steep mountainous slopes and crept, ooze-like, over the terrain. Again, lest you think this was all happening in what are now remote mountainous areas, you should know that places like Long Island, New York, and Cape Cod, Massachusetts, in the Eastern United States, are large piles of sand and gravel understood to have been scraped and "bulldozed" into position by the most recent continental ice sheet as it advanced southward. Even here in Hanover, New Hampshire, landlocked and on the border of Vermont, little Occum Pond, which provides a favorite little lunchtime walking loop for those of us who teach at Dartmouth College, also shows signs of glacier retreat. When the Earth finally emerged from the last ice age, the ice sheet melted and retreated northward toward colder climes over thousands of years, and the piles of bulldozed debris were left behind.

We are now in a period of environmental change associated with worldwide warming, which is, without doubt, at least in part the result of human activities. The upshot is simple, and irrefutable: the Earth's surface is warmed by *short-wavelength* radiation from the sun that passes relatively unaffected through the Earth's atmosphere. Since at least the Industrial Revolution, humans have discharged massive amounts of carbon dioxide and methane into the Earth's atmosphere as by-products of systematic land clearance, agriculture, manufacturing activities, and our everyday travel. Such gases act like glass in a greenhouse, trapping heat re-emitted by the sun-warmed Earth in the form of *long-wavelength* radiation.

By studying environmental change throughout Earth history, as well as by documenting ongoing changes now, geologists contribute to our understanding of what is yet to come. For example, geophysicists (geologists concerned with applications of physics to the study of the Earth) are monitoring the ongoing loss of ice in mountain glaciers and the Greenland ice cap to melting in our increasingly warmer world. Mountain glaciers are important sources of water for the people who live nearby. Loss of the Greenland ice cap to melting means that sea level will rise by up to a meter over the next hundred years or so; this development will affect the hundreds of millions of people who live along the coastlines of the world.

It's about Connections

By studying the links that exist across wide-ranging scales of space and time, geologists tackle many of the big questions about the Earth's form. For example, using our understanding of the controls on the melting temperature of rocks, controls that occur at the smallest scales of molecules and minerals, combined with the physics of floating bodies applied to whole continents made largely of those minerals, we answer such questions as "How high are the mountains?"

To get at this, let's start with the large-scale structure of the Earth. The Earth is layered like an onion; in this case the layers are distinguished by the speed and form of vibrations, generated by earthquakes and monitored by geophysicists around the world, as they pass through the different layers. These distinctions, in turn, reflect the chemical and physical properties of each layer. We know, for example, that there is a hot *core* composed mostly of iron and nickel, parts of which are solid (capable of deflecting certain earthquake-related vibrations) and parts of which are molten liquid (incapable of deflecting certain earthquake-related vibrations). Wrapped around the core is the *mantle*, composed of iron, magnesium, silica, and aluminum, and that is solid—well, sort of . . . That is, owing to the tremendous amount of heat released by naturally occurring, radioactive elements that make up a small but important fraction of the vast interior of the Earth, the mantle is so hot that, although not outright molten, it oozes and flows slowly when under pressure and over very long periods of time. The outermost layer of the Earth is a shell made up of frozen, rigid rock: "crustal rock," to be precise.

All rocks are made up of *minerals*, which are the solid, naturally occurring fusion of elements. Differences in rocks reflect differences in their minerals. The exact composition of minerals, including the flaws, contaminants, or water molecules in their rigid, lattice-like structure, affect the temperature at which a rock will melt. The most common minerals in crustal rock underlying the continents are *feldspar* and *quartz*, rich in the elements silica, aluminum, and oxygen. The melting point of rocks made up of these minerals lies in the range 500–1,000°C (for comparison, remember that water boils at 100°C), with the exact value depending in part on the abundance of impurities and water in the rocks.

The Earth's crust is, of course, warmed by the sun, but it is also heated from below, owing, as mentioned above, to the heat released by naturally occurring, radioactive elements within. In fact, if you were to descend into the crust down a very deep mine, you would feel a rise in temperature of about (on average, and

lessly sought, and ultimately found by some team of geologists. Thus, on the one hand, geology is about improving our understanding of the occurrence and the extraction of Earth resources. But on the other hand, increasingly, geology is also about understanding, monitoring, and reducing the impacts of our use of those resources.

In addition to benefiting from the Earth's livable environments and natural bounty, humans are constantly at risk of loss of life, health, and property from natural hazards. Worldwide between 2004 and 2013, just under 1 million souls perished in natural disasters: over 300,000 of these people lost their lives during episodes of severe weather, drought, and famine, in floods, in tornados, from lightning strikes, and in hurricanes. More alarmingly, in the same period, 650,000 people perished in earthquakes and resulting tsunamis, in mass movements like avalanches and wet flows of mud and debris, and during volcanic eruptions. In the face of such events, geology is also about the study of the occurrence of natural hazards, past and present, in the hopes of avoiding such catastrophic loss of life. Geologists aim to understand "where," "how," and (increasingly but still with difficulty) "when" natural disasters will happen. Geology is not just about rocks and resources; it is about people.

Geology Is about Big Ideas

Human history, however short in the long history of the Earth's past, is an account of the ingenuity of people overcoming difficult challenges, many of which define our well-being and even our existence. Now and increasingly for the future, many people feel that tackling such challenges requires a deep understanding and appreciation of the Earth, our home. In fact, it's not just about the Earth! Geologists ask questions about all the planets in the solar system—how they were formed, what they are formed of, what that means about their history and the history of the solar system and even the universe. It ranges from the terrestrial to the extraterrestrial!

In achieving these goals, geologists tend to be visual, four-dimensional (space and time!) thinkers who can accommodate wide-ranging scales of space and deep time, and who are comfortable with the challenge of interpreting flawed and incomplete observations in their study of the complex, natural world of the past and the present. We have also come to recognize that there are several big ideas that make special the study of the Earth. We have touched on some of these ideas here; they include:

The Earth is 4.6 billion years old, and the processes of the Earth's geological evolution and the development of life require millions, even billions of years.

Everything is connected; the Earth is a complex "system of systems." Physical and chemical principles have remained unchanged throughout the Earth's history and continue to drive gradual and catastrophic changes in the Earth environment and life.

Life is influenced by, and influences, the Earth environment. Humans depend on the Earth for natural resources, and they are at risk from natural hazards. Human activities can change the Earth environment in notable ways.

Taken all together, these big ideas suggest that geology is the study of the Earth's past so that we can better understand and thrive in the present, and to enable us to face an uncertain future with knowledge, wonder, and hope.

WHAT IS

History?

Robert Bonner

Imagine the oldest person you know. Now think about how that person lived as a kid or a teenager fifty, sixty, or even seventy years ago. If you can, set up a time to have a conversation between the two of you. If you are able to do that, you might be surprised about the memories that are shared. Growing up back then was in some ways not much different than growing up today. More than likely the person will tell you about playing with friends, doing chores because their parents told them to, going to a school and being taught by favorite (and least favorite) teachers, having fun when school was out in the summer.

You might find other parts of what it was like to be a young person back then a lot less familiar. People wrote letters instead of emails, so it took time to stay in touch with people far away. They listened to radio and couldn't see movies outside of the theater. Flying by airplane somewhere to take a vacation was not an option—even taking a long car trip was not something many families did. Politics worked in different ways too. There were a lot more arguments about whether the US Army should travel overseas (something largely taken for granted today). During the 1930s and 1940s, reporters ignored things that would be front-page news for us. Few people outside Washington knew that an American president needed a wheelchair and crutches to get around. (Franklin Roosevelt, a survivor of polio, still served more years in the White House than anyone else!) If this person grew up in another country, then all kinds of unfamiliar stories might be shared. In short, your friend is telling you stories from the past and giving you the opportunity to consider the passage of time through another's eyes and memories. As you ask these questions and consider the answers, you are working like a historian. You are "doing history"!

What Does It Mean to "Do History"?

Historians look backward across time as part of their job, and when they do that, they ask all sorts of questions with the aim of explaining how changes came about and how some things stayed the same. They are constantly arranging the framework of time as they track real people, actual societies, and forms of knowledge, power, and creativity over decades, and sometimes over centuries. One might think about what they do as a form of "mapping," which historians do with an overriding concern for the "temporal" (a fancy way of saying "time-based") dimensions of human experiences. Geographers, by their own mapping of territory, do something similar by attending to the "spatial" (or space-based) dimensions of human experiences.

You may assume that there is a special category of "historical" people, events, and trends, and that the stuff of the history textbook represents what "doing history" is all about. Yet historians take up a much wider set of issues and developments and factor these into powerful stories capable of yielding new insights about how past societies and cultures developed. Most historians take for granted the importance of monarchs like England's Queen Elizabeth I, military figures like Napoleon Bonaparte, or nationalist founders like Mahatma Gandhi, all of whom impacted their countries and the wider world. Some self-evidently important events similarly allow us to understand how and why wars began, how power passed from one interest to another, or how advances in technology, exploration, or law were achieved. But some of the most exciting work of history lies in connecting the actions of well-known people and events to the ordinary experiences recorded by those not nearly as frequently remembered. The best way to see how this works is to look back at how your meeting went (whether you knew it or not, you were practicing "oral history") and consider what was likely an intertwining of defining events of an era with personal details from an individual life. If the twists and turns of a presidential administration is "historical," so too are the "historical" anecdotes recalled by a single individual, even if those will probably never make it into the textbook.

Let me relate that point to my own work as a historian of the American Civil War. I find myself constantly circling around figures like Abraham Lincoln, Frederick Douglass, and Clara Barton; I also linger over "key" events like the Battle of Gettysburg, the issuing of the Emancipation Proclamation, or the move to create cemeteries for fallen soldiers. It is not because such people and events are "famous," or are included in every Civil War textbook, that they capture my attention. I consider them because they offer insight into what drove the dramatic consequences of this critical period of American history. Looking at the letters left by common soldiers, the narratives recorded by former slaves, or even the battle flags and poems created within local communities has allowed me to tell stories from different perspectives. In the end, I want that kind of material to broaden my readers' appreciation for what these years meant for the millions of people who experienced them.

Talking with real people who are still alive is only one way to find out about the recent past (it is one of the more interesting). In considering developments from centuries ago, historians of course don't have the option of arranging "live" first-person accounts and must use documents or other kinds of evidence as the basis for their work. Most historians are uncomfortable relying on a single piece of evidence apart from other sources that they can use to either support or contradict that version of the past. Here, consider what it would be like if you kept having chats with people alive fifty or so years ago. If you talked to ten people, you might have ten different sets of memories (this is probably what would happen, I think). Some of these might contradict each other. Which would you trust, and how would you decide which is most important? That's the kind of problem that historians regularly face as they do their work.

Historians learn to be good listeners as they sort out what look like conflicts between stories told about the same event or period. They do so whether they are interacting with actual people or taking notes from evidence collected together in archives. But historians are not through with their job when they have collected materials and thought about which are closest to the truth. They keep going until they turn all the things they hear into stories or narratives. Creating stories about the past is hard work, especially when they involve people who did not write things down themselves. The past was filled with people who shaped the direction of history. In becoming what we term *historical actors*, these countless individuals have caught the attention of historians concerned with what happened long ago and why it matters for us to continue to recall it.

That's the big picture of what historians do. Let me now break it down a bit.

Historians Tell Stories as They Seem to Have Actually Happened

Some years ago, maybe even around the time your older friend was a child, a historian named Carl Becker made a speech to a group of people whose job was to write history. He called this lecture "Everyman His Own Historian," and in it he explained what historians do in the form of a story that he made up. (In fact, I recommend you find a copy and read it yourself! It's a lovely essay.) His title made an important point—that everyone has been part of history, and almost everyone looks backward to make sense of what things were like, how things changed, and why we still live in the shadow of past struggles and accomplishments. It is easy to see that he was onto something. Even as children, we are able to put together an account of own lives. We learn about the life stories of our parents, grandparents, and other ancestors, alongside the biographies of our favorite sports stars, singers, or actors. All these ways of imagining the past help us to understand who we are and who we might become.

Histories as "real stories" share some things with made-up stories or stories told in the movies (where directors usually think it is okay to shift some of the facts for the sake of a more entertaining film). In each of them, vivid characters are put before audiences who are trying to imagine the past. It is the job of each of these kinds of narratives to explain reasons that people make certain decisions (taking up what historians call the *element of motivation*) and to explain why things happen (*the element of causation*).

History is a special category of storytelling, since its rules demand that we attempt to establish what "really happened" as accurately as possible. Historians don't blur the facts or try to shape things to make it easier to understand or fit together. This notion that history is, first and foremost, fact-based storytelling began more than two thousand years ago among the ancient Greeks. In a period when mythology and imaginative epic poetry were very popular, two writers offered alternatives, and this is what earned them a reputation as "founders" of history.

The lead here was taken by a writer named Herodotus (pronounced he-ROD-ah-tus), who was born about twenty-five hundred years ago. He gave an account of wars between the Persian Empire and soldiers from several Greek cities that had affected him personally. Driven from his hometown as a youngster, Herodotus traveled across areas that the rulers of Persia intended to conquer. He began to ask questions and take notes from people about what had happened and why. When he was about forty-five years old, he presented his "Historia" (the Greek word for "inquiry"), which explained its purpose in its very first few sentences. He wanted his book to pin down the causes of events and to leave a lasting record of the "great and wondrous deeds" accomplished both by the Greeks (his side) and by their enemies, the Persians. Appearing when it did, in the middle of a fifty-year Greek effort to block Persia's westward expansion, this was not a book that told the story from beginning to end. But it introduced a new style both in its aims and by the fact that it based its claims on the author's travels and on his efforts to gather evidence with a critical, objective aim (whether or not he was truly "impartial" remains a matter of debate).

A couple of decades later, a man named Thucydides (pronounced thoo-SID-a-dees) also used his own experience to write about military conflict between two power blocs within ancient Greece, pitting those allied with Athens (his own home city) against those fighting with Sparta. Thucydides had been a soldier in the wars between these two Greek rivals, but he wrote less about the fighting of battles than about the diplomacy that led to the wars. He re-created some speeches and debates that were not recorded; in that way, his work would not pass muster as legitimate history writing today. But he introduced a new way of portraying past actions by drawing characters and situations that were plausible and lifelike. Unlike earlier writers, he did not explain the outbreak of hostilities by typical formulas, such as appealing to the mythical intervention of Gods or offering self-serving explanations that made his side of the struggle seem "right." He was intent to show in his book the full complexity of human motivations at work. How those in the past struggled for advantage was, he helped to establish, not all that different from what humans do across time.

These two writers of ancient Greece developed a form of storytelling about un-folding events over time that mixed accounts of what happened with reflections about why and how events unfolded. In other words, they wrote histories in ways that we historians still offer them. Most of our best work takes up the question of who was responsible for bringing about change and considers the long-term effect of unexpected events. Historical work is never fully effective if it simply summarizes a series of events that occurred; what makes for good history is the accompanying explanation of why such things happened as they did, and with what long-term effects. They use the language of meaningful "consequences" of "contingent" events, terms which recognize that things might have turned out differently. When historians find an event or moment that leads to something bigger, they call it a historical "turning point." Lots of the best history focuses on these kinds of dramatic moments when something new happens. On the "temporal map" of the historian, these are the most important spots.

The beginning and end of wars, or the outcome of decisive battles, are a good example of the kinds of events that draw historians' attention. Thucydides brought into focus the breakdown in negotiations that led to war; Herodotus gave memorable accounts of famous battles like those fought at Thermopylae and Marathon. Nowadays, historians look at all sorts of other pivotal events when they think about how history has been made. The launching of a movement (think Rosa Parks aboard an Alabama bus) or a new realm (think Charlemagne and the Holy Roman Empire) are familiar events that set the course of history on a different path. Historians working in archives have from time to time uncovered more obscure moments that proved to be of vital importance in the long run (and only in retrospect). Those historians interested in the development of American atomic power had to comb through multiple archives before they fully understood the importance of a 1939 letter written by Albert Einstein to President Roosevelt urging an aggressive pursuit of this new technology.

History Looks to Evidence to Give Answers to Questions

Mapping the past—explaining how it was experienced, and when and how it changed—can be done by movies and fiction no less than from books written by historians. But historians stake out their claim as storytellers by drawing from material that they first consider as carefully as they can. Historians' emphasis on "evidence" as the bedrock of all of their claims is a fairly new principle, which was established as an essential part of their job about a century and a half ago, when the first graduate schools were set up to provide academic training in a "scientific" approach to history. Ever since, professional historians have employed an extensive footnoting scheme to assure that others can go back to the same evidence they considered. Historians now at work don't mind inviting others to go back and verify, or take a different look at, the same sources, so as to test the conclusion of their account of the past. Historians insist (on the basis of lots of evidence) that they are coming as close to things as they "really happened" as they can.

This emphasis on facts and evidence means that historians understand that even their own interpretations can change. New evidence can lead to new stories, or even to the acknowledgment that earlier accounts were just plain wrong. The notion that modern economic advances could be reduced to a so-called Industrial Revolution, driven by those famous belching coal-fired factories, is a case in point. Specialists in economic history increasingly emphasize developments in nonindustrializing cities (especially those who served as centers of a "financial revolution") and in a factory-free countryside (where wage labor, sophisticated markets, and advanced transportation technologies set the pace). That doesn't mean that the past changed, of course. What has shifted is our understanding of the past, and our appreciation that the story of modern economic development had as much to do with banks, farmers, and canals as with rich factory owners and an impoverished working class.

Stories told by a professional historian depend on the kinds of sources that he or she considers. Most evidence comes in the form of "primary" sources: information from earlier time periods that survived up to the present. Sometimes this evidence is in an archive that was carefully preserved to establish a record. Handwritten letters and diaries preserved in special collections are some of the best-known places to look for finding information about the past; my own work on common soldiers draws mostly from such materials. Government records are another key set of sources, so historians regularly find themselves traveling to public buildings to pore over files containing massive amounts of information. Material produced by religious officials furnish still another big body of sources. Until fairly recently, these people cared even more than governments about how people lived their lives. This sort of information is more and more being transformed into digital content and made available through the Internet. This allows some historians to join the move toward using so-called "big data" as a basis for their interpretations.

There are lots more places to find materials that provide clues about what happened and why. Everyone holds on to one item or another as a way to remember certain times in their own lives. Maybe here we can build on Carl Becker and point out that "Everyman" is an "archivist" of one sort or another. What we call "souvenirs" or "mementos" might one day be a "primary source" that will allow a historian to write about us! The sources historians use, assembled from all sorts of different places, are like pieces of a gigantic jigsaw puzzle—a really hard one. Even harder, a lot of the pieces don't exist anymore, so historians have to put the puzzle together the best they can by using just the pieces they have.

Working as a professional historian requires careful attention to asking multiple questions about primary sources that are brought together. In this way, the work of listening and telling stories overlaps with the historian's job to do the work of a detective who has a case to break or a scientist who has a theory to test. Some of the most important work in history involves expanding the kinds of sources that is brought together for inspection. Memories conveyed in interviews and sources found in public records or official archives sometimes cannot provide the sort of answers that historians really want to answer. Sometimes that leads historians to explore archaeological or even scientific evidence where new clues might be found about what happened and why.

A friend of Carl Becker by the name of Charles Beard gives us a helpful example to see how certain questions require historians to consider evidence previously ignored. More than a century ago, Beard wanted to ask about the motivations of those who created the US Constitution. He wondered whether these men's own explanations of patriotic duty gave the whole story. He began to consider whether their concern for their own personal property also was a factor in how they did their work. He scoured those personal papers and records that allowed him to piece together a different kind of story than their speeches and public writing. He saw that they owned certain kinds of property (especially debt in the form of government bonds) that they made more secure in forming a new, more powerful government. Beard's famous book was titled *The Economic Origins of the American Constitution*.

Charles was married to another very notable historian by the name of Mary Ritter Beard. Her work gives us another example of how our understanding of the past can be expanded by turning to new sources. Mary Beard's most famous work, which took many years to produce, was titled *Woman as a Force in History*. While Charles had revisited the motivation of powerful men, Mary wondered, as her title set out, whether American history had been shaped by women in ways that had been overlooked. After working with others to secure the vote for women (an effort that was successful in 1920), Mary Beard devoted most of her time to considering all the ways women influenced society even before they could participate in elections. She looked at their role in reform areas and religious movements, in the workplace as well as the public square. She was the first historian to take a serious look at a court system called "equity," which all previous historians had not thought very important. In an early period of American history, Beard showed how equity courts provided a route for married women to protect their interest. This was a time when nearly every other part of the legal system had been completely closed to them.

Historians like Charles and Mary Beard offered accounts of the past only after they have worked as detectives, seeking leads in places that others had not yet bothered to look. Attempts to establish "the facts" like an investigator was a way for them to establish a believable account of why people did what they did and with what results. Those are not the only sorts of questions that historians ask, and those kinds of narratives are not always the main goal of historical research. Another kind of exploration of the past attempts to ask really basic questions about the size and scope of certain large-scale historical realities. How many people were killed during the American Civil War? Historians of this period will tell you that the answer is different if you want to know the number of soldiers who died (something where the records allow for a pretty good estimate) or if you want to count civilians as well (where precise numbers are hard to come by). A similar puzzle involves the challenge of evaluating the number of victims of such criminal enormities as the African slave trade, the Holocaust, or the Chinese Cultural Revolution. To lay out with some precision the enormous scale of these horrors is part of the job that historians play as moral witnesses to past injustices (a theme I will expand on below).

Let's take a closer look at attempts to establish the scale of the African slave trade, since it gives an interesting example of how historical advances are possible. A short time before the Beards wrote their books, W. E. B. Du Bois finished his studies at Harvard (where he was one of the few African American students) by poring over records related to the slave trade from Africa to the United States. Du Bois was mostly interested in efforts to stop trade that made some people rich and condemned others to an unimaginably terrible fate. The best records here were laws, political debates, and court decisions. But he began to think about how many people were involved, and a few years after his book was done, he offered a very rough estimate that at least 10 million people had been taken into bondage. While we will never know the exact number for sure, work has continued, and the best estimates now count that around 12 million people were put on slave ships along the African coast. Of these, only about 10.5 million arrived alive after their horrible voyages.

Du Bois's speculation was a starting point for later historians to devote a lot more time to this issue. Working at some of the top universities, these scholars relied on the kinds of research assistance and support that he never had. Looking for new sources was a way for such research teams to establish the most accurate accounting possible. Over time, an enormous amount of work has been put into refining estimates and detailing this human tragedy. This research can now be tracked via the Trans-Atlantic Slave Trade Database, a very large website that documents more than thirty thousand slave voyages. Information about other migrants to the New World has been gathered too which has led to a very interesting set of comparisons. We now know that of all those who between 1500 and 1820 crossed the Atlantic, there were three times as many enslaved Africans as there were free immigrants from Europe. Stepping back and recognizing this pattern recasts how we often contrast "Old World" misery with "New World" opportunities. In sum, the story of relocation to the Western Hemisphere looks different when we appreciate that 75 percent of the migrants made the trip in chains.

Present Controversies, Past Destinations

Historians have the present in mind when they go about establishing how they want the past to be viewed. Beard knew that asking hard questions about the motivations of American founders would make some people angry. And boy, did it! Du Bois knew that his interest in drawing attention to the immense suffering of African American slaves would by ignored by many white Americans. He was right: this was a time when many still supported institutions like racial segregation, which denied black Americans basic opportunities. Only some fifty years after he wrote did scholars at the top history schools begin to build on his original questions. Notable scholars working today—such as Columbia University's Eric Foner, Yale's David Blight, and Pennsylvania's Stephen Hahn—each look back on Du Bois as one of America's most inspiring and rigorous historical writers.

If we look at countries other than the United States, we see historians also being criticized for calling into question common views about a glorious national past. The problem here is that countries tell stories about national heroes that routinely get the facts wrong. Sometimes this is on purpose. Mistakes made years ago put people in a bad light. Some believe it is better just to gloss over these areas, or just plain ignore them. Historians, of course, are trained to disagree with this approach and to follow the evidence where it takes them. This can make their job pretty difficult and open them to loud complaints, as lacking in proper respect for their ancestors.

Historians of France have been working over the past several decades to ask tough questions about the French "Vichy" government, which made an alliance with Adolf Hitler during World War II after the Nazi troops expanded control. There had been a tradition of assuming that only a small number of French people supported this government and that far more resisted the Nazis and tried to restore links to the anti-Nazi Allies. Documents gathered by the historian Robert Paxton suggest a different sort of story. The amount of support for Hitler within Germany has raised some of the same issues. You can watch a movie called *The Nasty Girl* about a youngster who begins to explore the local history of what people in her German hometown did during World War II. Like a good historian, she trusts the records of the past more than the memories of the present.

Historical controversies have moral dimensions, and the historian can emerge as a critic and commentator about right and wrong. The historian Caroline Elkins looked into what the British did in Africa fifty years ago, and what she found reflected very badly on the leaders there. It may not be surprising that historians who evaluate what happened a few decades ago can stir up strong emotions. But even those who probe very deeply into the past can upset people. In India, for instance, there is a tendency to learn about the distant past in terms of myth rather than history. When the historian Romila Thapar tried to produce a document-based approach to the country's earliest history, many accused her of depriving a new generation of the pride and civic instruction that came from considering an earlier "heroic age."

Why History Will Always Matter

These controversies discussed above remind us of an important issue when it comes to history—that it continues to "matter" in any number of different ways. Its appeal is a reflection of the fact that the human past, like the human present, is chock full of drama, tragedy, and very moving struggles against injustice and for opportunity. What draws us to these matters is the complexity of human endeavors as they have stretched across the immense span of historical experience.

Like other stories, readers of history simultaneously can be entertained by drama, characters, and suspense, moved by the tragedy, and disillusioned by the quest for wealth and power. Exploring these themes and the historical figures in vivid detail allows dozens of professional historians to reach audiences every bit as large as some of our age's most renowned novelists and journalists. Once we historians set ourselves the job of thinking about what has happened and why, we begin to think about bigger things than simply telling a good story. What we think about what happened years ago also can be a way to make things happen now. We consider the past not just on its own terms, but also in light of the deepest necessities of our present and future.

As you might have discovered through your interview with an older acquaintance, the more we think about the past, the more we learn to appreciate how some things change and others stay the same. One reason history attracts so many readers is related to this point. Fact-based narratives, constructed by imaginative historians, allow us to understand what is going on around us now more completely. Just as points on a map situate us in space, so points across the expanse of time situate us in a broader context. Sometimes it is our distance from what went before that stands out. Other times it is the similarity across time. Just because a person was a kid fifty years ago doesn't mean they don't have something to say to today's youngsters about growing up. There are some experiences that are constants about how we live our lives.

By launching serious engagement with past actions and experiences, historians give us a way to put ourselves beyond of our own world. With their work, we can imagine what things were like in times we would never experience firsthand. It is has been said that "the past is a foreign country" (though here it would be better to say it is countless foreign countries, separated widely by all sorts of fascinating peculiarities and particularities). This point helps to show how going back in time may serve the same purpose as going into other countries. Framed like this, it's hard to imagine that people will ever grow tired of wanting to travel back in time to see what things were like. Doing so can be among the most enjoyable, imaginative, and important experiences that we as humans can undertake. As long as this is true, it will be the job of historians to help chart these journeys. Maybe that will be you one day!

Docs your answer for question 1 match the region in the map where you grew up? As you can see, there are some exceptions here and there, but most of the people in the survey landed in three main categories: *pop* speakers across much of the northern United States, *Coke* speakers across the South, and *soda* speakers in the Northeast, California, and a few other places.

What was your answer for question 2? If you circled *sneakers*, you are most likely from the northeastern United States. *Tennis shoes* is most common for the rest of the country—even if you don't play tennis. The *sneakers* people show up in other scattered areas, along with *gym shoes* and other words. For question 3, *sub* is the most common across the United States as a whole, but most people in Pennsylvania and nearby areas say *hoagie*. The word *grinder* appears in some parts of the Northeast, but *sub* is getting more common.

Syntax

Individual words are interesting, but of course it's also interesting to learn how we string those words together to make sentences and see if there is variation in that too. This is called *syntax*. Try this question:

(4) Have you ever heard someone use *might* and *could* together, such as,
I might could help you?
a. Yes, and I speak that way, too.
b. Yes, but I don't speak that way.
c. No, I've never heard this before.

Question 4 suggests that syntax is another source of linguistic variation. It turns out that combinations like *might could* and *may could* are often found in the US South (although not everyone in the South talks that way, of course). It's a different way of speaking than you find among northerners, but it isn't worse or better; it's just different. You might want to think about why many people think it is wrong to say sentences like *I might could help you*. Dialect features like this can even affect the way people in other regions perceive each other. For example, what do you think about the word *y'all*? What about *ain't*? Is it "good English"? Does it sound "incorrect"? "Uneducated"? How about someone who speaks with a strong southern accent? Does it sound "friendly"? Does it sound educated or not? People's attitudes toward different dialects can differ across regions in North America. This type of research is called *perceptual dialectology*.

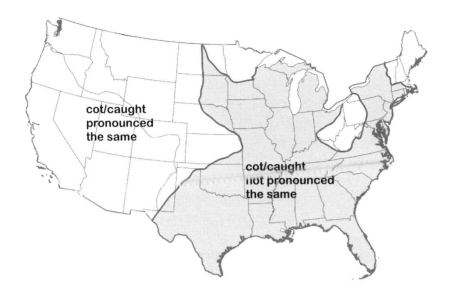

FIGURE 2 Map showing the regions that tend to pronounce *cot* and *caught* the same, and the regions that tend to pronounce them differently. Map adapted by Lucinda M. Hall, Dartmouth College Library, Dartmouth College. Based on the map in Bert Vaux's chapter in *Let's Go 2004: USA* (Let's Go, Inc.), using data from the Harvard Dialect Survey by Bert Vaux and Scott Golder

Pronunciation

There's much more to dialect research than just studying words and word combinations. Pronunciation is another interesting variable. Sometimes we find vowel differences that affect the pronunciation of hundreds of English words. Here are two other questions from the survey. Remember, there are no wrong answers!

(5) Do you pronounce the words *cot* and *caught* the same or different?
   a. Same
   b. Different
   c. Not sure

(6) Do you pronounce *marry*, *Mary*, and *merry* the same or different?
   a. Same
   b. Different
   c. Not sure

Question 5 is an example of this kind of vowel variation: the vowels in *cot* and *caught*. What was your answer? The map for *cot/caught* is shown in figure 2. As you can see, some regions pronounce these two words the same, but other regions don't. Where do you fit in this map? If you moved during childhood, then your dialect features may be more complicated, but focus on the region where you spent most of your childhood.

The *cot/caught* distinction goes much deeper than just those two words. It turns out that there is a whole class of English words with the *cot* vowel, such as *cot, lot, dot, Don, hot, not, rock, tot,* and thousands of other words, including longer words like *doctor, nominate, accomplish,* and so on. There is another whole class of words that have the *caught* vowel: *caught, talk, bought, dawn, thought, taught, law, awe, broad, dog, song,* and many more. You might notice that the vowel spellings in these *caught* words aren't all the same, such as *au* in *caught* versus *o* in *song*. But it's not about spelling; it's about how the vowels sound when we pronounce them. All of the words in the *caught* list are pronounced with the *caught* vowel, even if it is spelled differently in *song, talk, bought,* and so on. That's just a historical quirk of spelling. As far as the modern language system works in your mind, they are the same vowel.

People who grew up in the regions that pronounce *cot* and *caught* the same are likely to have just one vowel for both of these sets, while people in the other regions typically have two. This means that it isn't simply a matter of saying one word differently than another: people in the first region actually have a very different vowel *system* than people in the other region. That's why the *cot/caught* distinction is such a big deal for linguists in the United States. We call this *cot/caught* dialect feature the *low-back merger,* because these vowels are all pronounced with the tongue low and back in the mouth.

If you have the low-back merger, then you actually have one less English vowel than the people who pronounce *cot* and *caught* differently. But don't worry—you'll get through life just fine with one less vowel! It certainly doesn't affect your intelligence or your ability to communicate. Your English language is just organized in a slightly different way. It's not wrong; it's just different. In fact, it would be fair to say that your mind is organized is little bit differently than people in the other region. After all, vowel systems are part of how you think and organize information in your mind. In this way, the low-back merger is an example of *phonology,* the linguistic subfield that studies how speech sounds are organized in our minds and in different languages.

Figure 3 shows another kind of important geographic phonological distinc-

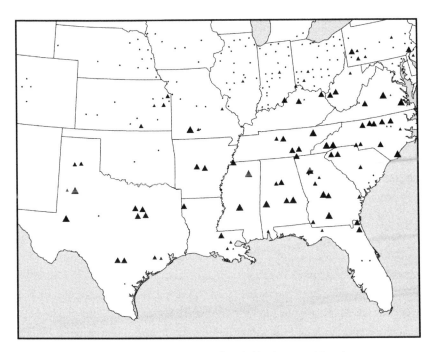

FIGURE 3 Southern pronunciation of words like *five, time, side,* and so on. Triangles represent people who pronounce these words like *faahv, taahm, saahd,* and so on. Map adapted by Lucinda M. Hall, Dartmouth College Library, Dartmouth College, based on William Labov, Sharon Ash, and Charles Boberg, *The Atlas of North American English* (Berlin: Mouton, 2006), 245

tion: North versus South. This is a map of the southern way of pronouncing the vowel in words like *five, time, side,* and so on, where the vowel is "flattened" a bit so that these words sound like *faahv, taahm, saahd.* The triangles represent people who pronounce it that way, and the little dots represent people who don't. Basically, figure 3 is showing us that there is a pretty sharp North/South border for this kind of pronunciation, and it's strongest in the interior parts of the South.

In addition to basic geography, the North/South divide of figure 3 may also make you think about modern maps of US politics and voting patterns that you may have seen on CNN: "red states," "blue states," and so on. It turns out that dialect patterns often reflect important *social* differences. Like other aspects of human culture, language is "transmitted" from parent to child over many generations (you might want to stop here for a minute and thank your parents or whoever raised you). We find that some of the twenty-first-century US dialect regions—and political regions—look a lot like the historical settlement patterns and social groupings from much earlier times. Some patterns trace as far back as the seventeenth or eighteenth centuries. In the 1700s, thousands of Scots-Irish people immigrated to America. As they looked for land and opportunities, they tended to settle in the interior hill country of the South, especially Appalachia. Almost three hundred years later, there are still sharp contrasts in dialect features—and political ideology—between the region that the Scots-Irish settled and the regions settled by other groups in nearby states to the north. Even now, after so many generations, a child growing up on the northern side typically acquires dialect features and *attitudes toward dialect features* that are the opposite of a child growing up on the southern side. Which side did you grow up on?

These kinds of historically related dialect differences can happen on a tiny scale, too, like Rhode Island. In fact, linguistics is almost like a time machine in this way. If you look back at figure 2 again, you can see that Rhode Island people tend to pronounce *cot/caught* differently, but most eastern Massachusetts people pronounce those vowels the same. Rhode Island and Massachusetts Bay were two separate colonies during colonial times, and that long-term social difference eventually led to dialect differences. Recently a researcher named Dan Johnson visited the neighborhoods right along the border of these two states to see whether the modern dialect boundary is as strong as the historical social boundary between the two former colonies. Dan made recordings of one hundred people in the area who were willing to be interviewed (it's hard to find that many people who are willing to be recorded!). When he analyzed the vowels, he found that the *cot/caught* border is quite close to the Rhode Island/ Massachusetts state border. That's a really sharp dialect boundary! In this way, we can use a New England linguistics "time machine" to look far back in time.

Studies like these make it clear that no language or dialect is "better" than another in any linguistic respect—that a good deal of how languages and dialects evolve is just due to twists of social history.

How Speech Works

How do people tell vowels apart when talking to each other? If someone said the word *bat* to you, how would you know it was *bat*, rather than *bit* or *bet* or something else? Our minds are able to figure it out almost instantly by identifying complex patterns in sound waves. Linguists explore this by measuring how people talk, using acoustic software and analyzing the results with statistics. If you were here in my office, I'd ask you to say some phrases into a digital recorder, and then I'd analyze your vowels with acoustic software. Figure 4 shows what this looks like. The ease with which we can do this is due at least in part to the strong interactions between computer science and some areas of linguistics!

Figure 4 shows the result of processing a recording of someone saying "my necklace." If you look at the word *necklace*, you can see that the first vowel in this word (marked as "EHI") has some semihorizontal dark bands above it. Those dark bands represent the amount of energy vibrating at different frequencies as you pronounce different sounds. These bands are called *formants*, and the computer has drawn a line of dots along each formant to make them easier to see. Counting from the bottom up in figure 4, the first dark band is the first formant (called "FI"), and the second dark band is the second formant ("F2"). The computer also helps us locate the individual vowels and consonants, which are marked with vertical boundaries in the lower half of the figure.

We pronounce different vowels by shifting our formant frequencies while we talk. As the sound vibrates between your larynx and your lips, some frequencies have more sound energy than others (resonant frequencies). Those frequencies are the vowel formants. Different tongue and lip positions produce different formant patterns, which we perceive as different vowels. All of this is an example of the linguistic subfield of *phonetics*.

We shift our formants all the time while we are talking. Try saying *see Sue see Sue see Sue see Sue*. Think about what your mouth is doing. What is different about the vowel in *see* compared to the vowel in *Sue*? You might notice that your lips become more rounded when you say *Sue*, but they are unrounded for *see*.

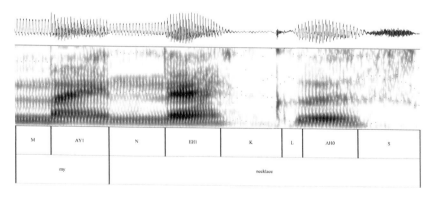

FIGURE 4 Acoustic analysis of vowel formants. Praat acoustic software,
Paul Boersma and David Weenink (2016). Praat: doing phonetics by computer (software).
Available from http://www.praat.org/

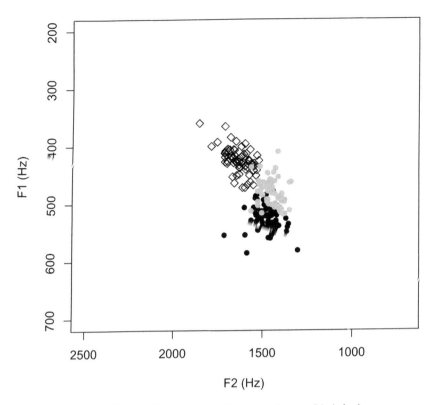

FIGURE 5 Plotting F1 versus F2 for *Mary* (squares), *marry* (black dots),
and *merry* (gray dots). Each dot shows the average for a single
speaker in South Boston. Illustration by the author.

You also might notice that your tongue moves forward for *see* and farther back for *Sue*. Those changes in your mouth and lips cause changes in the formants. Want to pronounce a French vowel? First, just say *deeeee* for a while. Now say *deeeee* again, but this time make your lips rounded. You just said the word *du* in French ("of the"). That's a front-rounded vowel, which is something that English doesn't have.

We can also use formants to learn about *marry/merry/Mary* (question 6). What was your answer for question 6? My students and I did some field research on *marry/merry/Mary* vowels on the streets of South Boston, and here is what we found (figure 5). We made a plot that shows the formants F1 and F2 for each person as they said those words. Each square is the average pronunciation of *Mary* for a single person. The black dots are the averages for *marry*, and the gray dots are *merry*. As you can see, these South Boston people show big differences in their vowel formants for *marry*, *Mary*, and *merry*. If you measured *marry/merry/Mary* vowels in the US Midwest or West, you would probably find that the three vowels are about the same, unlike our study on the East Coast.

Besides the positions of the tongue and lips, we can also measure little differences in the way you produce sounds in your larynx (your "voice box," halfway down your neck). Put your hand on your larynx and say [s] for a few seconds: *sssssssss*. Now say *zzzzzzzzzz*. Do you feel the difference? That vibration you feel while saying *zzzzzzzzzz* is called *voicing*. Now plug your ears and slowly alternate back and forth like this: *sssssssssszzzzzzzzzzzzzzssssssssssszzzzzzzzzz*. With your ears plugged, the voicing sounds like some kind of loud engine, right? Voicing happens when the muscles around your larynx pull your vocal folds close together and they begin vibrating very quickly, around one to two hundred times per second.

Now say [s] and [z] again, and think about what your tongue and lips are doing. The basic tongue position is the same for both [s] and [z]. The difference is that [z] is voiced and [s] is voiceless. For both [s] and [z], you can probably feel the noisy, turbulent air between your tongue and the roof of the mouth behind your teeth (the alveolar ridge). Consonants like [s], [z], [f], [v], and others all have this noisy friction, so we call them *fricatives*. Now try doing the same thing with *vvvvvv* and *ffffff* (plug your ears again). Which one is voiced? Which one is voiceless?

We can also measure voicing in a very precise way using a machine called an *electroglottograph*. We place small electrodes on either side of a person's larynx, ask the person to say some sentences, and measure the amount of electrical resistance across the tiny space between the vocal folds inside the larynx—thousands of measurements per second. The electroglottograph makes a plot showing exactly how the vocal folds open and shut for different speech sounds, different people, and different languages. For example, do you ever hear your friends sometimes talking with a little bit of a "creaky"-sounding voice? It's quite common. In English, people sometimes do this to make themselves sound more "cool" or relaxed or young. In other languages, this "creaky" sound can be a crucial part of distinguishing words. We can measure this in the sound waves coming out of your mouth using the software we discussed in figure 4. However, an electroglottograph gives us even clearer results because it makes measurements way down at the larynx, before the sound waves go up into your mouth.

Which Dialect Is the "Best"?

Now that we've been talking about different English dialect regions, which region do you think speaks the best English? As we said above, a linguist would say: "None of them. They're all equal." We all speak a dialect of some type. There is no linguistic reason to favor one dialect over another. In fact, linguists find that any language or dialect that is learned naturally as a child is a logical, orderly, rule-governed linguistic system. For a given country or society, the one dialect that gets to be viewed as "standard" is based on arbitrary social and historical reasons, political power, economics, and so on. It's true that national broadcast news anchors are sometimes trained to avoid certain regional dialect features, but that's just a matter of trying to fit in with social expectations. The only reason that some dialects sound more "prestigious" or "better" to our ears is that society chooses to view them in that way. This means that every dialect is worthy of respect, even if it is spoken by a group that is socially disadvantaged or prejudiced against, including ethnic minority groups.

We can even go a step further: the "nonstandard" dialects of a language are often more logical, orderly, and systematic than the standard dialect! Many of the formal English "rules" you have been taught in school are really just quirks of history—leftovers from earlier versions of English—not better or worse than "nonstandard" dialects in any linguistic way.

Here's an example:

(a) We don't like that restaurant.
(b) You don't like that restaurant.
(c) They don't like that restaurant.

What do you think about sentences a through c? Perfectly fine, right? Now look at sentences d and e:

(d) She doesn't like that restaurant.
(e) She don't like that restaurant.

I think you'd probably agree that *She don't like that restaurant* somehow feels like it's not as good as *She doesn't like that restaurant*. But why do we feel that way? Is there really anything "illogical" or "sloppy" or "unintelligent" about saying *She don't like that restaurant*? According to the rules of standard English, *She doesn't like that restaurant* is correct. But that's really just a quirky exceptional rule that only applies to *she/he/it* (third-person singular). It's just a small leftover from much older forms of English, when there was a more complex pattern. We don't really need it anymore, but it still hangs on in standard English.

You've probably read some Shakespeare in school. Were some of the words hard to understand? In Shakespeare's time, English had verb forms like *sayst, goest, goeth, doth,* and so on. Those forms sound really old-fashioned now. All languages naturally change over time, and sometimes those changes affect a whole *system* within the grammar, such as the system of verb endings. The English of Shakespeare's time (Early Modern English) had a system of verb endings to indicate whether the subject of the sentence was you, you plus other people, me, me plus other people, and so on. This set of verb endings simplified over time, so that modern English has just one left: the *s* that we put onto present-tense verbs when the subject is a single person other than you or me: *She sings a song. She doesn't like that restaurant.* It's a remnant of the older system of Shakespeare's time, but now it's just a quirky leftover—not part of a full system of verb endings.

If you think about the first group of sentences a through c a little more, you'll notice that *She don't like that restaurant* is actually more similar to sentences a through c than *She doesn't like that restaurant.* If someone says *She don't like that restaurant,* it matches sentences a through c in a nice orderly way: they have the word *don't* across the board. That's the most natural way to do it! From this viewpoint, a person who says *She don't like that restaurant* is just taking English to the logical next step: leveling it out a little bit so that *don't* is used with all of the pronouns. There's nothing linguistically "wrong" about doing that. It's a logical—and intelligent—thing to do. It's true that many people perceive it negatively, but that's simply because they buy into the idea that one type of English is somehow better than another. It isn't, at least not for any linguistic reason. People who grew up in communities that talk that way are worthy of respect just like anyone else. That's an important point, especially when you think about communities that tend to speak this way. They are often socially disadvantaged in other ways besides dialect features.

Of course, if you say something like *She don't like that restaurant* in a college admissions interview, the interviewer might think that you aren't well educated. That could be a big problem! Many people (including most college admissions committees) believe that one type of English is better than another, so they tend to view any "nonstandard" way of speaking as a negative trait. Sometimes it's necessary to use standard forms so that people don't misjudge you. That kind of judgment—the mistaken idea that one way of speaking a language is linguistically better than all others—is found in almost every industrialized society in the world. In some smaller communities where the local language isn't used in schools or other prestigious settings, all dialects are sometimes viewed as equal.

We've seen some examples where language change leads to simplified forms. In other cases, some aspect of a language can become more complex over time. Here's an example.

Fill in the blank:

me	→	us
her/him	→	them
you	→	_____

What do you think? Should it be the word *you* or something else? Of course, the word *you* is the standard form, but it's not very useful for distinguishing between one person and multiple people. That's why people sometimes say *you guys, y'all, yous, yas, yinz,* and so on. Those forms all sound pretty casual and nonstandard—maybe even "sloppy," right? But once again, these "nonstandard" forms represent a natural language change. In this case, the nonstandard form has found a way to "repair" a missing space in the grammar, making it a more complete system—but also making it more complex, since it has additional words in the system.

Shakespeare's English had two main ways of saying "you" as the object of a verb: *I see thee* versus *I see you. Thee* was singular, and *you* was plural. But now, in modern English, if you said *I see thee* to one of your friends, it would sound weird, right? The *thee/you* distinction is pretty rare now, except in older literature or church settings. For modern standard English, *thee* and *you* are now expressed by a single word, *you.* That's nice and simple, but it's a problem whenever we need to tell someone that we mean one person or more than one person. It's handy to be able to say something like *you guys* or *y'all* or *yous* or *yas* (my wife says *yas*). In a formal written essay at school, a teacher (at least a northerner) would probably correct any student who wrote *y'all.* Yet the word *y'all* is actually a very logical and practical development. Even so, many northerners view *y'all* negatively, so I wouldn't write *y'all* in a business letter.

Let's think about North and South a little more. Pretend that, in some parallel *Star Trek* universe, American history turned out differently, and the South won the Civil War, not the North. In that parallel universe, it wouldn't be too surprising to find the word *y'all* being taught in school as the correct form for second-person plural. Those schools might also tell children to say *might could* and other "nonstandard" forms, including double negatives. It's all about which social group's way of speaking is used as the model for these things.

In the *y'all/you guys/yas* example, we find once again that the standard dialect (*you* for plural) is lagging behind "nonstandard" dialects during the natural process of language change. Why does this keep happening? In both examples, the standard dialect preserved some patterns that were left over from earlier historical periods of the language—forms that no longer fit the modern system very well. These quirky or unbalanced grammar patterns often stay alive for a while because our society assumes that one version of a language should be favored above all the others. Standard dialects are supported by the weight of prestige, education, textbooks, teacher training, and so on. But language change is a natural process, not sloppiness. Anyway, the major world languages French, Spanish, and Portuguese once grew out of Latin, so they could really be viewed as "sloppy" versions of Latin! And Latin itself could be viewed as a "sloppy" version of the languages that came before it. But of course none of those languages are sloppy, and neither are any dialects of any language learned as a child. They are all orderly linguistic systems worthy of equal respect.

Still, in case you aren't quite convinced that nonstandard dialects are perfectly fine as linguistic systems (I don't think my mom is quite convinced about this), here's one more example for you. Double negatives are another case where a natural language change in "nonstandard" dialects give us a logical and clearer way to express ourselves. Most English schools teach that double negatives are incorrect, often explaining that double negatives are illogical because they "cancel each other out." After all, everyone knows that $-1 \times -1 = +1$. But is that really the right way to look at it? Suppose I was a defendant in a court case, and I told the judge, "I didn't steal nothin'." Would the jury say, "He just admitted that he's guilty!"? Does *I didn't steal nothing* mean *I did steal something*? That's obviously not what I meant. I meant that I did not steal anything. It's just a difference in dialect and emphasis. Even Shakespeare used a lot of double negatives, and we wouldn't want to say that Shakespeare was illogical or sloppy . . .

But let's pretend for a minute that double negatives (which linguists call *negative concord* or *multiple negation*) are actually illogical. What about major world languages that use double negatives all the time, like Spanish and Russian? Would a jury in Spain or Russia say I'm guilty of stealing if I said something like *I didn't steal nothing* in Spanish or Russian? No, because their language systems allow for multiple negation. It's not a matter of being illogical; it's just a different linguistic system.

What should we do about the old argument that double negatives are illogical because they "cancel out" (-1 x -1 = +1)? Well, if someone wants to use math analogies, then how about this: -1 + -1 = -2. This looks closer to what actually happens in languages with double negatives. In fact, it's probably more like this rule from middle school math: -1 x ($a + b + c + d$) = $-a-b-c-d$. In other words, languages and dialects with multiple negation are just spreading negation across the sentence: _Nobody won't never steal nothing nowhere_. In this sentence, multiple negation makes it very, very, very clear that the action of stealing did not happen. Now do you see why I might talk that way if you accused me of stealing?! So languages and dialects like standard English follow the -1 x -1 = +1 pattern for negation, while others follow another, equally logical, pattern: -1 x ($a + b + c + d$) = $-a-b-c-d$.

Conclusion

In this chapter, we've looked at some of the ways that linguists study languages. I couldn't cover everything in one chapter, but I hope you now have a better idea about what linguistics is. I think we're ready to answer the question in the title of this chapter: What is linguistics? From what we've seen in this chapter, I hope you'll agree with a definition like this: Linguistics is the scientific study of human language. Linguists systematically explore all levels of language: the sounds (phonetics), sound systems (phonology), words (lexicon), word structures like suffixes and prefixes (morphology), meaning (semantics), and sentence structure (syntax). We also look at how people put those things together in personal interactions (discourse, conversation analysis, pragmatics), how people use language in society and culture (sociolinguistics and anthropological linguistics), how language works in the brain and how people learn new languages and process linguistic information (neurolinguistics and psycholinguistics), how to classify different types of languages (typology), and how languages have changed across history (historical linguistics).

Another part of linguistics, computational linguistics, is a rapidly growing field that includes automatic speech recognition and language processing. If you use Siri or other voice recognition systems on your phone, you know that researchers have made some progress in teaching computers to understand spoken language—but there's a long way to go. Siri makes a lot of mistakes! Maybe you'll be the first person to invent a computer program that can accurately understand everything a human says on any topic.

Field research is another major area of linguistics. Linguists go all around the world making detailed recordings of diverse languages, carefully documenting the structures of these languages, and often working with communities to revitalize languages. There are over seven thousand languages in the world, and probably half or more of these languages will die out during this century, replaced by English, Spanish, Chinese, and other large languages. When a language dies, its speakers lose a valuable aspect of their personal and cultural identity. Many Native American communities, such as the Lakota people, say that language is a crucial part of their culture, and they are very concerned about the future of their Native languages. In many of these communities, few children are learning their heritage languages as they grow up. That's a big problem for the parent-to-child transmission of the language. For each language that is lost, we also lose valuable indigenous knowledge and scientific information about the structures that are possible in diverse human languages.

Linguistics and *The Planet of the Apes*

Personally, I think linguistics is fascinating because language is one of the key characteristics of human beings. When we study linguistics, we're studying ourselves! For example, this sentence that you're reading right now isn't especially challenging or unusual, but I guarantee that you couldn't teach an ape or any other animal to create a sentence like this—not in a million years. I don't know how they did it in *The Planet of the Apes*, but it wouldn't work in real life.

This makes us special on this planet. As the famous linguist Noam Chomsky likes to remind us, if you put a baby human and a kitten or baby chimpanzee or any other animal into exactly the same linguistic environment growing up, only the human will acquire language. And for the human child, it's an effortless and completely natural process. Apes, chimps, bonobos, and other higher primates can be taught to understand sets of simple words using hand signs, but only when there is a team of researchers actively teaching them and dedicating large amounts of time and money (a chimp in one of these projects was named "Nim Chimpsky" after Noam Chomsky!). More importantly, those nonhuman primates are *severely* limited in their ability to learn syntax and word structure, regardless of the time and effort. A two-year-old human toddler has already learned more syntax and word structure than an ape could ever learn. Humans are special in this way. *You* are special in this way, and you prove it to the world every time you use language.

Mathematics?

Dan Rockmore

Mathematics is many things. All of you have worked with numbers and played with shapes—and I hope you have enjoyed those activities! When you are adding, subtracting, multiplying, and even dividing (!) numbers, you are using mathematics. When you are confronted with shapes and try to describe them, you are thinking about mathematics. When you are glimpsing and wondering and seeing patterns in your playing and working with numbers and shapes, you are *doing* mathematics.

You see, mathematics is more than just working out lots of particular problems and getting good at arithmetic or recognizing shapes. Mathematics as a subject studies numbers and shapes like they were animals in the jungle or stars in the sky. Numbers can relate to one another in the same way animals relate to one another in the wild or astronomical objects relate to each other in space. Numbers have patterns of behavior and obey laws. Shapes have properties that distinguish them from one another in the way that a salamander is different from a newt or a frog (even though they are all amphibians) or the way that a planet is different from a comet that is different from a meteor that is different from a star. To "do mathematics" is to study these mathematical "things" and all of their properties and relationships.

There are lots of different kinds of mathematics, and depending on your interests and your skills, some kinds of mathematics might appeal to you, while other kinds might not, just like you like some kinds of movies, music, or books, but not others. Mathematics too is a matter of taste. Let's see some examples.

It All Adds Up—A First Formula

There is a very nice problem related to patterns in numbers that is famous for being a problem that was solved by the greatest of mathematicians, Carl Friederich Gauss—we all just call him Gauss—when he was a small boy. Let's try it out for ourselves: Legend has it that the precocious Gauss was always pestering his teacher for harder and harder problems to do. Exasperated, the teacher told Gauss to add up the first one hundred numbers (figuring this would keep him busy for a while):

$$1 + 2 + 3 + 4 + \ldots + 98 + 99 + 100$$

(We use those little dots to indicate that we're too lazy to write out the rest of the numbers between 4 and 98, but that we are pretending they are there!) Now you are all probably pretty good at addition, and I bet that if given a little time (and a snack and a drink) you could work your way through to the answer. But, as the legend goes, with just a brief moment's thought, Gauss said "5,050." And he was (and remains) correct! How did he do it so quickly?

Let's try a slightly simpler example—just adding up the first four numbers:

$$1 + 2 + 3 + 4$$

Okay, now you are very good at adding numbers, so you sit quietly at your desk and accumulate them and lo and behold arrive at the answer 10. Easy! But now let's go about this another way, a visual way:

Let's represent each of the numbers by an appropriate number of dots, as shown in figure 1.

Adding up the dots 1 through 4 will be equivalent to counting out the number of dots that we get when we put all these individual collections of dots together. Our "trick" will be to arrange them in such a way that we can quickly figure out the number of dots that we have without actually counting them one-by-one.

We can "double" this triangle and to get a rectangle like so (the lighter gray dots are the dots that we have tossed in), as in figure 2.

Now, we are already kind of clever, and we know from learning multiplication that the number of dots in this rectangle that now has 4 dots on one side and 5 dots on another side is 20. But this means that the number of dots in each of the triangles that make it up (which is going to be 1 + 2 + 3 + 4) is 10. Aha!!

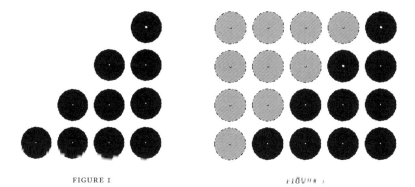

FIGURE I

FIGURE 2

I am hoping that you can see how this will help to add the numbers 1 + 2 + 3 + . . . + 100: Same idea, but we'll use our imagination to actually pencil in the dots. This time, we will make a rectangle out of our two triangles that has 100 dots on one side and 101 on the other. This multiplication problem is a bit more advanced (using three-digit numbers), but actually, since we are multiplying 101 by 100, we can just tack on two zeros to 101 to get 10,100. When we take half of that we get 5,050. Good one, young Gauss!

But now you see, there is a pattern here: we used our "chop the rectangle in half" trick to add up the numbers 1 through 4, and then we indicated (or, as mathematicians sometimes say, "waved our hands") how this would enable us to add quickly the numbers 1 through 100. That is, we saw a pattern and then used it to make a rule or a formula: if you are adding up the first several numbers, the answer is given by multiplying the biggest number in your list by the next biggest number and dividing that by 2. So if you're adding the first four numbers, the answer is (4 x 5) / 2, or 10, if adding the first 100 numbers, the answer is (100 x 101) / 2, or 5,050. Now here's the drum roll: if adding up the first N numbers (so, N can be any number we like—such as 10 or 100), written out as

$$1 + 2 + 3 + \ldots + N$$

the answer is $(N+1)N / 2$. This formula is also a pattern of numbers. It is a law that numbers obey, as surely as the planets obey the law of gravity. Figuring it out is part of doing mathematics. Notice how we did it—we experimented with a few examples and then generalized from our particular understandings to write down a law, which is our formula:

$$1 + 2 + 3 + \ldots + N = (N+1)N / 2$$

These kinds of "arguments"—which are sort of like arguing in front of jury made up of every mathematician in the world—are an important part of a lot of mathematics. Mathematicians are very concerned with being absolutely sure about their claims. For some of us, that's one of the things we like about math!

Gauss was very, very good at arithmetic and spent much of his life trying to understand all kinds of patterns in numbers, especially patterns about prime numbers, which as you may know are the whole numbers only divisible by themselves and 1—so the first several prime numbers are 2, 3, 5, 7, 11. When you spend your time uncovering patterns in numbers, you are doing number theory. Gauss called number theory the "Queen of Mathematics," and his life-long love of this kind of math (but he was good at all sorts of math) is probably one of the reasons that he is sometimes referred to as "The Prince of Mathematics."

It's All Connected—Euler's Little Problem

Not all of math is about numbers. Sometimes it can be about shapes or pictures or even little puzzles that might not seem like they are about "math"—but, after we strip them down to some kind of bare essence that is all logic and reasoning, we see that there is something mathematical about them. Here's a famous little problem that gave birth to the subject that we now know as "network theory"— the math of Facebook!

It all started with a little game that in the early eighteenth century people used to play in a town called Königsberg, which was then part of Prussia (but is now called Kaliningrad and is part of Russia). We'll call it by its old name.

Königsberg was a picturesque medieval town built around the Pregel River. In the middle of the river was a tiny town—really like an island neighborhood— called Kneiphof. Kneiphof was connected by bridges to the mainland and in this way was part of a beautiful parks system of the greater area. Figure 3 is a detail of an old map of the area with the bridges highlighted.

As you can see, there were seven bridges in all connecting the island with the city proper. As legend has it, residents would take on the challenge of trying to find a path through the parks that would enable them to use every bridge exactly once. Try it for yourself!

Euler (we pronounce it "oy-ler") thought about this problem and had a very clever insight, which might not seem like a big deal, but it started a revolution in

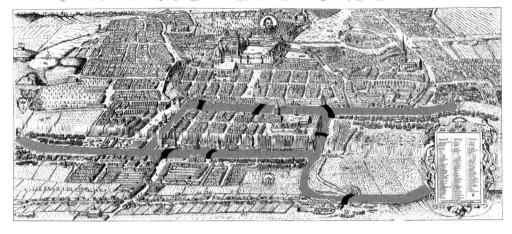

FIGURE 3 Detail of a map of bridges of Königsberg and the bridges to Kneiphof.
Wikimedia Commons, created by Wikipedia user Bogdan Giuşcă

mathematical thinking that today, almost four hundred years later has changed
the way in which we see our own lives and the world! How's that for the power
of mathematics? More on that later. For now, let's just return to our little problem
in the parks of Königsberg.

Euler realized that the woods, people, the birds, the little animals in the parks,
the babies, the food vendors, were all huge distractions from the problem that
he wanted to solve. All he cared about was how the various landmasses were
connected by the bridges. And of course he didn't even care particularly about
the bridges (whether they were made of wood or stone or long or short); all he
cared about was which parts of the park they connected. So instead of trying to
keep in mind the beautiful parks, he stripped it down into a very simplified representation of lines and dots—lines representing the bridges and dots representing
the various sections of the park—and, in doing so, turned the detailed map into
a very simple figure, as shown in figure 4. With a little more simplification, we
get the map in figure 5.

Mathematicians call this figure a *graph* or, as it is more popularly known
today, a *network*.

With all the distractions stripped away, Euler could now concentrate on
what we can call "The Park Problem." His goal was to use every bridge exactly
once. So let's imagine an attempt to do this: we would start at some part of the
park, make our way to a bridge and cross it and so on, hopefully crossing a last
bridge after having used all the bridges exactly once. But this would mean that

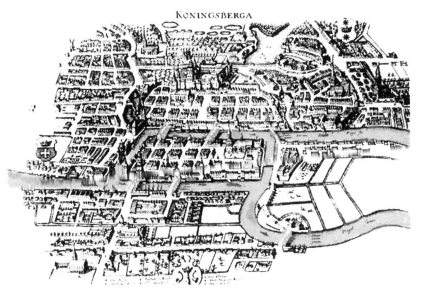

FIGURE 4 A first abstraction of the connection information for the bridges of Königsberg. Wikimedia Commons, created by Wikipedia user Chris-martin

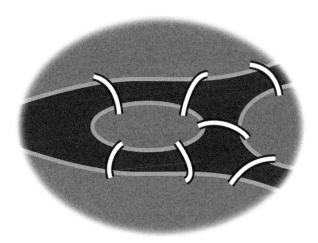

FIGURE 5 The mathematical "network" of the bridges of Königsberg. Wikimedia Commons, created by Wikipedia user Riojajar~commonswiki

every time we entered one of the regions of the park by one bridge, we would need to leave by a different bridge, so except for the first leg of our walk and the last leg, all the other stops in the walk would need to have an even number of bridges connecting them. Looking at the dots on our graph, we see that three of the areas have an odd number of bridges connecting them. So it can't happen.

Just like in our story about Gauss, while Euler may have settled the particular problem of the Königsberg bridges, his reasoning was such that it could be used much more generally: we could have a picture like this with any number of dots (maybe representing landmasses, but also possibly representing webpages or airports or people) and many, many connectors (maybe representing bridges, but also possibly representing web links or plane routes or friendships). Euler's way of settling the question—of realizing that all we care about is the connectivity of the landmasses and not their sizes—started a revolution, a revolution we call *topology*. This is the study of "objects" based only on their properties of connectivity. The study of topology is not just the study of networks—and in fact, that is such a rich area of work that it is really its own field of study today (this is the way math and all kinds of fields of study proceed—little problems give birth to big areas of work, whose specialties turn into their own areas of work, and so on and so on, like a family tree of ideas). The study of topology also is important for understanding the shape of the universe, and the coiling and uncoiling of DNA (part of a subject called "knot theory"). It is also a subject where all kinds of truly unimaginable shapes are thought about—shapes in many dimensions that bend back on themselves with holes and curves and interconnections—just for the fun and challenge of it! In fact, just a few years ago, a Russian mathematician named Grigori Perelman earned (and then turned down) a $1 million prize and the famous Fields Medal (which is sometimes called the "Math Nobel Prize") for disentangling a topological mystery that had stumped mathematicians for over one hundred years. And there are still many more topological questions to puzzle over!

Infinity

Infinity is a favorite topic of mathematics and mathematicians, and if you study mathematics, you will run into all sorts of mysteries that accompany thinking about infinity. Some people even say that mathematics is the *only* subject that truly studies the infinite. What do you think?

Many of us first make use of infinity on the playground:

EZRA: "I am stronger than you are!"

RACHEL: "I am stronger than you are + 1!"

EZRA: "I am stronger than you are + 2!"

RACHEL: "I am stronger than you are + infinity!"

EZRA: "Oh yeah?!"

"Infinity" is the word we use for anything that doesn't seem to have an end—an end in time, an end in space, an end in anything. Mathematicians have been trying to make sense of it for a long time—but not an infinite time! We even have a symbol for it—an 8 lying on its side: ∞.

This shape is a *lemniscate*. In 1655 it was introduced to represent infinity by the mathematician John Wallis. Some people trace this symbol back even further, to the Romans and Greeks. The history of why we use the symbols that we do use in mathematics is also very interesting, but something we don't have time to discuss here!

Counting is the place where most of us get us our first taste of infinity. We all know that there is no biggest whole number—given any number, then adding one to it gives us a number that is bigger, so the "number" of whole numbers is "infinite."

The mysteries of the infinite start quickly. What if we take only the even whole numbers:

$$2, 4, 6, 8, \ldots$$

It feels like there have to be fewer of these than of all the whole numbers—we're taking every other number, so it looks like about half as many, right? Hold on! One simple way to compare the sizes of each of these two number collections is to try to line them up, showing that for every even number there is a corresponding whole number. In fact, we can easily do that:

$$2, 4, 6, 8, \ldots$$
$$| \quad | \quad | \quad | \ldots$$
$$1, 2, 3, 4, \ldots$$

So, in this way of determining whether two collections have the same number of objects (we call that the "cardinality" of the collection), that is, by setting up a "one-to-one correspondence," we see that there are as many even numbers as there are whole numbers, even though the even numbers are clearly not all of the whole numbers!

Of course, there is nothing special about the even numbers. We could have done this will all the multiples of three: 3, 6, 9, 12, . . . or multiples of any number we like, or all kinds of other infinite collections that are among the whole numbers—like all the numbers that end with a 1: 1, 11, 21, 31, . . . In fact, one way to define a collection as infinite, is to say that it is possible to find these kinds of seemingly smaller collections within that can be put in one-to-one correspondence with the whole collection.

We can also play this game in the other direction, looking at collections that seem like they must be bigger than the whole numbers. Take, for example, all the numbers, both positive and negative and zero. We call the collection of all these numbers the *integers*. We do our usual trick with the dots to indicate how these go on forever in two different directions:

$$. . . -3, -2, -1, 0, 1, 2, 3, . . .$$

It looks like there should be "twice as many" integers as whole numbers. But once again, we use our one-to-one correspondence trick to see that it's not the case. We just need to be a little more clever about listing them out:

$$0, -1, \quad 1, -2, \quad 2, -3, \quad 3, . . .$$
$$| \quad | \quad | \quad | \quad | \quad | \quad | . . .$$
$$1, \quad 2, \quad 3, \quad 4, \quad 5, \quad 6, \quad 7, . . .$$

We are in fact touching on some very interesting, complicated, and fundamental ideas around the "foundations of mathematics"—the way in which we define what a number is. We are using the idea of "sets" and one-to-one correspondence as the key to defining numbers. Think about it!

The Russian mathematician Georg Cantor was one of the first mathematicians to think hard about infinity. He used the Hebrew letter aleph—the first letter in the Hebrew alphabet—to represent the infinity of whole numbers: $\aleph_0$

Using the first letter of the Hebrew alphabet to represent this infinity with a zero ("sometimes called "aleph-naught"), it begs the question, are their bigger infinities? Can something be even more infinite than the collection of whole numbers? The answer is yes! This is one of the amazing things that Cantor figured out—that in fact there is a whole range of infinities, almost like their own number system, a number system that is much more mysterious than our own number system (which is already pretty mysterious! We can't even predict where the prime numbers are!). It's kind of like an astronomer finding an alternate universe that vaguely resembles our universe, but not completely.

We say that any collection of things that can be put into a one-to-one correspondence with the whole numbers is "countable" or "countably infinite." So, the even numbers are countable, the multiples of three are countable, the prime numbers are countable. Basically, any infinite set that can be listed out is countable. Try this one on: take all the ordered pairs of whole numbers, which you may know we can think of as being points on the Cartesian grid:

$$\ldots \quad \ldots \quad \ldots \quad \ldots \quad \ldots$$
$$(4,1) \quad (4,2) \quad (4,3) \quad (4,4)\ldots$$
$$(3,1) \quad (3,2) \quad (3,3) \quad (3,4)\ldots$$
$$(2,1) \quad (2,2) \quad (2,3) \quad (2,4)\ldots$$
$$(1,1) \quad (1,2) \quad (1,3) \quad (1,4)\ldots$$

This is a countably infinite collection too! Why? Because we can list them in an orderly way: If we start at (1,1), then we can snake through this corner of the plane ticking off the points one by one: (1,1) (2,1) (1,2) (1,3) (2,2) (3,1) (4,1), . . . (can you see the pattern here? First we list all the points whose coordinates add to 2, then to 3, then to 4, and so on . . .). Notice that you can think of this as listing out all the positive fractions—the first number is the numerator and the second number is the denominator—with some repeats. So, there are as many positive fractions as there are whole numbers? Yes.

But now I bet you are getting pretty curious. Are all collections of things that infinite, countably infinite? Can we always be clever enough to find a way of listing out our infinite collection? This is where Cantor turned the world of mathematics upside-down. He answered with a resounding "*No!*"

Cantor discovered that if you take all the numbers between 0 and 1—and I mean *all* of them, that is, all the fractions, and all the *irrational* numbers too (you might remember that these are the ones whose decimal expansions go on without end)—that this collection can't be counted!

This set the world of mathematics into quite a tizzy! New notions of infinity, new number systems even—a world of *transfinite* ("trans-" is the prefix that means "beyond," so "beyond finite") arithmetic. Some mathematicians were even angry at Cantor for doing this, so angry that they made it difficult for Cantor to find a position where he could spend his time thinking about this mysterious new world of mathematics. Some of them argued that this wasn't really mathematics, that it was more properly philosophy. The strain of working under such bad feeling took its toll on Cantor, and he died quite young—and sad. Why would people get so upset over these interesting ideas about the infinite? That is a subject for another time.

A Wide World of Math Awaits!

I hope that this has given you a taste for the kinds of things that mathematicians think about and the ways in which they think. Sometimes the problems start off as very special problems that someone needs to solve in a single instance—like adding a collection of numbers or navigating a system of parks—and sometimes they can be pure flights of fancy, like pondering the infinite. The unifying themes are ones of finding patterns in ideas, patterns in relationships, patterns in patterns . . .

When you study a mathematical idea for its own sake—like trying to find a formula to produce prime numbers or pondering the infinite of the infinite—that is often called doing *pure math*, doing math for its own sake. Now you may have heard of something called *applied math*. Applied to what? That's a good question. When we talk about applied math, we mean that this is the study and creation of mathematics that has in mind the solution of a specific problem in the world. For example, for many years now, really centuries, people have been trying to figure out better and better ways to represent using equations the properties of liquids and gases. Some of the first work on this was done by our friend Euler, who was interested in making a mathematical description of model of the way in which blood flows in our body—sometime through relatively wide pipes and tubes like arteries and veins, and other times through very tiny tubes like capillaries. Going from wide to narrow creates all kinds of tensions on the flow of your blood and with that a wide range of phenomena, not unlike the eddies (whirlpools) and fast flows that you might find in a river that wanders in some places, and speeds along in others.

Applied math and pure math might start out with different motivations, but they still share much. What you now can see is that pure math and applied math actually share quite a lot. They are both about math, but they have different motivations: the "pure" stuff is generated by questions about the inner world of math and its object (numbers, shapes, etc.), and applied math usually starts with a question about something in the "outside world," or the "real world," as we sometimes call it. Euler was thinking about a very particular problem about bridges, and that gave birth to an area of mathematical research about "objects" that we can't necessarily even see. Mathematicians continued to study this even before there was anything like the Internet or Facebook. But once these technologies were invented, math was ready to jump in to help understand them. Four hundred years ago, discoveries were made about prime numbers—just because it was fun to think about prime numbers—and then someone realized that these pure mathematics discoveries would be useful for securing communication on the Internet. True story!

This shows again how different kinds of math appeals to different kinds of people. What we saw here is just the tip of the iceberg. If you like games of chance, then maybe probability is for you. If you enjoy pushing around x's and y's to solve equations, then maybe algebra is your game. If you like shapes and angles, then maybe geometry (a "cousin" of topology) is for you. The Internet, computers, and new challenges in technology have given birth to new areas of mathematics and even new subjects like computer science (check out the earlier chapter on this topic). The more we know, the more we realize there are things we don't know. Gauss, Euler, Cantor, and others were some of the early giants in the mathematics, and building on their work (and that of a bunch of others in between) there are new giants. In 2014 Maryam Mirzakhani became the first woman Fields Medalist!

There are lots of kinds of math, and if you are interested, then I bet there are kinds that will excite you.

Music?

Larry Polansky

"What is music?" seems like a simple question, but it turns out to be deeper than we think. This is odd. As far as we know, music is something all human cultures share. We evolved to do it. But we can't say exactly what it is. Trying to answer this question has inspired new ways of thinking about music, using ideas from physics, psychology, art, language, the mind, neuroscience, mathematics, evolution, philosophy, history, and culture. As the inspiration for so many interesting and beautiful ideas and activities, it's no wonder that so many of us are happy to spend a lifetime in its pursuit, and in its active practice and contemplation.

Although we have difficulty articulating an answer to our question, we generally recognize music when we hear it. Music is singing (in the shower, in a choir, to yourself while walking in the woods); drumming (on whatever you like); blowing through hollow things (dried kelp, ocarinas, kazoos, silver flutes, euphoniums); plucking and bowing strings (and hammering them, like on a cimbalom or a piano); even banging rocks together. We do "it" in nearly every conceivable way, all over the world, and we have been doing it since the first Neanderthals began chanting just to say, "Hey, we're in this together," and, maybe more importantly, "Our chant is different (and better) than those other folks' chant over in the next valley."

One could also say that music is something made and "listened to" by many other species, from gibbons and whales, to birds and frogs, and down to bugs. We even refer to the music of nonbiological entities: the music of the spheres, the night, nature, and the city. Music is the "food of love" and "soothes the savage breast." Why is it so hard to define?

One reason, perhaps, is that one person's music is another person's noise, just as one person's language is another's gibberish. We all hear things differently depending on culture, upbringing, language. When B. B. King plays guitar,

Ella Fitzgerald sings, an orchestra performs a Beethoven symphony, Esperanza Spaulding plays the bass, and U. Shrinivas plays the mandolin, I "know" that it's "music." And most of the time we generally agree, though we may not like or understand some particular kind.

But we don't agree *all* the time. Way back when, people said "rock 'n' roll" was not music. Today, many feel similarly about hip-hop, modern jazz, and twentieth-century classical music. The composer Edgard Varèse famously stated that "music is organized sound," but there are those, almost a century later, who still wouldn't call *his* "organized sound" music. When someone says (usually angrily): "That's not music!" they mean that they have some idea what music *is*, and they are pretty sure they're not hearing it.

Ironically, because music is so important to us, we want and need it to be familiar and understandable. If it isn't, it can't comfort us, evoke a memory, make us cry or smile. Music from a culture not one's own can be unsettlingly unfamiliar. The first time I heard Beijing Opera, I thought, "What's going on here? It sounds like a lot of banging and shrieking!" But I reminded myself that millions of people understand and love this extraordinary music—which is as virtuosic, complex, nuanced, and beautiful as any music on the planet.

All music *organizes sound*—pitch, color, rhythm, loudness, and orchestration—but different musics do so in very different ways. We usually like the music we've grown up with and become accustomed to, and dislike that to which we're not accustomed. But that's not the music's fault! Whenever we say, "I don't like [pick a kind of music]" we might keep in mind that somebody else does like it—very much.

The composer John Cage, along with other twentieth-century composers like Varèse, Lou Harrison, and Johanna Beyer who embraced percussion music, demonstrated that anything humans *intend* as music—noise, percussion, factory sounds, ambient environmental sounds—can be heard and understood as such. How we *hear* something is the important part. If we *choose* to listen to something as music—the antiphonic dawn chorus of the birds, the heterophony of a frog pond, the monotony of our neighbor yacking loudly on his cell phone, the cacophony of a chain saw, the regular polyphony of traffic sounds—it *is* music.

Is Music a Language?

Some people believe that music is a language. Languages and music certainly have a lot in common, in terms of both their medium (usually sound) and human evolution. Even so, I *don't* think music is a language. I'll explain why.

Clearly, music has *meaning* and *communicates*. Plato warned that of all art forms, music has the singular power to move us immediately and deeply. Music evokes feelings, associations, and states of mind and being that are hard, maybe even impossible, for language to call forth. Music triggers memories and creates moods, ones that neuroscientists are now just beginning to be able to measure. It compels you to dance, and enhances the meanings of the other arts. There are even common, probably cross-cultural and evolutionary characteristics of music that stimulate near universal responses. For example, slow, low, and quiet music tends to be associated with sadness and "negative" affects, while fast high, and loud music tends to be "positive," exciting.

But music has little, if any *specific semantic meaning* on its own in the way that natural languages do. "Semantics" means that individual units mean something "specific," or denote something. The word "cat" is a semantic representation of something that *is a cat*. But the sound of a 440 cps (cycles per second) tone itself denotes nothing specific, even though we can describe it (in English), specifically (in fact we just did, acoustically, but it's also colloquially called "middle A" on the piano).

This argues against music being what we generally think of as a language. But even more importantly, a language should be able, at least, to say: "There's a cat!" and hopefully, "There was a cat!" and "There was a black cat!" and "There was a big black cat on the couch!" and "There was a big fat lazy black cat named Max on that couch my Aunt Agnes gave me two days ago (I think!) sitting on my newspaper."

This is sometimes called (ironically, for music) *compositional meaning*. When specific meanings are put together in specific ways (syntaxes), they mean something more complex than just the sum of individual meanings. Imagine someone saying to you: "cat was two couch lazy big a named ago think . . .":—devoid of syntax, it's just a string of individual meanings, not very communicative. Natural human languages communicate complex, specific ideas by combining semantics and syntaxes. Wonderfully, we can tell when those syntaxes are being violated or toyed with, as in poetry or humor (did my Aunt Agnes give me the couch two days ago, or . . . ?). That's also, of course, somewhat true in music—we can usually detect a wrong note in a familiar song, or the difference between a Mozart and a Bartok string quartet, by the *relationships* of component parts, even though the component nonsemantic parts—pitches, rhythms, instruments—are more or less the same.

Languages also have verbs, nouns, modifiers, tenses, and pronouns. Languages are also *recursive*—one can embed and embed and embed (as in the above "cat" example). Music doesn't really have *any* of these features. You can't sit down at a piano and play "There's a [black] cat!" (You can't even play: "Cat!") unless you say ahead of time that what you're about to play means: "There's a cat!"

So music is not what we generally think of as a language. That's okay. In fact, to me, it's one of music's great virtues. The lack of semantics makes music unique and beautiful. Perhaps that's what Plato was worried about: music skips over the specifics of language and reaches a deeper realm of our consciousness, one that is intuitive, emotive, and physically powerful. It can't tell a story, it can't represent *anything*. But it can affect us in ways that words and pictures might not.

Maybe that's why the other arts often aspire to it. Poets talk about making their poetry musical. Painting, dance, and film often attempt abstraction, trying to move past representation, thinking "musically." Even when other art forms are abstract, we impose semantic perception on them. Is that a cat in the middle of the Jackson Pollock? Is choreographer Twyla Tharp's duet about two people falling in and out of love, or about two stars orbiting each other in space? The dance may not be "about" anything, but we can't help but try and discern a narrative in it.

Music refers to itself: form in time. We perceive, attend to, and are transfixed by its structure, its order. Music transports us to a different world, one in which there is *only* form, structure, and order. Abstract by nature, unlike most other arts it doesn't need to *attempt* nonrepresentation. As a composer, music theorist, performer, and teacher, this is one of the things that attracts me so much to its study, creation, and making. The meaninglessness is fascinating, endlessly engrossing, and magical. What else in human experience does this? It moves us, powerfully, and does so in ways we can't explain.

Talking about Music

But music is hard to talk about! We can discuss music's relationship to other music, historically and stylistically. We can try to articulate what's cool about Stravinsky, Balkan singing, or an Earl Scruggs banjo solo, or what makes a Carla Bley tune so surprising. We hear Jimi Hendrix play guitar, and try to figure out how to do that ourselves (good luck with that!). We can analyze and teach the harmonies, form, and orchestration of a Beethoven symphony, and try to explain, rationally, why it has the effect it does on us. Musicians, in all cultures, have specialized vocabularies. So do the other arts, but they always have the option of referring to things that are more concrete, more comprehensible, of real meaning ("The plot of that movie makes no sense!," "The characters in that novel are unrealistic!," "That doesn't look *anything* like a sunset!"). What kinds of things do we say about music? "That made me want to dance [cry, shout, make love . . .]!" But music has no sunset, no *Nutcracker* dancing-about, no nefarious and ingenious plot twist, no gun sitting on the mantelpiece that needs to be fired in the second act—no anything but music. The composer Laurie Anderson famously said that "talking about music is like dancing about architecture"! While it has always seemed to me that dancing about architecture is a wonderful idea, I believe she meant that talking about music—ironically, what I'm trying to do in this essay—is somewhat futile. There's nothing to *refer* to.

Pure Music?

The vast majority of music ever made by humans is not what we might think of as "pure" music. It's not people sitting in concert halls listening to string quartets, but overwhelmingly more often associated with something else: dance, theater, ritual, film, storytelling, or social, cultural, and a myriad of quotidian events. Music accompanies almost everything that humans do—shopping, driving, working, going to the dentist, attending a political rally or sporting event, cooking, eating. It is ubiquitous in human society, but ironically, we seldom devote our complete attention to it.

Most often music is inextricably connected to words, in song. We even frequently use the words "music" and "song" interchangeably (my undergraduate students, for example, will often refer to "that song of Beethoven's" when they're talking about a symphony!). In some languages, including American Sign Language, the words (signs) for "music" and "song" are the same. Jazz, Indian raga, Korean Pansori, Central Javanese karawitan, Celtic fiddle tunes, classical music (of any culture), and other musics without accompanying texts are rarely just "sat and listened to." Most people don't have the time, economic luxury, or patience to sit and listen to a full North Indian raga, a long Central Javanese gamelan piece, a jazz performance, or a Mahler symphony.

We generally listen to music while doing or watching something else. Most people are bored by music that is not associated with other channels of meaning—complex music, following its own internal rules, can be difficult to "follow." How many people sit and just *listen* to Bach's *Goldberg Variations*, which many musicians (myself included) consider one of the most magnificent achievements ever? Music itself is wonderful and powerful and universal, but (sadly) it rarely seems to fully occupy us. We want words, pictures, and action. This is music's blessing and curse.

Music's Universals

Anthropologists, ethnomusicologists, cognitive scientists, music historians, composers, and philosophers have long grappled with the question of what constitutes music. Musicologists study the history of music and musical styles, both ancient and recent, and more and more, how social and political factors affect it. Ethnomusicologists study music in culture—from both an insider and an outsider perspective. Music theorists try to explain the structure and form of music, both stylistically and, more recently, by working with psychologists, neuroscientists, and even mathematicians, to figure out how music perception and cognition help determine the music humans make. Almost all music, in today's world, is impacted by digital technology, so the study, transmission, and aesthetics of music are inextricably related to engineering and scientific ideas. Computation is now an important partner in musicology, composition, performance, production—every aspect of music.

I believe, though, that there *are* some quasi-universals of music that we *can* point to, things that are part of most of us (humans) call music? If some "sound in time" has at least a few of these universals, we might reasonably call it music. Some common ones are:

1. Music is made by *people, usually in groups*. Facility in a particular music-making activity (synchronous chanting, for instance) or familiarity with a musical culture ("I love emo," singing the "Star-Spangled Banner" at a Yankees game, clapping along with a band, an AC/DC T-shirt) helps to determine how people identify themselves and are identified by others as members of a group. We sing "Happy Birthday," "Auld Lang Syne," and "We Shall Overcome" together to express common—sometimes ordinary, sometimes extraordinary—sentiments. Political chants exploit simple musical rhythms ("Hell, no! / We won't go!"; "El pueblo, unido, jamás será vencido!") to unify large groups of people in a common goal. Cultures and groups define music in terms of styles, genres, instruments, and repertoires, as well as by where/how/why/when/by whom (professional/amateur? woman/man? socioeconomic class? age?). Within groups, different *forms* (song, symphony, ladrang, space-jam, chant, round, raga, hornpipe . . .) are used to organize and subcategorize musical repertoires.

2. Music is made most often by the *voice*, less often accompanied by *instruments*, and far less often by instruments alone. People work, tell each other things, fall in love, and (historically, about half of us) put babies to sleep. Cultures have their own lullabies, work songs, story songs, and love songs. These songs (and many others) are made by the human voice, usually simply, naturally, and unadorned.

3. *Pitch*, the relationships of frequencies to each other, plays an important organizational role in music. Pitch is generally limited and organized by some concept of *scale*: a set of pitches with an associated hierarchy. Scales are closely associated with what we often call *keys* or *modes*. For example, we say that a piece of music that uses the notes C-D-E-F-G-A-B is in the key of C major (C being the most "important" pitch). There are uncountably many scales and subscales (modes) around the world. The use of different scales is often what gives music its tonal character. Scales are, acoustically, a predefined set of frequency relationships, generally with some relation to simple whole-number ratios (see point 5 below). The frequency interval 2:1, or *octave* (or something close to that), is most commonly the frequency ratio at which scales repeat. Usually, two pitches separated by a ratio of 2:1 (or 1:2) are given the same name (such as, for example, all the different "C"s on a piano).

4. Some concept of *pulse*, or tempo, or regular *accents*, seems to be a nearly universal. Divisions of this pulse tend to be at simple numerical ratios (see point 5 below).

5. *Simple integer ratios.* This is perhaps the most subtle idea in the list, and points to the evolved and/or learned connections between our brains and music. *We prefer simple ratios to more complex ones.* Ratios like 2:1, 3:2, 4:3, and 5:4 predominate in both the pitch and temporal domains, across cultures. The simpler the ratio (smaller numbers, smaller primes, smaller exponents of those primes), the easier our brains can understand it. For example, 3:2 is simpler than 7:5 (3 and 2 are smaller primes than 7 and 5), and 9:8 is simpler than 27:16 ($9 = 3^2$ is simpler than $27 = 3^3$). This is most apparent in common rhythmic relationships. As an exercise, try tapping a regular pulse in one hand, and dividing that pulse in half with the other. That's easy. Now divide that regular pulse into three parts (harder). Now try to divide three pulses in one hand with five in the other! Ratios like 2:1 and 3:2 are more common than ones like 11:7 and 13:12. This is true in both rhythmic and pitch relationships. The simplest ratio, other than 1:1, is 2:1, which might explain the near universality of the octave's importance. This is of course not to say that musicians aren't capable of performing extremely

simple question

FIGURE I *Simple Question* (a round)

complex rhythms, and working with extraordinarily difficult pitch material. In fact, the intensive training that performers and composers undergo, which takes different forms (conservatories, apprenticeships) in different cultures, says a great deal about how much effort and commitment it takes to extend our basic predilection—for simplicity—to the exquisite flowering of complex and varied musics that humanity has produced.

A Music Primer

Now that we've talked about what music *can* be, some of its universals, and the relationship between music, language, and other art forms, let's address our initial question with an example—a piece of music.

I'd like, at this point, to play some music for you, instead of trying to describe it. But I can't, so I'll do my best by using *musical notation.* Throughout history, and across cultures, musical notation has taken and still takes many different forms. Most music is not notated at all. People generally learn music by listening to it. What we choose to write down, either for archival or mnemonic purposes, or so that others can replicate it, tells us something about what we consider important.

The form of notation above may be familiar to you: it's the one used in what we call (anachronistically and problematically) "Western music." If you can read it, try to sing or play the music on an instrument. If not, don't worry—you'll get the idea.

The vertical dimension, the five *ledger* lines, is called a *staff.* The placement of dots on the lines denote *pitch*—how high or low the sound is. In this system of notation, there are seven names for pitches (the white notes on a piano: C-D-

E-F-G-A-B). This is called a *C major* or *diatonic scale*. Five more pitches (the black notes on the piano), *flats* and *sharps,* are called *accidentals,* for a total of twelve. Most musical cultures—some with notation systems, some not—have names for pitches, which differ from culture to culture.

But pitch is not simply vertical. There are complex pitch organizations that we refer to by words like "harmony," "scale," and "mode." As I noted above, pitches are almost always *organized hierarchically* into scales. This means that different notes have different functions and are ranked, roughly, in importance. In *Simple Question*, for example, a slightly unusual mode is used, called G *mixolydian* (a famous example of this mode is its use in the Beatles song "Norwegian Wood"). This means it starts on the note G, and the notes are related to each other in a specific way, called *mixolydian*. Mixolydian is called a *mode*, because it's exactly like a *major scale* with a different hierarchy—in this case a C major scale (C-D-E-F-G-A-B-C, or the white notes on the piano) but starting and ending on G.

The horizontal dimension is rhythm—how time is divided up. In this example rhythm is described as *durations*—how long a note lasts before the next one enters. In this example there are only two different durations: quarter-notes ("What time . . .") and eighth-notes ("does the").

The idea that music, inscribed by notation, can be arranged along a horizontal axis is important: *Music is sound in time.* But just two simple dimensions—pitch and duration—are not enough. They don't, of course, explain everything, or even close. You can't write down the *sound* of Emmy Lou Harris's voice, but you can do a serviceable job of writing down the pitches and rhythms she sings. Notating only two parameters is shorthand, leaving much to be determined by performance and imagination.

Music need not even have recognizable pitches, or a fixed rhythm. Hand clapping, drums, even recited poetry, are all musical. We could also sing the pitches "out of time." Try that with a familiar song, like "Happy Birthday." Then just clap the rhythm. A familiar song is recognizable when either the pitches or the rhythms are left out (but not both).

Many other things crucially contribute to what this music actually sounds like. *Sound quality*, sometimes called *timbre*—the difference between one sound or instrument and another—is significant in our perception and performance of music. We can sing in a whisper or a yodel, through our nose, or in full voice. *Simple Question* might be sung by a woman, a man, a child, or played on a bassoon, sarod, and kazoo. Loudness, which is inextricably related to timbre, is also a salient artistic and perceptual parameter.

But certain transformations of these components won't change our perception of the music very much. Loudness is a good example: whether a song is sung a bit louder or softer doesn't affect how we "recognize" it. Similarly, and more interestingly, we can sing fast or slow, changing the underlying pulse, or *tempo*, while retaining the proportional relationships between durations. It's the same song. We can likewise *transpose* the pitches by some fixed frequency ratio (not adding frequencies, but multiplying and dividing them, like we did with durations), keeping the relationships the same. This is called changing the *key*. We still don't care—it's the same song.

All of these things—timbre, tempo, pitch transposition, loudness—and others are fundamental components of human music. The difference in the way these components are employed has much to do with what we call *style*. Javanese gamelan uses different pitches than Mozart piano music, as well as different timbres and rhythmic ideas. Yet while these two musics don't sound very similar to us, they have a lot in common, marking them both as music. The vast variety of the world's musics demonstrates the huge possibilities in how these fundamental components can be explored.

Music is the organization of these *components* in time. We don't just hear and remember music from moment to moment. Instead we perceive larger structures—form—over time. When we call something a twelve-bar blues, disco tune, sonata, jam, lied, fanfare, techno-groove, Sousa march, lullaby, folksong, fugue, New Age instrumental, hornpipe, rag, (Central Javanese) ladrang, hip-hop song, (Italian or Beijing) opera, ballad, bluegrass song, oratorio, chant, (Korean) pansori, hymn, or swing tune, we're usually talking about *form*—what happens musically, in many ways (harmony, rhythm, melody) over relatively large timescales. Form might be extremely simple—a repeating rhythm or melody (like an R&B riff, or a fiddle tune with an AABB repeat pattern)—or highly complex—like a baroque fugue or Indian raga. But all music has form, because it takes place in time.

Let's consider the *form* of *Simple Question*. It has a name: *round*. In a round (also called a *canon*), voices follow one another, repeating exactly, at some time interval. A round combines multiple lines into a texture where, we hope, they'll sound good together. This is called *polyphony*. In a round, one melody recombines with itself to form a more complex musical idea.

In *Simple Question* when the first voice arrives at the second measure, the second voice begins singing the first, and the third voice does the same thing with relation to the second voice. If we were to write down what is heard, it would look like figure 2.

simple question
(3 voice realization)

FIGURE 2 *Simple Question* realization in three parts

A fundamental and universal musical idea of this form is *imitation*. The musicians and listeners learn as they go! Someone sings something, and then someone else sings the same thing. Imitation is important, nearly universal, in music. And, as mentioned above, it's the main mechanism that people have always used to learn music—hearing it over and over.

The study of music is often the study of musical form. How do ideas get introduced and evolve? Do ideas introduced at the beginning return at the end? Do instruments or voices imitate, accompany, or oppose each other? Do they move in parallel, or in opposite and contrasting directions? Are there changes in density, in the amount of activity over some time span, in the tempo, in the dissonance or consonance of the material? Musicians are always inventing new forms and innovating new twists on old ones, as well as thinking about how to describe them. For a musician, working with form is like the way a writer develops characters and plot, or a painter plans out a canvas.

Coda

As you can see, we know a lot about what music is and isn't. We know what we generally mean when we talk about music, and what most music contains.

We've seen ways in which it intersects other kinds of disciplines, and with that we've seen that there are all kinds of ways to study it and create it. But we still haven't definitively answered our titular question.

Over the course of his life, John Cage was asked that same question many times. He offered several different answers, my favorite of which is simply "Work." I like to think Cage meant: "It's what I do." But he might have also been implying a kind of physics-oriented meaning, as in "Music is a force that displaces an object." In fact, the composer James Tenney used to joke that some aliens visited Earth, and they were able to explain why we eat, sleep, procreate, and make war, but there was one thing they couldn't understand: "Every so often they come together and vibrate the air!" Music moves us, and we need to be moved by it. Nothing else moves us in quite the same way, whatever way that is.

But . . . finally, I'd like to offer a simple definition, one whose veracity I'm quite certain of. Music is fun—to make, to listen to, to experience in every way. It feels good and it makes others feel good. It rarely does any harm (unless it's too loud, incites us to war, unites us toward some malevolent end, or encourages us subliminally to shop), and it seems to do a lot of good. Whether you're banging a drum, playing a koto, whistling, singing along embarrassingly with the radio at a red light, or playing ecstatically loud on a '57 Fender Telecaster electric guitar (my preference), you're doing something fine, joyful, beautiful, and fundamentally human. Go do it.

Philosophy?

Adina L. Roskies

If you ask one hundred philosophers "What is philosophy?" you will get at least one hundred different answers. "Wait!," you gasp in astonishment, but not because there is disagreement about what philosophy is. Your surprise is that there *are* one hundred philosophers to ask! Aren't all philosophers dead? Isn't philosophy ancient history? Well, I'll let you in on a secret, and it appears to be a pretty deeply guarded secret, at least until you get to college and maybe even beyond. Here's the secret: philosophy is a discipline that is alive and well, whose diverse practitioners engage with difficult, important, and interesting questions (some old, some new). Lots of people—women, men, young, old, people of color, Australians, Americans, and even a fair number of Icelanders—have jobs as philosophers! They are pushing the boundaries of knowledge even as you read this. And the things they think and write about may be as current and contemporary as stem cell research and voting rights, or as old and venerable a topic as *what there is*.

A lot of philosophy is geared toward figuring out what basic things to believe. And in that respect philosophy is really concerned with the fundamentals of all sorts of areas of inquiry. For virtually any field of study, for instance, there is (or could be) a corresponding area of philosophy, one that questions the assumptions that aren't usually questioned by those working in that field, or one that tries to figure out what logically follows from the accepted or potential doctrines in that field, or one that offers methodological critiques of the ways in which knowledge is sought and established in that field. Along these lines, *philosophy of biology*, *philosophy of physics*, and *philosophy of language* are all thriving areas of philosophy. In philosophy of biology, for example, philosophers argue about what natural selection operates over (what are the units of selection—are they genes, organisms, species, or populations?), whether the notion of "species" picks out a natural kind or meaningful division in the world, or whether there are any meaningful distinctions among people that correspond to the concept of "race." Answers to these questions could have far-reaching impact, for example on social structure and human relations, on science, and on the environment.

How can it then be, you might ask, that one hundred different philosophers will give you one hundred different answers to the question of what philosophy is? After all, it's about figuring out what to believe! Would you be even more disturbed if the one hundred philosophers gave you one hundred different answers to any philosophical question? Because they might! Isn't there one right answer to any question? Well, that itself is a philosophical question. And you will learn if you study philosophy, a lot depends on the assumptions you make, and the kinds of things you take to be fundamental. You'll also learn that philosophers can and will disagree about all sorts of things, so that even when they agree on the answer to a question, they may disagree about the *reasons* for which they agree! And for a philosopher, that is almost as deep a disagreement as the disagreement about the answer.

This may all sound so confusing! So let's take a step back, talk about just how philosophers approach their work, and then talk a bit about the kinds of questions they work on and think about. You'll see that it's an amazing world of ideas.

Methods

One thing (most) philosophers do share is a commitment to reasoned argument: we ought to believe things because we have good reason to believe them, and there are some rules about what good reasoning is. *Logic*, which I'm sure you've heard of, is a set of rules or recipes for how to reason so that you don't end up believing falsehoods when you've started out believing truths. If you follow the rules of logic (which really is both a branch of philosophy and a branch of mathematics) you can be sure that your conclusions will be true if your premises are. But how do you know whether your premises are true? That's a really hard question. Philosophers use a lot of tools to interrogate their assumptions, to try to determine whether things that seem true really are true. But this kind of reasoning is not iron-clad: no recipe can be followed that will ensure that your premises are true. However, with a little care you can increase your chances.

Philosophers prize *clarity*. Just like Horton the Elephant (of Dr. Seuss's Whoville fame), we strive to mean what we say and say what we mean. One kind of clarity philosophy seeks is clarity about the meanings of the terms or concepts we use. So a lot of philosophical effort is directed at trying to explain what we intend by the words and concepts we are using. To that end, a classic task for the philosopher is to give what is called "an analysis" or to engage in *conceptual analysis*. This involves reflecting on what our concepts refer to, and what their boundaries are. Let's try a quick example—how you would define a "game"? More precisely, what is the concept GAME such that for any given thing, we can determine whether or not it is an example of a game? Well, some but not all games are played with others; some but not all follow rules; some require props and others don't. What are the necessary and sufficient features? Give it some thought; it's not as simple as you might think, and the careful articulation of where the trouble spots are can have deep implications about a host of other ideas and even behaviors.

Historically, this kind of analysis was thought to be achievable merely by thinking, and thus could be undertaken from your couch or armchair. In some quarters, however, philosophers are increasingly skeptical about whether analyses of this sort are possible: first of all, whether any appreciable number of concepts (or any at all!) can be delineated by necessary and sufficient conditions, and second, whether clarification of concepts can really be done well from the armchair. A new but controversial trend in philosophy is called *experimental philosophy*, which some think is an oxymoron but others herald as a healthy methodological fix.

Experimental philosophy applies empirical methods to test philosophical intuitions, rather than relying on intuitions as bedrock for philosophical theorizing. Experimental philosophy has challenged some of the most well-accepted philosophical analyses to date, such as the analysis of knowledge as true justified belief (we explore this a bit below). Another very intriguing direction of work has been its use to investigate beliefs regarding free will, and, in particular, whether or not most people believe we have it. This usually is related to whether they believe free will is impossible (*incompatibilism*) or possible (*compatibilism*) in a deterministic universe, and whether they think the universe is deterministic. While this may seem extraordinarily ethereal, remember that much of science is based on finding laws of nature, down to the scale of the chemistry and physics that enables thought! So there is much to think about around human behavior and determinism. What experimental philosophy has found is that people's intuitions about free will tend to be unstable in a way that is unexpected, yet makes sense of the claims from both sides that their view is the intuitive or "folk" view.

The controversial status of experimental philosophy within the field illustrates that philosophy is a field in which one of the central problems is precisely the question of how to do philosophy! Experimental methods are new to the field, but other tools have been around much longer. A mainstay of the philosophical tool kit is the *counterexample*. Philosophers will often provide an argument for some positive claim, whether that be the analysis of a concept, some relation between concepts, or some theoretical explanation of a phenomenon. Others will try to undermine the claim, to show it to be false. This is really part of the scientific method: if we try to falsify what we believe to be true and can't, that should increase our confidence in the truth of our belief. The *counterexample* is aimed at demonstrating the falsity of a claim by producing an instance that seems to satisfy all the conditions of the claim but for which the conclusion is false. So, for example, suppose one claims that the concept BACHELOR can be analyzed as "unmarried man." A philosopher might suggest that this cannot be a correct analysis, since there is at least one counterexample: the pope is an unmarried man, but is arguably not a bachelor.

Although this particular counterexample is rather simple and straightforward, some counterexamples and philosophical arguments require the concoction of very strange or particular circumstances, the kinds of circumstances one cannot hope to observe in nature. They may involve notions of possibility, counterfactual conditions (those that could have happened but did not), or other judgments about the nonactual. These constructions are called *thought experiments*, for we try them out by imagining them, rather than by really carrying them out, as a scientist might test a scientific claim. The thought experiment is perhaps the most paradigmatic philosophical tool, and it has been the target of many a methodological critique. Perhaps the best-known and most celebrated thought experiment was one posed by physicist Albert Einstein. He asked himself what would happen if he were to ride on a train going at the speed of light. Working through this hypothetical and physically impossible scenario led him to develop the Theory of Relativity. Although his domain was physical theory, his method was distinctly philosophical (indeed, physics used to be called "natural philosophy"). Thought experiments, like all power tools, must be wielded with care, but used appropriately they can change the way we see the world.

At the heart of the thought experiment is the question "What if?" From that first question, the thought experiment will initiate a cascade of ideas whose implications may dramatically disturb a seemingly stable web of beliefs: Suppose I take some claim to be true: What other claims can be deduced from that (given my other assumptions), and how well does it fit with the other things I believe? Does it lead to contradictions with other things I think to be true? If so, which claim is likely to be the correct one? To return to Einstein, relativity was impossible to test given the scientific tools available at the time. But Einstein realized his theory implied that light would bend in a strong enough gravitational field, and he also realized the solar system would give him just the test he needed during an eclipse: the position of a faraway star would appear to change if the light it emitted passed by the sun. When an eclipse did occur, scientists were able to test his theory, which passed with flying colors. Like Einstein, philosophers try to work out what must follow from a claim or theory they think is plausibly true. Unlike Einstein, philosophers rarely have tests they can actually carry out; rather, they evaluate the plausibility of a claim largely on the basis of how well it sits with other claims the philosopher has good reason to believe.

A Few Philosophical Problems and Areas of Philosophical Inquiry

One of the attractive things about being a philosopher is that it allows you to retain a childlike perspective of curiosity and tenaciousness. Remember when you responded "Why?" to every answer your parents gave you? Constantly questioning the reasons given for things tends to fall out of favor with nearby adults at a relatively early age, and in some ways perhaps that is a good thing. But, in consequence, perhaps we all too readily accept what we are told, and stifle a curiosity and wonder that is a natural characteristic of our species by becoming too practical, too instrumentally minded, too accepting of authority, or perhaps just too embarrassed to press on. In philosophy it is always okay to dig deeper, to press harder, to question things that seem obvious. This insistent curiosity is at the heart of many deep problems in philosophy.

I remember, as a kid, wondering what color was, and puzzling over whether the experience of another child looking at the same object I was looking at was actually the same kind of experience as mine. Did she see the red apple in precisely the way I did (as a bright red color), or did she see colors differently? Did that very same apple look to her to have the color a blueberry seems to have to me? And if it did, could we ever find out? For, I reasoned, if she was taught to identify the apple's color with the label "red," then even if she experienced redness as I experience blueness, she'd call experiences of blueness "red." If we asked her, she'd say that the apple is red, regardless of how she saw it. So we couldn't find out just by asking her. Experiences seem to be strangely private: no one else can have ours! Wouldn't it be amazing if people across the world (not to mention animals) all experienced the world qualitatively differently, but just systematically called these different experiences by common names? Are there ways we could tell if this were the case? Is this color inversion even a coherent possibility? What would be a convincing answer to these questions, one way or another? As it turns out, this childhood reverie is actually recognized as a deep philosophical problem called the "Inverted Spectrum" problem. It concerns one of the perennially difficult topics in *philosophy of mind*: the nature of consciousness.

Another interesting illustration of the problems consciousness introduces is due to a thought experiment that posits the notion of a philosophical "zombie." A philosophical zombie is not the scary walking dead popular in horror movies and TV shows, but a less sinister but perhaps more troubling entity: the normally-behaving-but-not-conscious person. This person is not unconscious, in the sense of asleep or dormant. Instead it is mentally inert. The thought experiment asks you to imagine an exact physical duplicate of yourself who behaves exactly like you in all situations, but for whom it is *not like anything* to be them (think: a robot, an empty shell, an automaton). Your zombie doppelganger has no experiences, acts as if he feels things but does not really feel anything, has no inner life. So here's the first question: If such a thing is imaginable, is it possible? That is, does the fact that you can imagine it (whether or not you can in fact imagine it is itself a philosophical dispute!) imply that it is not necessarily false? And if it is possible, then might it be actual? Consider this unnerving possibility: that everyone around you is in fact a philosophical zombie: they merely act as if they are conscious, have feelings, enjoy the kind of mental life that you enjoy. This position is called *solipsism*: the view that no one else really exists (or has a mind) except yourself. After all, you are the only one for which you have that special kind of access—call it "first-person access"—to a mental life, and thus the only one for which you have convincing evidence of a mental life.

Of course, if you are willing to discount that possibility and accept that those around you are as conscious as you are, what is the reason for your acceptance? It is not evidence, for you have no evidence to distinguish those people from philosophical zombies. By hypothesis, both behave the same, and you only have access to behavior. But then what? By analogy with you? Other people are similar in shape, or in looks. But is that analogy strong enough to base your belief on? Why should looks matter? Because of shared biology? If so how far does it go? Monkeys are similar in many capacities and in much of their biology.

What about dogs? Rats? Octopuses? If it is biology, what is it that biology could possibly do that could make it the case that some brains have minds and some do not? (Here is one place where philosophy meets neuroscience.) Perhaps we need to then attribute consciousness all the way down the phylogenetic ladder. Or perhaps it is just something that goes along with a certain kind of collection of behavioral capacities, so that the notion of a zombie doesn't really make sense. But if that is the case, then an artificial robot that is complex enough should also be attributed consciousness. That would raise all sorts of ethical issues, and indeed one day it may! And as you can see, just a little philosophical theorizing can then connect to a variety of real-world issues, such as the ethics of eating animals, the possibility of conscious machines, and the question of what personhood is.

Here's another puzzle that used to keep me up at night. Sometimes you have a dream, and in that dream the things that happen to you seem real, even if they are—from our awake perspective—crazy and clearly dreamlike. It seems, then, that what we take to be reality is relative to our perspective, and some perspectives may not enable us to tell whether what we believe to be reality really is reality. But if we can't tell in a dream that we are dreaming and that what we dream is not real, who is to say that our entire lives aren't themselves just the extended dream-story of ourselves or even some other dreamer (maybe God?), and no more real than the dreams we have at night? Now, I suspect that many kids think about this same puzzle at some point in their lives, though most of them go on to replace that question with other more pressing things, like whether their favorite football team will make it to the playoffs, or what time *The Simpsons* is on, or how they are going to fill out their tax form by April 15. The writers of the movie *The Matrix* certainly thought about it.

Imagine my surprise when I discovered that some of the most famous philosophers actually wrote about precisely this question, and formulated entire philosophies around it! René Descartes, one of the central figures of the Enlightenment, used the realization that in dreams we don't know we are dreaming to call into question all sorts of beliefs that seem self-evident to us (a position called *skepticism*), and this pushed him to look for certain knowledge: things that couldn't be doubted even if we were dreaming. Descartes's desire to base all knowledge on indubitable premises (a form of *foundationalism*) led him ultimately to the claim he is most known for: "I think, therefore I am." For although it is possible to doubt the truth of many of our beliefs and the veridicality of our perceptions, Descartes reasoned that if we think we are thinking, then certainly something is thinking, and if something thinks, it must exist. We may not know what we are or what is real, but we can be certain that we are a thinking thing. Descartes's thinking formed the basis of a view about the nature of mind called *dualism*, the view that the mind is a different kind of thing than physical stuff. Cartesian dualism remained the dominant view on the metaphysics of mind for several centuries.

Only slightly less famous than Descartes is the philosopher George Berkeley, who did my childhood self one better by hypothesizing not just that *I* am a figment of God's imagination or dream, but that *everything that exists* is just an idea in the mind of God. This view, *idealism*, explains the whole world by reference to God's goodness and power. It is an example of metaphysical explanation. Questions about what the real nature of the world around us is—the most foundational questions about the world—are questions in *metaphysics*: What is there? What are objects? Is there a God? How, if the physical world is governed by natural law, and we are physical objects, can we have free will? Metaphysics is so fundamental Aristotle called it "first philosophy."

Epistemology is another major branch of philosophy. Epistemology is concerned with knowledge, what we can know, and how we know it. Descartes's brilliant reasoning about certainty, and discussions of solipsism, are examples of epistemological inquiry. Before we figure out what we can know, we ought to have a sense of what it is to know something, or what the standards are for knowledge. When can we say we know something, rather than just believe it? I might believe many things, and even be sure that I am right, but we generally don't think that thinking something is true is enough to establish it as knowledge. The ancients believed the Earth was flat, but they didn't know the Earth was flat, because it is not (and was not) flat. What more is needed? Truth, of course. The problem with the Flat Earth belief is that it was false. So knowledge requires true belief. But is that enough? Suppose I ask you what time it is. You look at your watch, and it says 6:07. So you say it is 6:07. In fact, it always says 6:07 because it broke last week at 6:07. But on the basis of your claim I form the belief that it is 6:07. Coincidentally, it just happens to be 6:07. Here's a case in which I have a true belief, but it doesn't seem right to say that I know it is 6:07, because my belief is true just by chance. Well, from the time of some of the earliest Greek philosophers, we had a good answer. They suggested that in addition to the belief being true, I had to be justified in believing it.

So, for a really long time, it was just accepted that knowledge is justified true belief. I'm talking *thousands* of years. And then, in my own lifetime, a relatively unknown philosopher wrote a short paper that upended virtually everyone's acceptance of this analysis of knowledge! Edmund Gettier offered a few compelling counterexamples to this definition of knowledge, sketching cases in which it seemed clear that someone held a belief that X, that his belief was true, and that he was justified in believing it. Nonetheless, in these examples it seemed obvious that our imagined true believer didn't *know* X, because the justification he had was not connected with the truth of X in the right way. Let's take a look the scenario Gettier dreamed up.

Suppose Smith and Jones are both interviewing for a job in a very big company, say, one with offices around the world. Smith knows that Jones has a relative working in the company. In addition, the company boss has told Smith that Jones will get the job. Smith therefore believes that the man who will get the job has a relative working there. However, as it turns out, some last-minute office politics will result in the outcomes that Smith, not Jones, will get the job! Also, unbeknownst to Smith, in one of the far-flung offices he too has a relation! (maybe it's his mother's third cousin, but so be it . . .). So Smith's belief, that the man who will get the job has a relative working there, is true and justified (because he was justified in believing what the boss told him). Yet we wouldn't call it knowledge (even if it is true and justified), because Smith of course thinks the wrong man will get the job.

So, what do we make of this? We have to conclude that knowledge is in fact something other than true justified belief. We still don't quite know how to articulate what knowledge is! (An alternative conclusion is that we don't understand what justification is.) Although maybe we have taken what seems to be a step backward, we now know that we don't yet understand the nature of knowledge (though many philosophers have offered proposals for how to fill the gap). Discarding false beliefs and knowing what you don't know gets you closer to the truth, so we view Gettier's result as a type of progress.

These are some directions of philosophical inquiry, but there are others. Philosophy is not only about understanding the way the world is (and the justification of our thought processes). It is also about how to live in the world. For example, *ethics* is branch of philosophy that deals with the questions of what is good or what goodness is, how we should live, and what we owe to others. These questions are *normative* questions: they ask about what ought to be, what is valuable, what is beautiful—in other words, these questions recognize the legitimacy of standards. Normativity itself is a puzzle: how do we understand the fact that some things are better than others, and how can value arise in a world that, science tells us, is just matter and energy? Other ethical questions are pressing because they demand action on our parts: in living our lives we are presented with options with various consequences, and we have to make choices. We are beset by emotions, affected by relationships, acting in dynamic situations with other actors. In the face of all these influences, we have to make decisions, often ones with weighty consequences: What principles should we follow? How should we value things that seem hard to put a value on, such as friendship or truth? What is more important, saving a life or obeying a law? Is euthanasia permissible? Are we obligated to give to charity?

Ethical questions also shape and inform *political philosophy*: What would constitute a flourishing society and how best should a polity be structured? What forms of government best cohere with our values? What kind of moral and cultural education should we provide our children in order for them to live a good life? What rights do people have, and when can they be infringed? Even timely and very applied issues like the ethics of drone warfare are deeply philosophical.

Philosophy—Just Do It!

The scope of philosophy is as broad as human inquiry; it can keep you busy and interested for a lifetime. It gives you a chance to participate in an extended conversation that unfolds over centuries, about whatever turns you on—whether it be love, goodness, power, or what have you—with many of the greatest minds in human history. Philosophy is not just something you read, it is something you *do*: by getting some practice using tools of careful thought and joining the conversation, you can be a part of and contributor to the give-and-take of the greater human project of understanding and bettering the world.

WHAT IS

Physics?

Miles Blencowe

When I was a kid growing up with my younger brother Ben in Vancouver, Canada, our grandfather Sam would come and stay with us for extended periods. Ben and I liked to raid Granddad Sam's room for loose change in order to provide for our snack habit, taking advantage of the seemingly limitless supply of quarters, dimes, and nickels to be found on his desk and on the floor, a result of him regularly emptying his trouser pockets of all their contents. Also scattered on Granddad Sam's desk and floor were sheets and sheets of paper covered with strange squiggly-looking symbols. I remember asking Sam what the symbols were about, and he would chuckle and then proceed to read out some of the symbols at random: "Eat-a Jane-not . . ." Despite sounding like gobbledygook to our ears, somehow at the time I knew that one day when I grew up, I would be doing the same thing as Granddad Sam, deriving pleasure from writing strange symbols on paper.

Well, that is exactly what happened: like my grandfather, I am now what is called a *physicist*. And I have a daughter, Cecilia, who likes to ask me what the symbols mean on the pages of calculations to be found on my desk. Cecilia has just started to learn about physics at school and has been coming home with some very interesting questions. But the question she asks me most often has to do with a physics problem that I have been working on for a while now. In fact, as I sit at my desk writing this, she comes up behind me and taps me on the shoulder: "Daddy, have you figured out how to be in two places at once yet?"

In a nutshell, physicists use mathematics as a language to describe and understand the behavior of the matter and energy world around us. By the world around us, we mean the whole universe—from the microscopic realm of subatomic particles to the macroscopic realm of clusters of galaxies and everything in between. No single physicist has enough time in the day to work on understanding every aspect of the universe, so as a community we divide into smaller groups and, depending on our interests, concentrate on trying to gain a deeper understanding of some aspect of the world around us. Also, physicists tend to be either experimentalists—working with instruments like particle accelerators, telescopes, and other types of equipment to measure precisely the behavior of the world—or theorists like myself, who attempt to explain using mathematics as a precise language the results of experiments, as well as predict the outcomes of future experiments.

In order to illustrate what physics is, I would like to tell you about what I have been working on—that question Cecilia keeps teasingly bringing up, the one about being in two places at once. The one thing I won't do, however, is use the convenient language of mathematics to explain my work, since I suspect most of you are not used to applying the algebra you started learning in math class to describe the world around you as a practicing physicist does. This would be a little like showing you a music score and expecting you to hear the music in your head while reading the score. Instead, I will try to explain what physics is by using only words and analogies, and by concentrating on one example that I hope you will find as fascinating as I do! But it is worth bearing in mind that, just as it is much more efficient to play music on an instrument such as a violin by reading a score than reading a description of how the music is to be played in words, so too it is much more effective to give our physics explanations of the world around us in terms of mathematics than in words. So, keep learning and practicing your mathematics!

Let us begin with an analogy. Take a look at figure 1, which shows gently flowing water in a cool stream somewhere in the White Mountains of New Hampshire. Imagine that you yourself are squatting on the stream bank contemplating the flowing water, particularly the ripples on the surface of the water. As you look at the ripples, you wonder what causes them. This wondering is exactly what physicists do when they work on a project; a large part of being a physicist is about being curious and asking questions concerning the phenomena occurring around us that we would otherwise hardly give a second's thought and coming up with elegant mathematical explanations for the phenomena. Another thing a physicist does in order to try to answer a question is to consider a simpler situation that displays the same phenomenon for which the math explanation won't be as complicated. Once we understand the simpler situation, we can then work toward understanding the more complicated situation. Figure 2 also displays water ripples, but in a simpler controlled situation that was carried out by an experimental physicist in a laboratory using a long, shallow tray contain-

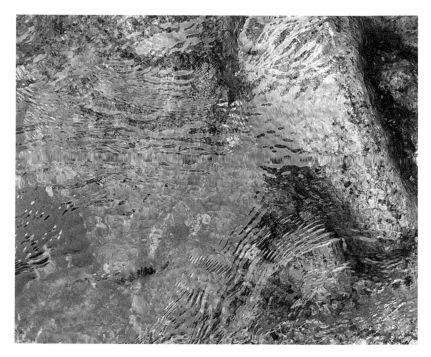

FIGURE 1 Water ripples

FIGURE 2 Water waves passing through two open channels and
interfering with each other

ing water. What figure 2 shows is a snapshot of water waves approaching two open channels or slits from the left. The approaching wave height maxima are illuminated as almost straight vertical bright lines. When the waves go through the two slits, they get scattered into circular waves: in the snapshot you can see successive wave height maxima to the right of the two slits as almost circular lines. But notice that the circular waves emanating from the two slits interfere with each other, creating alternating localized wave height maxima and minima appearing as bright and dark spots, respectively.

What this controlled experiment shows is that water waves passing through slits and also around objects interfere with each other, causing a ripple-like pattern. This in fact is exactly what is happening in the photo of the flowing stream in figure 1: the stones that can be seen just below the surface of the water cause the waves to scatter and interfere.

But water is not the only substance or form of energy that displays wave properties like interference—so do sound and light. Now with a little bit of equipment, you can demonstrate the wave nature of sound and light, working just like an experimental physicist does. I encourage you to try these experiments, because just as with math and the other sciences, it is most enjoyable to actively do physics. One way to demonstrate that sound has wavelike properties is to connect two small speakers to a laptop computer located in a reasonably large room, or, even better, outdoors. Place the speakers about a meter apart, both facing forward, and then, using any sound-generating software, get the computer to play through the speakers the musical note A above middle C, which corresponds to the frequency 440 Hertz (cycles per second). While the note is being played, walk around a few meters in front of the speakers, keeping one of your ears plugged, so that you can only hear through one ear. As you move around, you should notice that the sound alternates spatially between loud and quiet; in fact, if you mapped it out spatially, the sound intensity pattern would look almost identical to the water wave interference pattern shown in figure 2. What is happening is that sound emanates from both speakers as waves—compressions and expansions of the gas of air molecules—that interfere with each other. Almost exactly the same kind of mathematical expressions can describe the interfering sound waves as for the water waves. The only differences are in terms of the speed of sound in air versus the speed of surface waves on water, as well as the size of the waves, and these differences are not essential to the key understanding of the wave interference phenomenon.

One way to demonstrate the wave interference nature of light is to use a laser

FIGURE 3 Interference pattern for laser pointer light scattering either side
of a strand of human hair and projected onto a wall. Note the horizontal
bright bands separated by dark regions.

pointer (a green one is best because the light is usually brighter than for a red
laser pointer) and a strand of hair (yours, or a friend's if they don't mind!). Cut
a rectangular hole about a centimeter across and a few centimeters long in a
piece of cardboard and then tape the straightened-out hair to the cardboard so
that it splits the rectangular hole into two lengthwise slots either side of the hair.
In a darkened room and holding the piece of cardboard with a steady (!) hand,
direct the laser light onto the hair from a few centimeters away and look at the
resulting projected laser light pattern on a clear white wall a few meters in front
of you. If you can keep your hand steady enough, then you should see a pattern
on the wall like in figure 3. Notice the alternating thick bright and narrow dark
regions. This light interference intensity pattern is qualitatively the same as the
sound intensity pattern that you would experience by listening as you walk up
and down a straight line parallel to the two speakers.

With some simple geometry and algebra, it is possible to derive a mathematical formula that describes the distance between the light intensity maxima
projected onto the wall in terms of the distance between the wall and the hair
strand, the thickness of the hair, and the wavelength of the light. The wavelength
is defined to be the distance between light energy maxima of the incident laser
pointer light beam, like the distance between the water wave maxima of the
incident waves that you can see in figure 2 as parallel bright lines. Assuming you
know two of the quantities in the formula, for example the hair-to-wall distance
and hair thickness, you can use the measured distance between light intensity
maxima on the wall to determine the wavelength of the laser light, which turns
out to be about half a millimeter. Alternatively, if you already know the laser

light wavelength, you can use this experiment to determine the thickness of the strand of hair that you used!

At work in the examples described above are two aspects of physics that make it such a powerful way to understand and describe the world around us. One involves the use of experiments together with physics theories expressed in terms of math in order to determine properties of material and energy systems that otherwise would be practically impossible to know if we just used our own human senses: it is not easy to accurately measure the thickness of a human hair or the wavelength of light just by staring or squinting at the hair or the light beam! The second aspect we have already alluded to concerns a certain regularity (we might even go as far as to say a reasonableness) about nature in the sense that mathematical formulas can be written down that describe the behavior of very different material or energy systems.

Thus far we have seen that certain systems such as water, sound, and light have wavelike properties, and we can demonstrate these properties by doing relatively simple physics experiments. Now I am going to tell you about a different kind of system which under the right conditions also displays wavelike properties, but in a way that completely confounds our everyday view of the world—prepare to be shocked! What kind of system are we talking about? Well, really just very small particles such as electrons, atoms, or molecules. Let us begin by describing an experiment involving electrons that brings out their surprising wavelike nature. Remember that electrons are those negatively charged particles that orbit nuclei, making up atoms, and which can be set free from atoms if given enough energy (a process known as ionization). The experiment shown in figure 4 is in fact not much different from the two-slit experiments described above, although it requires much more sophisticated equipment to make it work and was carried out in a laboratory in Japan.

In the diagram showing the essential parts of the experimental apparatus, we have a source that shoots out a stream of electrons traveling at really large speeds of about 100,000 kilometers per second; with such speeds, you could travel around the Earth three times in one second! The electrons travel through a region called an electron biprism, which you can think of simply as two open holes or slits, much like the setup for the water waves or laser light described above. After passing through the biprism, the electrons hit a detection screen, producing bright spots that accumulate over time as more electrons hit the screen; about one electron hits the screen every one-hundredth of a second. In screen image (a), you just might be able to make out 7 spots—7 electrons; image

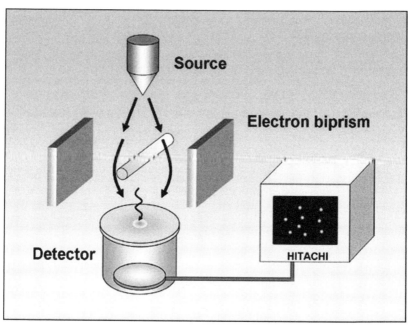

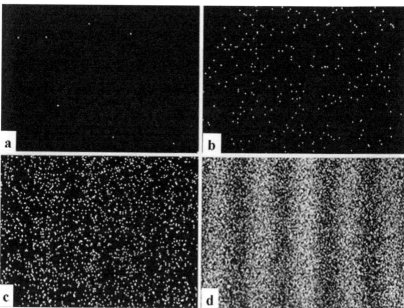

FIGURE 4 A two-slit interference experiment with single electrons.
Hitachi World-Wide Web Server, copyright Hitachi

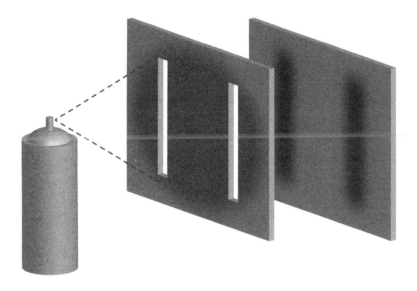

FIGURE 5 Spray-painting a screen through a two-slit stencil

(b) shows an accumulation of 270 electrons, image (c) an accumulation of 2,000 electrons, and image (d) an accumulation of 160,000 electrons. This last image, (d), represents an exposure time of about twenty minutes.

Now, when you look at, for example, image (a), you don't notice anything out of the ordinary; the electrons clearly appear to behave as particles, producing localized bright spots on the detection screen, much like hailstones landing on the ground during a hailstorm. Your intuition will tell you that those individual electrons arrived at the screen by going through either one or the other slit of the biprism—how could it be otherwise? But now shift your attention to image (d), showing the accumulation of a very large number of electrons (about 160,000 of them) hitting the detection screen. Notice the interference pattern? Such an interference pattern could not be produced if the electrons behaved like everyday particles such as sand grains, hailstones, pebbles, and other things that we are so familiar with. In particular, if the electrons really were traveling through either one or the other slit of the biprism, then we would get a pattern on the screen looking more like what I've drawn in figure 5 depicting the act of spray-painting a screen through a two-slit stencil.

When you use a spray-paint canister, you project a fine mist consisting of paint globules or particles about a thousandth of a millimeter (that is, a micrometer) in size. As we and graffiti artists alike all know so well, the image on the screen built up of spray-paint particles is just a projection of the two-slit stencil pattern. The particles must pass through either one slit or the other—there is no interference.

The only natural way explain the interference pattern in image (d) of figure 4 is to describe the electrons as *wavelike* in addition to being particle-like; depending on the situation, electrons can display both particle- and wavelike properties. As we mentioned at the beginning of this chapter, for a physicist the world around us is most effectively described using the language of mathematics. In the case of the electrons traveling from source to detector in the apparatus depicted in figure 4, we describe the electrons using the mathematics of waves, similar to the mathematics we use to describe light or water waves passing through two slits, or sound emitted from the two speakers. In the case of the electron, the wave flows through both slits, causing an interference pattern on the detection screen, just as observed in image (d).

However, the electron wave has a completely different interpretation than light, water, or sound waves. In the latter cases, the wave describes something material or energy-like that is changing at a given location in space over time, such as the water wave height, air pressure, or light energy density. For the electrons, on the other hand, we interpret the wave as giving the probability of detecting an electron at a given location in space and at a given time. It is important to ponder this radically different interpretation for a moment; the interpretation is about predicting the outcome of measurements, and not about some "real" material property of the electrons, such as what path they take. Our physics theory that mathematically describes material systems like electrons as waves and interprets the waves as giving probabilities to detect the electrons is called *quantum mechanics*.

And here is the shocking thing: while quantum mechanics can successfully predict the wave interference pattern made up of many single electron detection events shown in figure 4(d), it has nothing to say or tell us about how an individual electron traveled from the source to the screen; for the setup in figure 4 it makes no sense to ask, "Which slit did the electron go through?" The best way we can describe what happens in the biprism region is to say that the electron "went through both slits at once" or "was in two places at once"! The reason I have put these statements in quotes is that our thoughts and our language, which are based on our everyday observations of the world, are simply not capable of conceiving and describing the reality of the world of microscopic particles like electrons, which is why we physicists must resort to using mathematics as a language. In contrast to words and sentences, mathematics already has developed structure in the form of algebraic equations and expressions that are perfectly suited for describing the world around us, including the microscopic quantum world, whereas our everyday view of the world and our words for describing it fail us. It is remarkable that nature is so reasonable in allowing our mathematics (when suitably interpreted) to describe her innermost secrets.

From the above discussion, you may have gained the impression that the wave nature of electrons as described by quantum mechanics is only relevant in "exotic" experimental situations like the two-slit setup of figure 4. In fact, quantum mechanics is much more broadly relevant to explaining the world around us. One important consequence of the wave nature of atomic particles like electrons is that if you try to confine, say, an electron to a tiny region of space so that its location becomes more certain, then its motional (i.e., "kinetic") energy conversely becomes less certain; once you released the electron from its tight confinement, it would typically whizz away at high speeds. This is called *Heisenberg's uncertainty principle*, named after the physicist who first wrote down the algebraic expression for the principle. To give a somewhat loose and colorful analogy, this principle is a bit like confining a bee by cupping your two hands together. As you close your hands further, making the enclosure smaller and smaller, the bee gets more and more agitated, flying around the confined space at greater speeds and bouncing more rapidly off the insides of your hands. In nature, electrons are localized to small regions simply by being bound within atoms, due to the attraction between the positively charged nucleus and the negatively charged electrons.

Because of the wavelike nature of electrons as manifested in Heisenberg's uncertainty principle, this electrostatic attractive force is just balanced out by the effective repulsive force due to the large kinetic energy of the electrons. If it were not for this uncertainty principle, electrons would fall into the nucleus by radiating away their kinetic energy in the form of emitted light—all atoms would be unstable and the universe as we know it would not exist! Just think about this for a moment: without stable atoms, we could not have any molecules, fluids, or solid materials. Furthermore, the wave nature of electrons is essential for explaining the good electrical conductivity of some materials like copper and certain other metals, as well as the good electrical insulating properties of other materials, like quartz. Can you imagine a world where materials are only electrical insulators, or, conversely, a world where every material is a good conductor of

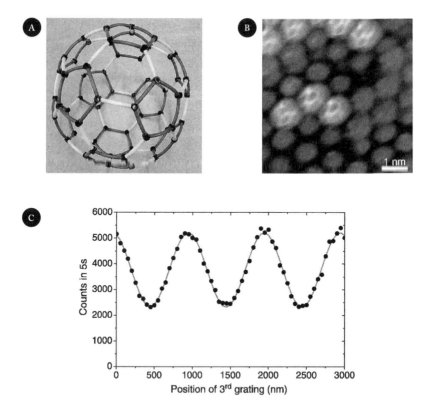

FIGURE 6. (a) A large-scale model of a C_{60} molecule showing the arrangement of the carbon atoms and bonds between the atoms. Reproduced with permission from J. Hare; http://www.creative-science.org.uk/c6omodel.html. (b) A microscope image of C_{60} molecules. From R. S. Pawlak, S. Kawai, S. Fremy, T. Glatzel, and E. Meyer, "High-Resolution Imaging of C_{60} molecules Using Tuning-Fork-Based Non-contact Atomic Force Microscopy," *Journal of Physics: Condensed Matter* 24, 084005 (2012); http://dx.doi.org/10.1088/0953-8984/24/8/084005. Copyright IOP Publishing. Reproduced with permission. All rights reserved. (c) Number of C_{60} molecules detected in a five-second time window versus the location of the slits relative to the molecule detector. Reprinted with permission from K. Hornberger, S. Gerlich, P. Haslinger, S. Nimmrichter, and M. Arndt, "Colloquium: Quantum Interference of Clusters and Molecules," *Reviews of Modern Physics* 84, no. 157 (2012); http://doi.org/10.1103/RevModPhys.84.157. Copyright 2012 by the American Physical Society.

electricity? In short, quantum mechanics is indispensable for providing the underlying reasons for the existence and properties of the material world around us.

So far, we have learned that we must describe electrons as wavelike—that is, obeying quantum mechanics—in order to explain the observed interference pattern on the detection screen in figure 4(d). On the other hand, micrometer-sized spray-paint globules behave like the ordinary, larger everyday particles that we are so familiar with, going through either one slit or the other to make the completely unsurprising paint pattern on the screen depicted in figure 5. The motion of each paint globule can be well described using the algebraic formulas of so-called classical mechanics, otherwise known as Newtonian mechanics after the scientist Sir Isaac Newton, who formulated the physics of the everyday motion of objects around us—from falling apples to orbiting planets—back in the eighteenth century.

But there is a mystery: according to our theory of quantum mechanics, there is nothing that prevents larger particles such as molecules, spray-paint globules, sand grains, hailstones, pebbles, baseballs, or even people such as you and I from behaving as quantum waves, that is, "going through two slits at once"! Consider how strange this would be: a steady stream of people somehow individually going through two side-by-side doors in a hallway at the same time, resulting in an interference pattern like that in figure 4(d) farther down the hallway! Of course, this never happens: classical Newtonian mechanics always perfectly explains what happens for larger particles like spray-paint globules. But how do we understand this coexistence of the micro quantum world of probability waves and the macro classical world of well-defined trajectories? Beyond the scale of what particle size should we use classical mechanics instead of quantum mechanics to describe their motion?

A large number of physicists around the world have been addressing these very questions, devising and carrying out ingenious experiments to determine whether particles much larger than electrons can display wavelike properties, as well as developing theories using mathematics to understand the results of these experiments and make predictions for future experiments. Figure 6(c) shows some experimental data from a group of physicists based in Vienna, Austria. Since the late 1990s this group has been sending progressively larger molecules through narrow slits. Under the right conditions, they find that molecules do behave as quantum waves, producing interference patterns at the detector. The data in figure 6(c) is from one of their first experiments, where they worked with molecules made out of sixty carbon atoms that are bonded together in a geometrical structure that very much resembles that of a soccer ball. Despite being about a million times more massive than a single electron, these microscopic "soccer" balls were found to cause an interference pattern and hence were "in two places at once" when passing through the slits. What is remarkable is that these molecules truly display both wavelike and particle-like properties in the sense that they interfere with themselves as evidenced in figure 6(c), while we can also "see" them as evidenced in figure 6(b), which is an actual microscope image of the C_{60} molecules. This image was not made with the kind of microscope that you are probably familiar with, the kind where you look through an optical magnifying eyepiece. Note the indicated size scale—a nanometer, which is 1 million times smaller than a millimeter; the wavelength of visible light is too large to be able to sharply resolve such small molecules. Instead, a special type of microscope was used, called an *atomic force microscope* (AFM for short), which was invented by physicists in the 1980s. The AFM looks a little bit like a miniature diving board, which is scanned close to and over the surface of the material system that is being imaged. Depending on the nature of the surface atoms, the diving board will bend toward the surface by different amounts as its tip is attracted by the forces exerted by the surface atoms. The displayed image shows the spatial variation of these surface forces.

While on this side subject of imaging, it is worth noting that physicists have played a major role in inventing new ways to see the world around us, beyond what our own eyes are capable of observing directly. In a broad sense, this is what carrying out precision physics experiments is all about, whether it be colliding particles together at ultrahigh energies using particle accelerators at large facilities such as CERN (the European Organization for Nuclear Research in Geneva, Switzerland) in order to learn about the inner workings of the atomic nucleus, or inventing new kinds of microscopes like the AFM to probe materials at the atomic and molecular scales, or designing new types of telescopes that enable us to see beyond our own solar system at wavelengths both shorter (e.g., X-ray) and longer (e.g., infrared, microwave, and radio wave) than visible light. Another remarkable example of seeing is our ability since 2015 to directly detect gravity waves emitted from the merging of pairs of black holes distant from our own galaxy using the Laser Interferometer Gravitational-Wave Observatory (LIGO), sited in Louisiana and Washington State; with the success of LIGO, we have opened for the first time a new window out to the universe and are now able to "see" not only with light, but also with gravity waves.

Our modern way of carrying out such precision experiments in physics means that we typically have a sophisticated instrument inserted between ourselves, the observer, and the system being studied. What we learn about the system, we learn indirectly, by noting the data that the instrument gives us as it probes the system—we are at the "back end" of the instrument, staring at computer screens that display images like in figure 6(b) or produce data plots like in figure 6(c) while the system is at the "front end" of the instrument, being sensitively probed by it. Our ways of thinking about and understanding the behavior of the system are based on this data. This is quite different from the way we typically experience the immediate, everyday world around us with our senses. Sometimes the systems that we precisely measure with our instruments behave, according to the data, in ways that cannot be explained in everyday terms. The best we can do in words is give imperfect analogies, and unavoidably we must rely on mathematics-based descriptions for our physical explanations of the data. The two slit experiments that we have been describing for electrons and C_{60} molecules are perfect illustrations of this; it makes no sense to think about which slit a C_{60} molecule went through, but we can use the wave mathematics together with the probability interpretation (i.e., quantum mechanics) to perfectly explain the data in figure 6(c). As humans we always hunger for a picture in our mind of what is going on, however imperfect it may be. But when we try to construct such pictures for the quantum world where particles have wavelike properties, we are confronted with the truly bizarre situation of a particle "being in two places at once," which does not really help clarify our understanding very much after all. Again, it is safer to resort to using mathematics to describe the outcomes of experiments; maybe in the distant future, our minds will have evolved in such a way as to better grasp the quantum world, but for now we have to live with this uncomfortable tension between our familiar, macroscopic classical world and the counterintuitive, bizarre microscopic quantum world that we can only indirectly access through sophisticated, sensitive experiments.

In 2013, the Vienna physicists demonstrated in an experiment that a certain molecule which is about fourteen times more massive than C_{60}—and about 18 million times more massive than an electron—could also "be in two places at once." These molecules are only one hundred times less massive than the smallest viruses, which really increases the uncomfortable tension between the quantum and classical worlds: can you even imagine what it would feel like for a living thing to "be in two places at once"? But while such molecules are impressively massive compared to a single electron, they are still much less massive than micrometer-sized living cells and spray-paint globules, which are about 100 million times more massive than a C_{60} molecule.

Since roughly the 1980s, physicists have worked hard to develop an understanding of why electrons and small molecules exhibit quantum wavelike behavior in controlled experiments (like the ones in figure 4 and figure 6) while certainly micrometer-sized and larger objects behave simply as particles under everyday conditions (like in figure 5). To explain this so-called "quantum/classical divide," it is useful to consider the "thought" experiment sketched out in figure 7 to determine through which slit a molecule went. By "thought" experiment, we mean some simplified, imaginary scheme for an experiment whose intention is to get the mind to focus on the essentials in order to develop an understanding of some phenomenon. Physicists often find thought experiments very helpful for this purpose. Figure 7(a) shows an incident molecule on its way to going through "both slits at once," interfering with itself as a wave and subsequently being detected on the screen, which shows the accumulated interference pattern of many previously detected molecules that went through both slits, much like the electron interference pattern in figure 4(d). As we discussed above, with the setup shown in figure 7(a) there is no way to determine through which slit the molecule went, and it makes no sense to even ask the question. On the other hand, figure 7(b) shows schematically how the experiment needs to be modified in order to obtain so-called which-path information. In particular, establishing through which slit a molecule went requires a sufficiently bright light source— or other source of sufficiently energetic particles—that must scatter off the incoming molecules and be detected by a sufficiently powerful light or particle detector (i.e., microscope), indicated symbolically by an eye. If the illuminating light source wavelength is smaller than the spacing between the slits, then we can resolve through which slit the molecule went. But notice the difference between the molecule detection pattern on the screen in figure 7(b) and the one in figure 7(a). The interference pattern has disappeared, replaced by the pattern we would get for everyday classical particles such as the spray-paint globules in figure 5!

Thus, in the act of detecting through which slit the molecule went, we destroy the wavelike interference pattern, and the particle resorts to going through either one slit *or* the other. At work here is the same Heisenberg uncertainty principle described earlier, where the more you try to locate a quantum particle, the more uncertain its speed will be, which is equivalent to suppressing the extended quantum wavelike interference nature of the particle. But here is the key insight that took physicists a while to appreciate: it is not really necessary for the eye (that is, microscope) to be present. All that is required to destroy the molecule quantum wave interference is that the scattering light or other scattering particles carry away sufficient information that could in principle be used to determine

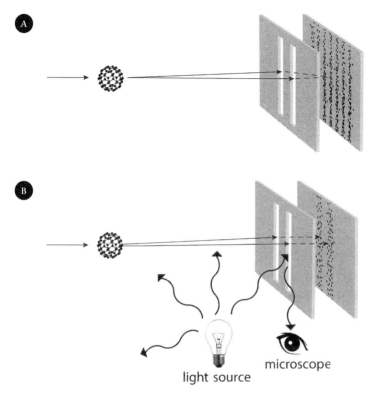

FIGURE 7 *(a)* Scheme for a molecular two-slit interference experiment where the molecule goes through one slit and the other slit "at the same time." *(b)* Resolving through which slit the molecule went destroys the interference pattern; the molecule goes through one slit or the other just like a regular classical particle.

through which slit the molecule went. More generally, any air molecules, dust particles, light, and so on—collectively termed "the environment"—that scatter off the molecule sufficiently to give "which-path" information will suppress its quantum wave nature. And for larger mass particles, such as paint globules, living cells, sand grains, pebbles, and the like, their environments typically interact so strongly as to induce extremely effective quantum wave interference suppression: the particles travel through one slit or the other with no interference.

So here we have an explanation as to why you "aren't in two places at once"! Bear in mind that this explanation is backed up with physics theories based on mathematical formulas that have been tested with a range of precise experiments. For example, in one relevant experiment, the Vienna group deliberately flooded their apparatus with air. As they increased the air pressure (i.e., air molecule density) and temperature, the interference pattern shown in figure 6(c) was suppressed precisely as predicted by the mathematical formulas that take into account the energetic air molecules scattering off the incident C_{60} molecules.

But this is not the end of the story. Suppose we could isolate our two-slit apparatus from everyday environments by putting it in an ultrahigh vacuum so as to remove wayward air molecules, cooling it down to close to absolute zero in temperature (-459.67 degrees Fahrenheit) so as to remove thermal radiation, and shielding it from light, microwaves, radio waves, and other external sources of low-energy electromagnetic radiation by encasing it in a metal container. Could we perhaps then put an arbitrarily large object in two places at once? Well, theoretical physicists like myself and experimental physicists alike are working hard on trying to address this question. As stated earlier, there is nothing in our theory of quantum mechanics that prevents us from doing this; it may be more a matter of what we can achieve in practice than in principle. One experimental approach involves sending ever-larger molecules through slits just as we have been describing. Another approach involves trapping and manipulating micrometer-sized and larger particles using magnetic fields. Yet another involves making micrometer-sized vibrating wires (much like a miniature guitar or violin string) and trying to make them display quantum wave nature by using certain small electronic devices. In all of these experimental approaches, the environments are carefully controlled, for example by cooling down the sample object under investigation in special fridges that provide an ultrahigh vacuum and also screen out the unwanted electromagnetic radiation, such as microwave noise from cell-phone towers and other electronic devices that surround us. Figure 8 shows a photo of such a setup called a *dilution fridge* that uses liquid helium to cool the sample to very low temperatures under ultrahigh vacuum, while at the same time allowing the sample to be manipulated and probed electronically from the comfort of the laboratory. Dilution fridges and other related low-temperature fridges are used extensively in physics laboratories around the world to investigate materials' quantum properties.

At the time of writing this chapter, we do not yet know the answer to the question "How large an object can be put in two places at once?" One idea that a number of physicists including myself are working on is that there may be a fundamental threshold mass or size scale for objects above which they follow well-localized paths: that is, behave classically. This idea is based on the fact that there is one environment that it is likely impossible to isolate a system from—gravity. While you are sitting comfortably, you are being prevented from

FIGURE 8 *(a)* Top side of a dilution fridge resting in a pit
below the floor. The fridge is cylindrical and more than six
feet long. *(b)* The dipstick on which the sample is located and
inserted into the top side of the dilution fridge.

drifting into outer space by the gravitational attraction between you and the Earth. And this attractive force increases as the mass of the system gets larger. But we now also know that gravity waves really exist, thanks to the LIGO gravity wave detector. As with the pervasive electromagnetic environment, it may be that we are bathed in a gravity wave environment that is so weak as to be practically invisible to everyday matter, and yet which would cause the rapid destruction of the quantum wave nature of any suitably large mass object that we tried to get to interfere with itself. But to be clear, we are really only at the early stage of speculation, without physics theories or experiment to back this up; much work remains to be done before we can answer the question that my daughter Cecilia keeps asking me.

Hopefully this example of quantum wave interference has given you a taste of what physics is. The practices and methodologies I have outlined apply to every area of physics: they are used by high-energy physicists exploring subatomic scales, by cosmologists exploring the origins of the whole universe, and by physicists investigating all energy and size scales in between. It is worth emphasizing that like the other sciences and humanities subjects, physics is a highly creative endeavor. Just as an artist might work with paint, a poet with words, and a musician with notes, a physicist works with mathematical equations. A large part of being a physicist is about coming up with original ideas for what experiments to do and what problems to work on, all with the goal of understanding nature (and certainly not to change it!). The pleasure is gained in working hard (with the inevitable ups and downs) to ultimately get experimental data that shows you the inner workings of nature in a way that hasn't been seen before. And for the theorist, the pleasure and enjoyment is in writing down and solving math formulas—sometimes simply with pencil and paper, and other times with the help of a computer—that actually tell us something new and unexpected about the world around us. Theoretical physicists sometimes prefer to work at arm's length from experimentalists, constructing their new theories based on previously experimentally validated theories. This is how Einstein came up with his general theory of relativity in 1916, which predicted the existence of gravity waves, and which had to wait nearly a century for their eventual direct detection by LIGO! At other times, theoretical physicists work closely with experimental physicists, developing theories to explain their experimental data and also suggesting and helping design new experiments to test those theories.

Physicists are driven not only by a desire to understand nature more deeply, but also by being part of a large community; our ideas and theories are not developed solely in isolation. We are inspired by interacting with fellow physicists through conversations as well as by reading their published work. Also, many areas of physics overlap with other quantitative fields, so you will often find physicists collaborating with biologists, chemists, computer scientists, engineers, philosophers, and social scientists—essentially, with colleagues in any field where developing physics models based on mathematics can yield new insights.

I would like to finish this chapter with a quotation from the famous theoretical physicist Richard Feynman. He made this statement during a conference in 1957, and it touches on the very question I have been discussing in this chapter. I have found this quote to very inspiring as I do my own work on the subject:

> It may turn out, since we've never done an experiment at this level, that it's not possible—that by the time you amplify the thing to a level where the gravitational field can have an influence, it's already so big you can't reverse it—there is something the matter with our quantum mechanics when we have too much *action* in the system, or too much mass—or something.

Maybe one day we will have a definite answer one way or the other to Feynman's speculation—a yet-to-be-written chapter in physics.

Political Science?

Russell Muirhead

Political scientists try to understand politics, and they make use of every method and technique that is useful in this quest: they borrow from philosophy, history, psychology, classics, economics, law, sociology, geography, statistics, and applied mathematics, even from literature. What binds political scientists together is not the way they "do" political science—this they will disagree about forever—but what they study: politics. Their methods may be quantitative (they may apply sophisticated statistical methods to large data sets) or qualitative (they may interpret ideas, history, and culture), but in their basic quest they are not that different from ordinary citizens. They simply try to understand the political world around them.

The most important reason to study politics is civic: ideally, it helps citizens understand their country and their world and thus make more informed and effective decisions. With this in mind, in what follows I will explain what politics is and the fundamental questions that arise when thinking about it, with a focus on democracy in general and American democracy in particular.

The First Question of Politics: *Who Rules?*

There is no good life for human beings without rule: without some bossing others, perhaps for their own private advantage, perhaps with a view to everyone's advantage. The only thing worse than bad rule is no rule, which is called *anarchy*. Anarchy, the absence of any rules and any power to enforce them, is a condition where life is (as the political philosopher Thomas Hobbes put it) "solitary, poor, nasty, brutish, and short."

Even if we cannot live well without some kind of rule, the question "Who rules?" does not answer itself for us as it seems to for other animals, like bees. The beehive has a natural order—there are drones, and workers, and a queen. But for us, there is no order that comes into being on its own and settles the question of rule without giving rise to an argument or contest.

You do not need to be a professor of political science to understand this. As soon as my twins learned to write—they were about three years old—they put a sign on their bedroom door: "LILA AND ALLIE RULE THIS ROOM." They grasped that the question of rule is a problem. And they understood that they might solve the problem by asserting themselves.

To rule, someone (or some group) must make a claim: *we rule this room.* Every assertion leads to an argument: *oh no you don't!* And every argument leads to counterarguments . . . and yet more arguments. Politics is argument without end (except in war—but when the war stops, the arguments restarts).

Some say that arguments about who should rule ought not to be taken *that* seriously. What matters, they say, is what gives people real power: a large following, money, or guns. What can an argument say to a gun?

But it turns out that even guns on their own are rarely enough to stabilize rule. There is no way to get rule and to keep it without convincing someone else that you should have it. If you want to rule, posting a sign on the door is only the first step: you must then persuade somebody else you deserve the power you assert.

This is why the study of politics is not a science in the way chemistry or physics is. The elements of the periodic table do not argue with each other about who should get the most atomic weight. The motion of the planets is not the outcome of a negotiation among the heavenly bodies. In politics, people argue with each other, and the arguments matter: you can't rule without them. So political science is never only about describing things simply as they are, as natural sciences do. Although many political scientists aim to discover the necessities that show how things must be, political science is also inescapably about describing things as they "should" be. The political world is full of shoulds and should-nots, claims and counterclaims.

The claims people make about what should and should not be accepted or enforced are, as I mentioned above, the focus of political theory (sometimes called political philosophy.) This is what I study and teach. It is the oldest part of political science, and goes back to the ancient Greeks, particularly Plato and Aristotle, who wrote in the fourth century BCE. Politics in ancient Greece was unstable, and many different kinds of rule (or "regimes") existed alongside one another; even in the same place, one form would often give way to another and then back again. This is why the classic questions of political science—who rules, and who should rule—were not academic questions reserved for the classroom, but real questions that mattered—urgently. The urgency of these questions recedes a bit when politics is stable (as in the United States since the Civil War), but they are never far from the surface.

As Aristotle observed, all the claims to rule can be reduced to three types: that one person should rule everyone else (which leads to kingship or tyranny); that some should rule others (which leads to *aristocracy* if the "best"—sometimes thought to be warriors or priests or even philosophers—rule, or an *oligarchy* if the rich rule); and *democracy*, where the people rule over themselves, more or less justly. Modern ideologies like communism or socialism might seem to have complicated Aristotle's scheme, but the basic question—*Who rules?*—still applies. They might be interpreted as attempts to make rule of the people more perfect by restricting the power of property; they also might be interpreted as attempts to empower a new self-serving elite of intellectuals (who think they possess the intellectual key to unlocking the way to a communist utopia).

Democrats All?

Today many people around the world affirm that the people should rule. Not many insist that we would be better off going back to the rule of kings, or that the wise and holy should rule, or that the rich *should* rule (many believe that the rich effectively *do* rule—but few openly argue this is the way it should be). There are some dissenters, but it is not a vast exaggeration to say that we, not only in the United States and Europe but across much of the world, are democrats all.

Although many believe in some form of democracy, it remains a kind of ideal that few actual democracies fully satisfy: in a literal sense, rule by the people is impossible. For one thing, the people are too numerous, scattered, and busy to rule themselves very actively. In the democracy of ancient Greece, citizens gathered every day in the *agora*, proposed laws, and voted on them. They could do this because they did not work—they made slaves, resident noncitizens, and women work for them. Today, democratic citizens are also workers themselves, and they are too busy to hang out in the park every day to directly exercise the power of rule. Instead, they vote once or twice a year to elect representatives who rule in their name.

To some, merely voting once in a while hardly qualifies as ruling. As the political philosopher Jean-Jacques Rousseau said of the British—who invented representative democracy, but whose democratic life did not always impress Rousseau—"The people of England regards itself as free, but it is grossly mistaken; it is only free during elections of members of parliament. As soon as they are elected, slavery overtakes it, and they are nothing." In a similar vein, the contemporary political theorist Benjamin Barber says that voting is a pale reflection of the power citizens in a strong democracy would exercise: voting, he says, "is rather like using a public toilet: we wait in line with a crowd in order to close ourselves in a small compartment where we can relieve ourselves in solitude and in privacy of our burden . . . and then, yielding to the next in line, go silently home."

When the institutions of American democracy were designed 230 years ago, voting for representatives was a necessity. There was no way for 3 million people, some living over a thousand miles apart, to hop on their horses and gather in one place. Today we can jump on our virtual horses and gather electronically. The Internet has collapsed the geographic space that separates us: citizens can read articles and essays as soon as they are written, they can talk with others hundreds and thousands of miles away at no cost, and they can vote directly on legislation, all online. These developments in communication are transforming democratic politics in ways we are only beginning to understand, and they might well make a new kind of democracy possible—though as yet, the digital revolution has not resulted in a new and better way of doing democracy. That task may fall to your generation.

There are a great many innovations we might try out to make democracy work better. The study of the way different countries work out their political institutions often falls to the field of comparative politics, though specialists in American politics and also in law have a lot to contribute. This includes designing new electoral systems and constitutions for emerging democracies.

The invention of new institutions tends not to affect American politics at the national level, since our national politics still takes its form from the 1789 Constitution that is both the object of great reverence and is very difficult to change. Eleven thousand amendments to the Constitution have been proposed since 1789; only thirty-three amendments to the Constitution have been passed by Congress and sent to the states; of those, twenty-seven have been ratified. More radical than a mere amendment is calling a new Constitutional Convention, which would occur if two-thirds of the state legislatures pass legislation demanding one. In recent years a number of state legislatures have called for such a convention, often to address specific issues like a balanced budget amendment.

There is no reason to think that a second Constitutional Convention would limit itself to specific concerns: it would be empowered to write a new constitution from scratch, just as the first Constitutional Convention did. Some think this would give us the opportunity to fix things (like the very unequal apportionment of representatives in the US Senate). Others think a new Constitutional Convention would be a wholesale disaster—a cacophony of deceptive propaganda funded by those with a lot to lose (and a lot to gain), culminating in . . . perhaps nothing except anger and distrust, if no agreement could be reached that the people ratified. Against that, many prefer to stick with what we know: a terse, enigmatic constitution whose separation of powers only gives control of the whole government to a large and durable majority.

As difficult as it is to change, the early decades of the twentieth century (called the *Progressive Era*) generated much constitutional experimentation. The national Constitution was amended four times, allowing for a national income tax, direct election of senators, Prohibition, and women's suffrage. Even more experimentation focused on the states, whose constitutions are more plastic than the national constitution: the California constitution, for instance, was amended more than five hundred times from 1911 to 1986. Amendments proliferate in California in part because citizens can directly propose and pass constitutional amendments (bypassing the legislature) through the initiative process. The initiative itself, along with the referendum (by which citizens can directly pass legislation or repeal a specific act of the legislature) and the recall (by which citizens can replace a public official before the end of his or her term of office), all go back to the Progressive Era. All of these reforms constituted a movement toward "direct democracy," born of the hope was that the people's wholesome good sense (guided by specialized experts) would check the corruption of state legislatures.

For their part, the American founders would not have embraced direct democracy (where people vote directly on laws) even if they had technological options that made it possible. They believed in representation as a way of improving democratic decisions: James Madison (the fourth president, the author of the Bill of Rights, and the most influential member of the 1787 Constitutional Convention) hoped that citizens would vote only for the best—for those who had done something admirable to make a name for themselves—and that these wise representatives in turn would "refine and enlarge" public views.

Democratic Performance

Few look at the US Congress today and trust that our representatives will refine and enlarge public views—on the contrary. Very few citizens today trust the government to "do what is right" most of the time: about 20 percent trusted the national government to this extent in 2012, versus 47 percent in 1970 and 57 percent in 1958.

Still, 76 percent trust the government to do what is right "some of the time " and in this respect, voting matters. Indeed, at a basic level, the threat of being voted out of office keeps rulers' attention focused on the people. Democracies malfunction and underperform in all kinds of ways, but even at their worst they can be good at the basics, such as ensuring that people in large numbers do not needlessly suffer: as the economist and philosopher Amartya Sen has observed, "No famine has ever taken place in the history of the world in a functioning democracy."

Scholars of international relations have highlighted another basic fact: democracies do not fight each other. Democracies trade with each other, depend on each other for their prosperity, and tend to be led by people who have some concern for human rights. Democracies are more likely to view each other as friendly, and rulers who are accountable to citizens are less likely to engage in very costly violence. It may be too soon to know whether the "democratic peace" is reliable, since modern democracy is a recent development. Prior to 1900, the world contained very few democracies. Even democracies were not very democratic: as of 1900 no country in the world gave *all* citizens the vote.

The act of voting itself is the most celebrated feature of democratic life: good citizens vote, and feel good about voting (even when they are not entirely happy about whom they get to vote for). It's easy to disdain voting, especially when the choices voters face are not very inspiring. But it is something people have had to fight for—first white men, then blacks, then women—and still the fight goes on.

Parties and the People

Apart from the difficulty in equipping the people to rule directly, there is a deeper problem with democracy: the "people" don't stand together as *one*. They disagree with each other about nearly everything, nearly all the time. About the best that can be hoped for is that a part of the people rules—the largest part. But even the largest part is only a part, a party. Modern democracy is rule not by the whole people over the whole people, but rule by part (parties) over the whole. Democratic government is party government.

Most democracies today use *proportional representation*, where even a party that only commands support from 10 to 15 percent of the population gets to enjoy some official representation in the legislature. The United States is unusual for its *two-party system*, where ballot laws and the electoral system conspire to reduce the number of viable parties to only two.

It is tempting to think that politics would go better without parties—the partisan contest can seem like a distraction from finding commonsense solutions to shared problems. After all, we agree about a number of important things: we all want peace, a comfortable life, respect, and a chance to do useful work. And since experts are said to know what the most advantageous foreign and economic policies are, it seems to some that there is no good reason we should disagree.

In my own work, I have defended the place of parties and partisan contestation in democracy. The hope for a democracy that escapes party and partisanship is mistaken, as I argue in my book *The Promise of Party in a Polarized Age*. The trouble is that we in fact disagree even when we disagree: we disagree about what kind of economic arrangements are fair, about the place of international institutions in securing peace, about what constitutes a threat. Expertise only compounds the problem, first because experts disagree with each other, and second because experts are often wrong. Common sense guided by expertise does not offer an escape from politics.

This is perhaps why every open society in the modern world has had parties—groups of people who disagree, often on principle, often on policy, usually on both. In most modern democracies, this disagreement can be generally described in terms of the left and the right. In the United States, "left" tends to mean "liberal," and "right" tends to mean "conservative." The "left/right" metaphor goes back to the French Revolution, when supporters of the king (defenders of tradition and religion) sat on the right in the Estates General, and opponents of the king (who saw their cause as enlightened and rational) sat on the left, looking out from the central podium.

Liberals and Conservatives

It is never easy to say exactly what "liberal" and "conservative" mean, and I first became interested in political science (and political theory in particular) in part because I wanted to figure out what they mean—and what they should mean in the future.

In general, liberals care more about equality. They look at the country and see it becoming too unequal: they worry more about the increasing inequality of money and wealth, for instance, because these threaten to introduce inequalities of power that undermine political equality. Liberals suspect that most social and economic inequalities are undeserved (what does the child of very rich parents do to *deserve* to be rich?). In the liberal view, morally arbitrary differences (in social background or natural luck) too often translate into unjust inequalities of power and influence.

Conservatives care relatively more about freedom than equality. One reason they care about freedom is because they care about the virtues—the qualities of mind and character—that sustain a free republic. They look at the country and worry about the erosion of virtues like commitment, the work ethic, and patriotism. Without people who are committed to family, work, and country, it will be difficult (conservatives argue) to maintain a free society. Conservatives tend to think that some people deserve more of the good things in life because they have certain admirable qualities of mind and character, and in the conservative view, good qualities and prudent habits are too often penalized (by taxes) and therefore discouraged. Where liberals often want to extend the spirit of equality, and conservatives fear that the spirit of equality will seep into our evaluations so completely that people will no longer be able to judge which of their desires and motives are good and admirable, and which are shameful.

This has a consequence for the way that liberals and conservatives think about risk. Liberals tend to think of government as a way of sharing risks that we cannot insure ourselves against individually—the risk that we might suffer from an expensive disease, the risk that we may be born to parents who make bad choices, the risk that what we do for a living will be rendered obsolete by technological change or trade. Conservatives, on the other hand, think that few good things come without some risk, and they want to give people an incentive to take on certain risks voluntarily—to start a new ice cream shop, to learn a new skill. In their view, when the government reduces the consequences (good and bad) that come from risky endeavors, people have less incentive to take risks that might pay off, since they do not get to enjoy the gains if they succeed, and more incentive to take risks that might lead to large costs, since they don't suffer from the results if they fail. All in all, conservatives say, if we do not get the rewards and pay the price of the risks we take, we will not learn how to make good use of freedom.

One could say a lot more about conservatism and liberalism, the two ideologies that dominate politics today. But it is important to see that ideologies are not merely philosophies that define what government is for. They are also ways of trying to bring people together, to build a coalition. They provide a reason for voting for this person or that person. And they link people who get elected to legislatures and other political offices, like governorships or the presidency. Without philosophies like these, it is very hard for people—hundreds of millions of individual citizens, for instance, in the United States—to communicate anything to those they elect. Just electing good women and good men to political office does not tell those good women and men what to do. Ideology is what gives good women and men a purpose, once they get elected.

The Vital Center

Yet many ordinary citizens do not think of themselves as either very liberal or very conservative. Even people who think about politics a lot often have a mixture of opinions, both liberal and conservative. Most people do not follow an ideological line when thinking about political questions. This is why some think that ideology is now *disconnecting* the government from the people. In this view, most people are pragmatic and centrist, but our elected representatives are ideological extremists. And ideological elites are betraying commonsense citizens who care less about ideological purity than they care about a government that works. In this view, centrist candidates would better represent the people than true believers in liberalism *or* conservatism.

If this view is right, then there is a majority, perhaps a very large one, of commonsense centrists who are waiting to be represented by centrist legislators and officials, but who are forced against their will to choose between extreme conservatives on one hand (who would shut the government down before approving a new tax) and extremist liberals (who would pass a new spending program before they would ever balance the government's budget). A government that is supposed to be *democratic*, that is supposed to let the people rule, has been captured by extremists.

This view might be right. When we look at the ways institutions can be corrupted—captured by small groups with an intense interest, captured by those with money and resources, or captured by those whose strange sense of self-righteousness eliminates their ability to hear the other side of an argument—we begin to see how very difficult it can be to structure a political system in a way that ensures the people rule. The people are easy prey for small, well-organized, well-funded minority groups. James Madison called such groups "factions" and hoped that the United States Constitution would make rule-by-faction impossible.

Madison hoped that large and diverse legislative districts would liberate representatives from factions and special interests: in a district with many competing interests, no one interest could command a majority and control the district's representative. Yet today technology has perfected the art of the *gerrymander*, where the boundaries of legislative districts are drawn in a way that benefits one party over the other. Many worry that the creation of "safe" districts (districts that will *only* elect a Democrat or a Republican, and rarely swing between the two) also elects more ideologically extreme candidates. Republicans from safe Republican districts do not fear Democratic opponents—they fear a more conservative challenger in the Republican primary election. To guard against this, they become more extreme. The problem of gerrymandering is compounded by primary elections, which are held at unfamiliar times and draw a relatively small number of more committed (and more ideologically extreme) voters. The two—gerrymandering and primary elections—combine, some worry, to produce more ideologically extreme members of Congress who disdain compromise in the name of maintaining their ideological purity.

This is why California and Washington State have abolished *partisan* primary elections, replacing them with a *top-two primary*, in which the top two candidates, even if they are from the same party, proceed to the general election in November. The theory behind this innovation is that voters in "safe" districts will have a choice between a more centrist and a more extreme candidate from the same party, rather than face a choice between a liberal Democrat and a conservative Republican. If voters are really centrist—more so than their representatives—they will elect the more centrist candidate.

The Art of Politics

California and Washington's political innovation is too recent to assess whether it will be successful at moderating American politics. But there is good reason to doubt that it will succeed, as there is reason to doubt that "the people" have been entirely disempowered by a small hyper-ideological minority. For one thing, if the people stood together in some commonsense centrist way, there would always be an incentive for at least one party or one (well-financed) candidate to appeal to the people (and win) rather than appealing to the ideologues.

The deeper problem, as I have noted, is that it is very difficult to get people in any large number to stand together. Rather than seeing "the people" as one group with a coherent centrist view, it might be more accurate to see them as a messy collection of tens of millions of individuals, none of whom completely agrees with anyone else. To get "the people"—even a bare majority of the people—to stand together, even for a moment, is a daunting task, one made more difficult because people increasingly sort themselves into like-minded friendships and residential enclaves, and consume news only from sources whose ideological slant they agree with.

Yet in order to work, democracies need people to stand together in a group that is large enough to govern legitimately. This generally means a majority, or something larger (the US Constitution defines a constitutional majority in a way that requires it to be dispersed in space and enduring in time, in order to control both the House of Representatives, the Senate, and the presidency—and perhaps the Supreme Court too).

In American politics, it is even more difficult than usual to assemble a durable governing majority (this is even more acutely the case in many other countries around the world). Liberals cannot bring people together behind a liberal vision of rule. Conservatives cannot unify people behind a conservative vision. And if centrists agree about things, no one quite knows what those things are. So we want to rule ourselves, but we cannot come together long enough to succeed. As a result, contemporary democracy leaves everyone frustrated, looking for something—a good we hold in common—that they cannot quite find.

Political Science: A House of Many Mansions

My focus on American democracy is not to suggest that American democracy is the most important regime to understand, even if the United States is the single global power of the age. The focus of this essay reflects my own work, in which I blend *political theory*, which studies rival understandings of justice as they arise both in contemporary politics and the history of political thought, and *American politics*, a broad subfield that combines the study of American political institutions, American political behavior (why people vote the way they do), American public opinion, and American political history.

Of course, different countries have different problems, priorities, patterns of political institutions, societal divisions, traditions, and lines of ideological disagreement. *Comparative politics* attends to these differences by focusing on politics as it is organized and operates in countries around the world. Sometimes specialists of comparative politics focus on one country or region (like European politics, or African politics), and sometimes they actually compare across a large number of countries from various regions. *International relations* is the study of the relation between states: the agreements that states enter into with each other to facilitate cooperation, the way states negotiate their disagreements to avoid war, and the conflicts and diplomatic failures that lead to war. Another specialty, *formal theory and quantitative methods*, focuses on game theoretic reasoning and statistical methods both to build models of strategic behavior and to develop statistical techniques that allow political scientists in all subfields to properly assess the data they gather. *Public law* centers on courts and constitutionalism, using both empirical and theoretical methods.

At some universities, political science is also called "government" or "politics." Regardless of the name, the aim is the same: to discover ways of getting people to cooperate for their mutual advantage, against the predatory forces of self-seeking elites, and despite the asocial tendencies of the people themselves. The stakes are always high. To fail courts grave and unnecessary suffering—hunger, disease, and violent death. To succeed can bring security, hope, comfortable living, and justice. The art of politics remains to be mastered, which is why political science is the one science all citizens have a reason to study.

WHAT IS

Psychology?

Thalia Wheatley

Have you ever wondered what it means to be you? I'm not talking about how you might describe yourself. I'm talking about what it means to be the only you that will ever exist—the only person that you, and no one else, ever could be. The fact that each of us has a unique mind—or *psyche*, in Greek—has been a source of fascination for thousands of years, stretching back to the even older concept of having a soul. When we die, our bodies remain but we are gone. Our mind, more than any other part of our body, is the bit that makes us *us*.

But what actually *is a mind* and what makes it tick? These are the primary questions of psychology, the study of the mind.

What Is a Mind?

Plato, and later Descartes, believed that the mind exists separately from the physical body. This view is called dualism (mind and body are dual entities) and it is appealing because *who we are* feels greater than the mere product of biological machinery. Daydreaming about a loved one or deciding on college doesn't feel like billions of neurons flickering on and off in a pattern. It *feels* separate—transcendent even.

Yet if I looked inside your skull I would only see a brain. The brain, sometimes called *wet matter*, weighs about three pounds and has the consistency of cooked oatmeal. Everything we do, think, and feel is caused by waves and patterns of electrical and chemical activity coursing through that oatmeal.

Does that lose some of the magic? If you think it does, try thinking of it this way: three pounds of brain tissue somehow creates art and music, produces feelings of joy and pain, generates insight and humor, connects with others, and plans for the future. The world's fastest computers can only do a tiny fraction of the things our brains do every day. How the brain does all of these things and more is one of the deepest mysteries in science. Figuring it out will keep psychologists and neuroscientists busy for a very long time.

But if we don't know how the brain works, then why are scientists so confident that mind and brain are inseparable? One reason comes from case studies of people who have brain damage. These cases revealed that if you damage the brain, you damage the mind. And different kinds of brain damage change the mind in different ways. Let's look at three of psychology's most famous patients.

Phineas Gage: Losing Oneself

One September day in 1848, Phineas Gage was working as a railroad foreman in Cavendish, Vermont. His job that day was setting blasting holes, which entailed digging a hole, filling it with gunpowder and sand, and tamping the mixture down with a heavy three-foot-long iron rod. While Phineas was tamping down one of the holes, the gunpowder ignited, turning the heavy iron rod into a missile. Unfortunately for Phineas, his head was in the way. The rod shot up through his cheek, behind his left eye, and out the top of his skull. Along the way, the front of his brain—the area just behind his forehead—was obliterated.

The blast threw Phineas backward, but he reportedly never lost consciousness. Instead, he got up, walked over to an oxcart, and was driven into town to see the doctor. After a few weeks of painful recovery, he seemed to be fine. A famous physician at the time declared him "quite recovered in his faculties of body and mind" and in "full possession of his reason." However, his friends noticed a change. The Phineas Gage after the accident was not the Phineas Gage from before. The same physician that noted his miraculous recovery would later add: "He is fitful, irreverent, indulging at times in the grossest profanity (which was not previously his custom), manifesting but little deference for his fellows, impatient of restraint or advice when it conflicts with his desires . . . A child in his intellectual capacity and manifestations, he has the animal passions of a strong man . . . His mind was radically changed, so decidedly that his friends and acquaintances said he was 'no longer Gage.'"

Phineas Gage's condition was one of the first times that physical brain matter was linked to something purely *psychological*. When Phineas lost part of his brain, he kept much of his mind but lost who he once was.

Henry Molaison: Losing Memory

Henry Molaison also lost part of his brain, but with a completely different outcome. When he was a child, he suffered from epileptic seizures—uncontrollable spasms that result from large amounts of random electrical activity that spread through the brain. By age twenty-seven, his seizures were so severe that he sought help from a neurosurgeon, who found the part of Henry's brain that triggered the seizures and cut it out. The good news was that the surgery cured him from having seizures. The bad news was that the surgery also made Henry incapable of making certain kinds of new memories. On first meeting Henry, you might not notice anything unusual about him. He would shake your hand and say hello, and you and he would have a conversation. But if you left the room and came back, he would reintroduce himself, having no memory that the two of you had spoken just five minutes earlier.

Psychologists kept trying new things with Henry to see just how bad his memory really was, and they made an interesting discovery. Henry could still learn new tasks. One task they gave him was drawing a star by looking at his hand in a mirror. Have you ever tried drawing something while looking in a mirror? It is really hard! Henry also found it difficult at first, but he got better over time. This was interesting because getting better meant that he was *remembering*.

Even though Henry's memory for new places and things was abysmal, he could still learn and remember *how* to do things. He still had the kind of memory you use whenever you get on a bike. You remember that to start, you kick the pedal up to the top of the chain and push down hard. You remember to lean into a turn. All of this requires memory. And just as with learning to ride a bike, Henry would get better each time he did the drawing task. Every time, though, he would claim that he had never seen the task before. Thanks to Henry and some clever psychologists, we know that a structure in the brain called the *hippocampus* (Latin for "seahorse," because it is shaped like a seahorse) is critical for our ability to remember where we went, what we ate, and who we met, but not *how* we do something. It meant that memory is not one thing—that there are different kinds.

Patient SM: Losing Fear

Of the three patients mentioned here, the third is still living and is therefore only referred to in print by her initials. Patient SM never feels afraid. She has no fear of snakes or spiders and no fear of walking into a dark tunnel at night.

Psychologists have given her lots of tests that evoke fear in almost everyone, such as anticipating getting an electric shock. Imagine every time you heard a buzzer you would get a painful electric shock a few seconds later. Pretty soon just hearing the buzzer would make you sweat, your heart race, and your pupils dilate. Not SM—SM hears the buzzer and just waits calmly for the shock. There is nothing wrong with her ability to learn (she learns that the buzzer means a shock is coming), and there is nothing wrong with her experience of pain (she finds shocks as painful as you would). The only thing that is different between you and her is a complete lack of fear. SM has damage to two small, almond-shaped brain areas called the amygdalae.

People with damaged, small, or low-functioning amygdalae not only tend to have a reduced fear response; they can also have difficulty recognizing when *others* are afraid. This particular difficulty has been associated with psychopathy. When the psychologist Essi Viding asked one prison inmate to identify the facial expressions of people in photographs, she was struck by that inmate's inability to name one particular emotional expression. The inmate became increasingly agitated by being stumped, finally declaring: "I don't know what that expression is called, but I know it's what people look like right before I stab them!"

What is the opposite of psychopathy? It turns out that altruism is also associated with the amygdalae. People who have donated one of their own kidneys to a stranger tend to have larger-than-average amygdalae and be more sensitive to expressions of fear in others. Thus, whether you are trusting or uncaring, selfish or generous, is in part a function of two little almond-shaped parts of your brain.

Psychologists study many kinds of patients. Some patients have bizarre disorders like believing that their left hand belongs to someone else or believing themselves to be dead. Others have more common problems with motivation or controlling their emotions. So far, all have been shown to result from disruptions of brain activity. Does this mean we are merely a product of our biology? Are we simply born who we are and who we will become?

Not at all.

The Power of the Environment

You may have heard about the nature/nurture debate. This debate in psychology asks how much our thoughts and actions are shaped by our biology (what we are born with) versus our environment. So far we have only considered biology (nature), but psychologists know that the environment plays an equally important role. More importantly, psychologists know that there is no firm line separating nature and nurture; rather, our biology and our environment shape each other.

Take intelligence. In affluent neighborhoods, genes explain a lot about how people do on intelligence tests. In these communities, high-IQ parents tend to have high-IQ kids, and low-IQ parents tend to have low-IQ kids. In poorer neighborhoods, there is little to no relationship between the IQ scores of parents and their kids. How could this be?

It turns out that having the biological potential to have a high IQ is just that: *potential.* Without a nurturing, safe, and enriching environment that potential cannot be fully realized. An old English saying goes "Mighty oaks from little acorns grow." Now imagine that a little acorn gets wedged under a rock. There may be potential in that acorn to become a mighty oak, but its environment (the rock) makes it impossible to realize that potential.

Scientists have noted that with every generation, people are becoming taller and smarter overall—a rate of growth that is much too fast to be explained by evolution. Here is the acorn example again. With every generation, nutrition, health care, and education are getting better, and this progress is akin to moving the rock, little by little, off our acorn. Who knows what people generations from now will be able to do. All we know for sure is that they will be taller and smarter than we are now. Environments not only help us realize our potential but can also shape our minds in particular ways. This is especially true of the social environment. The study of how people affect us is called *social psychology.*

Have you ever tried facing the "wrong" way in an elevator, toward the other passengers instead of the doors? It is surprisingly hard to do for more than a couple of seconds. Of course, it is not *physically* more difficult than standing in the normal direction; the discomfort is purely social. Going against the grain is difficult because we are wired to care what other people think. Next time you are in an elevator, you might see how high you can count while standing the wrong way before you break down and face the door. If you can do ten seconds without feeling awkward, take it up a notch by doing deep knee bends. Even when we know that we will never see these people again, it is very difficult to not be affected by them. The people around us guide our behavior and constrain what we do.

In this example, it is easy to argue that using others as a guide for behavior is fine. Indeed, it makes the whole boring-but-necessary act of elevator riding a maximally efficient experience. But let's consider a different example of social influence that is far less innocuous.

Imagine you see someone being attacked. You are a safe distance away and you have no danger of being seen yourself. Would you try to help? Would you call

9-1-1? In 1963, Kitty Genovese was stabbed to death over several hours, outside her apartment building in Queens, New York. Even more troubling was the fact that thirty-seven people watched her die from their bedroom windows. Not one even called the police. Why?

At the time, the favored explanation was that New Yorkers were cold-hearted, hardened by city life. It was a theory that fed on intuitions about how big cities create uncaring strangers. But social psychologists wondered if there was another explanation. Could the number of people watching have actually made it *less* likely that Kitty would get help?

Bibb Latane and John Darley tested this theory by staging an accident like a painter falling off a ladder and manipulating whether people witnessed the accident alone or with other people (actors) who did nothing. They found that the greater the number of people who witnessed a crime, the less likely any one person would help. It turns out that the presence of more witnesses makes any *one person* feel less responsibility to do something. In the case of Kitty Genovese, neighbors could see each other looking out of their windows, and everyone assumed that *somebody else* had called the police. Unfortunately for Kitty, because everyone made the same calculus, no one made the call. The other reason that more witnesses can lead to less helping is that we take the *inaction* of others as information. If others are not doing anything, we assume that they know more than we do. We assume either that the situation is not an emergency or that nothing can be done. We assume that other people know the appropriate behavior, and just like in the elevator situation, we follow suit.

It is likely that Kitty Genovese would be alive today if only one person had seen the crime. In part, she died because the presence of thirty-seven witnesses meant that no one did anything.

How do we stop this from happening? Well, one way is to tell people about it. Psychological studies have shown that just *knowing* about this phenomenon makes people more likely to help in a later emergency. So now that includes you! If you find yourself in a situation in which someone may need help, don't look to see what others are doing. Instead, block them out and think: "What would I do if I were the *only* person seeing this?" And know that, if you help, you won't be alone for long. Just as inaction is infectious, action is too. When one person breaks the paralysis created by other people, it frees others to act as well.

If other people can stop us from helping someone, can they also cause us to actively hurt someone? What if someone asked you to kill a person? Would you do it? Would you kill someone simply because someone asked you to?

Social psychologist Stanley Milgram was gripped by this question. In particular, he wanted to better understand how the Nazi Holocaust happened in World War II. At the time, it was widely assumed that such atrocities could never happen in the United States. It was believed that Americans, as a people, were less authoritarian than Germans. This should sound familiar. Think back to the original theory for why thirty-seven New Yorkers didn't help Kitty Genovese. In both cases, it took psychological research to reveal that the situation can shape us in ways that can even go against our personal conscience.

In Stanley Milgram's famous obedience experiment, people came to his laboratory to take part in a study about learning. When they arrived, they met an experimenter in a white lab coat and another person who was pretending to be another participant. The two participants drew lots to find out who would be the "learner" and who would be the "teacher." The draw was fixed so that the real participant was always the teacher. The learner (an actor called Mr. Wallace) was taken into a room and had electrodes attached to his arms. The teacher and experimenter then went into a room next door that contained an electric shock generator and a row of switches marked with various settings, beginning at 15 volts ("Slight Shock") and progressing to 375 volts ("Danger: Severe Shock"), and ending at 450 volts ("xxx").

The experimenter explained that the teacher would teach the learner a series of word pairs (e.g., "horse, blue") and later test the learner's memory. If the learner got a question wrong, the participant would give the learner a shock. The shocks started out relatively small, but with each wrong answer, the participant was told to move to the next higher shock level. At 150 volts the actor started crying out as if in pain. The cries were a ruse. The learner never received the shocks that the participants believed they were giving him. With higher levels of shock, the actor's cries became screams, until the actor stopped responding altogether, leading many participants to believe he was unresponsive and possibly dead.

If you were a participant in this experiment, at what point would you stop shocking the learner? Milgram found that some people stopped midway, refusing to give the most painful shocks. But he also found that the majority of people—around two-thirds—continued to the end, giving what would have been lethal levels of electric shock. Milgram discovered that most people would give someone a lethal electric shock simply because a man in a white lab coat told them to do so. When asked at the end why they kept going, many of Milgram's subjects offered the same excuse heard at Nazi war tribunals: "I was just following orders."

Now, it was not that Milgram's participants enjoyed the experience. In fact, the situation made participants terribly anxious—they sweat profusely, complained, and argued with the experimenter. They even pleaded for the experimenter to stop the experiment and check on the learner. Each protestation was met by the experimenter calmly telling the participant to continue, which in most cases they did. Milgram did many versions of his famous study. In one of the more troubling scenarios, participants did not flip the shock lever themselves; instead they took orders from the experimenter and instructed a third person to flip the switch. In this version, almost everyone obeyed until the highest switch was thrown. But Milgram also found some good news. When participants saw another participant (actually yet another actor) resist the orders and quit the experiment, they were much more likely to quit as well.

Psychologists have shown that other people powerfully shape what we think and do. On one hand, it sounds like we are all just puppets of the social situations we find ourselves in, but think of it another way. Remember that in the bystander situation, if any one person helps, he or she breaks the paralysis, freeing others to help as well. In Milgram's obedience experiment, when one person quit, others gained the strength to stand up for what was right. One person can make a big difference. And knowing these facts about human behavior makes that person more likely to be you.

Over the last hundred years, psychologists have demonstrated that many of our intuitions about how people tick are wrong. Have you ever heard that "opposites attract" and that "absence makes the heart grow fonder"? How about that "birds of a feather flock together" and "out of sight, out of mind"? Do you see the problem? Look at the first phrase in each sentence. Now look at the second phrase in each. Folk intuitions about behavior are often contradictory. A deep understanding of when and why people think and act the way they do takes careful scientific research.

New Frontiers in Psychology

Psychologists have made great progress over the last one hundred years in determining what makes people tick. We have learned that particular patterns of brain activity are associated with particular kinds of thought and behavior. We have also learned that situations can shape our behavior in powerful ways. But there are many big, unanswered questions left. For example, what was special about the few people in Milgram's obedience experiment that gave them the strength to say no? Why does being abused in childhood lead to mental illness in some people but not others? What is consciousness? Why do we dream? These questions, and many others, are wide open for future generations of psychological scientists. It is an exciting time. Not only are some of the biggest questions still open, but rapidly evolving technologies are also giving us a closer and closer look at the inner workings of the mind.

A hundred years ago, psychologists inferred what parts of the brain did what by finding a patient with a mental disability and waiting until they died to look at their brain. Often they found diffuse brain disease, making clean diagnoses impossible. Only rarely would a relatively straightforward case come along, as in the case of Phineas Gage, whose tamping iron near-surgically removed part of his frontal lobe. Today we don't have to rely on patients alone or wait for autopsy results; we can monitor the brain activity of healthy people while they think and do things. One of the most widely used technologies is *functional magnetic resonance imaging* (fMRI), which uses magnetic fields to track oxygen levels in the blood while people do specific tasks, like trying to remember a six-digit number. This works because oxygen is magnetic, and when neurons fire they eat up oxygen. Depleted oxygen in a brain area is like a smoking gun—it tells us that neurons had just been firing in that area. Although tracking oxygen gives us a good sense of *where* activity was happening in the brain, the indirect and delayed nature of the measurement means figuring out *when* the neurons were firing is difficult. *Electroencephalography* (EEG) can measure the electrical activity directly, and therefore gives better "when" estimates, but is worse than fMRI at locating where that firing occurred. *Magnetoencephalography* (MEG) aims to combine the best of both techniques, and new technologies are being invented as I write this to provide even better and more mobile measurements. This kind of *noninvasive* (not sticking anything in your head) and *in vivo* (measurement while you are alive) testing is a huge advance!

These technological advances have even allowed us to communicate with people in a coma, even those who have been comatose for years. In one clever study, comatose patients were scanned while being asked yes/no questions like "Is your father's name Thomas?" and "Do you have any brothers?" Sometimes the correct answer was yes, and other times no. But wait, didn't I just say that the patients had not communicated in years? How could they answer the questions? Remember that different mental states are associated with different brain areas. The scientists told the patients that if the answer was yes they should imagine playing tennis, thereby activating the motor imagery area at the top of their brain. If the answer was no, patients were to imagine walking through the rooms of their house, thereby activating the spatial navigation area at the bottom of their brain. For several comatose patients, the results were unmistakable. "Yes" questions were followed by activation of motor cortex; "no" questions were followed by activation of the navigation area. For the first time in years, these patients were given a channel of communication. Once believed to be lost, their minds were found to have been there all along.

The merging of brains and computers used to be the sole purview of science fiction. Today electrodes inserted in the brains of Parkinson's patients send pulses of electrical activity that alleviate uncontrollable shaking. *Deep brain stimulation* has also helped patients with intractable depression, and brain activity can even be harnessed to move prosthetic limbs. None of these cases would appear to change the definition of mind. But imagine many more electrodes, perhaps in brain circuits that control memory or personality. Is there a point in our future when a person's mind will be more the product of machine that biology?

Consider also the advances in artificial intelligence. Every year, we make computers that learn more like human beings, even beating us at our own games. Do these computers have minds? Would we feel differently if they looked like us? Would interacting with them affect our behavior as other people do now? These are wide-open questions that will only increase in importance as we develop smarter robots and other machines.

Technological advances also increasingly let us decode the thoughts and feelings of other animals. Imagine a computer that could decode the brain activity of a pig, allowing us to know, for example, when the pig was in pain or hungry. If we could understand what other animals thought and felt, would it change how we think of animal minds and how we treat them?

For thousands of years, our understanding of what a mind is and does relied on intuition and religious doctrine. Over the last one hundred years, psychology has countered intuition with science, resulting in a more modern and sophisticated understanding of how biological and environmental forces shape what we think, feel, and do.

We are at the beginning of a new era in psychology. It is an era in which we will learn much more about the mind than we have at any other time in human history. Part of this is due to the fact that psychology has become a much larger, more collaborative, and more interdisciplinary science. Collectively, across the world, scientists are contributing to the Human Connectome Project—an effort to compile thousands of brain scans in one big database. Such a large database would provide enough data to map out the entire network structure of the human brain (*connectome* means "network map"). Understanding how these networks connect different brain areas and how information flows through them could lead to new discoveries about how neural networks are altered by disorders like Alzheimer's and schizophrenia. Engineers are working with neuroscientists to design new equipment to help us measure the workings of the brain. Even biologists, chemists, and physicists are getting in on the act of understanding that three-pound thought-producing object! Mathematicians, computer scientists, and statisticians are working hard to help us make sense of the huge amounts of data that experiments are generating.

It is also a time in which we will have to think through what we do with this knowledge. If you knew, for example, that someone was likely to commit a violent crime based on a brain scan, would you act on that knowledge? It is easy to imagine a world in which criminals are treated more humanely and the public is safer. But it is also easy to imagine a world in which there is no privacy and a thought can land a person in jail. This is a heady responsibility and a space where ethics and philosophy come into play. The psychological science of the future will grapple not only with what we *can* learn about the mind but also with how we should use that knowledge to make the world a better place.

WHAT IS

Religion?

Susan Ackerman

What is religion? Every time I teach my college's "Introduction to Religion" course, I ask my students this question on the first day. Perhaps most often, their answers focus on belief: "Religion is about a belief in God or in gods," or "Religion is about believing in something superhuman/transcendent/oth-erworldly," or "Religion means to believe in higher powers." My students also often describe religion as having some explanatory power: "Religion explains things that humans can't know or don't understand"—things like where the world came from, why we humans are here, and what happens after we die. Relatedly, students suggest that in the past, before the advent of scientific worldviews, religion explained natural phenomena that otherwise mystified and more often than not terrified human beings: famine, floods, pestilence, disease. Frequently, students propose that religion in addition has some connection to ethics and morality: "Religion provides a rulebook, or guidelines on how to live one's life"; "Religion furnishes a system of laws for human behavior"; "Religion articulates the values for living a moral life."

When I listen to these answers, I hear two things. First, I hear my students telling me that religion is hard to define: it is a complex and multifaceted phe-nomenon that means different things to different people. Indeed, according to one scholar, trying to answer the question "What is religion?" is a little like the traditional Indian story of the six blind men who are asked to define an elephant by feeling different parts of its body. For the blind man who feels the leg, the elephant is like a pillar; for the blind man who feels the ear, the elephant is like a fan; for the blind man who feels the tail, the elephant is like a rope, and so on. The moral of the story is that no one of the blind men is right, but that when they put all their impressions of the elephant together, they do have a definition of an elephant.

But note that to get to an accurate definition of an elephant, it takes six blind men touching the elephant all over (head, tail, legs, side, tusk, trunk), and this brings me to the second thing I hear when I listen to my students try to answer the question "What is religion?" on the first day of class: these students usually haven't learned enough at that point to talk about religion all over the globe. Rather, the parts of religion they tend to describe come very much out of what they have "touched" or been touched by in their lives, which is to say: their answers to the question "What is religion?" overwhelmingly reflect their own experience and the worldview of the communities they live in. Because most of my students are American, this means they tend to describe religion based on their experience of Christianity, the religious tradition that dominates in the United States. Indeed, according to the Pew Research Center "Religious Landscape Study," about 71 percent of Americans identify as Christians, while only 6 percent identify as members of other religious traditions—the rest identify as unaffiliated. What's more, the Pew "Religious Landscape Study" tells us that about two-thirds of these American Christians are a part of Christianity's many different Protestant denominations.

This helps me understand why my students, when I ask them to define religion, respond most often with answers that focus on belief ("religion means believing in higher powers" or the like): it is because principles regarding belief are cornerstones of the Protestant Christian traditions that my students as Americans (whether they themselves are Protestants or not) know best. In fact, according to the founder of Protestantism, the German theologian Martin Luther (1483–1546), the "doctrine by which the church stands or falls" is the conviction that salvation comes to Protestants "when they *believe* that they are received into [God's] favor and that their sins are forgiven" (emphasis mine). Luther called this precept *sola fide*, or the doctrine of salvation through "faith alone"; also foundational for Luther was the doctrine he called *sola scriptura*, or the doctrine that maintains all Christian dogma and teaching must be derived from "scripture alone." By scripture, Luther means the Christian Bible, both the Christian Old Testament and New Testament, but for him the New Testament, with its focus on Jesus, Christianity's founder and savior, clearly has priority. Jesus's teachings in the New Testament, moreover, largely concern issues of ethics and morality. For example, the New Testament frequently speaks of Jesus's commitment to help the poor, the ill, and other marginalized members of society.

No wonder, then, that my students, under the influence of the Protestant traditions that dominate their world, so readily identify ethics and morality as key components in their definitions of religion. No wonder, too, that my students' definitions of religion so frequently focus on the relation between religion and science, as this has been a concern of Protestantism and of Christianity more generally for at least the past five hundred years. Think of the friction that resulted when Nicolaus Copernicus (1473–1543) and later Galileo Galilei (1564–1642) proclaimed their views that the Earth revolved around the sun, in opposition to the Earth-centered model of the universe championed by the Roman Catholic Church. Or think of the tensions that still manifest themselves today concerning the theory of evolution that Charles Darwin published in 1859, as opposed to the more traditional Christian (and especially Protestant) claim that the world and all its life-forms was created in only six days.

If we are to define fully the complex and multifaceted phenomenon of religion, however, we need to touch more parts of the elephant than its Christian components, meaning we need to move beyond a Protestant-centered worldview to take other religions into account. Consider, for example, Buddhism, for while Buddhists affirm the existence of various gods and other divine beings (for example, demons), belief in those gods is not of primary importance in the religion. Indeed, Buddhism is sometimes called a nontheistic religion because what matters most to Buddhists are not the religion's gods, but the teachings of its human founder, the Buddha, and especially the question whether they can, like the Buddha, achieve the state that Buddhists call *nirvana*. This is the state of awakening to the knowledge of the fundamental truths of existence that the Buddha revealed. Indeed, to achieve this state of awakening is a goal even of Buddhism's gods and other divine beings, although in order to achieve that goal, the gods—consistent with Buddhism's human-centered worldview—must ultimately die to their divine life and be reborn as humans. Then they can join other humans in striving to understand the Buddha's teachings about the ephemeral nature of existence and how to escape from the suffering that Buddhism believes is intrinsic to life.

Or consider Islam. Just as Protestantism has its set of foundational principles such as *sola fide* and *sola scriptura* (plus another one, two, or three of these *solae*, depending on which Protestant authorities one follows), Islam has a set of five foundational principles, the so-called Five Pillars of Islam. The first of these, moreover, seems quite reminiscent of the Protestant focus on the importance of belief in some sort of higher power: it reads, "There is no God but God, and Muhammad [the founder of Islam] is his prophet." The four other pillars, though, concern not what a Muslim is to believe, but what a Muslim is to do.

What's more, while the third pillar, which commands Muslims to offer charity (especially to needy Muslims), brings to mind Protestant concerns with living an ethical and moral life, the other three pillars require the performance of specific ritual acts that have no obvious moral or ethical component. The second pillar mandates that Muslims pray five times a day, in the early morning, at noon, midafternoon, and sunset, and in the evening. The fourth pillar specifies that Muslims should fast between sunrise and sunset during the ninth month of the Muslim calendar, which is called Ramadan. The fifth pillar states that at least once during his or her lifetime, every Muslim, if physically and economically able, should undertake a pilgrimage, called the *hajj*, to Islam's holiest city: Mecca, in Saudi Arabia.

What is indicated here is how important ritual activities are within many religious traditions—and not ritual in a mundane, routinized, or even automatized sense (such as my morning ritual of brushing my teeth), but ritual as prescribed formal behaviors that move the ritual actor outside the mundane, the routinized, and the ordinary in order to focus the actor's attention on that which is extraordinary. In Islam's case, for example, a Muslim focuses on submission before God during the day's five prayers; on God's revelation of the Qur'an, Islam's Holy Scriptures, during the month of Ramadan; and on the foundational figures of Islam—Muhammad, and also the prophet Abraham, his wife Hagar, and their son Ishmael—during the pilgrimage to Mecca.

Also important to note here is that religious rituals are more often than not undertaken communally. A Muslim, for example, cannot just embark on the hajj to Mecca at whatever time during the year is convenient: rather, the hajj takes place during the eighth to the thirteenth days of the last month of the Muslim year, and all Muslims going on the pilgrimage in any given year—these days, more than 2 million people—must go during the prescribed time. Furthermore, between the eighth and thirteenth days, there are prescribed actions for every day, so that all 2 million pilgrims are performing the same component of the hajj ritual—for example, making seven circles around Islam's holiest shrine, the Ka'aba—at the same time.

Similarly, although Muslims can pray alone during the five daily prayers, more typically practitioners—especially Muslim men—come together communally to pray. In Judaism, in fact, the three daily prayers (in the morning, afternoon, and evening) cannot be fully performed unless there is a *minyan*, or a gathering of ten worshippers (traditionally, ten men) who are thirteen years of age or older. The text of the prayers that the members of this *minyan* recite, moreover, are found in a prayer book called a *siddur*. The thrice-daily prayers, that is, are not the spontaneous utterances of each individual; instead, every member of the praying community is reciting the same words at the same time. This is also true for the five daily prayers in Islam.

Another religious tradition in which ritual, and ritual in community, is especially important is Hinduism. As in Judaism and Islam, these rituals can involve prayer-like devotions that are directed toward Hinduism's gods: this, indeed, is the essence of the Hindu rite of *puja*, which involves directing prayers, invocations, and offerings of incense, flowers, water, fruits, and other foods toward a deity or divine spirit. This deity or divine spirit is typically represented in the temples, outdoor sanctuaries, and household shrines where puja takes place through a sculpture, a painting, or some other object that represents the god. But Hinduism is also notable for the way in which ordinary human practices, such as eating, are made extraordinary by being ritualized. At large gatherings, for example, Hindus eat sitting in a row, rather than facing one another, and food is served on banana leaves instead of plates. What one eats (especially whether one eats meat or not), with whom one eats, and who cooks the food are important considerations as well.

What drives these various aspects of food preparation and eating are Hindu notions of purity and pollution. Most crucial for understanding these Hindu concepts is to realize that purity and pollution are ritual, as opposed to moral or ethical states; indeed, in Hinduism, one could be a moral cad yet still ritually pure, so separate are one's moral or ethical character from one's status as pure or polluted. Rather, what determines one's state as pure or polluted is, first, birth, as Hindus understand themselves to be born into a particular caste, or *varna*. These varnas are hierarchically ranked; moreover, within the four main varnas are multiple subunits, called *jati*s. Again, one is born into a particular jati, and again, these jatis are hierarchically ranked. This hierarchy, however, does not play itself out in terms of the status markers of which many in today's world might most naturally think—for example, wealth or power. Instead, the main way the caste system's hierarchical ranking plays itself out is in terms of purity and pollution: members of the highest caste or varna are considered to be purer than members of lower castes, and within any given caste or varna, members of higher-ranked jatis are considered to be purer than those of lower-ranked jatis. One is thus born—based on one's caste or varna and one's jati—into a particular status in terms of purity, and since one cannot move between jatis or castes, the purity status of one's birth defines an individual through his or her entire life.

The second factor that determines one's purity status are the happenings of day-to-day life, for one's purity status based on birth can be (and inevitably is) compromised by various life activities and events. A woman's purity is compromised, for example, whenever she menstruates. In addition, the pollution this woman incurs is contagious—as is all pollution—so a menstruating woman should neither cook nor serve food during the time of her menses, lest she pollute those who eat any food she touches. Lower-caste Hindus can also transmit their impurities to upper-caste Hindus, and while contact among various castes or varnas cannot be avoided, Hindu tradition does take steps to minimize this contact and especially to regulate occasions where the transfer of impurity is particularly likely. Since the body's orifices are major pathways via which one person's impurities can move beyond that individual to pollute another, occasions that involve the breach of bodily orifices—which happens, for example, when people put food into their mouths—are especially important to police.

At multicaste gatherings, Hindus thus eat sitting in a line, rather than face-to-face, so that the danger of transmitting pollution via the eaters' open mouths is minimized, and within the line, members of different castes and jatis sit separately to minimize the risk of cross-caste pollution. Meals are served on banana leaves, which are discarded when the meal is done, rather than on plates, so that one does not risk eating from a dish that had been previously used, and thus polluted, by a lower-caste person. Also, Hindus typically eat with their hands, rather than a fork or spoon, so as to avoid using a potentially polluted utensil; more specifically, Hindus eat with their right hands, as the left hand is used to wipe oneself after going to the bathroom, and one would not want to introduce the pollution that accrues to urine and excrement into one's mouth. Pollution also accrues to blood (as we saw above concerning menstrual blood), and so Hindus of higher castes or varnas do not eat meat. Still, it is important to note that once polluted, one can rid oneself of the impurity through various means: a common way to do so is through ablutions or bathing. The act of washing oneself is thus another ordinary human practice that becomes extraordinary in Hinduism by being ritualized.

Traditionally in Hinduism one's varna and one's jati not only determined the purity status into which one was born; various castes and jatis are tied to various professions, and, again, there is no mobility. If one is born, then, into a family of farmers, one will be a farmer; a blacksmith's son will be a blacksmith. One also must marry within one's caste. Or at least this was true historically among Hindus; in modern-day India, the land where Hinduism originated and where it remains centered, traditions regarding caste are rapidly changing, especially in urban areas. In the past, however, and among many of India's rural communities still today, caste as a religious institution is inextricably intertwined with Hindu culture's economic order and with other aspects of social organization. For my students, who, again, generally speak out of an American perspective, this can be somewhat hard to understand, as the us Constitution enshrines a separation between religion and the state and thus, by implication, suggests a separation between religion and all sorts of other systems that constitute human communities. But in point of fact, religion for most of the world's people does not exist in a vacuum, but must be analyzed in conjunction with all of a culture's organizing principles—political, economic, juridical, and so on.

In ancient Egyptian religion, for example, the king, or pharaoh, is considered a god, a clear coming together of the culture's religious convictions and its political institutions. This bringing together of religion and politics has significant implications, moreover, for ancient Egyptian society. The mighty power ascribed to the gods, for example, was understood to accrue also to the pharaoh, with the result that political insurrections in ancient Egypt—coups and the like—were rare, for who would dare rebel against the representative of the gods on Earth? Ancient Egyptian pharaohs were also able to use their position as gods to commission for themselves the sort of monumental structures otherwise reserved for deities: most famously, the pyramids (envisioned in Egyptian tradition as a ramp the pharaoh would ascend upon his death to join his divine counterpart, the sun-god, in the sky), but also elaborate temples served by a priestly staff who made offerings to the pharaoh—especially dead pharaohs—just as they would to the gods of the Egyptian pantheon.

The doctrine of the divine right of kings that was promulgated in late medieval and early modern Europe similarly assumed that the spheres of religion (specifically Christianity) and politics were fundamentally connected, by asserting that a monarch's authority was derived directly from God and that kings were therefore not answerable to any earthly authority (be it the people, or the aristocracy, or a governing body such as a parliament). In our world today, moreover, we still find multiple examples of the deeply intertwined nature of religion and politics. Israel, for example, defined itself as a "Jewish state" in its 1948 declaration of independence, and many of its recent leaders continue to use this term. Also, a certain number of Israel's laws are based on the legal codes articulated in Jewish sacred texts, such as the Hebrew Bible (the Christian Old Testament), the second-century collection of legal materials known as the Mishnah, and the fifth-century expansion and elaboration of the Mishnah known as the Talmud. For example, Israeli law, basing itself on the biblical book of Leviticus holds that it is illegal for an Israeli Jew who is thought to be descended from the priestly lineage of biblical days (a *kohen*) to marry someone who has converted to Judaism (Leviticus 21:7). Islam, like Judaism, has its own long and rich tradition of religious law, called *shari'a*, and many countries with majority Islamic population have either instituted or have considered instituting juridical systems that incorporate at least some precepts of shari'a law.

So what is religion? Religion, as we have seen, is an essentially communal phenomenon, so much so that one scholar writes of religion as "attested *only* within social groups" (emphasis mine) and "requir[ing] such groups for [its] maintenance." Religion is also a system of thought, whose adherents affirm various propositions that they hold in common. These can include propositions about belief, but also propositions about adherents' hopes, fears, desires, and the like. However, unlike the beliefs, hopes, fears, and desires we may have about many other things that matter to us—our hopes for our nation's well-being, say, or our beliefs about the superiority of some political ideology—religious beliefs, hopes, fears, and desires are explicitly related to supernatural or superhuman beings.

Supernatural beings include the one God of Judaism, Christianity, and Islam, or the many gods and goddesses of religions such as Hinduism and the religion of the ancient Egyptians. In addition, supernatural beings can be demigods, angels, devils, and demons. Some religious traditions also attribute supernatural or superhuman abilities to their community's deceased ancestors, or—as in Australian Aboriginal tradition—to long-ago ancestral beings who shaped the cosmos and defined Aboriginal norms and customs at the very beginning of time. Humans with beyond-human abilities, too, can serve as the beings to which a religion's beliefs, hopes, fears, and desires relate, as in Buddhism, where the Buddha, although a human being (born as Prince Siddhartha Gautama), is nevertheless a human of extraordinary abilities: he walks and speaks, for example, at the moment of his birth.

Religious adherents, moreover, do not only affirm certain propositions—beliefs, hopes, fears, desires—that relate to supernatural or superhuman beings. They also engage in formally prescribed behaviors—rituals—that relate to those same supernatural or superhuman beings and that coordinate with their propositions of belief, hope, fear, and desire to form a coherent whole. Religion, in short, is a communal and coordinated system composed of propositions—beliefs, hopes, fears, and desires—and of rituals that are related to supernatural or superhuman beings.

Religion is also, as we have seen, a communal and coordinated system of propositions and rituals that is intimately intertwined with all the other systems—social, political, economic, and juridical—that define human communities. And like these social, political, economic, and juridical systems, religion is an integral and fundamental element within human communities. In fact, the same religion scholar I quoted above who insists that religion exists only in groups has also insisted that along with the systematic manufacture of tools and the development and employment of complex, abstract language, "people are distinguished from all other living things . . . by the creation and maintenance of religion." To be sure, that claim, for some, may go too far. Still, religion is arguably a feature of every human community on Earth today and every community of the past that we have been able to study and come to know.

Indeed, in a speech he gave in August 2013, US secretary of state John Kerry stated, "If I went back to college today, I think I would probably major in comparative religion, because that's how integrated it is in everything that we are working on and deciding and thinking about in life today." Religion, that is—no matter how hard it may be to define—is a ubiquitous part of our human experience, and our efforts to understand it are crucial to our efforts to understand ourselves.

WHAT IS

Sociology?

Janice McCabe

Have you ever wondered why kids group together the way they do at your school? Or whether it's a coincidence that you read three books in a row about boy animals? Or if your parents are the only ones with friends who are quite similar to them? Thinking about those patterns and investigating them in a systematic way is *sociology*.

In 1959, the American sociologist C. Wright Mills coined the term "sociological imagination" to refer to the ability to connect seemingly personal experience with broader social forces. By using your sociological imagination, you will come to look at your own life through a different lens. You will start to see patterns in people's experiences according to history, biography, and social structure. Another way to think about this is that although we certainly make choices that impact our lives—such as deciding on a favorite color or who to be friends with—larger structural forces shape these choices. In other words, some choices are more likely and seem more "natural" than others. Gender, race, and class background are three of the main structures at play in our society. Sociologists uncover the structures organizing social life.

Becoming Socialized

You were born into a society. But you were not born knowing how to act in society. You learn through watching and listening to people around you. Sociologists speak about *socialization* as the process through which people learn *cultural norms*—in other words, the values and behaviors deemed appropriate within a society. Socialization is a lifelong experience, but it's often invisible to us except when we violate cultural norms or are unsure about what they are. It's in these new situations, such as entering a new school or visiting a country for the first time, that we discover these cultural norms. For example, when I first moved to the South from the Midwest, I realized that although we still spoke English, there were things that I did not understand. One that stands out to me was when I went to the grocery store and the clerk asked if I wanted a "buggy." I stood there trying to figure it out, thinking that I did not have a baby with me, so he wasn't asking if I wanted a "baby buggy," so maybe this was a new kind of food? He must have sensed my confusion, so he pushed a grocery cart toward me and again said, "Would you like a buggy?" I realized that a "buggy" was what I called a "shopping cart" or "grocery cart" and came to expect this as I went to the grocery store again. This was no isolated event. I also learned that "Coke" was what we midwesterners called "pop" and that if I just ordered an "iced tea" it would arrive heavily sweetened. I soon learned to order "unsweetened iced tea." In short, my new neighbors quickly socialized me so that I became one of "them"—at least linguistically!

Language is just one kind of behavior to which we are socialized. We often don't notice socialized behaviors until either someone breaks a norm or we experience unexpected norms in a new situation—in other words, when we see someone who behaves "out of the ordinary." This often happens when you travel or, even better, live abroad. I taught and lived for a summer in Florence, Italy. Immediately I noticed a very different response from the Italians (or at least the Florentines) when I took my eleven-month-old son out into the city than I generally received when doing the same in the United States. When my son started fussing while we were waiting in line at the local grocery store, I was worried that we were disturbing the other customers (that's what I had come to expect at home), so I looked around to assess how disruptive we had become, ready to apologize. To my surprise, several other customers met my gaze with wide grins and started to walk our way. They got within a few inches of us and began talking and singing to my son in Italian. He immediately calmed down, relishing the attention. This happened each time he started fussing when we were in public. It made outings quite enjoyable. Another surprising behavior was the frequent sharing of food with my son. The first time it happened was a little cracker at the corner bakery, then a banana at the farmer's market, a cookie from a stranger's purse on the bus, and a mini-cone at the gelato stand. Each and every day we were out in the city, my son got at least one piece of food from a shopkeeper or stranger. At the café around the corner from our apartment, they had a special type of bread specifically for small children. It was over a foot long! The waiter also told us that he would like the ribollita, a tomato and bread soup, and he did. At the pasta stall at our farmer's market, the cashier suggested pasta in very small shapes, which we later found out was made especially for babies. I began to see that what I first thought were odd but fun experiences were really part of structural differences between us and Italian culture. That's my sociological imagination at work. As it turns out, our experiences fit with sociologists' extensive observations, based on years of fieldwork, showing that Italian culture—like most of Western Europe—is more communal, celebrates childhood more, and integrates children and adults more highly compared to us culture, which is more individualistic.

Social Construction

These are just a few of the many examples of quite different behaviors that are all assumed to be "normal" in different places. Each society that we find ourselves in is organized in particular ways. We often take for granted that the ways our own society is organized is "of course" the way things are done. However, sociologists uncover how many of these ideas are *socially constructed*. Looking across time to examine the forces of history, as the sociological imagination urges us to, often reveals other possibilities for how social life can be organized.

One important and interesting context for understanding social construction is the concept of gender. Take, for example, the notion that pink is for girls and blue is for boys. This seems obvious, right? But it wasn't always the case. Until the early twentieth century, all babies wore white. There was no color-coding because in order to get clothes clean, they needed to be boiled. White was practical in this way. Baby boys and baby girls also wore the same outfits, which were dresses. Nurseries were not color-coded either. In the early twentieth century, when color separation started to take hold, pink was the preferred color for boys because of its association with red and strength. Blue was the preferred color for girls because of its association with the Virgin Mary. So although it may seem obvious today that pink is a girls' color, this association is socially constructed.

Before you were born, the most frequent question your parents were asked about you was whether you were a boy or a girl. This distinction is one of the starkest in society today: people are classified from birth as either male or female. Your sex is noted on your birth certificate. Biological sex is typically identified by the external genitalia noted by the doctor when a baby is born. And for most people, the sex we are assigned at birth corresponds with the gender category with which we identify—in terms of children, classification as a boy or a girl. This notion, that gender is a *binary* attribute, has a long tradition. Specific behaviors and appearance are associated with each of these categories. In general, we expect that girls like pink, princesses, and dolls, and act more passively, and we expect that boys like blue, superheroes, and trucks, and act more aggressively. However, I'm sure we all know boys and girls who violate these gender expectations. We generally tolerate small transgressions, such as a boy wearing a pink shirt or a girl who likes trucks. Typically, though, other people let us know that we have violated these cultural norms surrounding gender, perhaps by joking or teasing that we are "acting like a boy" or "looking like a girl."

What happens when people consistently violate cultural norms surrounding gender? Two groups of people who do so are *transgender* and *genderqueer* individuals. *Transgender* individuals are people for whom the sex they were assigned at birth does not correspond to their gender identity. Just as there is a wide range of behaviors and appearances associated with gender, there is a similarly wide range of ways to be transgender. Caitlyn Jenner (previously Bruce Jenner, already a public figure as an Olympic gold medalist) famously transitioned to a woman and appeared on the cover of *Vanity Fair* magazine. Transgender individuals, however, do not always undergo surgery or hormone therapy. Some may undergo a gender transition by dressing according to their gender identity and adopting a name and gender pronouns that are consistent with their gender identity. Some transgender individuals "come out" as transgender to the people they meet as well as family members and friends. Others prefer to keep their gender transition quiet and are sometimes referred to as "stealth" transgender individuals. Some transgender individuals prefer romantic relationships with people of the same gender, others prefer the opposite gender, and others do not have a preference. The shift in cultural norms around gender can be seen in the new attention being directed toward transgender rights. In spring of 2016, the Obama administration released a letter providing guidance to schools on providing an environment that is "welcoming, safe, and inclusive for all students." The guidance includes allowing transgender students to use names, locker rooms, and restrooms that correspond to their preferred gender—that the US Supreme Court will soon consider in the case of *Gavin Grimm v. Gloucester County School Board*. Time will tell if and how these changes are implemented and whether they reduce discrimination and violence against transgender youth. Using our sociological imagination to understand this issue, we can see that gender is a profoundly personal issue and a category that is socially constructed and changing.

Genderqueer identification also reveals the social construction of gender. Genderqueer individuals do not identify as male, female, man, woman, boy, or girl. Instead, they identify as a blend of these binary categories or as a third gender. Genderqueer individuals challenge the organization of society in an even deeper way than transgender individuals. Which restroom should they use? Which pronouns should we use to refer to them? Who are they allowed to marry?

As we ask these questions and many others, we realize how the structure of our society is built on a gender binary—that is, on the idea that there are two and only two genders. However, as we look at other cultures, we find that there are other possibilities. For example, many, but not all, Native American societies recognize sex or gender in a nonbinary way, whether by recognizing a third gender or by categorizing people as both male or female, such as *nàdleeh* among the Navajo, *alyha* among the Mahave, or *two-spirit* among urban Native American gays and lesbians.

Tracking Cultural Representations

Sociologists study not only categories of people, but also the culture itself. For example, I was part of a team of sociologists who examined almost six thousand children's picture books for whether males or females were included in the title of the book (like *Winnie the Pooh* or *Olivia*) or as central characters in the book.

What do you think we found?

Left to pure chance, you would figure roughly it should be split 50–50, right? Well, in the six thousand books that we looked at (a fairly comprehensive set) we found clear patterns of male/female inequality. Males are included in titles nearly twice as often as females. Males are featured more than one and a half times more often than females as central characters (meaning that there are three male central characters for every two female central characters). The largest inequality is for animals (nonhuman), where male animals are central characters almost three times as often as female animals. Males appear more often than females not only in children's books, but in every aspect of children's media that has been examined—from cartoons to video games to G-rated films to coloring books. People are often surprised by these findings because our socialization blinds us to these patterns.

As you read books, watch movies, or engage with other forms of media, you can do your own content analysis. How often are males or females included? You can also do this with other groups to see how often various racial or ethnic groups are included, or people with disabilities, or different types of families.

Here is another fun exercise you can do. As you read books, watch movies, listen to music, or look at advertisements, pay attention to whether the words or images reinforce or violate *cultural norms*. When it comes to men and women, who is portrayed as more independent? Who is more focused on romantic relationships? Who takes care of children? Do you find exceptions to the general patterns? What does this tell us about our culture?

After you start to use your sociological imagination, it can be hard to shut it off. Students often tell me that after a sociology class, they find it difficult to flip through magazines or watch movies without noticing patterns in race, class, and gender.

Popularity and Status in Schools

Friendships are—next to family—the most fundamental social relationship. Friendships are very different from family relationships. As the saying goes, "You can't choose your family, but you can choose your friends." Understanding how those choices are made and whether there are patterns to them is super-interesting and a thriving context for using our social imaginations.

Even before they enter formal schooling, children start to form friendships. At first, being friends means simply playing together. With this definition, friendship is fleeting, but there are also endless possibilities, as anyone you play with would be your friend while you play together.

As children get older, the rules surrounding friendship start to get more complex. In addition to individual friendships, *cliques* start to emerge. Cliques are groups of people who interact with each other on a regular basis. Cliques in themselves are not a problem. They provide people with companionship and support. Many people, however, experience them as a problem when they feel excluded by or looked down upon by members of certain cliques.

Schools are often—or maybe even always—places where these cliques emerge. You've probably either experienced this phenomenon or seen it in a movie or a TV show. There are the "cool kids," the "nerds," the "jocks," and so on. Some may seem more powerful than others—or, as a sociologist might put it, schools also have their own *status systems*. You might be surprised to learn that status systems emerge in elementary school. In a well-known study of elementary school status systems Patricia and Peter Adler interviewed and observed children (including their own) in a single town over an eight-year period. The children attended seven public and five private schools. The researchers found many commonalities across these schools, including that a status system exists at each grade and within each grade, and there was one for boys and one for girls. The status system was perceived as ranging from the "popular clique" at the top, followed by the "wannabes," then "middle-rank friendship circles," with "isolates" at the bottom.

The relationships children form with their classmates differ according to where they happen in the status system. At the top, the popular clique commands the most attention and is closed to outsiders. In other words, the popular clique is cliquish. Popular clique members are typically quite aware of their high status and concerned with maintaining this status, which results in competitive relationships within the group, including the distinction between leaders, second-tier members, and third-third "followers." Going down the status hierarchy, the next group is wannabes, who hang around the popular clique hoping to be included. Wannabes are sometimes temporarily included, particularly when the popular clique needs more people to play a game or when they agree to fetch things for children in the popular clique. But they're even more frequently rejected. The existence of the wannabes reaffirms the high status of the popular clique, and their ties to the popular clique also reaffirms the lower status of the middle-rank friendship circles and the isolates. The middle-rank friendship circles make up about half of the grade, organized into smaller friendship circles. Most of these children recognize their middle-level status but don't try to be accepted by the popular clique. Unlike cliques that closely guard their boundaries, the middle-rank friendship circles are generally open to anyone who wants to join. These circles also reinforce loyalty among members, creating quite intimate and intense relationships. At the bottom of the status hierarchy are social isolates. With no real friends, isolates are chronically left out of games and rarely interact with others, except when they're being teased. Rather than forming their own group of isolates, isolates tend to reject each other, which further reinforces their low status.

By using your sociological imagination, you can see how children's experiences and friendships are not only personal, but also structured by children's position in the status hierarchy. For example, children in the middle-rank friendship circles have low prestige but strong peer relationships. Children in the popular clique have high prestige but greater anxiety about how they fit in.

By high school, status systems have become more complex. Instead of just one clique at each status level, multiple groups exist at the same status levels. There is still a "top," which is composed of popular kids, often including star athletes. And there is a "bottom," usually composed of isolates but sometimes also "nerds" or other low-status groups. The top and bottom are typically better defined than the middle. However, in the middle are kids referred to as "normals" (or sometimes "regulars" or "average students") along with a range of other groups, such as "alternatives," "skaters," "rednecks," and "thugs." The specific groups and labels vary from school to school, but the general structure of multiple groups in the middle was found in most schools. The barriers around these different groups make it hard to get to know people from other groups. Yet some students, referred to as "drifters" or "floaters," move between groups and befriend students in multiple groups. Can you map out the status system in your school? Has it changed as you've grown older? Where do you fit? If you can see yourself in this hierarchy, you are using your sociological imagination!

Patterns in Friendships

Friendships are often built around something that you and your friend have in common. For example, boys are more likely to be friends with boys, and girls more likely to be friends with girls. This is true among elementary school children as well as people in retirement communities. Friends are also more likely to be of the same racial or ethnic group.

One reason that many of our friendships are *homophilous* is that we are more likely to come into regular contact with people who are similar to us. In other words, sociologists point out that friendships are more likely to form when we share physical space (which they refer to as *propinquity*). This explains why people are more likely to befriend their neighbors than people who live across town (or even why we befriend the people who live across the hall rather in an adjacent building). Think about your own friendships. What do you share in common? What differences do you find? What brought you together? You might also look at the friendships of people who you know, including your classmates and family members. Do you see evidence of homophily and propinquity in their friendships?

Although it can often feel easier to be friends with people who are similar to us, there are also benefits of diverse ties. Research shows that college students who reported positive, diverse interactions with peers also had higher scores on complex thinking, cultural and social awareness, and concern for the public good. Diverse friendships can be good for you and for society.

Friendship relationships have always been of huge interest to sociologists, and we are responsible for the idea of the social network—that is, the web of connections between people. I would be happy to wager that anyone reading this

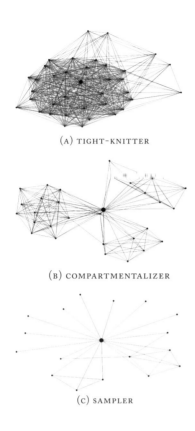

(A) TIGHT-KNITTER

(B) COMPARTMENTALIZER

(C) SAMPLER

FIGURE 1 Three styles of individual (ego) networks. In each case the large node is the central individual (ego) and smaller nodes are friends of "ego." Lines between nodes indicate that friends know each other. In (a) we see an example of a "tight-knitter": that is, generally ego's friends are themselves connected, so that ego's network is highly dense. In (b) we see an example of a "compartmentalizer," where the friends of ego split off into easily recognizable smaller networks that don't mix. In (c) we have an example of a "sampler," wherein ego has friends, but they rarely mix at all, so that ego "samples" from the various social networks around him or her. Courtesy of Janice McCabe / Dartmouth

essay often refers to his or her own "social network" and has maybe even seen a visualization of their social network on some social media platform.

Network analysis—or the mathematical analysis of networks—was pioneered by sociologists and is now a huge area of research. By using a little mathematics you can find very interesting patterns in social networks. For example, in some recent work I interviewed sixty-seven college students to try to get some understanding of how people might be different in the way that they form their social networks. Based on what they told me about their friends and which friends knew each other, I discovered that the networks of these sixty-seven students clustered into three types that I call *tight-knitters, compartmentalizers,* and *samplers.* Tight-knitters have one densely woven friendship group where nearly all their friends know each another. Compartmentalizers' friends form two to four clusters, where friends know each other within clusters but rarely across them. And samplers make a friend or two from a variety of places, but their friends are unconnected to each other. As shown in figure 1, tight-knitters resemble a ball of yarn, compartmentalizers resemble a bow-tie, and samplers resemble a daisy. Which type are you?

Sociologists examine not only friendship, but other kinds of connections as well. We have found that *weak ties*—that is, people we do not know intimately—are more important sources for finding a job than are *strong ties*, like friends. Using network analysis, you can map out the connections between almost anything—friendships, job offers, college applications, trade patterns among countries, and so on.

Thinking like a Sociologist

Now you should have a better idea of what it means to think like a sociologist. The patterns that sociologists investigate in our social world, however, go far beyond what I had room to discuss in this essay. Here are a few more examples: Using surveys, sociologists investigate patterns in public opinion or behavior, such as documenting changes in attitudes about homosexuality among the US public or differences in student loan debt by people's age and racial background. Sociologists travel to historical archives to examine common pathways in the revolutions of the past and those today. Sociologists design experiments to gain deeper insights into how people's stereotypes influence how they work with and evaluate others in small groups. Sociologists interview welfare recipients before and after new government policies to see their impact on families. As you can see, sociologists use a variety of research methods—surveys, archival analysis, experiments, interviews, ethnographic observations, content analysis, and statistics—to investigate patterns in society.

Throughout this chapter, I've suggested ways for you to exercise your sociological imagination. As you continue to develop your sociological imagination, you'll continue to find more patterns in our social world, to ask questions about why society is patterned in the way it is, and to notice as our categories and understandings change. There is always more to uncover.

WHAT IS

Theater?

Daniel Kotlowitz

When I was fifteen, my father (who had been dragging me kicking and scream-ing to the opera for years) took me to see a production of *Carmen* at the New York Metropolitan Opera. I remember being awestruck by the images created onstage: the scenery was red and white and all curves, the lighting was blin-dingly white and hot, and of course there was Georges Bizet's fiercely passionate music. The opera had all of the elements that make a great story: love, jealousy, betrayal, and death. However, there was something else about that production that caught my attention. On that particular evening, the air conditioning at the Met failed, and as the opera progressed, the theater got hotter and hotter, until it was almost impossible to breathe. The audience was drenched in sweat, and the smells, sounds, sights, and sensations of this hot, dry theater began to make me feel as if I were right there in the white-hot summer sun of southern Spain.

I remember thinking that this was unlike anything that I had ever experienced. I was dazzled by the immediacy and impact of this world onstage. It wasn't like television or the movies. I didn't feel as if I was just watching a story—I felt like I was actually another character within that story. It never occurred to me that the lack of air conditioning and general discomfort in the theater was not on purpose. Feeling so immersed in the action and music was unexpected and exciting. I was part of a living world, and even though I was just an observer, I was also a participant: the music, the heat, and the raw emotions onstage felt real and boldly theatrical. On first glance one might think that "real" and "theatrical" are contradictory—but in fact (as I shall hopefully reveal) it is the very nature of theatricality that makes theater "real."

Though I didn't know it at the time, this was the moment when I decided to devote a good deal of my life to thinking about and creating theater as a theater designer. Sometimes I worry that I started my career based on a misunderstanding, but forty-four years later, here I am, still awestruck by theater.

Theater can be many different things, but I'll go out on a limb and say that one thing that all (or most) theater people would agree with is that

THEATER IS LIVE PERFORMANCE.

Notice how I put that sentence in the middle of the page, in capital letters with a pleasing font . . . That is because, like all theater folk, I love dramatic entrances.

Theater Is Live Performance and More . . .

This is a pretty broad view of theater, and I think that musicians might take some offense. They might say that what they do is not theater; however, because I am a theater person, I will disagree. Have you ever yelled at your parents or a friend and stomped around in anger, maybe slammed a few doors, thrown a plate, sighed loudly, and sobbed for so long that you forgot why you were crying? This is all theater. Let me expand this definition just a little, because there is something else about theater that is important, which I haven't yet mentioned. That is the telling of stories. So . . .

THEATER IS LIVE PERFORMANCE
THAT TELLS A STORY.

Stories are everywhere. For example, when you yelled at your parents and stomped around, you were telling your parents a story. It was a story about your anger. When you sighed loudly, your story was about how disappointed you were. Stories don't always go in a straight line; they don't always start at the beginning and follow with a middle and then the end. Some stories never get past the beginning, some start at the end, while others don't have a middle. Your anger story only had a beginning: "I AM ANGRY!" (Your parents probably supplied the middle and the end.)

Usually when we talk about theater, we are talking about theater as an "art form." As an "art form," theater has certain responsibilities connected to the relationship between the art and the audience. When "civilians" (that's what we in the trade call the non-theater-trained audience!) attend the theater, they unknowingly sign an implicit contract with the theater artists. It is a simple contract, but one that has nasty repercussions if not followed. This contract reads: "We, the artists, promise to create an experience that will engage and interest you. If that happens, then you, the audience, agree to suspend your disbelief and forget that you are in a theater."

This is a sacred contract that, when broken, usually means the closing of a show, the loss of employment, and even the possibility of tomatoes being thrown toward the stage. And yes, I have actually seen all of that happen. It's also worth pointing out that there is a lot embedded in this contract. The experience that the theater provides is composed of many different pieces: players, staging, words, movements, each of which can and will vary over time, space, and context. What the audience brings to the work also affects the experience. Every time a work of theater is performed, that performance is something new—there may be twenty productions of Shakespeare's *Macbeth* all going on at the same time in different parts of the world, and you can be sure that none of them will look, sound, or feel the same! Similarly, within the run of a single production, the performances will change nightly—each performance being shaped by the response (or lack thereof) of the audience. Theater is never the same thing twice.

Theater embodies the human condition. It is about what we feel, what we experience, and how we react. It is about our strengths, our weaknesses, our courage, and our fears. It is about our future, our past, and our present. It is about us, and, I would venture to say that we, as imperfect, emotional, and spiritual beings, have not changed all that much in the last three thousand years. Yes, of course, the world around us has changed dramatically, but the things we experience, such as love, hate, anger, sadness, joy, pleasure, pain, hunger, gluttony, contentment, stress, anxiety, birth, and death, these things haven't really changed that much over the years. So when Shakespeare's Othello kills his wife Desdemona, egged on by the nasty Iago, we are frustrated by Othello's confusion and deep regret. We are lifted up by Desdemona's courage, deeply disturbed by her murder, and angered by Iago's cruelty. The play still moves us, it still touches us, and we still learn from Shakespeare's words. Theater is a living, breathing art form, and with each new production of a piece of theater, life is again breathed into the story. We realize that these are not historical relics: they are stories about us—you and me—and they continue to teach, inform, inspire, and move us. The reason theater people keep doing theater and audiences keep coming to see theater is that we see so much of ourselves in the work.

Every production is new. Theater is an ethereal medium. Like smoke, it billows out, often beautiful and graceful, sometimes just annoying. Yet then, just as quickly, it dissipates and disappears forever. A theater production, when it closes, is done. No audience will ever see that production again. For theater artists, this impermanence is frustrating, but also empowering, because we are never forced to repeat what has been done before. Theater happens, then it is gone. Now you see it, now you don't.

Questions, Not Answers

Generally, in the theater, we have found that it is more interesting to simply raise questions than to try to answer them. This is not because we are lazy, but because when you leave a question unanswered, you provoke your audience to think and act for themselves and, in effect, become a part of the experience. These are not broad, open-ended questions like "How was your day?" Rather, they are directed questions that push and provoke, like "Why did you ignore that homeless person?" One of the best feelings in the world is to watch an audience streaming out of a show during intermission or at the end of a performance, arguing loudly about what they saw. This sends a shiver of delight down every theater person's spine, because it means that our audience members are digging for answers to the questions we have raised.

These questions offer us an opportunity to consider ourselves from a different viewpoint—like looking at a mirror and seeing the back of your head. This is something you don't often see, and it can make you think of all sorts of different and sometimes interesting ideas. This is really what art is meant to do: ask questions. Sometimes these are questions everyone is afraid to ask, questions no one ever thought to ask, or perhaps they are questions we are all asking. The point is to make us think, and to sometimes act as a reflection of not just what we are, but who we are, and maybe who we might become.

Theater has a long and vibrant recorded history that goes all the way back to the Greeks, to the classic plays of Aeschylus, Sophocles, and Euripides. In fact, it goes back even further, to ancient Indian Sanskrit drama. These great Greek and Sanskrit dramas are still performed today. Why would anyone want to perform a play written twenty-five hundred years ago? Why do we continue to see productions of Shakespeare, who died over four hundred years ago, or Molière, who wrote over three hundred years ago? Because the questions they ask are universal and timeless.

Shakespeare was a master question-raiser. His work is timeless because of the universality of the questions he forces us to confront. Every generation of theatergoer and theater-maker is able to reinterpret his work for their own time. Even now the questions that Shakespeare raises remain relevant and meaningful. For example, take *Macbeth*. In 2008, there was a marvelous production of *Macbeth* directed by Rupert Goold with Patrick Stewart in the title role. I saw this production in New York, and there was one particular scene that had such power that even years later the images remain clear in my mind. Macbeth and his wife have just killed their king, Duncan, and the next in line for the crown, Banquo. Immediately after Banquo's death they sit for a feast with Macbeth's minions. As they eat, Banquo's ghost appears: covered in blood, he steps up and walks on the banquet table. Macbeth (the only one who can see Banquo) recoils, and Lady Macbeth tells him to pull it together:

> O proper stuff!
> This is the very painting of your fear . . .

Lady Macbeth is telling her husband that his overwrought guilt and imagination are "painting" his fear and that he should just get a hold of himself. After Banquo leaves, Macbeth declares: "It will have blood they say; blood will have blood."

For Macbeth, Banquo's appearance is not merely a manifestation of his guilt. Rather, it foretells the natural order of things: bloody acts will be paid for with bloody acts. The words are powerful in and of themselves, but this production takes this scene one step further—and this is what I will never forget: we first watch the scene with Banquo's ghost physically present, covered in blood and looking quite dead; then the scene is done again—without Banquo actually being present. The first scene is seen through Macbeth's eyes, the second through the eyes of Lady Macbeth and the banquet guests. Now when Macbeth recoils in response to Banquo, Banquo's ghost is not there. I have seen more productions of *Macbeth* than I can count, but I have never felt so clearly the horror within Macbeth, and the frustration of Lady Macbeth. Yet I still walked away questioning: "Does Macbeth really see the ghost of Banquo, or is it all in his head? And if the ghost is real, then are all acts of evil eventually paid for in kind . . . and, more to the point, is that payment delivered by an omniscient being (God?), or by our own sense of right and wrong (Guilt)?" Tough questions.

Beginning, Middle, and End?

Many works of "Classic theater" (the plays of Shakespeare, for example) possess a structure that goes back all the way to ancient Greece. This pattern of narrative requires a beginning, a middle, and an end, but some forms of stories don't have this classic structure. Dance provides a good example of other ways to tell a story. Sometimes dance, ballet for instance, can have a clear story line, as in *The Nutcracker* or *Swan Lake*. Ballet is often driven by convention and traditional stories; specific movements and techniques are combined in unique ways that are expressive and tell stories. However, modern dance often relies less on conventional stories and instead subverts conventional narrative form to tell a story of rhythm, or of the vertical length of a body, or about the great power of gravity pulling us all downward, or the even greater power of the human spirit to lift us up. These are stories that don't follow a straight line. I remember watching Suzanne Farrell, when she was a principal dancer at the New York City Ballet. She was dancing a solo to Maurice Ravel's *Boléro* (a glorious piece of uplifting music, which I am listening to at this very moment).

Farrell confined her movements to a small area (eight feet in diameter), lit by a single round pool of cool, white light. Ravel's music is very simple, repeating the same melody over and over for seventeen minutes. During this time, the music slowly, almost imperceptibly builds in volume, orchestration, and rhythm, starting insubstantially (almost too quiet to hear) and becoming larger and louder and faster. Throughout, Farrell dances in this simple pool of light to this simple music. Her legs, already long and powerful, extend and increase their height as she goes up "on pointe" (standing on the very tip of her toes, very difficult to do—try it!). Her arms reach up higher and higher, extended even further by her long and graceful hands and fingers. It was as if she were expanding ever higher and higher toward the source of light. I felt like she was slowly growing, expanding up and up, getting taller and taller. As with Shakespeare, it's not just about the extraordinary physical performance of the artist/dancer, synchronized with this uplifting music; it's larger and grander than what is visible and audible. At the peak of Ravel's music and Farrell's movement, I felt an extraordinary sense of achievement and purpose, a hint of what is possible not just on the stage, but in life, of what we can attain when we reach beyond what we think is possible. That was the story I was experiencing, and it was, in some measure, the story the artists (the dancer, orchestra, choreographer, lighting designer, conductor, and others) were telling me; it was at that moment a story about the extraordinary potential and purpose of humankind. Although there was no conventional plot line with a beginning, middle, or end, it was a journey that made me feel something very real and substantial. This is what great theater and art can do—it makes us feel.

There is a very exciting British theater company called Punchdrunk doing work that doesn't yet have a single identifying genre title—it could be called devised theater, immersive theater, and/or spectacle. ("Devised theater" is theater that starts without a script and is "devised" in collaboration by the theater artists. "Immersive theater" happens when the boundaries between audience and performer are gone and the audience is "immersed" in the experience). In 2013 Punchdrunk produced an enormous spectacle of a show called *The Drowned Man: A Hollywood Fable.* The production was performed in a four-story warehouse in London that was transformed into a Hollywood studio, village, forest, hotel, bar, and desert. The audience all wore masks and wandered around on their own initiative, stopping to watch scenes being played out all over the warehouse. For an audience member the experience was frustrating, exhilarating, scary, funny, confusing, and revelatory. A group of viewers might congregate around a small scene being played out by actors—then suddenly one actor would break away and a few audience members would follow that actor to some other scene. The audience decided how they were going to experience the story—and no one person had the same experience. Here was a story that had a beginning, a middle, and an end, and then another beginning, another end, a new middle, and yet another beginning . . . and on and on. Finally, at the end, all of the audience collected in the same area and the final end scene is experienced by the entire audience together, for the first time. After the show I was exhausted; I had not just "watched" an event, I had been fully 'immersed' within the work. It left me unsettled and changed, and three years later I still think about it.

Audience

If you record theater on your iPhone and play it back, is it still theater? I say no. The one thing that you cannot take away from a performance (and still call it theater) is that it is live. There must be an audience. This is the theater version of the age-old question "If a tree were to fall in a forest and no one is around to hear it, does it make a sound?" A theater practitioner would say no, because you *need* an audience.

Why is the audience so important?

The audience is crucial because they are actually a part of the performance.

Audience members are much more than just passive observers—they are participants. Ask any actor, musician, dancer, singer, or politician. The audience changes the way they perform. An actor says a line and the audience laughs. The actor pauses until the laughter is done. Then, in wanting more laughter, the actor speeds up the next three boring lines in order to get to the next laugh. Thus, the audience has changed the performance.

The other unique and often frightening thing about live performance is that *anything* can happen, and anything often does. I once worked with a Japanese dance company named Sankai Juku. Someone in the audience took a picture in the middle of the show and the camera flash went off. The leader of the dance company, who was dancing at the time, stopped, looked up at the audience, and then suddenly leapt off the stage and into the audience looking for the person with the camera. Amazingly, this dancer found the person and demanded that he open the camera and expose the film. (Um, so, in the old days, we didn't have digital cameras. If you opened up the camera, it would ruin the film.) Incredibly, the dancer then bounded back onto the stage and resumed the performance. The audience was absolutely silent throughout the entire episode, and only a few of us knew that this was not a part of the performance . . . Or maybe it was?

Nothing beats the sheer untouchable electricity of live people in a live environment being watched and responded to by a community of live theatergoers. This interaction of audience and performance is unlike any other artistic medium that I have experienced. I have worked on shows where all five hundred people in an audience shifted in their seats at the same moment because of something they were watching onstage. I have seen audiences laugh, sigh, shout, and weep in unison. When five hundred people all weep together, that becomes a part of the performance. The audience and the performance becomes thoroughly enmeshed into a single reality.

I recently designed the lighting for a musical called *Chicago* and began the production by suddenly bumping up a row of lights that were pointed directly into the audience's eyes. The stage was filled with smoke, and the pipe that held the lights slowly rose up into the air. On opening night when this happened, everyone in the theater shifted ever so slightly in their seats. I know it sounds odd, but the energy of four hundred people all shifting in their seats at the same moment is one of the most exciting things in the world, because you know that you have touched all of those people just enough to make them move. For that one brief instant, you have shifted their reality.

For the artist, theater can be a glorious explosion of an audience celebrating our work, and it can also be a horrific implosion of audiences rejecting our work. Everything we do onstage makes us very vulnerable. The rewards are great and the punishments are swift and brutal.

Theatricality

Another thing about live performance is the idea of *theatricality*. Sometimes when we look at someone we might say, "Oh, they are very *theatrical*," and generally we mean they are flamboyant or bigger than life. But when I use this term I am talking about a presentation that takes specific advantage of the power of theater as a *live* event. It is one thing to watch a transformation in a movie or on television, where editing, special effects, and scale can distance us from the actual event. In the theater, these transformations happen right in front of your eyes on the stage. This is live, on a human scale. We are a part of it. It is truly magic. In addition, theater has all of the audience members' senses at its disposal: sight, hearing, smell, touch, and even taste. I know I have experienced theatricality when I think, "What I just saw could only happen in the theater." It is about letting theater be theater.

Collaboration

With all the moving parts that theater requires, you might have already guessed that as an artistic process theater is grounded in collaboration. Collaboration—at its best—represents the sharing of a process. Theater collaborators include a wide range of artists, artisans, and managers. There are the performers, actors, singers, dancers, clowns, acrobats, writers, directors, choreographers, musicians, composers, set designers, lighting designers, costume designers, sound designers, projection designers, stage managers, carpenters, electricians, properties persons, sound engineers, backstage crews, light and soundboard operators, house managers, marketing teams, general managers, production managers, and dramaturgs. All of these people work together to create a vivid and meaningful world that starts from nothing.

Collaboration can be both the most rewarding and the most difficult aspect of the production process, at times exhilarating and terribly frustrating. The best collaborations make seemingly contradictory demands on their participants. First, they demand the strength and confidence of an artistic ego capable of supporting a purposeful and meaningful vision. They then call for the generosity to willingly give up a certain measure of that very same ego so that the vision of the production can become a unified whole. Theater is not created in seclusion and silence. Theater is a loud and hurried art form, defined by conflicting and often intoxicating artistic temperaments, urgent deadlines, and a necessary spirit of community.

I tell my students that if they don't like to collaborate, they shouldn't do theater. If you do like to collaborate, then you need to learn how to do it right. Here are a few simple things to remember:

RULES FOR COLLABORATION

1. Learn to listen. This is not an easy task. This means that when someone is talking, you are actually listening to what they are saying, and not, as we so often are, thinking the entire time about your own response.

2. Trust your collaborators. This is an even more difficult task than listening. When we do theater, we are often working with complete strangers. It is hard to trust a stranger. So we work extra hard to create a bond. We do this by talking very deeply and honestly about our lives, confessing sins, and revealing unpleasant and distasteful character traits. We do this immediately after meeting our collaborators, and then, because we know the worst of each other, we become fast friends. In fact, we often become friends for life.

3. Acknowledge that collaboration does not mean compromise. Rather than being a dilution of an idea, collaboration is the adding of many ideas together that build and grow.

The Magic of Theater

The theatrical worlds that result from this collaboration have all the sights and sounds of a real world—the people, the words, the history, the events. There are sunsets, sunrises; shafts of supernatural light from the heavens; the sounds of crickets, birds, and thunder; toilets flushing; the buzz of electricity. Sometimes lives are underscored by sounds or music. The characters in these worlds live in houses with chairs and tables, napkins, forks, books, guns, diapers. They have wallets and keys in their pockets; they wear shirts, skirts, hats, and pants with worn holes at the knees; sometimes they are naked, and sometimes their clothes don't quite fit. They have deep and sad inner thoughts, bad memories, happy memories, dark unthinkable ideas. They cry, they laugh, they love, they steal, they share, they hate, they dream, they kill, and sometimes they die. All of this is created out of thin air, it is alchemy and it is magic, but it always comes from collaboration.

Genres

There are many different approaches to making theater, and all are valid. These different approaches are often called *genres*, but it gets complicated, as genres intermix and combine. Each basic genre, at its foundation, represents a different craft or style. In *straight theater* (which doesn't refer to a line) artists rely on text and the craft of acting; words are the primary tool. *Dance* is another genre, where we rely on the craft of movement to create expression. In *opera*, we rely on music and spectacle—the craft of singing. In *musicals*, we use all the genres listed so far: text, movement, and music. Then there is a relatively new genre of theater that we call *devised theater*. This is theater that starts without a text of any kind—there is only an idea. The "creative team" must then "devise" the work from this nothingness. There are of course many variations of genres and theater work that could fall into any of the genres. The truth is, when we make theater, we don't spend too much time thinking about the genre in "which we are working." In fact we often, when possible, prefer to defy genres—which is mostly because theater people tend to be contrary. For example, when we think of musicals we tend to imagine stories that are told through singing and dancing, but this "genre" didn't fully reveal itself until *Oklahoma* opened in the 1940s. This was the first "musical" where each song and dance served to further the story—it changed what we thought of as "musical theater." Music had always been a part of theater—but until *Oklahoma* the music stood apart from the plot and the characters.

Another example of shifting genres can be seen in our ever-changing perception of what we consider *naturalistic*. (Naturalism is defined by the viewpoint that everything occurs via natural rather then divine or supernatural causes.) In any case, naturalism really grew as a convention in the theater in the late nineteenth century with playwrights like Henrik Ibsen and Anton Chekhov—so as theater history goes it is relatively new. Prior to Chekhov and Ibsen, theater tended to have a larger-than-life quality—it was very "dramatic." What felt naturalistic in the theater before the nineteenth century would not feel so naturalistic now. For example, look at a new *Star Wars* movie: it all feels "real," the spaceships feel solid as if they are really moving through space, and the aliens look like living, breathing beings. Then watch an old *Star Wars* movie: the spaceships don't seem to move quite right, and the aliens look like actors wearing heavy costumes and makeup. Genres are continually modified and redefined; even now, *Hamilton* is redefining the style and content of the American musical. *Hamilton* has taken advantage of the great casting possibilities created in a diverse and varied nation like the United States; the impact of *Hamilton* will be felt for decades.

Genres are long-lasting—they change and evolve in response to cultural needs and expectations, and may even become unrecognizable, but I am hard-pressed to think of any genre of theater that no longer exists in some form today.

Why Theater Is Fun to Do

The greatest thing about theater is that it demands deep critical thinking as well as making and creating. Some people find deep satisfaction and meaning in the study of theater as both an art form and a cultural reflection and voice for the human condition. It is even possible to look at most activities in life in the context of performance: weddings, births, deaths, sacred religious rituals, wars, political rallies, school, sports, and most any human activity. We call this *Performance Studies*.

At first, making theater is fun because of the sense of community created by many people working toward one goal. I have been making theater for thirty-five years, and what really sustains my interest is the storytelling. Every show I work on is a new exploration of a story. The first thing I do when working on a show is to learn as much about the "story" as I can. I do this through research. Sometimes this research is in libraries, but I have also gone to prisons, coal mines, hospitals, subway systems, the seashore, movies, law offices, churches, synagogues, concentration camps, movie studios, museums, anyplace that would offer a clue to the world I had to create. So, while we *do* theater, we also have the privilege of exploring lives and places different than our own. We are always learning. We are always examining our own lives, experiencing the lives of others, and trying to understand what is going on around us. In some ways it is very much like what we all did as children—we try to understand a confusing and confounding world by creating make-believe worlds that help explain and explore the mysteries around us. What could be more fun than that?

WHAT IS

Women's and Gender Studies?

Ivy Schweitzer

Can you imagine a time when a woman could not win a major party's nomination for US president? Hillary Clinton shattered this glass ceiling in June 2016, but it was, in fact, the reality ever since our democracy was founded over two hundred years ago. Think about it: despite the famous declaration that "all *men* are created equal," it has taken over two centuries for a major political party to even consider a woman as a candidate for the highest elected office in the land. I highlight the word "men" in Jefferson's iconic phrase from the Declaration of Independence because I don't think our Founding Fathers meant to include women in their vision of equality.

Listen to this exchange from letters written by John and Abigail Adams, one of our founding "couples," from March/April 1776. They are writing during the tense run-up to the Declaration. John is attending the Continental Congress in Philadelphia and preparing to publish an essay titled "Thoughts on Government," which proposes new laws for the new nation. Abigail, who remained at home, writes, "I long to hear that you have declared an independency." And in the new set of laws her husband will propose, she asks him to "remember the Ladies . . . Do not put such unlimited power into the hands of the Husbands" as did the laws and customs of the time, which she felt made women practically "vassals of your Sex."

In his response, our future second president fends off Abigail's plea in a joking tone that flatly refuses her request and, more infuriating, makes men into the victims:

Depend upon it, We know better than to repeal our Masculine systems. Although they are in full Force, you know they are little more than Theory. We dare not exert our Power in its full Latitude. We are obliged to go fair, and softly, and in Practice you know We are the subjects. We have only the Name of Masters, and rather than give up this, which would completely subject Us to the Despotism of the Petticoat, I hope General Washington, and all our brave Heroes would fight.

Could women really be "masters" over men and "despots in petticoats" when they didn't have the vote and were unable to elect their representatives and determine their political fate—which was the entire *point* of fighting the American Revolution? Let alone not being able to attend college or get training in a profession, give evidence in court, own property after marriage or have custody of their children? Furthermore, does "men" here include all men, such as Native Americans and enslaved Africans, or just the white men in power? If not, do women want to adopt that as our standard of equality? The tools developed in Women's and Gender Studies (WGS) allow us to analyze the power plays in John's charmingly dismissive response and also resist the sexist and racist worldview it assumes, in which white men are the universal—and also the particular. These tools help us understand how John's attitude toward women, what we now call "male chauvinism," shaped the development of this country and its people.

Origins of Women's and Gender Studies

Women's and Gender Studies is an academic field and an interdisciplinary approach that seeks to make visible the lives, concerns, and impact of the half of society that had been effectively overlooked and silenced for centuries. The field began around 1970 as "Women's Studies" (I will discuss the name change later on), the academic arm of the growing women's liberation and feminist movements, which had their origins in the maelstrom of social upheavals of the 1960s and 1970s. I use the plural here because the loosely affiliated groups and organizations that made up these movements were never homogeneous or linear. While the media made middle-class white women, like Betty Freidan and Gloria Steinem, the official faces of feminism, in reality women of different ethnic identities, classes, and sexual persuasions brought a range of issues to public attention and advocated different strategies for action. As we will see, this diversity resulted in contention and ongoing, heated debates.

Many young women, black and white, joined the civil rights movements of the 1950s and the anti–Vietnam War, free speech, student power, and New Left movements of the 1960s, where they learned about grassroots organizing and critiqued traditional forms of authority. But many of these young women found their efforts to enact change blocked by male comrades who did not welcome women into leadership positions and thought their roles should be limited to serving men in the movement by typing minutes, copying flyers, making food, providing moral support, and even giving sexual satisfaction.

Women experienced this male chauvinism even in radical groups, such as the Student Non-Violent Coordinating Committee, Students for a Democratic Society, and the Black Panther Party. Apparently a revolutionary analysis of society did not, in most male minds of the time, extend to the "private" realm of intimate relationships. Stung by this betrayal of their radical vision for society and accusations of "whining," young women began talking together and writing about the sexism they experienced. Even the federal government agreed that sexism was real. In 1963, President Kennedy convened a Commission on the Status of Women and named former first lady and human rights activist Eleanor Roosevelt as its chair. The commission's report officially documented discrimination against women in almost every area of American life.

These young, disgruntled activists created what we now call the "second wave" of US feminism. (The first wave got a similar start in the 1830s among black and white women abolitionists who experienced gender discrimination in that movement, organized a series of Women's Rights conventions, and agitated for change and female suffrage.) During the 1960s, women met in small groups across the nation and began to discover that they weren't alone in their experiences of sexism and discrimination, a practice that came to be known as "consciousness raising." Women (and some men) began to ask searching questions about the "naturalness" of male privilege and female subordination and the constricted roles women were required to play. They questioned why society translated biological differences between the sexes into women's inferiority. Why women did not hold prominent political offices and were paid less than half as much as men for the same work. Why women did not have control of their bodies and reproduction. Why rape within marriage was not illegal in many states.

It may be difficult to imagine now, but less than fifty years ago, high schools and universities did not offer courses that studied women's lives and achievements. This omission subtly reinforced traditional ideas about female intellectual inferiority as well as women's social, economic, and political marginality. Fired up by their discoveries of what poet Adrienne Rich calls "a common language," women began organizing and publicly protesting the inequalities they faced in the home and workplace, movements initially labeled "women's liberation."

More women were also attending college in this period and, energized by these movements, began demanding lectures and classes on women and insisting on their inclusion in the traditional curriculum. These started first on a community and ad hoc basis, with tattered mimeographed texts being shared around, but soon moved into college classrooms. In the late 1960s and early 1970s, hundreds of Women's Studies courses were offered across the United States.

It was an exciting and heady period of discovery and revelation. Scholars began searching through archives, unearthing "herstories" and works of literature and art by women and about women that the male-dominated academy had devalued and ignored. Students could study the origins of gender discrimination and learn about the seemingly lost histories of women's struggles for rights and equality in the United States and around the world. In 1970, the first formal Women's Studies programs in the United States were created at San Diego State University and Cornell University. Despite predictions that this was a fad, as of 2016 one website lists more than nine hundred Women's/Gender/Feminist Studies programs, departments, and research centers across the globe.

Methods

What grew out of the extensive grassroots movements and burgeoning scholarship was the central idea undergirding feminist thinking and pedagogy in the United States: that "the personal is political." This theory argues that the personal problems women face are not all their fault or, as we had been told for years, the result of our inferiority, weakness, madness, hysteria, having our periods, being pregnant, or "all in our heads." Rather, many of these problems are the result of real inequalities that hamper women, as individuals and as a group, from achieving our full potential. This slogan is also a call to collective action, reminding us that what we thought was individual and isolated (the "personal") is often actually built into the structures of systems and institutions that shape our lives. These structures only look natural and unchanging (the "political").

Reflecting this belief, Women's Studies begins with the assertion that girls and women matter and that our own assessment of our experiences constitutes the starting point for discussion, analysis, and the production of knowledge. This simple but radical idea and the connection of Women's Studies as an academic field with identity politics and movements for social change give it a strongly experiential, self-reflective, and democratic character. Unlike with other fields of study, Women's Studies scholars come from many different disciplines, bring different points of view, and practice various methods of conducting research. What they have in common, though, is the goal of understanding the causes, workings, and effects of power inequalities in societies of the past and the present. These inequalities shape the claims and assumptions a white and male-dominated academy has made about girls and women as well as boys and men.

A prominent method in Women's Studies is called *feminist standpoint theory*. It emerged in the 1970s from Marxist feminists who, embracing the political theories of Karl Marx (the founder of communism), saw capitalism and the system of private property as a central force in subordinating women, and included feminist social scientists looking at how gender operates in social trends. Feminist standpoint theory makes three important claims:

> First, that knowledge is not "objective" or free of values. When we do our scholarship, we all bring our particular biases to the knowledge we produce. That has been true of the male-dominated academy, but it is also true of feminist work. Thus, feminists pioneered inclusion of an announcement of the position and character of the speaker ("As a white, Jewish woman from Brooklyn . . ."). Though easy to parody, this serves the crucial purpose of "locating" the speaker and making her position visible.
>
> Second, that privilege blinds us to our privileged situation, and that marginalized groups, because of their "outsider" status, have a clearer awareness of oppressive circumstances.
>
> And third, that analysis of power relations should begin with the lives of the marginalized. Thus, feminists routinely ask: who is speaking, from what location or position of power, and who will benefit? By implying that "objectivity is not, as we have been taught, a gender-neutral view that encompasses everyone, this theory challenges one of the very pillars of traditional academic learning. Feminists contend that by erasing differences among us to ensure fairness, such an approach holds everyone to a masculine, white, and Western standard. The question is, how do we make space for differences and still regard or treat people as equals?

An important method that addresses this quandary is "intersectionality." It developed in response to women of color who criticized some of the early women's movements for ignoring issues of race and class and seeing gender as the primary factor in determining women's fates. Many early "women's libbers" were white middle-class women concerned with issues like reliable birth control, equal pay, and "the problem that has no name." This is the phrase Betty Freidan used in *The Feminine Mystique*, her 1963 bestseller that is often credited with sparking the second wave of feminism, to describe the misery of women who were told that their total happiness in life should come from marriage, motherhood, and managing households. In contrast, many women of color experienced forced sterilization, could not get jobs other than as maids and housekeepers, and were therefore *always* working outside the home. In order to accurately describe the complicated situations of black women, the legal scholar Kimberlé Crenshaw used the term "intersectionality" in a 1989 essay to describe not just multiple and interrelated forms of oppression based on gender, race, class, and sexuality, but the interlocking systems and patterns that particularly burden women of color.

Although intersectionality has been an extraordinarily productive approach in explaining differences, some theorists now argue that it has lost its critical edge. In this political moment, they say, the liberal status quo embraces difference and multiculturalism but only in order to "manage" and accommodate them. Intersectionality, they contend, does not capture the dynamism of lived experiences in the quickly shifting geopolitical climate of the twenty-first century. Rather than seeing the components of our identities, such as gender, sexual orientation, racial identity, class position, as static entities and attributes, feminists now argue that they are events, actions, and encounters. In this view, identity is a process constantly in process, rather than an imaginary crossroads.

Another important method and practice is *transnational feminism*, an approach that grows out of examinations of the violent histories of colonialism and imperialism around the world. Transnationalism recognizes that the increasing movement of people, goods, finance, and ideas across national borders requires a globalized analysis that does not put Western and First World realities at the center. Heated debates over the politics of female circumcision, veiling, and Western women intervening to "save" women in Islamic cultures, for example, have promoted a necessary reevaluation in WGS's understandings of what it means to be a woman and a person. A Western notion of what "liberation" looks like (freedom to exhibit one's body or slut walks, for example) does not necessarily apply to women in other cultures. Thus, transnational feminism calls for recognizing differences across cultures and building alliances and coalitions among women instead of expecting a romanticized commonality and offering salvation.

Major Questions

A basic question in WGS is the meaning and relation of the terms "sex" and "gender," which has been called "the nature/nurture" debate. In the 1960s and 1970s, scholars used these terms to mean separate and distinctive things. Sex (aka "nature") meant the biological stuff of males and females that we think of as fixed and immutable: chromosomes, genes, and the physical characteristics that follow from them. Gender (aka "culture" or "nurture") referred to the socially conditioned and historically determined characteristics like dress, roles, and activities societies impose on people to express biological differences—the attributes that make us feminine or masculine.

Women's Studies scholars distinguished sex and gender because it helped them with the activist mission of the field. If we understand biological differences as given and "natural," scholars argued, we can do nothing about them. But if we understand gender differences as constructed or imposed by social custom, we can challenge those customs and work to undo the differences or at least undermine them.

The publication of Joan Scott's *Gender and the Nature of History* in 1988, however, refocused attention on what she calls the "sex/gender system," its historically specific (and thus changing) character, and its interaction with power and knowledge. Using this model, feminist theorists began dismantling the distinction between sex and gender. For example, the philosopher Judith Butler argues that even the biological category of sex is culturally gendered and not, as previously thought, fixed or immutable.

In addition, we now have much more information about queer and transgendered people. Biologist Anne Fausto-Sterling identifies more sexes than the basic two, making the male/female binary inaccurate and problematic at best. Queer theorists argue for the importance of distinguishing gender identity (how we identify ourselves genderwise) from sexual orientation (who we are attracted to). Uncovering the pervasiveness of heterosexism, they have championed unsettling the fixity of the customary sex/gender binaries for a "gender-queer" fluidity that eschews the "either/or" for the "both/and."

Another related question that was crucial in determining feminist political strategies is what the feminist legal scholar Martha Minow calls "the dilemma of difference." Many early second-wave feminists emphasized women's differences from men, whether those differences were the result of biology or the society (parents, schools, religion, media) training us to be masculine or feminine. These theorists highlighted "women's ways of knowing," "women's different voice," "maternal thinking," and women's distinctively relational moral reasoning and caretaking capacities. They called for radical changes that would embrace and integrate these formerly devalued characteristics into all aspects of society. A separatist feminist culture, strongly influenced by radical feminism and political lesbianism, sprang up in which women created their own "women-identified" institutions: banks, garages, co-ops, restaurants, bookstores, households, and families.

But this strain of thinking emphasizes qualities that in the past earned women an inferior social status. Furthermore, it is not clear that all women share or should share these characteristics. Finally, women's commonality implies a harmful ignorance of racial/ethnic, cultural, class, and sexuality differences among, between, and within women. Still, many feminists held what political theorist Hester Eisenstein described as "the ideological and political conviction that women were more unified by the fact of being female in a patriarchal society than we were divided by specificities of race or class."

By contrast, another strain of feminist thinking arose, springing from the work of Mary Wollstonecraft, an early feminist foremother and author of *A Vindication of the Rights of Woman* (1792). These feminists believed the surest means to social equality for women was to argue for their similarities with men and to work to dismantle the differences between the sexes. Often called *liberal*, *equality*, or *power feminism*, this strain highlights the individual and her attributes and presses for the integration of women into existing male-dominated institutions, such as women in all aspects of the military.

But this view accepts masculine social norms, and again, we have to ask, which men are considered "the norm"? Simply integrating women into the dominant order may not change or reform that order and its discriminatory structures. It's clear that, in dealing with differences, Western culture finds it difficult not to create hierarchies that disparage and subordinate what it considers different. Can we redefine equality not as sameness but as an evolving parity or equity that rests on an acknowledgment of differences? In response to this dilemma, a third strain has lately emerged in feminist thought that focuses on fluidity and multiplicity (both/and) rather than binaries (either/or). The predominance of queer theory exemplifies this trend in the way it challenges and unsettles narrow sex and gender binaries. It argues that people shouldn't have to choose one static sex or gender identity but should be free to move between and among these identity markers fluidly within their lives.

A version of this dilemma has also internally affected feminist movements and WGS, which have struggled from the beginning to adequately address racial and sexual differences among women. As soon as radical feminists identified the enemy as "the patriarchy" (by which they meant male-dominated institutions but which many interpreted as "all men") and called for female solidarity to resist it, women of color and lesbians began demanding recognition of their specific issues, finding both racism and homophobia among their "sisters," and sharing struggles with their "brothers" and gay men, WGS acknowledges how incomplete our analyses of gender are without considering other identity factors such as race, class, sexuality, ability, and location.

Ongoing Debates

One of the ongoing debates in the field is the very status of its name. People have criticized the name "Women's Studies," arguing that the apostrophe is ambiguous (does it mean the study *of* women or *by* women or both?), that it implies that we can study all women together without considering ethnicity and class, and that it does not take into account either lesbian or transgendered identities. New knowledge and developments in medical treatments and sexual identity have called the whole category of "women" into question. Does it include butch lesbians who adopt masculinity or transwomen with male genitalia or surgically constructed female genitalia? Furthermore, as the field developed, it became obvious that studying gender must also include discussions of boys, men, and masculinity.

To address these concerns and the reality of course content and research agendas, many programs began including the term "Gender" in their names. "Women's and Gender Studies" remains the most popular solution. Still other programs became solely "Gender Studies" (a name that loses the historical focus on "women"), the more politicized "Feminist Studies," or also included "Sexuality" as a separate but related category of study.

What may seem like fussy arguments over academic terms indicates the continuing evolution of the field. In the 1970s feminists debated the reality of "sisterhood," an almost mystical sense of female commonality and potentially coercive expectations of emotional support and political solidarity. In the 1980s university administrations responding to student pressure and the amazing proliferation of feminist scholarship recognized the need for such programs and authorized funding that created tenure lines and positions. Despite the defeat of the Equal Rights Amendment in 1982, affirmative action policies succeeded in bringing more women and minorities into higher education, making "diversity" a desired goal and giving WGS an institutional foothold. Women made important gains but by the 1990s experienced profound backlash, even the assertion that the struggle is over and we are in a "postfeminism age." Many factors contributed to the turn away from feminism, including the rise of individualism and corporate culture, campaigns against affirmative action, the restructuring of universities as businesses, and the emphasis on vocational training rather than humanistic study.

In this contentious atmosphere, feminists continue to debate several long-standing questions. Whether Women's and Gender Studies is an approach or a discipline, and whether it should remain its own program or department or be integrated into the entire academic curriculum, or both. Some feminists support allying WGS with other cultural/ethnic studies programs, like African American and Native American Studies. Nor do feminists agree on whether we should strive to reform the system from within or call it into question altogether; whether WGS should continue the activist approach on which it was built or focus on the analysis of discourse, culture, and history; whether it should become less "political" in order to be taken "more seriously." These debates have profoundly shaped what scholars research and how they teach—and what students take away from courses or degrees in WGS.

Finally, the influence of LGBT and queer studies has been a challenging but vibrant force in shaping WGS. Lesbian feminists struggled with latent and not-so-latent homophobia among feminists and disagreements within their own ranks, but offer a strong theoretical and activist challenge to questions about the role of sexuality, pleasure, pornography, sex work, and transgenderism in the academy and in feminist scholarship. The upshot of these interventions has been to unsettle the category of "women." Some transwomen—biologically born males who have transitioned into women—argue that they are more "authentically" women than cis-women—biologically born females—because they have chosen their gender.

Where We Are Now

A new wave of feminism, called "the third wave," gained momentum in the 1990s and continues strongly today. It arose partly in response to what young women perceive as the failures of second-wave feminism to embrace women of many backgrounds and identities. Rebecca Walker, the daughter of well-known author and "womanist" Alice Walker, coined the phrase and defined the movement's focus on queer women and women of color. While some third-wavers reject the label "feminist" as exclusive, elitist, or insensitive to the fluidity of gender, others have embraced and redefined the term to avoid the "political correctness" associated with some forms of second-wave feminism. They argue there are many different ways of "doing feminism," or "feministing," as one popular website calls its version of ongoing consciousness raising and political activity around gender issues.

Despite its contentious history, WGS remains a force for innovation and social change. In June 2016, *Elle* magazine published a list titled "63 College Classes That Give Us Hope for the Next Generation." In the current climate, saturated with stories of rape and sexual assault on college campuses, *Elle* finds cause for celebration in the vast number of WGS courses offered at both small private liberal arts colleges and big public universities. They are particularly impressed with the wide range of women's experiences represented in these classes. Many focus on specific ethnic, cultural, and regional groups and a variety of gendered practices and uses of social media, blogs, and websites, expressed through titles such as "#Sayhername: Intersectionality and Feminist Activism," "Pleasure, Power and Profit: Race and Sexualities in a Global Era," and "Leaning In, Hooking Up: Visions of Feminism and Femininity in the Twenty-First Century," to name only a few.

Two other forms of feminism have emerged recently as important sites of activism and scholarship. The first is ecofeminism, an activist and academic movement based on the connections between the exploitation of nature and the domination of women. The second is "the new materialism" or "materialist feminism," an expansion of feminist thought into the biological sciences. This approach shifts focus away from the field's dominant concerns with agency, social construction, and intersectionality toward bodily matter, the limits of the human and our relation to the nonhuman world, using the concept of "assemblages"— performances that emphasize the uneven daily encounters that produce identity.

How these new forms will shape WGS in the future remains to be seen.

Acknowledgments

Any project with the kind of breadth found here can only come about through the cooperation and contributions of many people. First and foremost, I want to thank my colleagues who contributed to this volume. Writing for a general audience poses all kinds of challenges, and I very much appreciate the generous spirit with which they took this on and their collaborative engagement with the editorial process. With any luck at all, the many friendships that were in place prior to beginning this project are still in place at its completion. Thanks also to the graphic artist Annelise Capossela, whose graceful and clever artwork adorns the chapters and cover.

This project came to UPNE with the help of Jeff Horrell, when he was Dean of Libraries at Dartmouth College. It would have never happened without Jeff's guidance and advice. His presence on the Dartmouth campus is already missed. Thanks to Dartmouth College Dean of Arts and Sciences Michael Mastanduno for his support in all ways and over many years and also to Richard Pult for having faith in the idea of this book and taking it on at UPNE.

My position as Director of the Neukom Institute for Computational Science has put me in the lucky position of coming into contact with a wide range of colleagues and projects on the Dartmouth campus. I gratefully acknowledge the generosity of former Dartmouth trustee Bill Neukom, which supports this vibrant intellectual nexus.

Many individuals came through with important advice and comments at various times and in various ways. Miles Blencowe would like to acknowledge the support of the National Science Foundation under Grant No. DMR-1507383. Sienna Craig dedicates her essay on Anthropology to Mr. Larry Goodman (Dartmouth '47), in gratitude for his unflinching support of the subject, and acknowledges her colleagues Sabrina Billings, Jesse Casana, and Jeremy deSilva, for their contributions to the chapter, and her father, Steve Craig, for his editorial feedback. Larry Polansky thanks Amy Beal and Dard Neuman for their comments (and the latter for a couple of choice phrases); he also thanks Adrian Chi for her comix "Bite the Cactus" in the punk magazine *Razorcake* for her retelling of this joke by her father. Christopher Snyder would like to give special thanks to James Feyrer and Douglas Irwin for their insights on macroeconomics and the Great Depression; he is also grateful to Patricia Anderson and Ada Cohen for insightful conversations, and to Henry Senkfor for able research assistance. Of course any lingering errors are the responsibilities of the authors. Special thanks to Sarunas Burdulis for some final image rendering. I'd further like to give particular thanks to Katinka Matson and Steve Strogatz for their timely encouragements.

As with any thing that I manage to bring to completion, I can only do so with the support, love, and advisements of my wife Ellen. She has had to live with this project for as long as I have. I have so appreciated her thoughtful and insightful comments and calming advice at various critical moments.

This project was inspired by my children: Alex, Shayna, and Rachel. Their pure spirit of inquiry and wonder, and their constant asking "What is . . . ?" gave birth to this volume. Their eye-rolling whenever I begin an answer with "Well, it's complicated . . ." helped to shape its form. Trying to see the world as they do and then trying to help them to understand it is one of the great joys of my life and an ongoing gift.

Finally, on behalf of all the contributors, I'd like to thank family and friends and teachers and mentors who turned each of us on to a world of ideas and encouraged us to explore that world, each in our own way. We hope we can pay that favor forward. This book is dedicated to them.

Dan Rockmore

Notes

WHAT IS AFRICAN AMERICAN STUDIES?

Page 1   *"If there is no struggle there is no progress . . . never will."* Frederick Douglass, "West Indian Emancipation," in *Frederick Douglass: Selected Speeches and Writings*, ed. Philip S. Foner and Yuval Taylor (Chicago: Lawrence Hill Books, 1999), 367.

Page 2   *Supreme Court Justice Roger Taney . . . to respect.* Don E. Fehrenbacher, *Slavery, Law, and Politics: The Dred Scott Case in Historical Perspective* (New York: Oxford University Press, 1981), 190.

Page 2   *Take for example . . . than 26,000. The Ohio State University Archives*, "The Ohio State University: A Historical Timeline." www.tiki-toki.com/time line/entry/69886/The-Ohio-State-University-A-Historical-Timeline# vars!date=1862-06-01_10:55:21!. Accessed July 8, 2016.

Page 3   *African American Studies . . . arts, and humanities.* Alan K. Colón, "Critical Issues in Black Studies: A Selective Analysis," in *The African American Studies Reader*, ed. Nathaniel Norment Jr. (Durham, NC: Carolina Academic Press, 2001), 520–527.

Page 5   *Christian authorities . . . good and evil.* Ivan Hannaford, *Race: The History of an Idea in the West* (Baltimore: Johns Hopkins University Press, 1994), 87–126.

Page 5   *Common Christians, . . . blood Christians.* Ibid., 100–125.

Page 5   *By slotting . . . political economy.* Sylvia Wynter, "1492: A New World View," and Valentin Y. Mudimbe, "Romanus Pontifex (1454) and the Expansion of Europe," in *Race, Discourse and the Origin of the Americas: A New World View*, ed. Vera Lawrence Hyatt and Rex Nettleford (Washington, DC: Smithsonian Institution Press, 1995), 5–57, 58–65.

Page 6   *The sudden . . . the Europeans. The Trans-Atlantic Slave Trade Database*, www .slavevoyages.org. Accessed July 8, 2016. Walter Rodney, *How Europe Underdeveloped Africa* (Washington, DC: Howard University Press, 1972).

Page 6   *Economic competition . . . are inferior.* Anthony Pagden, *The Fall of Natural Man: The American Indian and the Origins of Comparative Ethnology* (Cambridge: Cambridge University Press, 1982); Anthony Pagden, *Lords of All the World: Ideologies of Empire in Spain, Britain and France c. 1500–c. 1800* (New Haven, CT: Yale University Press, 1998).

Page 6   *Demonstrating his . . . body and mind.* Thomas Jefferson, *Notes on the State of Virginia* (Boston: Bedford/St. Martin's, 2002), 175–180.

Page 9   *Banneker's deliberate . . . African Americans.* Benjamin Banneker, "I Freely and Cheerfully Acknowledge, That I Am of the African Race," in *The African American Experience: Black History and Culture through Speeches, Letters, Editorial, Poems, Songs, and Stories,* ed. Kai Wright (New York: Black Dog and Leventhal, 2009), 109–111.

Page 9   *The expansion . . . if necessary.* David Walker, *Appeal, in Four Articles; Together with a Preamble, to the Colored Citizens of the World, but in Particular, and Very Expressly, to Those of the United States of America* (1830; Baltimore: Black Classic Press, 1993), 34.

Page 10   *"African American novelist . . . white man's dilemma?"* Ralph Ellison, "An American Dilemma: A Review," in *Shadow and Act* (New York: Vintage Books, 1995), 315–316.

Page 11   *Langston Hughes's 1925 . . . I, too, am America,* Langston Hughes, *The Collected Poems of Langston Hughes,* ed. Arnold Rampersad and David Roessel (New York: Random House, 2004), 46.

WHAT IS ECONOMICS?

Page 121   *Huge gains from Altria stock investment.* Author's calculations using historical stock-return data from the Center for Research in Security Prices. Jeremy Siegel first identified Altria as the highest performing among S&P 500 stocks in his book *The Future for Investors: Why the Tried and True Triumphs over the Bold and the New* (New York: Crown Business, 2005).

Page 125   *In any event, the label "dismal science" has stuck.* Robert Dixon, "The Origin of the Term 'Dismal Science' to Describe Economics," University of Melbourne Department of Economics working paper no. 715, available at https://ideas.repec.org/p/mlb/wpaper/715.html. Accessed August 22, 2016.

Page 125   *"Nowhere, in that quarter of his intellectual world, is there light; nothing but a grim shadow of hunger."* Thomas Carlyle, *Collected Works,* vol. 1 (London: Chapman and Hall, 1870), 181.

Page 130   *Christina Romer . . . hit on the idea of looking at recessions outside of the span of the Great Depression.* Christina Romer, "What Ended the Great Depression?," *Journal of Economic History* 52 (1992): 757–784.

Page 133   *Stacy Dale and Alan Krueger, two economists working in Princeton, New Jersey, took a clever approach to estimating the causal effect of prestigious colleges on salaries.* Stacy Dale and Alan Krueger, "Estimating the Payoff to Attending a More Selective College: An Application of Selection on Observables and Unobservables," *Quarterly Journal of Economics* 117 (2002): 1491–1527.

Page 143 *"Architectural design and structural engineering have a symbiotic relationship: a close and essential union in which one relies upon the other. In the ideal structure, the lines between science and aesthetic are blurred."* William F. Baker et al., "Integrated Design: Everything Matters—The Development of Burj Dubai and the New Beijing Poly Plaza," in *Structures Congress 2009: Don't Mess with Structural Engineers: Expanding Our Role*, ed. Lawrence Griffis, Todd Helwig, Marc Waggoner, and Marc Holt (Reston, VA: American Society of Civil Engineers, 2009), 1485–1494. Also at www.civil.ist.utl.pt/~cristina/EBAP/FolhasEdifAltos/burj-dubai/162.pdf. Accessed August 15, 2016.

WHAT IS GEOGRAPHY?

Page 171 *Go ahead . . . having fun.* Seterra Geography, http://online.seterra.net/en/vgp/3063. Accessed November 6, 2016.

Page 173 *But now, with climate change and global warming, we do.* Arthur Neslen, "Carbon Dioxide Levels in Atmosphere Forecast to Shatter Milestone," *Guardian*, June 13, 2016, https://www.theguardian.com/environment/2016/jun/13/carbon-dioxide-levels-in-atmosphere-forecast-to-shatter-milestone#img-1. Accessed June 26, 2016.

Page 174 *how Western consumers have changed their ideas about perishable foods and just what is "fresh" and desirable.* Susan Freidberg, *Fresh: A Perishable History* (Cambridge, MA: Harvard University Press, 2009).

Page 175 *"Wild pigs . . . domestication."* Ian Frazier, "Hogs Wild: Suddenly, Feral Swine Are Everywhere," *New Yorker,* December 12, 2005.

Page 176 *This law might only be several decades young.* Waldo R. Tobler, "A Computer Movie Simulating Urban Growth in the Detroit Region," *Economic Geography* 46 (1970): 234–240.

Page 179 *"structural linchpin of US race relations."* Thomas F. Pettigrew, "Racial Change and Social Policy," *Annals of the American Academy of Political and Social Science* 441 (1979): 114–131.

Page 181 *built the Island Detention Project.* Alison Mountz, The Island Detention Project (2016), https://legacy.wlu.ca/page.php?grp_id=2599&p=21545. Accessed June 17, 2016.

WHAT IS GEOLOGY?

Page 189 *Consider too . . . That is, in 2015 humans worldwide consumed hydrocarbons at a rate that would fill Yankee Stadium about every forty minutes.* Internal Energy Agency, "About Us," www.iea.org/aboutus/faqs/oil/. Accessed December 5, 2016.

Page 189   *For example, lithium . . . Humans currently use lithium, in other words, at a rate that would fill Yankee Stadium about every six years.* "Lithium" entry, *Wikipedia*, last modified November 2016, https://en.wikipedia.org/wiki/Lithium.

Page 189   *Humans pump . . . The bulk of this water is drawn from underground reservoirs occupying naturally occurring open spaces and fractures in rock, making it a geological resource of fundamental importance.* UNESCO, "Water Cooperation 2013," www.unwater.org/water-cooperation-2013/water-cooperation/facts-and-figures/en/. Accessed December 5, 2016.

WHAT IS LINGUISTICS?

Page 205   *You might recognize some of these questions from a* New York Times *online dialect survey that went viral a few years ago. You can take the full survey on this site:* http://www.nytimes.com/interactive/2013/12/20/sunday-review/dialect-quiz-map.html?_r=0. The survey was designed by Josh Katz, using dialect data from Bert Vaux and Scott Golder.

Page 216   *Thee was singular, and* you *was plural.* There was also a formal/informal difference between these pronouns during this time period, but I'll let you explore that extra bit of history on your own.

WHAT IS MATHEMATICS?

Page 229   *the prime numbers are countable.* A simple proof of this fact can be found in many places and in particular, is sketched in Dan Rockmore's *Stalking the Riemann Hypothesis* (New York: Pantheon, 2006), 32–33.

WHAT IS MUSIC?

Page 243   *"In fact, the composer James Tenney used to joke that some aliens visited Earth, and they were able to explain why we eat, sleep, procreate, and make war, but there was one thing they couldn't understand: 'Every so often they come together and vibrate the air!'"* Thanks to Adrian Chi for relating that anecdote to me.

WHAT IS PHYSICS?

Page 273   *It may turn out . . . or something.* Richard Feynman, "Critical Comments," in *The Role of Gravitation in Physics: Report from the 1957 Chapel Hill Conference,* ed. Dean Rickles and Cécile M. DeWitt (Berlin: epubli, 2011), at http://www.edition-open-access.de/sources/5/toc.html. Accessed December 5, 2016.

Page 276   *As Aristotle observed . . . where the people rule over themselves, more or less justly.* Aristotle, *Politics* (325–323 BCE), translated, with introduction, notes, and glossary, by Carnes Lord, 2nd ed. (Chicago: University of Chicago Press, 2013).

Page 277   *"The people of England regards itself as free, but it is grossly mistaken; it is only free during elections of members of parliament. As soon as they are elected, slavery overtakes it, and they are nothing."* Jean-Jacques Rousseau, *The Social Contract and Other Later Political Writings,* ed. Victor Gourevitch, Cambridge Texts in the History of Political Thought (1762; Cambridge: Cambridge University Press, 1997), book 3, chapter 15.

Page 277   *"is rather like using a public toilet: we wait in line with a crowd in order to close ourselves in a small compartment where we can relieve ourselves in solitude and in privacy of our burden . . . and then, yielding to the next in line, go silently home."* Benjamin R. Barber, *Strong Democracy: Participatory Politics for a New Age* (Berkeley: University of California Press, 1984), 188.

Page 277   *Eleven thousand amendments to the Constitution have been proposed since 1789; only thirty-three amendments to the Constitution have been passed by Congress and sent to the states; of those, twenty-seven have been ratified.* National Archives, "National Archives Opens Amending America Exhibit" (press release), December 2, 2015.

Page 279   *Very few citizens today trust the government to "do what is right" most of the time: about 20 percent trusted the national government to this extent in 2012, versus 47 percent in 1970 and 57 percent in 1958.* American National Election Survey, *The ANES Guide to Public Opinion and Electoral Behavior,* "Trust in the Federal Government, 1958–2012," available at http://electionstudies.org /nesguide/toptable/tab5a_1.htm. Accessed June 21, 2016.

Page 279   *"No famine has ever taken place in the history of the world in a functioning democracy."* Amartya Sen, *Development as Freedom* (New York: Anchor Books, 1999), 16.

Page 279   *Scholars of international relations have highlighted another basic fact: . . . in very costly violent conflicts.* Michael W. Doyle, *Liberal Peace: Selected Essays* (New York: Routledge, 2011).

Page 280   *In my own work, I have defended the place of parties and partisan contestation in democracy. The hope for a democracy that escapes party and partisanship is mistaken, as I argue in my book.* Russell Muirhead, *The Promise of Party in a Polarized Age* (Cambridge, MA: Harvard University Press, 2104).

Page 280   *Expertise only compounds the problem, first because experts disagree with each other, and second because experts are often wrong.* Philip E. Tetlock, *Expert Political Judgment: How Good Is It? How Can We Know?* (Princeton, NJ: Princeton University Press, 2006).

Page 282   *This is why some think that ideology is now disconnecting the government from the people.* Morris P. Fiorina (with Samuel J. Abrams), *Disconnect: The Breakdown of Representation in American Politics* (Norman: University of Oklahoma Press, 2011).

WHAT IS RELIGION?

Page 297   *Indeed, according to one scholar, trying to answer the question "What is religion?" is a little like the traditional Indian story of the six blind men who are asked to define an elephant by feeling different parts of its body.* Gerald A. Larue, "What Is 'Religion'?—Well, It's Hard to 'Say Exactly,'" posted at the site "Teaching about Religion in Support of Civic Pluralism," http://www.worldvieweducation.org/whatisreligion.html. Accessed November 16, 2016.

Page 298   *according to the Pew Research Center.* "Religious Landscape Study," Pew Research Center, www.pewforum.org/religious-landscape-study/. Accessed November 16, 2016.

Page 298   *"doctrine by which the church stands or falls" is the conviction that salvation comes to Protestants "when they believe that they are received into [God's] favor and that their sins are forgiven."* Martin Luther, *The Augsburg Confession of Faith* (1530), Article 4, 1–3.

Page 304   *one scholar writes of religion as "attested only within social groups" (emphasis mine) and "requir[ing] such groups for [its] maintenance."* Ziony Zevit, *The Religions of Ancient Israel: A Synthesis of Parallactic Approaches* (London: Continuum, 2001), 11.

Page 305   *"people are distinguished from all other living things . . . by the creation and maintenance of religion."* Ziony Zevit, *The Religions of Ancient Israel: A Synthesis of Parallactic Approaches* (London: Continuum, 2001), 11.

Page 305   *"If I went back to college today, I think I would probably major in comparative religion, because that's how integrated it is in everything that we are working on and deciding and thinking about in life today."* John Kerry, "Remarks at the Launch of the Office of Faith-Based Community Initiatives," U.S. State Department website, http://www.state.gov/secretary/remarks/2013/08/212781.htm. Accessed November 16, 2016.

WHAT IS SOCIOLOGY?

Page 306   *In 1959, the American sociologist C. Wright Mills coined the term "sociological imagination" to refer to the ability to connect seemingly personal experience with broader social forces.* C. Wright Mills, *The Sociological Imagination, Fortieth Anniversary Edition* (New York: Oxford University Press, 2000).

Page 310   *For example, many, but not all, Native American societies recognize sex or gender in a nonbinary way.* Serena Nanda, "Multiple Genders among North

American Indians," in *Gender Diversity: Crosscultural Variations*, 2nd ed. (Long Grove, IL: Waveland, 2014).

Page 310   *a team of sociologists who examined almost six thousand children's picture books for whether males or females were included in the title of the book (like Winnie the Pooh or Olivia) or as central characters in the book.* Janice McCabe, Emily Fairchild, Liz Grauerholz, Bernice Pescosolido, and Daniel Tope, "Gender in Twentieth-Century Children's Books: Patterns of Disparity in Titles and Central Characters," *Gender and Society* 25, no. 2 (2011): 197–226.

Page 311   *In a well-known study of elementary school status systems.* Patricia A. Adler and Peter Adler, *Peer Power: Preadolescent Culture and Identity* (New Brunswick, NJ: Rutgers University Press, 1998).

Page 313   *Research shows that college students who reported positive, diverse interactions with peers also had higher scores on complex thinking, cultural and social awareness, and concern for the public good.* Sylvia Hurtado, "Linking Diversity with the Educational and Civic Missions of Higher Education," *Review of Higher Education* 30, no. 2 (2007): 185–196.

Page 314   *I discovered that the networks of these sixty-seven students clustered into three types that I call tight-knitters, compartmentalizers, and samplers.* Janice McCabe, *Connecting in College: How Friendship Networks Matter for Academic and Social Success* (Chicago: University of Chicago Press, 2016).

For More Information

WHAT IS AFRICAN AMERICAN STUDIES?

The New Jim Crow: Mass Incarceration in the Age of Colorblindness, Michelle Alexander (New Press, 2010).

The Black Revolution on Campus, Martha Bioni (University of California Press, 2012).

That's the Joint!: The Hip-Hop Studies Reader, ed. Murray Forman and Mark Anthony Neal, 2nd ed. (Routledge, 2012).

Racism: A Short History, George M. Fredrickson (Princeton University Press, 2002).

Stamped from the Beginning: The Definitive History of Racist Ideas in America, Ibram X. Kendi (Nation Books, 2016).

The African American Studies Reader, ed. Nathaniel Norment Jr. (Carolina Academic Press, 2001).

Not Just Race, Not Just Gender: Black Feminist Readings, Valerie Smith (Routledge, 1998).

WHAT IS ANTHROPOLOGY?

What It Means to Be 98% Chimpanzee: Apes, People, and Their Genes, Jonathan Marks (University of California Press, 2003).

The Vulnerable Observer: Anthropology That Breaks Your Heart, Ruth Behar (Beacon, 1997).

Infections and Inequalities: Health, Human Rights, and the New War on the Poor, Paul Farmer (University of California Press, 2004).

Wisdom Sits in Places: Landscape and Language among the Western Apache, Keith Basso (University of New Mexico Press, 1996).

Sweetness and Power: The Place of Sugar in Modern History, Sidney Mintz (Penguin Books, 1986).

Life in the Pueblo: Understanding the Past through Archaeology, Kathryn Kamp (Waveland, 1997).

WHAT IS ART HISTORY?

Look! The Fundamentals of Art History, Anne D'Alleva, 3rd ed. (Prentice Hall, 2010).

Stories of Art, James Elkins (Routledge, 2002).

Art History: A Critical Introduction to Its Methods, Michael Hatt and Charlotte Clonk (Manchester University Press, 2006).

Critical Terms for Art History, ed. Robert S. Nelson and Richard Shiff, 2nd ed. (University of Chicago Press, 2003).

WHAT IS ASTRONOMY?

Galaxy: Mapping the Cosmos, James Geach (Reaktion Books, 2014). This is a fascinating and accessible overview of the science of galaxies and the large-scale structure of the universe.

Black Holes and Time Warps: Einstein's Outrageous Legacy, Kip Thorne (W. H. Freeman, 1995). A great scientific and historical introduction to the physics of general relativity and black holes.

Investigating Astronomy, Timothy F. Slater and Roger Freedman, 2nd ed. (W. H. Freeman, 2014). An introductory and up-to-date college textbook that is concise and enjoyable to read and covers all the important concepts in astronomy.

WHAT IS BIOLOGY?

Lives of the Cell, Lewis Thomas (Viking, 1974). A classic on discovery in the life science and what it is to do biological science.

Cell Biology by the Numbers, Ron Milo and Rob Phillips (Garland Science, 2015). A new textbook on quantitative measurements in cell biology.

www.microscopyu.com. Nikon's educational online resource, with interactive tutorials on all kinds of microscopy principles and applications.

WHAT IS CHEMISTRY?

The Sceptical Chymist or Chymico-Physical Doubts and Paradoxes, Robert Boyle (CreateSpace Independent Publishing Platform, 2015), www.gutenberg.org/ebooks/22914. Reprint of the 1661 classic where Boyle published his hypothesis of matter as composed of atoms.

Elements of Chemistry, Antoine Lavoisier (Dover Books on Chemistry, 1984). Reprint of the 1789 classic, which has been called the first chemistry textbook.

The Periodic Table, Primo Levi (reprint, Random House, 1996). A tour of elements, inspired by an extraordinary life, by one of the great writers of our time who was both a chemist and Holocaust survivor and memoirist.

Elements: A Visual Exploration of Every Known Atom in the Universe, Theodore Gray and Nick Mann (reprint, Black Dog and Leventhal, 2012).

Molecules: The Elements and the Architecture of Everything, Theodore Gray and Nick Mann (Black Dog and Leventhal, 2014).

WHAT IS CLASSICS?

Classics: A Very Short Introduction, Mary Beard and John Henderson (Oxford University Press, 2000).

1177 B.C.: The Year Civilization Collapsed, Eric Cline (Princeton University Press, 2015).

The Archaeology of Greece: An Introduction, William Biers (Cornell University Press, 1996).

The Ancient City: Life in Classical Athens and Rome, Peter Connolly and Hazel Dodge (Oxford University Press, 2000).

Translations of some ancient texts that should be appealing to students interested in ancient Greece and Rome:

Homer: The Iliad and The Odyssey, translated by Robert Fagles (Penguin Classics, 1999).

Virgil: The Aeneid, translated by Robert Fagles (Penguin Classics, 2008).

Livy: The Early History of Rome (Books 1–5), translation by Aubrey De Sélincourt (Penguin Classics, 2002).

Suetonius: The Twelve Caesars, edited by J. Rives, translated by Robert Graves (Penguin Classics, 2007).

WHAT IS COMPUTER SCIENCE?

Nine Algorithms That Changed the Future: The Ingenious Ideas That Drive Today's Computers, John McCormick (Princeton University Press, 2013).

WHAT IS ECOLOGY?

Ecological Society of America, "What Does Ecology Have to do with Me?," http://www.esa.org/esa/education-and-diversity/what-does-ecology-have-to-do-with-me/.

Understanding Evolution, "An Introduction to Evolution," http://evolution.berkeley.edu/evolibrary/article/evo_02.

WHAT IS ECONOMICS?

Freakonomics: A Rogue Economist Explores the Hidden Side of Everything, Steven Levitt and Stephen Dubner (Harper, 2005). Popular bestseller that gives a great introduction to the range and reach of economic research through fascinating case studies.

Microeconomic Theory: Basic Principles and Extensions, Walter Nicholson and Christopher Snyder, 12th ed. (South-Western Cengage Learning, 2017). In particular, chapter 1 explains the core concepts of costs and market equilibrium in more detail and also provides more depth on the evolution of theories of value.

WHAT IS ENGINEERING?

The Art of Tinkering, Karen Wilkinson and Mike Petrich (Weldon Owen, 2014); see also http://tinkering.exploratorium.edu/art-tinkering.

Creative Confidence: Unleashing the Creative Potential, Tom Kelley and David Kelley (Crown Business, 2013); see also www.creativeconfidence.com/about.

The Engineering of Structures around Us. Free online course through edX: https://courses.edx.org/courses/course-v1:DartmouthX+DART.ENGS.02.X+2T2016/info.

WHAT IS ENGLISH?

English Studies: An Introduction to the Discipline(s), Bruce McComiskey, ed. (NCTE, 2006).
Wikipedia, "English Studies," https://en.wikipedia.org/wiki/English_studies.

WHAT IS FRENCH?

French Lessons: A Memoir, Alice Kaplan (University of Chicago Press, 1994).
Course in General Linguistics, Ferdinand de Saussure (reprint, Open Court Classics, 1998).
Is That a Fish in Your Ear? Translation and the Meaning of Everything, David Bellos (reprint, Farrar, Straus and Giroux, 2012).
Lost in Translation: A Life in a New Language, Eva Hoffman (reprint, Penguin Books, 1990).
Le Ton Beau de Marot: In Praise of the Music of Language, Douglas R. Hofstadter (reprint, Basic Books, 1998).

WHAT IS GEOGRAPHY?

Fresh: A Perishable History, Susan Freidberg (Harvard University Press, 2009).
"The Map as Intent: Variations on the Theme of John Snow," Tom Koch, *Cartographica* 39, no. 4 (2004): 1–14.
"The Enforcement Archipelago: Detention, Haunting, and Asylum on Islands," Alison Mountz, *Political Geography* 30, no. 3 (2011): 118–128.

WHAT IS GEOLOGY?

Wikipedia, "History of Earth," https://en.wikipedia.org/wiki/History_of_Earth. Nice summary of the history of the Earth!
Wikipedia, "Natural Resource." https://en.wikipedia.org/wiki/Natural_resource. Nice summary of our "natural resources."
American Association for the Advancement of Science Atlas of Population and Environment, "Population and Natural Resources," http://atlas.aaas.org/?part=2. AAAS Atlas of Population and Environment website that gets at the important effects of natural resource usage.
Earth Science Week, "Big Ideas: Activities," http://www.earthsciweek.org/big-ideas. Wonderful resource explaining the many things that geologists (and their relatives) do.
The Earth Science Literacy Initiative, "Earth Sciences Literacy Principles," http://eo.ucar.edu/asl/pdfs/es_literacy_brochure.pdf. Great summary document of the "big ideas" of earth sciences.

WHAT IS HISTORY?

History: A Very Short Introduction, John H. Arnold (Oxford University Press, 2000). Provides one of the best and most compact accounts of history's storytelling aspect.

The Landscape of History: How Historians Map the Past, John Lewis Gaddis (Oxford University Press, 2004). Compares and contrasts historical thinking to work in the natural and physical sciences.

Historians' Craft, Marc Bloch (Knopf, 1953). The Nazis murdered the French historian Marc Bloch as he was working to complete this book; this tragedy gave a uniquely brilliant unfinished work its own gripping story.

The Allure of the Archive, Arlette Farge (Yale University Press, 2015). Evocatively relates how discovery and revelation enliven the nitty-gritty work of digging through records.

WHAT IS LINGUISTICS?

The 5-Minute Linguist, ed. E. M. Rickerson and Barry Hilton (Equinox, 2006). This collection of sixty short essays by linguists covers a wide range of interesting topics and is a good place to start your exploration of linguistics.

The Atoms of Language: The Mind's Hidden Rules of Grammar, Mark Baker (Basic Books, 2002). Syntax expert Mark Baker explores how sentences work in different languages around the world.

Language Change: Progress or Decay?, Jean Aitchison, 3rd ed. (Cambridge, 2002). This book provides an interesting and readable introduction to historical linguistics.

Do You Speak American?, www.pbs.org/speak/. This PBS website contains short readings, videos from a TV series, and other information about US English dialects.

Rising Voices. Shown on PBS in 2015, tells how Native American communities are working to revitalize their languages. See also http://risingvoicesfilm.com/the-project/.

WHAT IS MATHEMATICS?

What Is Mathematics?, Richard Courant and Harold Robbins (Oxford University Press, 1996, newly edited by Ian Stewart). Reprint of a 1941 classic text surveying the world of mathematics.

The Joy of "x": A Guided Tour of Math, from One to Infinity, Steven Strogatz (reprint, Mariner Press, 2013).

The Grapes of Math, Alex Bellos (Simon and Schuster, 2015).

The Math Life, Wendy Conquest, Bob Drake, and Dan Rockmore (distributed by the Films Media Group, 2002). This documentary aired on PBS. It gives a sense of the kinds of problems mathematicians think in the words of a wide range of a people who study mathematics.

Mathematics Illuminated, a thirteen-part video series that gives a survey of the world of "higher mathematics" aimed at a broad math-curious audience. Funded by the Annenberg Foundation and freely available online at www.learner.org/courses/mathilluminated/.

WHAT IS MUSIC?

Music, Language, and the Brain, Aniruddh D. Patel (Oxford University Press, 2007).

WHAT IS PHILOSOPHY?

Think: A Compelling Introduction to Philosophy, Simon Blackburn (Oxford University Press, 1999).

What Does It All Mean? A Very Short Introduction to Philosophy, Thomas Nagel (Oxford University Press, 1987).

The Life You Can Save: How to Do Your Part to End World Poverty, Peter Singer (Random House, 2009).

Philosophy Bites podcast, www.philosophybites.com/.

Stanford Encyclopedia of Philosophy, http://plato.stanford.edu/.

WHAT IS PHYSICS?

"How Big Can Schrödinger's Kittens Get?," Philip Ball, *Nautilus*, 2015, http://nautil.us/issue/29/scaling/how-big-can-schr246dingers-kittens-get.

"Physicists Eye Quantum-Gravity Interface," Natalie Wolchover, *Quanta Magazine*, 2013, https://www.quantamagazine.org/20131107-physicists-eye-quantum-gravity-interface/.

Physics Central: Learn How Your World Works, www.physicscentral.com.

WHAT IS POLITICAL SCIENCE?

Politics, Aristotle (325–323 BCE), translated, with introduction, notes and glossary by Carnes Lord, 2nd ed. (University of Chicago Press, 2013).

Strong Democracy: Participatory Politics for a New Age, Benjamin R. Barber (University of California Press, 1984).

Liberal Peace: Selected Essays, Michael W. Doyle (Routledge, 2011).

Disconnect: The Breakdown of Representation in American Politics, Morris P. Fiorina with Samuel J. Abrams (University of Oklahoma Press, 2011).

The Promise of Party in a Polarized Age, Russell Muirhead (Harvard University Press, 2104).

Expert Political Judgment: How Good Is It? How Can We Know?, Philip E. Tetlock (Princeton University Press, 2006).

Development as Freedom, Amartya Sen (New York: Anchor Books, 1999).

WHAT IS PSYCHOLOGY?

The Social Animal, Elliot Aronson (Worth Publishers, 2011).

Brain Rules: 12 Principles for Surviving and Thriving at Work, Home, and School, John Medina (Pear Press, 2014).

Phantoms in the Brain: Probing the Mysteries of the Human Mind, V. S. Ramachandran and Sandra Blakeslee (William Morrow, 1999).

The Mind Club: Who Thinks, What Feels, and Why It Matters, Daniel M. Wegner and Kurt Gray (Viking Press, 2016).

WHAT IS RELIGION?

Harvard University, "The Pluralism Project," http://pluralism.org/. This is a very good source for information about religious diversity (especially in the United States)

Pew Research Center: Religion and Public Life, www.pewforum.org/. An excellent place to start thinking about religion in our world today.

ReligionFacts.com, "Definitions of Religion," www.religionfacts.com/religion. This is among the several good websites that discuss how difficult it is to define religion (and then lists various alternatives).

WHAT IS SOCIOLOGY?

Modern Romance, Aziz Ansari (with Eric Klinenberg) (Penguin Books, 2015). Written by a stand-up comedian in consultation with a sociologist, this book uses a humorous approach along with sociological research methods, including focus groups and interviews with hundreds of people, to investigate romance today and how technology has changed how we search for love.

Freaks, Geeks, and Cool Kids: American Teenagers, Schools, and the Culture of Consumption, Murray Milner Jr., 2nd ed. (Routledge, 2016). Using insights from students attending hundreds of high schools, this book provides an in-depth look at the high school status system along with peer relationships, fashion, and consumption.

We're Friends, Right? Inside Kids' Culture, William A. Corsaro (Joseph Henry Press, 2003). This book provides a unique look at the peer worlds of preschool children. The author, a sociologist, seeks to understand young children through becoming a member of their classrooms, documenting the complexities of their interactions with each other, their schools, and their communities.

Dude, You're a Fag: Masculinity and Sexuality in High School, C. J. Pascoe (University of California Press, 2007). This sociological investigation provides deep insights into daily life at a California high school, especially how gender norms are reinforced through language and interactions.

Sociological Images, https://thesocietypages.org/socimages/. This blog includes contemporary imagery and short commentary to encourage people to develop their sociological imagination.

WHAT IS THEATER?

Poetics, Aristotle, available at http://classics.mit.edu/Aristotle/poetics.html.

The Empty Space: A Book about Theatre: Deadly, Holy, Rough, Immediate, Peter Brook (Touchstone, 1995).

The Dramatic Imagination: Reflections and Speculations on the Art of Theater, Robert Edmond Jones (Routledge, 2004).

Peer Gynt, Henrik Ibsen, available at https://archive.org/stream/peergyntdramaticooib seuoft/peergyntdramaticooibseuoft_djvu.txt.

Any of Shakespeare's plays, all of which are available at http://shakespeare.mit.edu/.

WHAT IS WOMEN'S AND GENDER STUDIES?

A Room of One's Own, Virginia Woolf (1929; reprint, Albatross, 2014). See also http:// gutenberg.net.au/r books02/0200791.txt. This short, brilliant essay by one of the great modernist writers and feminist foremothers addresses the status of women, women artists, education, and economic and emotional independence at a time when few women had any of these.

Sister Outsider: Essays and Speeches, Audre Lorde (1984; reprint, Crossing Press, 2007). An important collection by the outspoken black lesbian feminist author and activist.

Gender Trouble: Feminism and the Subversion of Identity, Judith Butler (Routledge, 1990). In this key text of queer theory, Butler, one of the leading feminist theorists, questions the category of "women" by arguing that gender is performative—that is, it is not stable but rather a set of repeated acts with no original that constitute an illusion of identity.

Backlash: The Undeclared War against American Women, Susan Faludi (Crown Publishing Group, 1991). Written by a Pulitzer Prize–winning researcher, this is one of the best explanations of the changes wrought by the feminist movements of the 1970s, how men and women responded to them, and the media-driven backlash against them.

Transgender Warriors: Making History from Joan of Arc to Dennis Rodman, Leslie Feinberg (Beacon, 1996), www.transgenderwarrior.org/. By uncovering the extensive global history of gender-variant people and their resistance to transphobia, and offering a hopeful vision for trans liberation, this book became a rallying cry for transgender rights in the late 1990s.

Manifesta: Young Women, Feminism and the Future, Jennifer Baumgardner and Amy Richards (Farrar, Straus and Giroux, 2000). An articulation of third-wave feminism that opens with a compelling "Prologue: A Day without Feminism," in which the authors imagine it's 1970 and re-create the life and limitations of girls and women for all who take feminism and its advances for granted.

Transnational Feminism in the United States: Knowledge, Ethics, Power, Leela Fernandes (New York University Press, 2013). In this series of five loosely connected case studies, Fernandes uncovers the problems US feminists encounter in their attempts to use a transnational feminist approach to produce transformative knowledge and more ethical practices.

Contributors

SUSAN ACKERMAN is the Preston H. Kelsey Professor of Religion and Professor of Women's, Gender, and Sexuality Studies and professor of Jewish Studies at Dartmouth College. She is the current president of the American Schools of Oriental Research as well as the past president of the New England and Eastern Canada Region of the Society of Biblical Literature. Among her many writings is the book *Warrior, Dancer, Seductress, Queen: Women in Judges and Biblical Israel* (Doubleday, 1998).

MILES BLENCOWE is a professor of physics at Dartmouth College. In addition to his National Science Foundation supported work on large-scale manifestations of quantum phenomena, he is working on a book, *Mechanical Systems in the Quantum Regime* (Oxford University Press).

ROBERT BONNER is the Kathe Tappe Vernon Professor in Biography and a professor of history and chair of the History Department at Dartmouth College. He is the author of four books, including *The Soldiers' Pen: Firsthand Impressions of the American Civil War* (Hill and Wang, 2006).

ADA COHEN is a professor of art history and the Israel Evans Professor in Oratory and Belles Lettres at Dartmouth College. She is the author of *The Alexander Mosaic: Stories of Victory and Defeat* (Cambridge University Press, 1997) and *Art in the Era of Alexander the Great: Paradigms of Manhood and Their Cultural Traditions* (Cambridge University Press, 2010).

THOMAS H. CORMEN is a professor of computer science at Dartmouth College and former director of the Institute for Writing and Rhetoric at Dartmouth College. An ACM Distinguished Educator, he is the coauthor (with Charles E. Leiserson, Ronald L. Rivest, and Clifford Stein) of the textbook *Introduction to Algorithms* (3rd ed., MIT Press, 2009) and the author of *Algorithms Unlocked* (MIT Press, 2013).

SIENNA R. CRAIG is an associate professor of anthropology at Dartmouth College. As a cultural anthropologist, the major focus of Sienna's research, writing, and teaching is the social study of medicine. Her most recent book is *Healing Elements: Efficacy and the Social Ecologies of Tibetan Medicine* (University of California Press, 2012).

WILLIAM B. DADE recently retired from the faculty of earth sciences at Dartmouth College. His research interests include environmental flows and sediment transport in rivers and the sea.

AMY GLADFELTER is an associate professor of biology at the University of North Carolina, Chapel Hill, and was formerly an associate professor of biology at Dartmouth College. Her research combines live cell microscopy and computational approaches with genetic and biochemical analyses to understand the development of cellular structure and receives funding from the National Science Foundation and National Institutes of Health.

RYAN HICKOX is an assistant professor of physics and astronomy at Dartmouth College. He is a recipient of an Alfred P. Sloan Research Fellowship in 2014 and a National Science Foundation CAREER award in 2016.

DANIEL KOTLOWITZ is the Leon E. Williams Professor of Theater at Dartmouth College. He has designed the lighting for over 250 professional productions in New York and in regional theaters all over the United States and Europe. His design for *GHOSTWRITER* at the Merrimack Repertory Theater was nominated for the Boston IRNE award, and his design for *Twelfth Night* at the Berkeley Repertory Theater was nominated for a Bay Area Critics Award.

F. JON KULL is the Rodgers Professor of Chemistry at Dartmouth College and dean of Dartmouth's School of Graduate and Advanced Studies. He is a widely published structural biologist who studies molecular motor proteins and regulators of bacterial pathogenesis.

THOMAS H. LUXON is a professor of English at Dartmouth College. Besides the usual scholarly projects, he is general editor of *The John Milton Reading Room*, an online edition of Milton's poetry and selected prose. From 2004 until 2013 he served as the Cheheyl Professor and founding director of the Dartmouth Center for the Advancement of Learning.

VICKI V. MAY is a professor of engineering at the Thayer School of Engineering at Dartmouth. Thousands of students of all ages have participated in her massive open online course, "The Engineering of Structures around Us."

JANICE MCCABE is an associate professor of sociology at Dartmouth College. Her recent book, *Connecting in College: How Friendship Networks Matter for Academic and Social Success* (University of Chicago Press, 2016), and other research focuses on how gender, race/ethnicity, and social class operate as social identities and how they shape social networks.

MARK A. MCPEEK is the David T. McLaughlin Distinguished Professor of Biological Sciences. He has worked for thirty-five years on all manner of problems related to ecology, evolution, and behavior.

RUSSELL MUIRHEAD is the Robert Clements Professor of Democracy and Politics and professor of government at Dartmouth College. His recent book, *The Promise of Party in a Polarized Age* (Harvard University Press, 2014), is on the ethics of party spirit in modern democracy, with special reference to American politics.

LARRY POLANSKY is the Emeritus Strauss Professor of Music at Dartmouth College and professor of music at University of California at Santa Cruz. He is a composer, performer, writer, and theorist who has been awarded a Guggenheim Foundation Fellowship and a Mellon New Directions Fellowship (for the study of American Sign Language poetry) and was the inaugural recipient of the American Music Center Henry Cowell Award.

DAN ROCKMORE is the William H. Neukom 1964 Professor of Computational Science, director of the Neukom Institute for Computational Science, and a professor of mathematics and computer science at Dartmouth College. His book *Stalking the Riemann Hypothesis* (Random House, 2005) was longlisted for the 2006 Aventis Science Writing Prize.

ADINA L. ROSKIES is a professor of philosophy and chair of Cognitive Science at Dartmouth College. She has been awarded the Stanton Prize and William James Prize from the Society of Philosophy and Psychology.

IVY SCHWEITZER is a professor of English and past chair (twice!) of the Women's, Gender, and Sexuality Studies program at Dartmouth, specializing in early American literature and culture. She is the editor of *The Occom Circle*, a digital edition of primary texts by and about Samson Occom held at Dartmouth (https://www.dartmouth.edu/~occom/).

CHRISTOPHER SNYDER is the Joel Z. and Susan Hyatt Professor and Chair of the Department of Economics at Dartmouth College. His two widely used undergraduate textbooks, now each in its twelfth edition, have been translated into four languages.

JAMES N. STANFORD is an associate professor of linguistics at Dartmouth College. He researches language variation and change using quantitative sociolinguistic methods. He coedited *Variation in Indigenous Minority Languages* with Dennis Preston (John Benjamins, 2006).

ANDREA TARNOWSKI is the chair of the Department of French and Italian at Dartmouth College, where she also codirects the first-year Humanities course sequence. She has recently completed an English translation of Christine de Pizan's *The Long Road of Learning*, originally written in fifteenth-century French.

ROGER B. ULRICH holds the Ralph Butterfield Professorship in the Department of Classics at Dartmouth College. He is the author of *Roman Woodworking* (Yale University Press, 2007, 2013) and editor of *A Companion to Roman Architecture* (Wiley-Blackwell, 2013).

THALIA WHEATLEY is an associate professor in the Department of Psychological and Brain Sciences at Dartmouth College. She uses a broad range of methodologies, from neuroimaging to cross-cultural studies, to better address questions such as "How does the human brain understand other minds?" and "How do our social networks change the way we think?" Professor Wheatley collaborates widely with professors in other disciplines such as computer science, music, and business.

DERRICK E. WHITE is a visiting associate professor of history and affiliated with the African and African American Studies Program at Dartmouth College. He is the author of *The Challenge of Blackness: The Institute of the Black World and Political Activism in the 1970s* (Florida, 2011) and coeditor of *Winning while Losing: Civil Rights, the Conservative Movement and the Presidency from Nixon to Obama* (Florida, 2014). He is currently working on a book tentatively titled *Blood, Sweat, and Tears: Sporting Congregations and Black College Football at Florida A&M University.*

RICHARD WRIGHT holds the Orvil E. Dryfoos Chair in Public Affairs and has been a professor of geography at Dartmouth College since 1985. With support from the Guggenheim, National Science Foundation, and Russell Sage Foundation, he has authored more than seventy scholarly papers. His research, like his teaching, focuses on housing and labor markets, migration and immigration, and race.